Television and the Crisis of Democracy

Television and the Crisis of Democracy

Douglas Kellner

Westview Press

Boulder • San Francisco • Oxford

Interventions: Theory and Contemporary Politics

Copyright © 1990 by Westview Press, Inc.

Published in 1990 in the United States of America by Westview Press, Inc., 5500 Central Avenue, Boulder, Colorado 80301, and in the United Kingdom by Westview Press, 36 Lonsdale Road, Summertown, Oxford OX2 7EW

Library of Congress Cataloging-in-Publication Data
Kellner, Douglas, 1943–
    Television and the crisis of democracy/Douglas Kellner.
        p.   cm.—(Interventions—theory and contemporary politics)
    Includes bibliographical references and index.
    ISBN 0-8133-0548-9. — ISBN 0-8133-0549-7 (pbk.)
    1. Television and politics—United States.   I. Title.
II. Series.
HE8700.76.U6K45   1990
324.7′3′0973—dc20   90-39829
                                                                                                      CIP

Printed and bound in the United States of America

The paper used in this publication meets the requirements
of the American National Standard for Permanence of Paper
for Printed Library Materials Z39.48-1984.

10   9   8   7   6   5   4   3   2   1

Every man thinks he has a concern in all public matters; that he has a right to form and a right to deliver an opinion on them. They sift, examine, and discuss them. They are curious, eager, attentive, and jealous; and by making such matters the daily subjects of their thoughts and discoveries, vast numbers contract a very tolerable knowledge of them, and some a very considerable one. . . . In free countries, there is often found more real public wisdom and sagacity in shops and manufacturies than in the cabinets of princes in countries where none dare to have an opinion until he comes into them. Your whole importance, therefore depends upon a constant, discreet use of your own reason.

—Edmund Burke

A popular government without popular information or the means of acquiring it is but a prologue to a Farce or a Tragedy; or perhaps both. Knowledge will forever govern ignorance; and a people who mean to be their own governors must arm themselves with the power which knowledge gives.

—James Madison

The press, designed for freedom's best defence,
And learning, morals, wisdom to dispense,
Perverted, poisoned, lost to honor's rules,
Is made the sport of knaves, to govern fools.

—Philadelphia *Public Ledger,* 1839

There is no need of a law to check the license of the press. It is law enough, and more than enough to itself. Virtually, the community have come together and agreed what things should be uttered, have agreed on a platform and to excommunicate him who departs from it, and not one in a thousand dares utter anything else.

—Henry David Thoreau

*To the One in a Thousand
Who Spoke Out*

Contents

ix

Preface and Acknowledgments

In 1973 David Rockefeller and other corporate leaders founded the Trilateral Commission, which sought to discover ways to stabilize the capitalist democracies of the United States, Western Europe, and Japan. Within two years, the commission had more than 300 members, drawn from the elites of the corporate, government, labor, and media sectors of these countries. In 1975 it released a report entitled *The Crisis of Democracy* (Crozier, Huntington, and Watanuki 1975). According to the authors of this work, too much democracy in the Western capitalist societies was making them increasingly difficult to govern. The media were allegedly promoting an "adversary culture" that was undermining leadership, challenging authority, and delegitimizing established institutions (ibid., 6–7).

The report concluded that the media, especially television, were promoting excessive democracy (ibid., 33ff., 98ff.). Huntington argued that the media constituted the "most notable new source of national power in 1970" and were spreading a "democratic distemper" that threatened the stability of existing capitalist societies. An imbalance had occurred, Huntington argued, between democratic demands and social order. Likewise, he deemed the media to be too critical of state policy, thus requiring the restoration of "a balance between government and media" (ibid., 181). Accordingly, the Trilateral Commission Report argued that the media, Congress, the educational system, and other major institutions must curb the "democratic distemper" to promote order and stability. Less democracy was therefore necessary to "save" democracy.

In this book, I argue that the goals of the Trilateral Commission were realized during the 1980s at the expense of democracy itself. My position is the reverse of that of the Trilateral Commission. Although I agree that there is indeed a crisis of democracy in the United States today, I claim that it is precisely because there is not enough democracy and that the media, especially television, have subverted the very foundations of democratic government. My argument is that television and the media not only have failed in recent years to carry out the democratic functions of providing the information necessary to produce an informed citizenry but also have promoted the growth of excessive corporate and state power. In this book

xiii

I shall accordingly describe how the commercial television networks were taken over by corporate conglomerates and have become instruments of corporate power that have undermined the foundations of democracy in the United States. From this perspective, the conglomeratization of television can be seen as part of the restructuring of the capitalist system that has occurred during the transition from an economic order based on industry and manufacturing to a new high-tech media/information society. In this new socioeconomic configuration, television and the entertainment/information industries have in the last decade achieved a significant increase in economic, political, social, and cultural power. Corporate control of television, I shall argue, has greatly increased the power of the dominant conservative and corporate forces while undermining democracy. Development of this theme involves analysis of the relations among business, the state, and the media, combined with analysis of how the new configurations of media power constitute a clear and present threat to democracy in the United States.

My aim is twofold: to produce a critical theory of television that provides comprehensive perspectives on the system of commercial television in the United States and to develop proposals for reconstructing the medium so as to make it more democratic. For more than fifteen years, I have been working on developing a theory of the nature, social functions, and effects of television. Systematic inquiry began in 1975 in a study group in Austin, Texas, and my theoretical position is indebted to members of this group: Lynn Carr, Bill Gibson, John Gibson, Jim Greene, Stuart Hersh, Frank Morrow, Harry O'Hara, and Jack Schierenbeck. An earlier version of Chapter 3 appeared in *Theory and Society* (Vol. 10, No. 1, 1981), and I am grateful to the late Alvin Gouldner for his critical comments and encouragement. Parts of Chapter 5 on public access television appeared in different forms in *Making Waves* (Vol. 16, 1985), Donald Lazere's *American Media and Mass Culture* (1987), and Vincent Mosco and Janet Wasko's *Democratic Communications in the Information Age* (1990). This section is especially indebted to my work on a public access program with Frank Morrow, "Alternative Views," which we have undertaken from 1978 to the present.

The sources for this book include a vast number of published books and articles on all facets of television; the most important of these are listed in the Bibliography. I have also drawn on newspaper and magazine articles that are listed in the text so as to avoid an excessively large bibliography. Other sources include interviews and discussions with media theorists, critics, and members of the industry; government and public interest group reports and documents; and, of course, television programming itself.

For critical scrutiny of this manuscript I would like to thank Spencer Carr, Harry Cleaver, Jim Combs, Emile de Antonio, Gloria Gannaway, C. A. Kellner, John Lawrence, Yahia Mahamdi, Vincent Mosco, Richard Ryan, Herbert Schiller, and John Stockwell. Special thanks go to Stephen Bronner, who read and carefully edited several versions of the manuscript, and to Robert Antonio, Steve Best, and Jack Schierenbeck, who provided vigorous critiques of the penultimate version, which strongly influenced the final product. For superb copyediting I am grateful to Christine Arden.

This book is dedicated to those members of the press and broadcast media who dared to speak out rather than conform to the dictates of those who own and control the system of information in the United States.

Douglas Kellner

1

Toward a Critical Theory of Television

Television will be of no importance in your lifetime or mine.
—Bertrand Russell

Once television is truly national it will become the most important medium that exists. Everything that it does or does not do will be important.
—Norman Collins

Chewing gum for the eyes.
—Frank Lloyd Wright

The luminous screen in the home carries fantastic authority. Viewers everywhere tend to accept it as a window on the world, and to watch it for hours each day. Viewers feel that they understand, from television alone, what is going on in the world. They unconsciously look to it for guidance as to what is important, good, and desirable, and what is not. It has tended to displace or overwhelm other influences such as newspapers, school, church, grandpa, grandma. It has become the definer and transmitter of a society's values.
—Erik Barnouw

In excess of 750 million TV sets in more than 160 countries are watched by 2.5 billion people per day. Although there is no consensus regarding television's nature and impact (as the quotes that open this chapter attest), the ubiquity and centrality of television in our everyday lives are obvious. At present, almost every home in the United States has a television set that is turned on for more than seven hours per day. Individuals spend more time watching television than in any other leisure activity and, cumulatively, far more time in front of the television than in school; only work absorbs more waking time. Furthermore, polls reveal that more people depend on television for news and information than on any other source, and that it is the most *trusted* source of news and information.[1]

Given television's penetration into everyday life, the controversy surrounding it is not surprising. The controversy intensifies in the light of debates over its social and political functions. Television has been deeply implicated in post–World War II presidential elections, the cold war, the Vietnam War and other struggles of the 1960s, and the major political controversies of its era, sometimes referred to as the Age of Television (Bogart 1956). There is little agreement, however, concerning television's social and political effects. Some commentators argue that television has overwhelmingly defended conservative economic and political interests. Others have argued that television has had a primarily liberal bias, bringing down such conservatives as Joseph McCarthy and Richard Nixon, undermining the U.S. intervention in Vietnam, and promoting a liberal agenda of social reform and change.[2]

A series of equally heated controversies surround television's impact on everyday life. Whereas some claim that television promotes violence, others maintain that its effects are primarily "pro-social." Defenders of the industry see television as promoting a democratic, egalitarian, populist culture; critics argue that it is creating a vast cultural wasteland. Some see it as a "tube of plenty" that provides a wealth of entertainment and information; others attack it as promoting ideological domination and manipulation of the masses by dominant social groups and forces. And some social scientists perceive television as a powerful instrument of socialization, while others dismiss it as harmless entertainment, "chewing gum for the eyes."[3]

1.1 Theorizing Television

Despite these and other controversies, few attempts have been made to provide a systematic theory of television that articulates its relations with the chief institutions of contemporary capitalist society and defines its impact on social and political life. Surprisingly, it has not received the sort of systematic theoretical scrutiny that has been directed toward other major institutions, such as the state, the corporation, the military, the family, and the education system. Of all contemporary institutions, the system of television is the one most neglected, mystified, and undertheorized.

Of course, many books on television have emerged. Several detail the history and economics of television, and a growing number are concerned with analyzing its influence on contemporary politics. Its impact on socialization has been widely studied, and many criticisms of its effects have been mounted, ranging from attacks on its promotion of sex and violence to its alleged political biases. In addition, there are countless books about the television industry as well as about its programming and personalities.

An even greater amount of material is published daily in newspapers, magazines, and journals, ranging from scholarly and academic studies to TV reviews and gossip. Yet there are few critical theories of television that situate it within the institutional and systemic framework of the existing social order.

Television thus has many critics, commentators, and celebrants—but few theorists. The critiques themselves have largely been determined by the political views of the critics. Conservatives, for example, claim that television is a liberal medium that subverts traditional values. Liberals and radicals, by contrast, often criticize television for its domination by business imperatives and conservative values. Liberals decry trends toward monopoly in television, restrictions on freedom of the press, and what they see as distortions and misuse of television in certain instances (Skornia 1965, 1968; Bagdikian 1987). Radicals argue that television reproduces a conservative status quo and provides powerful tools for managing social conflict and for selling the values and life-styles of corporate capitalism. Theories of television thus tend to focus on television's political functions and values, and often reproduce the political perspectives of theorists.

The Politics of Theory

Conservatives frequently criticize new forms of popular culture and mass media that they see as a subversive threat to traditional values and institutions.[4] In the 1960s conservative values were under attack by the new social movements of that era and, as noted, some conservatives saw television as a primarily liberal medium. In 1969, for example, Vice President Spiro Agnew carried out an assault against "Eastern-establishment" news media. Noting that a recent Vietnam speech by Richard Nixon was followed immediately by critical analysis on the television networks, Agnew complained that the president's talk had been "subjected to instant analysis and querulous criticism . . . by a small band of network commentators and self-appointed analysts, the majority of whom expressed in one way or another their hostility to what he had to say." Agnew claimed that a "small group of men" decide what the country will learn each day, and that they have acquired the power to make or break politicians or policies. These journalists, Agnew continued, are highly parochial and share the same liberal biases. Such concentration of cultural power is intolerable, he argued, and should be carefully scrutinized by the government (Agnew, cited in Emery and Smythe 1972, 309ff.).

In later speeches, Agnew referred to this "Eastern, liberal-biased" media establishment as an "effete corps of impudent snobs" and as "nattering nabobs of negativism" (Barnouw 1975, 443ff.) A variety of conservative scholars and commentators have subsequently taken the position that network television has a "liberal bias." In a study of the 1968 election, Edith Efron (1972) concluded that television was overwhelmingly prejudiced against Richard Nixon and in favor of Hubert Humphrey, given the positive and negative presentations of the two candidates on the nightly news programs. Ernest Lefever (1974) found that CBS's coverage of defense-related issues in 1972–1973 reflected unfavorably on the U.S. military and was slanted toward detente with the Soviet Union. Still others argue that, according to their research, reporters for the major news media were overwhelmingly liberal in their political orientations (Lichter, Rothman, Lichter 1986). (Some of these claims, however, were contested: see Stevenson, et al. 1973.)

These conservatives critiques have formed part of the ideology of the "New Right," which emerged in the late 1970s. The New Right became increasingly critical of the "new class" within the media, claiming that its biases are liberal, "collectivist," and "anti-free enterprise." This position was promoted for several years by *TV Guide*, which employed conservatives such as Edith Efron, Patrick Buchanan, Kevin Phillips, and others who argued that television subverted traditional values and promoted a left-liberal sociopolitical agenda. Efron, for instance, claimed that television became a mouthpiece for "ecological stop-growth types," "nuclear Luddites and plutonophobes," and "Third World and socialist tyrannies," all the while exhibiting hostility toward "U.S. business, U.S. labor, the U.S. military and U.S. technology." In short, she claimed, it promotes the agenda of the New Left (*TV Guide*, October 8, 1977, pp. A5–A6).

In a series of corporate ads, Mobil oil corporation claimed that "leading reporters and editors of major newspapers and television networks have distinct hostilities toward businessmen" (cited in Dreier 1987: 64). A similar position concerning television entertainment was advanced by Ben Stein (1979), who attacked television programming for promoting antibusiness, antimilitary, and antitraditional values. Stein contends that the Hollywood community, which produces TV entertainment, is an "extremely energetic and militant class" that uses its cultural power to attack competing social elites and to propagate its ultraliberal views. Segments of the New Right have focused their critiques on television entertainment as well, claiming that it subverts traditional religious values while promoting "secular humanism."

Another group of critiques emerged in the 1970s. For instance, Daniel Bell (1976) argued that television and the mass media have been instrumental in promoting a new consumer ethic and hedonistic life-style that contradict the older capitalist-protestant production ethic with its emphasis on hard work, saving, delayed gratification, the family, religion, and other traditional values.[5] "Neoconservative" critics such as Daniel Moynihan, Robert Nisbet, and Samuel Huntington maintain that television has eroded respect for authority by exposing political scandals (as well as business corruption and failures) while fostering cynicism, distrust, and disrespect for the system as a whole. These critics complain that the media have gone too far in their "adversary" function and have eroded the president's power, thus "seriously and dangerously" weakening "the state's ability to govern" (Moynihan 1973, 315). The neoconservatives claim that television has helped produce an "adversary culture," and Crozier et al. (1975) specifically assert that it has promoted a "democratic distemper."

The liberal approach to television and popular culture is divided into two camps. One critical position focuses on television's institutional setting and function within contemporary capitalist democracies (Siepmann 1950; Friendly 1967; Skornia 1965; and Bagdikian 1987). The other, more pluralist position focuses, often affirmatively, on the cultural and social functions of television. Liberal critics usually document the abuses of television caused by excessive corporate control of television and the placement of profit above all other values and goals. They hold that if television were both more fully competitive and in the service of democratic goals, the medium could be embraced as an important institution in a pluralist, democratic social order.

The liberal pluralist position is detailed, along with some conservative and radical critiques, in the anthology *Mass Culture*, edited by Bernard Rosenberg and David White (1957). White presents television and popular culture as parts of a democratic, pluralistic cultural system that provides a marketplace of ideas and entertainment as well as a diversity of choices. This position is also elaborated in Herbert Gans's (1974) study of "taste cultures," which celebrates the liberal pluralist view of culture—and television—in the United States. The affirmative liberal position is reflected as well in James Carey's (1988) description of television and popular culture as a "communalistic ritual" in which a culture celebrates its dominant values, institutions, and way of life. This view is elaborated by Paul Hirsch and Horace Newcomb (1987), who present television as a "cultural forum" in which society presents, debates, and works out its values, problems, and identity. The liberal position also shapes some of the work being done by members of the Popular Culture Association, which views television positively as an important expression of dominant values in the United States.

Although liberals have not developed a distinct and systematic institutional theory or critique of television, most sociological studies of how news is produced tend to take a liberal bent. These studies see the production of news as a consequence of complex organizational imperatives, which in turn result from the interplay of economic and ideological constraints by management, professional codes and news values, and the interaction of a variety of reporters. Most of these liberal sociological studies (Epstein 1973; Altheide 1976; Gans 1979) see news in terms of a liberal consensus produced through a series of compromises and complex interactions. They call into question the conservative claim that television has a liberal bias by emphasizing how the allegedly liberal bias of reporters is countered by the processes of gatekeeping and filtering, which tend to exclude socially critical stories and radical points of view. The studies also point to the ways in which the constraints in news production force the news media to rely on establishment sources and, hence, to disproportionately favor pro-business and pro-government points of view.

Radicals have variously conceptualized television as part of "an ideological state apparatus" (Althusser, 1971), as a "mind manager" (Schiller 1973), as "the cultural arm of the industrial order" (Gerbner 1976), as an instrument that "maintains hegemony and legitimates the status quo" (Tuchman 1974), as a "looking glass" that provides a distorted and ideological view of social life (Rapping 1987), as an instrument that "invents reality" according to the needs and imperatives of corporate capitalism (Parenti 1987), and as a propaganda machine that "manufactures consent" to the existing sociopolitical order (Herman and Chomsky 1988; Herman 1988; Chomsky 1989). In a sense, only the radicals have attempted to provide even a rudimentary account of television's place in the system of institutions established in the United States and to analyze its sociopolitical functions and effects. The conservative critique focuses on television's alleged liberal bias, and I have seen no systematic liberal attempt to theorize television as a key institution within contemporary U.S. society.

The Logic of Accumulation and Exclusion

In this book, I shall generally take the radical position, although I argue that television has contradictory social functions and effects: Sometimes it reproduces the status quo in a highly conservative manner, and sometimes it promotes (liberal) change and social reforms. Against models of contemporary U.S. society that project a pluralist concept of television as a major institutional force between big business and big government, I argue that, in a capitalist society, the state, media, and other major institutions are predominantly controlled by business—that is, by the capitalist class. A capitalist society is a system of commodity production defined by a set of social relations marked by private ownership of the means of production and production for private profit. In such a society, workers are forced to sell their labor power to the capitalists, who own the means of production; and the capitalists extract at least part of their profit from unpaid labor time (Marx and Engels 1978).

A capitalist society is therefore a class society divided between those who own and control the means of production and those who do not and are thus forced to sell their labor.[6] This class division is often described as an opposition between the ruling (or capitalist) class and the working class. The ruling class, in turn, is divided into various class sectors, just as capital is divided into various fields. The capitalist class is divided between big and small business sectors and between transnational and national corporations. Big business is divided into various sectors such as heavy manufacturing, finance, communications, and oil.

The ruling class often competes internally, as when struggles erupt between big business and small business or between the manufacturing and finance sectors. In a competitive market society, competition among different firms within a sector constitutes another form of conflict. Business sometimes unites to struggle against workers or reform movements; but, on the whole, capitalist society is characterized by conflict and struggle among the different class sectors and classes. In a highly competitive society, such conflict is inevitable—especially if certain groups are oppressed or exploited. Thus, tension, structural antagonism, and struggle are permanent and constituent features of capitalist society.

Marx and Engels argued that the ruling ideas in a given society are those of the ruling class, and that these ideas express the interests of the dominant class in an idealized form (1978, 172). Thus in feudal society, the ruling ideas were those of chivalry, honor, valor, and spirituality—precisely the ideas of the ruling strata. In capitalist society, individualism, competition, winning, material success, and other capitalist ideas are highly esteemed and likewise reflect the interests and ideas of the ruling class.

"Ideology" smooths over differences between classes and presents idealized visions of class harmony and consensus. Ruling classes attempt to present their ideas as universal and their interests as the common interests; thus ideology presents historically contingent ideas, such as the "innate" aggressiveness and egotism of human beings, as the "ways of the world." Ideas such as competition and the right to accumulate unlimited amounts of money and property, which reflect the interests of the capitalist class, are presented as the interests of everyone, as universally valid ideas. The media—one of a series of "ideological apparatuses" along with the state, the church, schooling, and the family (Althusser 1971)—produce ideology and thus serve the interests of the ruling class by idealizing existing institutions, practices, and ideas. In this context, ideology refers to a set of ideas that legitimate the existing organization of society and obscure class/gender/race domination, oppression, exploitation, inequality, and the like (Kellner 1978).

Ideology thus attempts to obscure social antagonisms and conflicts—a function that the media carry out in their entertainment and information programs. In opposition to liberals and others who conceptualize U.S. society as a pluralistic system that maintains a balance and harmony of power, I view U.S. society as a terrain of struggle, as a terrain contested by various economic, gender, and racial groups and forces that is nevertheless dominated by the state, media, and big business. My working assumption is that the capitalist mode of production structures dominant institutions, technologies, media, social practices, and ideologies into a capitalist system. But I also assume that individuals will struggle against their exploitation and oppression, that the interests of capitalists and workers are fundamentally opposed, and that tension and struggle are thus inherent features of capitalist society.

Capitalism is a system of production of commodities in which private corporations attempt to maximize their profits through accumulation of capital in a system of private enterprise. To protect their interests and to expand their wealth and power, the most powerful capitalist forces attempt to control such institutions as the state and the media. Television enters into this terrain and mediates between different institutions and social forces, all the while growing in power and influence within the contemporary sociopolitical scene in the United States. In capitalist society, the logic of capital accumulation is the key constitutive force in the economy. By the same token, in the system of commercial broadcasting that has developed in the United States, capital accumulation is the primary motor of the television industry. In this system, the commercial television corporations are primarily business enterprises concerned with the maximum accumulation of capital. Like other corporations, they are organized to extract the maximum of profit from the production process. This involves producing programming that will attract large audiences for the advertisers who support the commercial system of television in the United States. It also involves, like other enterprises, exploitation of producers and consumers, though the process of exploitation is more subtle in the extraction of profit in the television industry. Like other productive enterprises, the television industry will obviously pay their employees cumulatively less than the total amount of value produced by their labor. Yet exploitation in the television industry is highly uneven, as top executives are regularly paid over one million dollars a year and celebrities, ranging from newscast anchors to top-dollar stars, are paid in the millions. Thus exploitation of the labor force concentrates on lower-level employees such as technicians, researchers, secretaries, writers, and the like.

In addition, exploitation takes place through the extraction of higher prices from consumers for the products advertised on television. Networks charge the corporations who purchase advertising time according to how many viewers watch a given ad and, in some cases, which viewers in specific demographic categories are supposedly viewing a given program (i.e., upscale women from 30–45). The corporations in turn pass these charges on to the viewers in the form of higher prices; because businesses can still, incredibly, take tax write-offs from advertising expenses, viewers pay for their "free" television with both higher taxes and the growing public squalor caused by a system in which corporations have paid a dramatically lower tax rate since the beginning of the reign of the pro-business Republican administrations of Reagan and Bush (see Harms/Kellner 1991).

Yet the television industry is different from other businesses in that it has the crucial ideological functions of legitimating the capitalist mode of production and delegitimating its opponents (e.g., socialist and communist governments, Third World liberation movements, labor, and various anti-capitalist social movements). As I argue in Chapters 2 and 3, television's dual functions of accumulation and legitimation sometimes conflict, but for the most part they work together in defining television's specificity as an institution within corporate capitalism.

Television's logic of accumulation dictates a logic of exclusion that condemns to silence those voices whose criticisms of the capitalist mode of production go beyond the boundaries allowed by the lords of the media. Although specific politicians, corporations, and business practices can be criticized, television does not undertake criticism of the capitalist system in terms of any positive alternatives (such as socialism) and rarely questions foundational capitalist values (such as the right to accumulate unlimited amounts of wealth and power). The opinion spectrum that dominates television thus includes only those liberals and conservatives who tacitly agree that all discourse must take place within the framework of the existing system of production and representative democracy, from which more radical views are rigorously excluded.

This logic of exclusion helps determine which views are aired on television and which are not. As Herman and Chomsky (1988) have demonstrated, the media in the United States usually follow the foreign policy agendas advanced by the existing government and exclude views critical of its policies. They demonize the official enemies of the state while idealizing the client states of the U.S. empire. For example, Chomsky argues that the media consistently projected negative images of Nicaragua, deemed an enemy by the Reagan and Bush administrations, while glossing over the crimes of U.S. client states such as El Salvador or Guatemala (Chomsky 1989). Yet ideological hegemony is neither one-dimensional nor conflict-free. If there are significant differences among political or corporate elites on specific policies, then this debate will be reproduced in the media, which otherwise systematically exclude criticism of the existing economic-political system and its institutions and policies.

To be sure, the logic of exclusion shifts and reflects social struggles and changes. Blacks were excluded from television almost completely during the 1940s and 1950s, in part because television executives feared that affiliates in the South would not play programs featuring blacks or dealing sym-pathetically with their problems. By the same token, views critical of U.S. policy in Vietnam were excluded until significant cracks had occurred in the consensus and debate over the policy itself, and positive views of the Soviet Union were excluded until Gorbachev provided the impetus for more sympathetic and even positive coverage.

The range of ideas allowed by the media depends on the level of social struggle and crisis. Because television is a ubiquitous eye that focuses on social existence twenty-four hours a day, challenges to existing policies and values will occasionally be aired. Such challenges help legitimate television as an independent voice of criticism, which in turn helps produce a balance of power in a democratic society. In the following pages, however, I shall question this view of television and argue, instead, that television has taken on the function of systems maintenance within the structure and dynamics of corporate capitalism and liberal democracy—that is, within the dominant economic and political institutions that together constitute technocapitalist societies in the present age.[7] Accordingly, the development of a theory of television requires one to situate television within a theory of society.

1.2 Critical Theory, the Culture Industries, and the Public Sphere

A critical theory of television should provide analysis of the historical development, socioeconomic structure, and political effects of the system of commercial television. The concept of "critical theory" used in this book derives from the work of the Institute for Social Research, which has provided radical perspectives on the transition from enterpreneurial market capitalism to the system of state corporate capitalism (Jay 1973; Kellner 1989a; Bronner and Kellner 1989). In exile from Nazi Germany, the Institute moved in the 1930s from Frankfurt, Germany, to Columbia University in New York. In the United States, the Institute theorists (Max Horkheimer, T. W. Adorno, Herbert Marcuse, Erich Fromm, Leo Lowenthal, and Frederick Pollock, among others) developed a critical theory of society, which consisted, in part, of analyses of the new synthesis between the state and economy in the configuration of state and monopoly capitalism that emerged during the 1930s in both fascist and democratic forms. These critical theorists also developed one of the first critiques of the roles being played by mass culture and communication in contemporary capitalism, one of the first theories of the consumer society, and one of the first appreciations of the new forms of science, technology, and instrumental rationality in the constitution of a "totally administered society." In addition, they developed theories and methods that can be used to analyze the ways in which culture, social institutions, the state, and the economy work together to form a capitalist system (Kellner 1989a).

These critical theorists conceptualize the mass media as a "culture industry" that systematically indoctrinates individuals with the ideological values and ways of life of established society (Horkheimer and Adorno 1972 [orig. 1947]; Marcuse 1964). The media, according to this account, thus serve as instruments of social control and mass deception. Generalizing from the fascism that the theorists observed in Germany and the rise of the consumer society that they experienced in the United States, they initially postulated a model of a monolithic capitalist society in which the media served as powerful instruments of domination in the hands of the ruling class. In the process, they focused on popular entertainment and its ideological nature and functions, to the exclusion of media presentations of news, information, and actual political struggles. They assumed that mass culture was a powerful instrument that integrated the working class into capitalist society and managed their consciousness, needs, and behavior. Yet, although their study provided important insights into capitalist modes of domination, it lacked specificity and empirical analysis of the history, political economy, and effects of the media in actual historical constellations.

The limitations of this model of the culture industry were somewhat overcome by a second-generation critical theorist, Jurgen Habermas. In his first major book, *The Structural Transformation of the Public Sphere*, Habermas (1989 [orig. 1962]) analyzed the transformation of the public sphere under the pressure of a rising system of mass media. During the eighteenth century, he claimed, the democratic public sphere initially provided a free space of mediation between state and everyday life in the construction of liberal bourgeois societies. Habermas analyzed the role of newspapers, literary and political clubs, coffee houses, and institutions of political debate and discussion in producing what he calls a "bourgeois public sphere." The media composed of the press, journals, and books fostered this public sphere and thus produced at least a potential space for political debate, opposition, and struggle.

A free press, according to Habermas, is an essential component of a democratic social order. In his account, a critical press began to emerge in England during the late 1600s and, during the 1700s, became an important voice of political opposition and criticism. Official state recognition of "freedom of speech" was initially restricted to parliament, but the press eventually won this right. In the Virginia Bill of Rights, written a month before the Declaration of Independence in 1776, George Mason recognized that "[t]he freedom of the press is one of the great bulwarks of liberty and can never be restrained but by despotic governments" (Mason, cited in Stoler 1986, 19–20). The First Amendment of the U.S. Constitution institutionalized this freedom by stating that Congress shall make no law abridging freedom of speech, of the press, of religion, and of the people to assemble peaceably. Likewise, in the French Constitution of 1791, which adopted the "Declaration of the Rights of Man and of Citizens" of August 26, 1789, it was written that "[t]he free communication of ideas and opinions is one of the most precious rights of man. Everyone can therefore speak, write, and print freely, with the proviso of responsibility for the misuse of this liberty in the cases determined by law" (cited in Habermas 1989, 70).

The press was deemed necessary as a source of information that would enable citizens to democratically participate in public affairs. It was also intended to provide a balance of power, as a bulwark against excessive state power. In practice, the press during the nineteenth century was often partisan, providing support or opposition to existing regimes. In 1832 the Englishman Lord Macaulay wrote that, in addition to the estates of the "Lords Spiritual," "Lords Temporal," and "Commons" in the British Parliament, "[t]he gallery in which the reporters sit has become a Fourth Estate of the realm." Thereafter, the term *fourth estate* was popularly used to describe the press. It came to signify that the press was a major institution in a democratic society that would serve as a watchdog against government abuse of power or corruption (Hulteng and Nelson 1983).

Habermas argues, however, that in the late nineteenth century, the state increasingly intruded into the public sphere, censoring groups and publications that challenged its interests and agenda while operating as an instrument of political indoctrination. In addition, private corporations began taking control of the state and the media to promote their own interests and power. Advertising became a crucial component of mass communication, providing the advertisers with power over these media and the depoliticized public of the consumer society that emerged after World War II. Not only were the media subject to new forms of state and economic control, but the very space of the public sphere receded with the development of new suburbs, consumerism and shopping malls, new electronic media, and a declining interest in both book culture and politics. Under these conditions, the public was transformed from participants in political and cultural debates into consumers of media images and information.

The result, according to Habermas, was a crisis of the public sphere and a threat to democracy. Democracy required a vital and well-informed public, eager to participate in debates and struggles concerning political issues of common interest. In a privatized society, however, individuals withdrew from the public sphere and contented themselves with consumption, private family lives, and individual pursuits and pleasure. In this book, I shall delve further into television's contributions to this crisis of the public sphere. The focus of my analysis is the United States, in contrast to Habermas's wide-ranging, multisocietal study.

The crisis of the public sphere is arguably much more intense in the United States than it was in 1962, when Habermas published his text. Transnational entertainment and information conglomerates have streamlined cultural production to an extent far beyond that analyzed by Horkheimer and Adorno (1972) and earlier critical theorists. New technologies have been developed and introduced by communications and electronic conglomerates that are attempting to control vast sectors of the information and entertainment industries. This development is part of a new configuration of technocapitalism, which combines new technologies with neocapitalist forms of economic organization. Whereas the individual firm in a single industry was the model during the earlier phase of competitive capitalism, today giant corporate conglomerates such as the television networks, Time-Warner, Murdoch communications, and other transnational corporations control huge segments of the communications, information, and entertainment market (Bagdikian 1987, 1989).

Centralized corporate control gives these corporations enormous power to decide what people will read, see, and experience. Moreover, the conglomerization of media and communications seriously threatens democracy and gives the major transnational corporations massive political, economic, and cultural power. The entertainment and information industries in particular have rationalized cultural production and produced new forms of cultural hegemony through the new electronic media. Television stands at the center of the new media in that cable and satellite delivery systems, video-recorders, disk systems, and computer/information systems also operate through television, providing it with even more power than it had during the era of over-the-air broadcasting.

The new media experience, which is primarily imagistic (i.e., grounded in image production and proliferation), is producing new forms of experience, culture, and hegemony. Interestingly, in the same year that Habermas's *The Structural Transformation of the Public Sphere* was released, Daniel Boorstin (1962) published *The Image* in which he analyzed the growing role of image in many domains of life in the United States. Boorstin included some discussion of advertising and the media, but he was mainly concerned with contrasting the bad new modes of experience and culture with the good old ones. Indeed, he saw nothing progressive in any of the new forms of culture and experience. A similar conservative nostalgia marked the earlier critique of the cultural industries by Horkheimer and Adorno (1972), who bemoaned the demise of elite culture and the highly prized forms of individuality in the new mass societies.

More recent "postmodern" theory has conceptualized contemporary capitalist society in terms of proliferation and dissemination of images. In this new image culture, "reality" is effaced and the media constitute a new realm of "hyperreal" experience where images replace reality and the distinction between reality and irreality blurs (Baudrillard 1983a, 1983b). As I have discussed postmodern theory in detail elsewhere (Kellner 1987; Best and Kellner 1987; Kellner 1989b; Best and Kellner 1990), I shall limit my discussion in this book to a consideration of postmodern theories of the politics of the image (see Chapter 4). Extreme postmodern theory claims that in a media society it is impossible to delineate institutional structures, historical trajectories, or political effects (Baudrillard 1983b); it also views the media as a black hole that absorbs all content, social reality, politics, and so on, into a vortex of noise, meaninglessness, and implosion. Although this articulation may well express the experience of some media-saturated denizens of the TV world, I contend that the effects of television are quite different and considerably more specific.

1.3 Contested Terrain and the Hegemony of Capital

In contrast to postmodern media theory and the study by Horkheimer and Adorno (1972), I shall take a multidimensional approach, discussing both the regressive and progressive potential of new media and forms of culture. According to the first-generation thinkers of the Frankfurt School and many of their followers, the very forms of mass culture are regressive, exemplifying commodification, reification, and ideological manipulation. Commodity culture, from this viewpoint, follows conventional formulas and standarized forms to attract the maximum audience. It serves as a vehicle of ideological domination that reproduces the ideas and ways of life in the established order, but it has neither critical potential nor any progressive political uses.

The classic "culture industry" analysis focuses on mass culture as a cultural form. Whereas the critical theory of the 1930s developed a model of social analysis rooting all objects of analysis in political economy, the critical theory of mass culture neglects detailed analysis of the political economy of the media, conceptualizing mass culture merely as an instrument of capitalist ideology. My aim, by contrast, is to develop a critical theory that analyzes television in terms of its institutional nexus within contemporary U.S. society. Moreover, rather than seeing contemporary U.S. society as a monolithic structure absolutely controlled by corporate capitalism (as the Frankfurt School sometimes did), I shall present it as a contested terrain traversed by conflicting political groups and agendas. In my view, television— far from being the monolithic voice of a liberal or conservative ideology— is a highly conflictual mass medium in which competing economic, political, social, and cultural forces intersect. To be sure, the conflicts take place within well-defined limits, and most radical discourses and voices are rigorously excluded; but the major conflicts of U.S. society over the last several decades have nonetheless been played out over television. Indeed, contrary to those who see the logic of capital as totally dominating and administering contemporary capitalist societies, I contend that U.S. society is highly conflictual and torn by antagonisms and struggles, and that television is caught up in these conflicts, even when it attempts to deny or cover them over, or simply to "report" them.

My response to the first generation of critical theorists (Adorno, Horkheimer, Marcuse, and so on) is the argument that the capitalist system of production and its culture and society are more riven with conflicts and contradictions than are present in the models of "one-dimensional society" or the "totally administered society" presented by earlier critical theorists. In addition, I stress that U.S. society is not only a capitalist society but also (in part) a democratic one. *Democracy* is perhaps one of the most loaded and contested terms of the present era. In its broadest signification, democracy refers to economic, political, and cultural forms of self-management. In an "economic democracy," workers would control the work place, just as citizens would control their polity through elections, referenda, parliaments, and other political processes. "Cultural democracy" would provide everyone access to education, information, and culture, enabling people to fully develop their individual potentials and to become many-sided and more creative.

"Political democracy" would refer to a constitutional order of guaranteed rights and liberties in a system of political decisionmaking, with governance by rule of law, the consent of the governed, and public participation in elections and referenda. The form of representational democracy operative in the United States approximates some, but not all, of these features of political democracy. (See Barber 1984 for another model of "strong democracy.") While I admit that full-fledged democracy does not really exist in the United States, I shall argue in this book that conflicts between capitalism and democracy have persisted throughout U.S. history, and that the system of commercial broadcasting in the United States has been produced by a synthesis of capitalist and democratic structures and imperatives and is therefore full of structural conflicts and tensions (see Chapter 3). As we shall see, television *is* its contradictions.

Furthermore, I stress the importance of conflicts within the ruling class and challenges to liberal and conservative positions by radical movements and discourses more than do previous critical studies of television. Given the ubiquity and power of television, it is a highly desired prize for ruling groups. Unlike most critical theorists, however, I attempt to specify both the ways in which television serves the interests of dominant economic and political forces, and the ways in which it serves to reproduce conflicts among these groups and to mediate the various antagonisms and conflicts that traverse contemporary capitalist societies. Accordingly, I shall attempt to present a more comprehensive and multidimensional theoretical analysis than the standard Marxist and neo-Marxist accounts, which tend to conceptualize the media and the state simply as instruments of capital. I shall also discuss current efforts at restructuring capitalist society in relation to the movements of the 1960s and 1970s, the world economic crisis of the 1970s, and the challenges of utilizing new technologies and media as additional sources of profitability and social control. In contrast to mechanistic "instrumentalist" accounts, which conceptualize the media merely as instruments of capital and of the ruling class and class domination, the "hegemony" model presented in this book provides an analysis of the ways in which television serves particular class interests in forging specific forms of hegemony at specific points in time.

Hegemony, Counterhegemony, and Instrumentalist Theories

The hegemony model of culture and the media reveals dominant ideological formations and discourses as a shifting terrain of consensus, struggle, and compromise, rather than as an instrument of a monolithic, unidimensional ideology that is forced on the underlying population from above by a unified ruling class.[8] Television is best conceptualized, however, as the terrain of an ever-shifting and evolving hegemony in which consensus is forged around competing ruling-class political positions, values, and views of the world. The hegemony approach analyzes television as part of a process of economic, political, social, and cultural struggle. According to this approach, different classes, sectors of capital, and social groups compete for social dominance and attempt to impose their visions, interests, and agendas on society as a whole. Hegemony is thus a shifting, complex, and open phenomenon, always subject to contestation and upheaval.

Ruling groups attempt to integrate subordinate classes into the established order and dominant ideologies through a process of ideological manipulation, indoctrination, and control. But ideological hegemony is never fully obtained; and attempts to control subordinate groups sometimes fail. Many individuals do not accept hegemonic ideology and actively resist it. Those who do accept ideological positions, such as U.S. justification for the Vietnam war, may come to question these positions as a result of exposure to counter-discourses, experiences, and education. Accordingly, hegemony theories posit an active populace that can always resist domination and thus point to the perpetual possibility of change and upheaval.

Hegemony theories of society and culture can therefore be contrasted with instrumentalist theories. The latter tend to assume that both the state and the media are instruments of capital, and to play down the conflicts among the state, the media, and capital. Examples include the structuralist Marxist theories of Althusser (1971) and Parenti (1986). Instrumentalist theories tend to assume a two-class model of capitalist society divided into a ruling class and a working class. These theories see the state and media as instruments used to advance the interests of the ruling class and to control the subjugated class. The model assumes a unified ruling class with unitary interests. A hegemony model, by contrast, posits divisions within both the working class and the ruling class and sees the terrain of power as a shifting site of struggle, coalitions, and alliances. Instrumentalist theories of television tend to be ahistorical in their assumption that television, under capitalism, has certain essential and unchanging functions. The hegemony model, by contrast, argues that media take on different forms, positions, and functions in different historical conjunctures and that their very constitution and effects are to some degree the result of the balance of power between contending groups and societal forces.

Hegemony itself takes different forms at different historical junctures. After the disruption of the conservative hegemony of the 1950s in the United States by the radical political movements of the 1960s, the 1970s witnessed intense struggles among conservatives, liberals, and radicals. The radicals were eventually marginalized and the liberals defeated with the victory of Ronald Reagan in 1980. During the 1980s it became clear that television had been taken over by some of the most powerful forces of corporate capitalism and was being aggressively used to promote the interests of those forces (see section 2.5 and Chapters 3 and 4 for documentation).

Gramsci and Hegemony

The term *hegemony* is derived from the work of the Italian Marxist theorist Antonio Gramsci.[9] In analyzing power relations, Gramsci (1971) distinguished between "force" and "consent," two ways in which the ruling class exercises power and maintains social control. Whereas institutions such as the police, military, and prisons use force to maintain social control, ideology wins consent for the social order without force or coercion. Hegemonic ideology attempts to legitimate the existing society, its institutions, and its ways of life. Ideology becomes hegemonic when it is widely accepted as describing "the way things are," inducing people to consent to the institutions and practices dominant in their society and its way of life. Hegemony thus involves the social transmission of certain preconceptions, assumptions, notions, and beliefs that structure the view of the world among certain groups in a specific society. The process of hegemony describes the social construction of reality through certain dominant ideological institutions, practices, and discourses. According to this view, experience, perception, language, and discourse are social constructs produced in a complex series of processes. Through ideological mediation, hegemonic ideology is translated into everyday consciousness and serves as a means of "indirect rule" that is a powerful force for social cohesion and stability.

For a hegemony theory, therefore, all beliefs, values, and so on, are socially mediated and subject to political contestation. In every society, there is a contest over which assumptions, views, and positions are dominant. In Gramsci's (1971) analysis, ideologies "cement and unify the social bloc" and are embodied in everyday experience. Specific cultural forms—such as religion, philosophy, art, and common sense—produce consent and serve as instruments of ideological hegemony. In Gramsci's view, hegemony is never established once and for all but is always subject to negotiation and contestation. He pictures society as a terrain of contesting groups and forces in which the ruling class is trying to smooth out class contradictions and incorporate potentially oppositional groups and forces. Hegemony is opposed and contested by efforts to produce a "counterhegemony" on behalf of such groups and forces.

For Gramsci, it was the communist movement and party that provided the genuine progressive alternative to bourgeois/capitalist hegemony. A counterhegemonic movement would thus attempt to fundamentally alter the existing institutional arrangements of power and domination in order to radically transform society. The concept of hegemony has recently been reconstructed by theorists such as Laclau and Mouffe (1985), who root counterhegemony in new social movements struggling for democracy. Television in the United States helps establish capitalist hegemony—the hegemony of capital over the state, media, and society. Because of the power of the media in the established society, any counterhegemonic project whatsoever—be it that of socialism, radical democracy, or feminism—must establish a media politics (see Chapter 5).

According to the hegemony model, television thus attempts to engineer consent to the established order; it induces people to conform to established ways of life and patterns of beliefs and behavior. It is important to note that, from the standpoint of this model, media power is *productive power*. Following Foucault (1977), a hegemony model of media power would analyze how the media produce identities, role models, and ideals; how they create new forms of discourse and experience; how they define situations, set agendas, and filter out oppositional ideas; and how they set limits and boundaries beyond which political discourse is not allowed. The media are thus considered by this model to be active, constitutive forces in political life that both produce dominant ideas and positions and exclude oppositional ones.

Media discourse has its own specificity and autonomy. Television, for instance, mobilizes images, forms, style, and ideas to present ideological positions. It draws on and processes social experience, uses familiar generic codes and forms, and employs rhetorical and persuasive devices to attempt to induce consent to certain positions and practices. Yet this process of ideological production and transmission is not a one-dimensional process of indoctrination, but, rather, is an active process of negotiation that can be resisted or transformed by audiences according to their own ends and interests.

Gramsci's work is important because it provides as a model of society one that is made up of contending forces and groups. It thus avoids the monolithic view of the media as mere instruments of class domination. The two most prolific radical critics of the media, Herman and Chomsky (1988), come close to taking an instrumentalist position, assuming that the media are "adjuncts of government" and the instruments of dominant elites that "manufacture consent" for the policies that support their interests. Herman and Chomsky also argue that a series of "filters" control media content, beginning with the size of the media and their ownership and profit orientation, and continuing through advertisers, media sources, pressure groups, and anticommunist ideology. All of these forces filter out content and images that would go against the interests of conservative powers and characterize the media as a propaganda machine. To document their thesis, Herman and Chomsky carry out a detailed analysis of mainstream media coverage of U.S. foreign policy, including studies of television coverage of Vietnam and Indochina, Central America, and the alleged plot to assassinate the pope, as well as studies of the individuals deemed worthy or unworthy to be represented as victims of their respective governments.

Lacking a theory of capitalist society, Herman and Chomsky tend to conceptualize the media as instruments of the state that propagandize on behalf of ruling elites and their policies. Whereas they see ownership of the media and commercial imperatives as filters that exclude views critical of established institutional arrangements of power, I would argue that the media are organized primarily as capitalist media and only further foreign policy and other perspectives that are perceived to be in the interests of the groups that own and control the media. Nonetheless, Herman and Chomsky quite rightly contest the self-image of the media as robust and feisty critics that help maintain a balance of power and promote liberal democracy. Arguing instead that the media are primarily propagandists for the status quo, they conclude:

> A propaganda model suggests that the "societal purpose" of the media is to inculcate and defend the economic, social, and political agenda of privileged groups that dominate the domestic society and the state. The media serve this purpose in many ways: through selection of topics, distribution of concerns, framing of issues, filtering of information, emphasis and tone, and by keeping debate within the bounds of acceptable premises. (1988, 298)

The concept of *hegemony*, rather than that of *propaganda*, better characterizes the specific nature of commercial television in the United States. Whereas propaganda has the connotation of self-conscious, heavy-handed, intentional, and coercive manipulation, *hegemony* has the connotation, more appropriate to television, of induced consent, of a more subtle process of incorporating individuals into patterns of belief and behavior. By the same token, the propaganda model assumes that its subjects are malleable victims, who willy-nilly fall prey to media discourse. The hegemony model, by contrast, describes a more complex and subtle process whereby the media induce consent. It also allows for aberrant readings and individual resistance to media manipulation (Hall et al. 1980).

The ideological effects of television are not limited to its content, contrary to the dictates of the propaganda model. The forms and technology of television have ideological effects too, as I shall argue in this book. I therefore present perspectives different from those of Parenti (1986) and Herman and Chomsky (1988), who tend to utilize a somewhat monolithic model of capitalist society in their interpretation of the media as mere instruments of class rule and propaganda. My viewpoint also differs from that of radical critics of the media who focus on cultural imperialism and on the nefarious effects of the importation of U.S. television throughout the world. I supplement this important work by emphasizing the roles of commercial television within contemporary U.S. society, and my case study (Chapter 4) indicates the ways in which television has processed domestic politics during the 1980s. Much of Parenti's work, and almost all of Herman and Chomsky's work focuses on how U.S. television presents foreign affairs and how its anticommunist bias reflects the dominant lines of U.S. foreign policy while ignoring, or obscuring, unpleasant events that put U.S. policy and alliances in question. The works of Parenti and of Herman and Chomsky are indeed valuable as damning indictments of U.S. foreign policy and of the ways in which the media serve the interests of dominant corporate and political elites in these areas. But a more comprehensive theoretical perspective on television would focus on television's domestic functions and political effects and the ways in which it is structured by the conflicting imperatives of capitalism and democracy.

Critical Theory and Television

This book provides a more differentiated model of power, conflict, and structural antagonisms in contemporary capitalist societies than previous radical accounts. Although television can be seen as an electronic ideology machine that serves the interests of the dominant economic and political class forces, the ruling class is split among various groups that are often antagonistic and at odds with one another and with contending groups and social movements. Under the guise of "objectivity," television intervenes in this matrix of struggle and attempts to resolve or obscure conflict and to advance specific agendas that are prevalent within circles of the ruling strata whose positions television shares.

Because television is best conceptualized as a business that also has the function of legitimating and selling corporate capitalism, a theory of television must be part of a theory of capitalist society. Contrary to those who view television as harmless entertainment or as a source of the "objective" information that maintains a robust democratic society, I interpret it as a "culture industry" that serves the interests of those who own and control it. Yet, in contrast to Horkheimer and Adorno (1972), whose theory of the culture industry is somewhat abstract and ahistorical, I analyze television's mode of cultural production in terms of its political economy, history, and sociopolitical matrix. In the process, I stress the interaction between political, economic, and cultural determinants.

From the perspective of critical theory, in order to adequately understand a given object or subject matter, one must understand its historical genesis, development, and trajectory. Chapter 2 accordingly outlines the history of television in the United States, focusing on the ways in which powerful economic and political forces have determined the course of the established commercial broadcasting system. Indeed, the broadcast media have served the interests of corporate hegemony from the beginning and took on even more blatantly pro-corporate agendas and functions during the 1980s. Chapter 3 follows with a sketch of my theoretical perspectives on television in the United States. Here I discuss the ways in which the capitalist mode of production has structured contemporary U.S. society and the system of commercial television. I also analyze the methods and strategies with which corporations and the state have attempted to control broadcasting; the ways in which commercial imperatives have shaped the organization, content, and forms of commercial broadcasting; the structural conflicts between capitalism and democracy in constituting the system of commercial television in the United States; and the major conflicts among broadcasting, government, and business over the past several decades.

A critical theory of society must not only ground its analyses in historical and empirical studies but also develop a comprehensive theoretical perspective on the present age. Chapter 4 accordingly reveals the role of television in maintaining conservative hegemony in the United States during the 1980s. In this chapter I document the conservative turn in the media during this decade and suggest that television promoted the Reagan/Bush agenda of deregulation, tax breaks for the rich and for the biggest corporations, and pursuit of a pro-business and interventionist foreign policy agenda. Television's role in the 1988 election, especially, dramatizes the current crisis of democracy in the United States. Indeed, television has increasingly reinforced conservative hegemony during an era in which corporate capitalism was aided and abetted by a political administration that was aggressively pro-business and hostile to the interests of working people as well as to those of progressive organizations and social movements.

Normative and political perspectives are also crucial to the conception of critical theory, which has traditionally been structured by a dialectic of liberation and domination that analyzes not only the regressive features of a technology like television but also its emancipatory features or potential. Critical theory promotes attempts to achieve liberation from forces of domination and class rule. In contrast to the classic critical theory of the Frankfurt school, which is predominantly negative in its view of television and the media as instruments of domination, this book follows Benjamin (1969), Brecht (1967), and Enzensberger (1977), who conceptualize television as a potential instrument of progressive social change. My studies thus maintain a doubled-edged focus on the media in which the progressive and democratic features are distinguished from the negative and oppressive aspects.[10]

Critical theory is motivated by an interest in progressive social change, in promoting positive values such as democracy, freedom, individuality, happiness, and community. But the structure and system of commercial network television impedes these values. In Chapter 5, I have proposed an alternative system that promotes progressive social transformation and more democratic values and practices. This alternative system embodies such values as democratic accountability of the media, citizens' access and participation, increased variety and diversity of views, and communication that furthers social progress as well as enlightenment, justice, and a democratic public sphere.

In short, critical theory criticizes the nature, development, and effects of a given institution, policy, or idea from the standpoint of a normative theory of the "good society" and the "good life." Capitalism defines its consumerist mode of life as the ideal form of everyday life and its economic and political "marketplace" as the ideal structure for a society. Critical theory contests these values from the standpoint of alternative values and models of society. In this way, critical theory provides a synthesis of social theory, philosophy, the sciences, and politics. Accordingly, I shall draw on a range of disciplines to provide a systematic and comprehensive critical theory of television. To elucidate the nexus between television and the crisis of democracy, I begin by situating television within the fundamental socioeconomic processes of corporate capitalism and by charting its growing influence and power in contemporary U.S. society.

Notes

1. The number of TV sets in the world was cited in the documentary "Television," broadcast in 1989 by the Public Broadcasting Service (PBS). In 1988, 90.4 milion homes in the United States (i.e., more than 98 percent of the population) had televisions, with 1.651 viewers per TV home (*Broadcasting/Cable Yearbook* 1989,

G16). By the end of the 1980s, televisions were turned on more than 7 hours per day, and the average adult watched television more than 32 hours per week. Eight out of 10 people spent 2 or more hours watching television every night (Gilbert 1988). The Roper Organization Poll indicated that 64 percent of the people questioned chose television as their chief source of news; that from 1959 to 1980 there was a dramatic reversal in the number of people who chose television over newspapers (Roper 1981, 3); and that television was deemed the most "believable" news media by a large margin (Roper 1981, 4). The results are consistent with those reported in Bower (1985). They also concur with Gilbert (1988, 234), who states that 44 percent of the people polled chose television as their preferred source for local news and 60 percent chose it as their preferred source for national and international news. A whopping 96 percent believed that local TV news is "very or fairly" accurate, while 89 percent believed that network news was "very or fairly" accurate (ibid.).

2. For some characteristic conservative attacks on television's "liberal bias," see Efron (1972), Lefever (1974), Phillips (1975), Herschensohn (1976), and Lichter, Rothman, and Lichter (1986). The terms *conservative* and *liberal* are constantly being redefined. Whereas conservatives were once allied with state institutions against the emerging capitalist economy and liberals defended a laissez-faire political economy and criticized state regulation, conservatives today tend to be critical of big government and liberals defend government programs and state intervention in the economy. Previous U.S. conservatives were isolationist in their foreign policy, but since World War II they have been generally interventionist. In this book I characterize "conservatives" as those individuals who criticize big government and liberal welfare state measures while championing deregulation, a relatively unrestricted free market, an interventionist foreign policy, and traditional social values. By contrast, I identify "liberals" with welfare state reform measures, redistribution of wealth, less interventionist foreign policy (although this often shifts), egalitarian reform of social values, and more permissive attitudes toward social and cultural change. And, finally, I describe "radicals" as those who champion more extensive social transformation, ranging from socialist attempts to reform the capitalist economy to feminist attempts to dismantle the institutions of male dominance.

3. Meyer (1979) argues that television is pro-social, whereas Gerbner and Gross (1976) maintain that it promotes violence and a "mean world" vision that supports conservative ideologies. Apologists for television include industry spokespeople, their academic allies, and TV fans who publish "fanzines" and celebrate TV trivia.

4. For discussions of earlier conservative critiques of popular culture, see Swinge-wood (1977) and Brantlinger (1983).

5. On "neoconservatism" and the New Right, see Crawford (1979). Bell (1978) is sometimes labeled a neoconservative because he defends traditional values against the movements of the 1960s and new cultural forms such as television; Bell himself admits that he is a cultural conservative but also a liberal in politics and a socialist in economics (1978, xi). Still, his critique of television and of contemporary hedonist, "sensate" culture parallels the neoconservative critique.

6. For theories about capitalist society, see Marx and Engels (1978), Marcuse (1964), Baran and Sweezy (1966), Mandel (1975), Lash and Urry (1987), and Kellner (1989a), which discusses the Frankfurt school's theories of capitalist society.

7. By "technocapitalism" I mean contemporary, transnational, corporate capitalism in which the capitalist mode of production and new technologies are creating new products, a new organization and structure of labor, and new forms of society, culture, and experience. For a preliminary delineation of the concept of technocapital, see Kellner (1989a). As the television industry is a crucial component of techno-capitalism, the present book can be read as an attempt to theorize the nature, form, and structure of contemporary capitalist societies via the perspective of television.

8. This position is elaborated in Kellner (1979, 1980, 1982), in Best and Kellner (1987), and in Kellner and Ryan (1988). By contrast, the present book provides a more critical/institutional analysis of television. (I shall later devote a separate book to analysis of television as a cultural form.)

9. On hegemony see Gramsci (1971) and Boggs (1986), and on ideology and hegemony see Kellner (1978, 1979). Among those others who utilize a hegemony approach as opposed to a capital logic or instrumental approach to conceptualizing the media in relation to the economy and society are Stuart Hall and the Birmingham school (see Hall et al. 1980) as well as Gitlin 1980, and Rapping 1987.

10. Brecht (1967), Benjamin (1969), and Enzensberger (1974, 1977) developed perspectives in which new technologies, as in film and broadcasting, could be used as instruments of liberation—by "refunctioning" the media to serve progressive goals. The present volume follows this tradition, which attempts to develop progressive uses for existing technologies and media. I should note that the first generation of the Frankfurt school also discussed emancipatory uses of popular culture and new technologies (Kellner 1989a), but for the most part they took a negative stance toward mass culture and communication.

2

Broadcasting and the Rise of Network Television

Resolved, that it is the sense of the conference that radio communication is a public utility and as such should be regulated and controlled by the federal government in the public interest.

—First National Radio Conference

This is one of the few instances that I know of in this country where . . . all of the people interested are unanimously for an extension of regulatory powers on the part of the Government.

—Herbert Hoover

I believe that television is going to be the test of the modern world, and that in this new opportunity to see beyond the range of our vision we shall discover either a new and unbearable disturbance of the general peace or a saving radiance in the sky. We shall stand or fall by television—of that I am quite sure.

—E. B. White

A vast wasteland.

—Newton Minow

The first three decades of the twentieth century witnessed the emergence of new communication technologies and industries that provided the basis for the system of commercial broadcasting in the United States. These communication industries quickly became important social and political forces, and the corporations that developed and controlled them became some of the most powerful institutions in the country. This chapter details the process by which commercial imperatives structured the form, content, and effects of broadcasting in the United States. We shall see how the network system of television evolved from the corporate and technological structures of radio broadcasting, and how television came to play an indispensable role in economic, political, social, and cultural life.

The story of broadcasting is one in which ever-more powerful corporations attempt to control leisure, entertainment, information, and mass communication in the interests of corporate profit and social control. These broadcasting corporations produced cultural industries that became an indispensable feature of corporate capitalism. A critical theory of broadcasting must accordingly analyze the interactions among technological inventions, economic imperatives, individual and group efforts to utilize the new technologies, and systemic needs and imperatives that together have created a specific type of commercial broadcasting in the United States.[1]

2.1 The Origins of Broadcasting

Television eventually emerged from a set of inventions and the development of a network system of commercial broadcasting. At the turn of the century, individual inventors such as Guglielmo Marconi developed new communication technologies that were appropriated by corporate enterprises, which in turn emerged as key institutions of transnational capitalism. Marconi's "wireless" sent messages through the air via the dots and dashes of Morse code. Reginald Fessenden developed a "continuous wave" technology that allowed the transmission of sound through the air. And Lee De Forest invented the "audion tube," which made possible dramatically improved reception and so served as the foundation for the emerging electronics industry. De Forest also envisaged radio broadcasting, and both he and Fessenden demonstrated their new technologies by airing music and speech—features that would become central to later radio broadcasting (Barnouw 1966; Douglas 1987).

These inventions appeared as the products of technological entrepreneurs who worked alone or with small teams. The new technologies were of interest to individuals wishing to utilize and develop them; they were also of interest to corporate and military powers. Almost immediately, however, major corporations came to monopolize broadcasting by their control over key patents. Early on, such corporations as American Telephone & Telegraph (AT&T), General Electric (GE), Westinghouse, and American Marconi began manufacturing radio receiving sets and transmitters and also assumed control over the new broadcast technologies.

In the decade before World War I, transnational corporations such as United Fruit were interested in radio technology because it represented a way to coordinate their foreign investments. During the same period, the U.S. military sought to use electronic communications in the planning and execution of warfare. The usefulness of radio became apparent when the military perceived that radio signals were not as vulnerable to destruction as telegraph wires. The military was given monopoly control over radio during World War I. All patents were put in a pool, amateur broadcasting was forbidden, and the U.S. navy was placed in charge of developing and administering the use of radio technology. After the war, the navy petitioned to obtain a state monopoly over radio, arguing that its successful development and administration of radio technology during the war justified its continued control of the new technology.

After World War I, powerful economic forces with allies in the navy eventually began developing a commercial system of broadcasting (Archer 1938, 156ff.). General Electric worked with American Marconi to buy patents from British Marconi in order to set up a U.S.-owned and -controlled communications industry. Certain political and military interests worried about British control of the communications cables, which were the lifeblood of international communication, and wanted to ensure that the United States had its own alternative system of over-the-air broadcast communication. Others envisaged the centrality of communications in the development of the American empire. GE executive Owen D. Young, who became first chairman of the Board of Directors of the Radio Corporation of America (RCA), later reported that he was told by officers in the navy that President Wilson

> had reached the conclusion, as a result of his experience in Paris, that there were three dominating factors in international relations—international transportation, international communication, and petroleum—and that the influence which a country exercised in international affairs would be largely dependent upon their position of dominance in these three activities; that Britain obviously had the lead and the experience in international transportation—it would be difficult if not impossible to equal her position in that field; in international communications she had acquired the practical domination of the cable system of the world; but that there was an apparent opportunity for the United States to challenge her in international communications through the use of radio; of course as to petroleum we already held a position of dominance. The result of American dominance in radio would have been a fairly equal stand-off between the U.S. and Great Britain—the U.S. having the edge in petroleum, Britain in shipping, with communications divided—cables to Britain and wireless to the U.S. (Young, cited in Archer 1938, 164)

This account indicates that the United States was keenly interested in empire after World War I, and that government officials were enlisting big industry and mass communications to pursue strategic geopolitical goals. It also points to the emerging importance of communications in the new international world order and thus explains why both government and private corporations would be willing to invest in risky new businesses such as radio and television. In light of the perceived importance of communications in the world economic and political order, RCA was formed in 1919 to guarantee control of radio by U.S. corporations. The new company, formed in large part by GE, bought out American and British Marconi. After securing patent and corporate alliances with AT&T, Western Electric, and Westinghouse, RCA developed a monopoly over "radio telegraphy."

Initially, RCA used radio technology for broadcasting messages—that is, as an auxiliary to the telegraph and telephone services; but the popularity of home radio entertainment and information directed it toward over-the-air broadcasting of music, news, sports, and talk for home receivers. Earlier, David Sarnoff (while serving in 1916 as assistant manager of the American Marconi company) had proposed development of a "Radio Music Box," which would "make radio a 'household utility' in the same sense as the piano or phonograph" (Archer 1938, 112–113). At first, RCA resisted radio broadcasting. However, after Westinghouse began broadcasting regular programming from its radio station in Pittsburgh, RCA followed suit, thereby beginning the dramatic "radio boom" of 1920–1922.

Radio was thus introduced within the framework of the capitalist system. Its needs and imperatives structured and dominated the system of commercial broadcasting soon to come. Radio was developed as a commercial enterprise during a period when corporate capital was expanding its system of mass production and consumption, and mass communications eventually came to play a central role in stabilizing, reproducing, and strengthening this system of consumer capitalism. By the 1920s capitalism had come to master the art of mass production with assembly lines, scientific management of the labor force, and the rationalization of production and distribution of its products. But it needed to discover new techniques for producing mass consumption, to integrate a restive and militant working class into the capitalist system, and to resolve the recurrent economic crises that had plagued the capitalist system from the beginning. The most forward-looking corporate leaders saw the importance of developing and controlling new communications technologies; as indicated by the earlier quote from Owen D. Young of GE, for the captains of industry, communications would come to be of central importance to the expansion of the business empire and the organization and coordination of markets.

The new technologies also sold citizens on the virtues of consumer capitalism and helped legitimate the capitalist system as the producer of new forms of technology and entertainment that promised to create a better existence for all. Radio in particular was universally perceived as a marvelous instrument of magical and fascinating voices when it first appeared. Like electricity, the automobile, airplanes, and cinema, all of which developed within the same time frame, radio was an exciting new technology that promised new experiences and gratifications. All were introduced by big corporations, thus helping to legitimate capitalism as a force of modernity and progress. These big corporations, in turn, sought both to control the new technologies and, in the case of broadcasting, to sell the virtues of new products and, eventually, of the consumer society itself.

Indeed, when radio appeared during the "Roaring Twenties" it was part of a series of new technologies and cultural forms that were bringing modernity into everyday life. Products and services offered to the masses started to proliferate. The automobile, airplane, and new communications technologies were breaking down barriers of time and space; radio, in particular, was delivering messages and entertainment simultaneously to thousands of homes across a large geographical area. In this new era of advertising, public relations, and new corporate management strategies, a commercial structure for broadcasting was eventually produced.

Thus, it was not merely the production of technological innovations and the "natural" inclinations of individuals and businesses to pursue profit that led to the development of commercial broadcasting. Also implicated was the desire of powerful corporations to control key technologies and markets and to legitimate the system as one that provided desirable goods and services. As Raymond Williams notes, "the key question about technological response to a need is less a question about the need itself than about its place in an existing social formation. A need which corresponds with the priorities of the real decision-making groups will, obviously, more quickly attract the investment of resources and the official permission, approval or encouragement on which a working technology, as distinct from available technical devices, depends" (1974, 19).

The new broadcasting corporations followed the main lines of capitalist development by seeking monopoly control of the market by giant firms, thus following the lead of oil, steel, railroad, and other major industries, which, as sectors of capital, were controlled by monopoly firms.[2] Indeed, the communications industry was heavily monopolized very early: AT&T controlled the telephone industry; Western Union monopolized the telegraph industry; RCA, Westinghouse, and GE dominated the industries producing radio and electric appliances; and NBC and CBS commanded radio broadcasting. In this way, the communications industry became increasingly powerful within the emerging system of monopoly capitalism, and broadcasting was (indeed, still is) dominated by these corporate forces.

Mergers with major corporations fueled the establishment of the system of commercial broadcasting. In 1921 the RCA consortium merged with Westinghouse and United Fruit, and established a virtual monopoly on radio patents. It forced many retail outlets to accept only RCA tubes and radio sets, whereas AT&T monopolized production of radio transmitters and dictated who could purchase them. In 1923 AT&T began what it called "toll broadcasting"; by leasing its New York station WEAF to anyone who had a commercial or other message to communicate to the public, it helped establish a commercial basis for broadcasting. It also began leasing its telephone lines to companies that wanted to "network" stations, but it reserved the most powerful transmitters for its own stations.

A variety of individuals and institutions struggled to take advantage of the radio boom. Early radio operators sent out regular programs from technically crude "studios," and department stores and businesses soon began sponsoring regular broadcasts of music and other forms of information and entertainment. In 1922 many educational stations and churches started using the service to disseminate their messages (Barnouw 1978, 12–13). Indeed, from 1922 to 1925 the proportion of American households with radios grew from a tiny fraction to more than 10 percent, and investment in radio receivers and parts jumped from $5 million to almost $500 million dollars (Barnouw 1966, 154, 210).

Radio broadcasting was fast becoming an important social force in the United States. But the chaos created by the proliferation of often overlapping broadcast signals led to a demand for government regulation. In response, Secretary of Commerce Herbert Hoover convened several Washington Radio Conferences to deal with the problem. Radio licenses were required for transmission, and wave-length frequencies were assigned; the biggest commercial enterprises obtained the most desirable wave lengths. But monopolistic practices were also attacked at the conference, where the following declaration was made: "Resolved, that it is the sense of the conference that radio communication is a public utility and as such should be regulated and controlled by the federal government in the public interest" (Barnouw 1968, 250).

Radio was thus conceived initially as a public utility, and the phrase concerning "public interest" was part of the rhetoric of public-utility regulation of the day—a discourse that officially continues to define the relations between broadcasting and government. Despite the conservative ethos of hegemony in the 1920s and the election of Republican presidents in 1920, 1924, and 1928, traces of progressivist and antimonopoly sentiment remained. Members of Congress, sectors of the press, and the public frequently attacked big monopolies (Hofstadter 1955; Pells 1973). From the beginning, the broadcasting industry itself was subject to criticism for its monopolistic tendencies. Small businesses that wanted to participate in the broadcasting explosion were inhibited by the control of key patents by the radio trust.

The intellectuals, educators, professionals, and radicals who had been the soul of the Progressive movement also wished to use radio to further their goals, as did religious figures. But their attempts to do so were frustrated by corporate control of broadcasting. Indeed, the biggest monopoly corporations aggressively continued to develop commercial broadcasting in their own corporate interests. AT&T expanded its operation, linking its New York toll station to one in Washington via its telephone wires; thus it commenced a sort of "chain broadcasting" experiment. However, its refusal to allow others the use of its cables (Barnouw 1978, 19) angered its corporate partners, who resented AT&T's attempt to gain a broadcast monopoly. Moreover, as broadcasting was mostly entertainment oriented, educators and reformers who wanted to use it for higher intellectual and cultural purposes were angered as well.

In short, antimonopoly sentiments were actively voiced both by businesses desiring to compete with the broadcast monopolies and by members of Congress and the public who favored antitrust legislation. The Progressive era had publicized the evils of monopoly and legitimated trust-busting regulatory activity. In light of these trends, it was not surprising that government antitrust action was initiated in 1924. The Federal Trade Commission went against the broadcast monopoly, charging that the four radio corporations had "conspired to create a monopoly in broadcasting and the manufacture of radio devices" (Barnouw 1978, 21).

This government action led to settlement of the corporate conflicts between the broadcasting interests. After protracted secret bargaining, AT&T agreed to sell its "toll stations" and to withdraw from broadcasting if the radio stations of its partners would use its telephone lines. As a result, RCA became the dominant force in broadcasting. In 1926 it launched the first broadcasting network, the National Broadcasting Company (NBC), which quickly expanded to two networks—the "red" and "blue" networks named after the color-coding system by which NBC charted its affiliates and network connections. During 1927, William Paley established the Columbia Phonograph Broadcasting System (now CBS). The three networks that would dominate broadcasting in the United States were now in place. (As we shall see, NBC was later forced to divest itself of the "blue" network, which became the American Broadcasting Company [ABC].)

It was also in 1927 that the Federal Radio Commission (FRC) was established, thus providing a governmental body to regulate broadcasting. The FRC temporarily suspended and then reallocated radio licenses, assigning the best frequencies to stations owned by the largest commercial interests. Educational stations were forced to share less powerful and thus less desirable frequencies. As a later summary of the career of the FRC concluded, "the point seems clear that the Federal Radio Commission has interpreted the concept of public interest so as to favor in actual practice one particular group. While talking in terms of the public interest, convenience and necessity the Commission actually chose to further the ends of the commercial broadcasters. They form the substantive content of public interest as interpreted by the Commission" (Herring, cited in Barnouw 1966, 219).

Nonetheless, broadcasting was initially conceptualized as a public trust (i.e., as a resource owned by the people), and advertising was either banned from radio or strictly limited. Inevitably, however, radio was used for commercial messages and soon became dominated by those corporate sponsors who produced the most popular programming and gained total control over its content. As advertising proved to be the best means of financing radio, corporate sponsors demanded control over programming and funded only what they considered "popular entertainment"; the commercial system thus inevitably arose on the basis of advertiser-financed broadcasting (Barnouw 1978; Horowitz 1989). Although the Radio Act of 1927 stipulated merely that all sponsored programs must announce which "person, firm, company, or corporation" had actually paid for the program, advertising eventually became what radio manufacturer Harold La Fount called "the life blood of the industry" (Mosco 1979, 8–9). Moreover, the corporate networks that resolved to use broadcasting for commercial purposes received the most advantageous frequency spectrums and came to constitute a system of strictly commercial broadcasting.

Still, government officials such as Herbert Hoover criticized commercial intrusion for cluttering up broadcasting during its formative period. In 1922, at the first National Radio Conference, Hoover stated that radio represented one of the few instances in which the public unanimously supported an extension of federal governmental powers. Moreover, both Hoover and Calvin Coolidge were in favor of a public-utility attitude toward broadcasting (Hoover, cited in Fly and Durr et al. 1959, 10). Hoover went so far as to claim that "[r]adio is not to be considered merely as a business carried on for private gain, for private advertisement, or for the entertainment of the curious. It is to be considered as a public trust, and to be considered primarily from the standpoint of the public interest" (ibid.). At a subsequent Washington Radio Conference, Hoover criticized the AT&T "toll broadcasting" concept and argued that it was against the public interest to "broadcast pure advertising matter" (Hoover, cited in Barnouw 1978, 15). Czitrom, however, suggests that although Hoover criticized advertising, his policies encouraged development of advertising-supported media (1982: 76ff.). Indeed, advertising executives of the period saw broadcasting as a powerful new field for managing consumer demand and consciousness (ibid.).

Early radio, however, was a contested terrain. Corporations wanted to use it for commercial purposes; educators and intellectuals wanted to use it for cultural purposes; and private individuals wanted to use short-wave radio to talk to one another. Initially, then, radio was employed as an instrument of communication and required a somewhat active orientation on the part of its audience, who had to work to tune in the receiver to the proper frequency and to experiment to discover the most interesting stations. As many listeners acquired technical knowledge and became radio "tinkerers" and ham-radio operators, radio became, in effect, a popular technology, used and appropriated by individuals for their own purposes. Although noncommercial uses predominated during the early years of radio, commercial interests inevitably took over and relegated noncommercial broadcasting to the margins of the system (Smythe 1981, 77ff.). Thus, while it appears "natural" to us today to have a commercialized system of broadcasting in the United States controlled by corporations and used for advertising, this configuration is in fact merely one of many forms of broadcasting that emerged as a victory over other conceptions of noncommercial broadcasting. The latter continued for decades to be the model employed by most European countries.

Indeed, early proposals to finance broadcasting included suggestions that radio be endowed by wealthy contributors, or that it be financed by municipalities or public subscription. Even David Sarnoff, president of NBC, initially envisaged a nonprofit broadcasting service that would be financed by the sale of radio sets and equipment, with RCA, GE, and Westinghouse contributing 2 percent of their profits (Siepmann 1950, 9ff.). Yet the commercial system of financing radio by advertising prevailed. By the 1930s "sponsors" were producing and controlling most of the entertainment broadcast over the radio, whereas the networks themselves were limiting production to music and educational programming. As Barnouw puts it:

> In the sponsor-controlled hours, the sponsor was king. He decided on programming. If he decided to change programs, network assent was considered *pro forma*. The sponsor was assumed to hold a "franchise" on his time period or periods. Many programs were advertising agency creations, designed to fulfill specific sponsor objectives. The director was likely to be an advertising agency staff employee. During dress rehearsal, an official of the sponsoring company was often on hand in the sponsor's booth, prepared to order last-minute changes. (1978, 33)

Sponsors produced what they considered to be the most popular type of programming in order to maximize the audiences who would be exposed to their "messages." Thus radio adopted the genre system of film, regularly broadcasting episodic series that fit into genres such as soap operas, cowboy and gangster series, comedy series like "Amos and Andy" or "Jack Benny," music shows, and some talk and discussion programming. During the Depression, escapist fare became especially popular and radio became the most popular form of home entertainment (MacDonald 1979). Indeed, entertainment came to dominate the airwaves during the "golden age of radio," as broadcasting served to divert audiences from the suffering of the Depression.

The Triumph of the Commercial System

By 1930 "more than six hundred radio stations were broadcasting to more than twelve million radio homes, about 40% of the total number of American families" (Czitrom 1982, 79). Radio provided the first form of simultaneous mass communication. It helped overcome ethnic, regional, and class differences by producing a shared culture dominated by commercial messages. In a sense, then, radio "united" the United States of America by creating its first national culture. Unlike Europe, the United States had neither a national press nor even a national news magazine at the start of the 1930s. The country consisted of widely divergent regions and contained significant immigrant cultures. Radio provided the unifying voice of national culture, dominated by the networks.

Radio also helped promote a homogeneous consumer culture. The commercial system guaranteed that broadcasting would be a vehicle for advertising, which in turn would constantly plug consumerism. The major radio sponsors hired advertising agencies to develop and produce programming, and the major corporations tried to create national markets for products and to convince consumers not only to buy their products but also to practice brand loyalty. Because these corporations sponsored popular radio programs, they were able to buy good will by providing the public with "free entertainment." In this way, radio produced a new mode of legitimation for corporate capitalism; through its entertainment it emerged as an ultramodern and beneficent force that served the public. Through radio commercials the corporations, too, were presented as salutary forces that provided not only remedies for the body (such as toothpaste, soap, and antiacid pills) but also products that reduced household labor or provided new sources of enjoyment. The magical voices of the air became the voices of corporate capital. Commodities now talked and sang and were celebrated by beloved celebrities. Capital had indeed found a powerful new tool of cultural hegemony.

The commercial system also established the hegemony of national networks over local outlets. Local stations all across the country were affiliated with the giant broadcasting networks. NBC, for instance, reimbursed stations for the sponsored network programs they broadcast. And CBS offered programming free to the affiliates in exchange for a commitment to schedule programming that would be paid for by sponsors. The sponsors, in turn, were guaranteed that a certain amount of affiliates would carry their programming.

The broadcasting corporations prospered under this arrangement, even during the Depression. Indeed, the power and profitability of broadcasting were enhanced as more and more people turned to radio for cheap entertainment and escape from the troubles of the period. But it was also during the 1930s that some attempts were made to create a more diverse and democratic system of broadcasting. In 1930 the Justice Department commenced antitrust proceedings that, by 1932, had forced a split between RCA and its corporate partners, including GE and Westinghouse (Archer 1939, 353ff.). RCA emerged from the separation as the top broadcasting system and came to dominate, as well, the manufacture and sale of radio equipment during the decades following the antitrust split (Archer 1939, 380ff.).

The commercial system of broadcasting continued, however, to come under pressure toward reform and democratization. Reformers attacked the commercial system and called for increased educational radio facilities. In 1934 the Hatfield-Wagner Act was introduced in the Senate. It called for the allocation of 25 percent of broadcasting facilties to be licensed for noncommercial radio, for use by "educational, religious, agricultural, labor, cooperative, and similar non-profit-making associations" (Barnouw 1970, 23ff.). Religious leaders and educators supported this move: Dean Thomas Brenner of the University of Illinois claimed that the Depression had brought a "sickness" to American culture and that a revitalized broadcasting system was necessary to cure it. Intellectuals and labor leaders increased their criticism of the commercial broadcasting system and called for an alternative structure of broadcasting.

In 1934 commercial interests organized against the Hatfield-Wagner Act, whch was defeated in the Senate. During the same week, the Communications Act of 1934 set up a new Federal Communications Commission (FCC), which was mandated to regulate broadcasting in "the public interest, convenience, and necessity." Although this clause was ambiguous, the act clearly defined broadcasting as a public good, subject to regulation by a government agency. The act also required that the government grant licenses only to responsible organizations and that the FCC suspend or revoke such licenses in the event of abuse. Specific abuses (obscenity, lotteries, monopoly, etc.) were documented, and Section 315 required equal access to candidates running for political office. The FCC was also mandated to "study new uses for radio, provide for experimental uses of frequencies and generally encourage the larger and more effective use of radio in the public interest." A subhead of Section 307 required that the FCC study the proposal for the allocation of a certain percentage of nonprofit radio (Siepmann 1950, 15ff.).

The Communications Act of 1934 thus appeared to establish a democratic foundation for broadcasting, inasmuch as the airwaves were declared a public utility to be used in the public interest. Yet, as Barnouw argues, the new Communications Act "represented an almost total victory for the status quo" (1970, 26). Although it contained much democratic rhetoric and was eventually used in occasional attempts to reform the commercial system, the regulatory apparatus largely served the interests of the corporations it was supposed to regulate. The FCC itself rarely revoked licenses or attempted to reform the system of commercial broadcasting. For the most part, it was dominated by commissioners who were sympathetic to the existing broadcasting interests and system, and who did little to change or modify the commercial structure (Horowitz 1989).

The commercial system of broadcasting provided an ideological voice for corporate capital during an era when protracted economic crisis led to calls for radical restructuring of the capitalist system. As noted, radio entertainment provided a diversion and escape from the problems of the Depression, but it excluded radical political discourse. Radio broadcasting was dominated by entertainment, and its control by commercial interests served to reproduce dominant ideological codes through a celebration of the same hegemonic values central to Hollywood films—family, romance, material success, individualism, patriotism, and so on. Radio relentlessly promoted a star system that produced national celebrities and intensified the individualism that anchored the national ideology. It tended to ignore the suffering of the Depression and failed to address race divisions and inequalities, massive unemployment, and the problems created by a capitalist economy out of control. Corporate control ensured that there would be no broadcasts of messages that might challenge the existing capitalist system of production, commercial control of broadcasting, and other major institutions. Labor and all left-wing parties were also rigorously excluded from network broadcasting (Barnouw 1970). In short, the logic of accumulation dictated a logic of exclusion, which in turn guaranteed that broadcasting would reproduce the dominant values of corporate capitalism and block discourses that challenged capitalism.

The most popular genres of radio entertainment helped advance a homogenized hegemonic set of values in the United States, in effect producing a "mainstream" culture in a large, diverse nation wth varying regional, ethnic, and traditional values. Soap operas projected proper role models for men and women as they dramatized the pain and suffering brought about through violation of social norms (Herzog 1941). In the world of the soap opera, extra-marital sex invariably brought unwanted pregnancies and social ostracism, and every series had a villainess, or villain, who attempted to disrupt happy marriages or romances. Westerns and gangster series idealized male authority figures and, like their cinematic counterparts, legitimated violence as a way to eliminate threats to the existing order. Along with comic books, radio circulated the exploits of new superheroes such as The Lone Ranger, Superman, Batman, The Shadow, and The Green

Hornet, who represented American values against those who threatened existing institutions and traditional ways of life (Jewett and Lawrence 1988).

Radio also promoted certain political personalities who learned how to use the new technology and thereby personalized political discourse. President Roosevelt used his fireside chats to calm the nation and to promote his New Deal programs, Father Coughlin advanced a brand of American fascism, and Huey Long articulated a type of charismatic populism. At the same time, in part because of pressures from newspapers, severe restraints were placed on news programming: Broadcasters agreed in the 1930s that no news item could exceed 30 seconds and that news bulletins could provide material only for two 5-minute news broadcasts a day (Barnouw 1968, 18ff.); and the Associated Press news service agreed to provide news clips for free in exchange for a pledge by the radio networks not to establish news-gathering teams and departments (Czitrom 1982, 86). Rising interest in the events in Europe during World War II, however, eventually led broadcasters to increase their news output (Charney 1948).

Ideological commentary abounded nevertheless. It ranged from Du Pont's "Cavalcade of America," which celebrated corporate capitalism's triumphs, to the right-wing commentaries of Boake Carter, Father Coughlin, and Fulton Lewis, Jr.[3] Of course, not all radio entertainment and information was conservative and rightist. As Barnouw (1978, 34ff) points out, isolationist and profascist commentators were countered by such antifascists as Edward R. Murrow, Raymond Swing, and William Shirer. "The Pursuit of Happiness," and other such programs, "made a point of its ethnic diversity, introducing such talents as the black ex-convict 'Leadbelly' (Huddie Ledbetter), the 'borscht circuit' comedian Danny Kaye, the hobo laureate Woody Guthrie, and scheduling a radio premiere of 'Ballad for Americans' in a powerful rendition by Paul Robeson" (ibid., 36). To a very limited degree, then, broadcasting allowed some political debate and served as a "cultural forum" in which contesting cultural forces could participate—within certain limits. Yet, despite its growing strength, labor was never allowed a voice in mainstream broadcasting; nor (with rare exceptions) were socialist, communist, and other radical political groups.

Monopoly Capitalism, Struggles for Corporate Hegemony, and the War

With the invention of television, the struggle for dominance of the telecommunications industry reached a fever pitch in the 1930s. In their book, *Television: A Struggle for Power*, Frank Waldrop and Joseph Borkin (1938) recount how AT&T and RCA battled for supremacy in the communications industry. AT&T wanted to use telephone lines to broadcast television into homes, whereas RCA wanted to use wireless, over-the-air broadcasting to maintain control of radio and to secure control of television. As indicated in an in-house memo, certain AT&T executives envisaged control of broadcasting: "[Although the corporation had not] stated to the public in any way . . . the idea that the Bell system desires to monopolize broadcasting . . . the fact remains that it is a telephone job, that we are the telephone people . . . and it seems the clear, logical conclusion that must be reached is that sooner or later, in one form or another, we have got to do the job" (cited in Berkman 1988, 36).[4]

RCA also had hegemonic dreams of control over the entire communications system of the United States. During the late 1920s RCA President Sarnoff envisaged about six superstations so powerful that they could cover the entire country: "These super-power stations . . . will radiate the same program with a power to reach every home in the United States" (Sarnoff, cited in Berkman 1988, 40). Later, during the mid-1930s, RCA considered not only developing facsimile electronic reproduction, which would deliver newspaper and other print material into the home, but also introducing two-way televisual phone communication via broadcast waves. In addition, RCA sought ways to deliver movies to homes or theaters via broadcasting. These developments, in conjunction with control over broadcasting, would have given the network almost total control over the communications industry. The two corporate giants, RCA and AT&T, were thus seeking monopoly control of all forms of mass communication, thereby reproducing earlier attempts by the "robber barons" to dominate the major industrial and financial institutions.

In the 1930s and 1940s AT&T and RCA reached a compromise, dividing between themselves and other big corporations the field of communications. This compromise established the basis for the present system of television. AT&T retained control of telephone lines, and RCA dropped development of over-the-air two-way televisual phone communication. The introduction of facsimile reproduction was postponed, and publishing interests retained control of print material. For these concessions, RCA was allowed to remain the foremost corporate power in broadcasting.

There were several reasons for the delay in introducing television in the United States. As Brian Winston states:

"[T]he capital necessary to diffuse TV was then being applied to the movies—by now the talkies—and to radio. The very same firms were interested in all three areas, and judged that TV would be a threat to current business but had interesting future possibilities. . . . A major factor in the delay in the United States was that RCA so controlled the patents that the Federal Communications Commission was worried about the survival of the other firms that could make TV equipment. It therefore stood in the path of RCA's development of TV from 1936–1941. The FCC was trying to prevent the

AT&T telephone monopoly from being reproduced by RCA in this area. By 1941 the necessary agreements had been struck, but U.S. entry into the war that year halted further development." (Winston in Downing 1990, 65)

U.S. involvement in World War II contributed to the postponement of the introduction of television because crucial electronics resources and personnel were enlisted in the war effort. When the United States intervened in the war, partisan debate of all sorts subsided in favor of a unified war effort. Broadcasting played a crucial role in this effort, by explaining the reasons for U.S. intervention, entertaining the troops, and keeping up morale at the home front. Many broadcast executives joined the war effort, advertisers entered the Office of War Information and the War Advertising Council (Fox 1975), and radio news commentators such as Edward R. Murrow became trusted "voices of truth" and reassuring sources of information.

During World War II, radio played a key role in mobilizing the country for the rigors of a war economy and mobilizing public opinion in support of U.S. involvement in the war. It was also during this period that state monopoly capitalism emerged as the economic and political structure dominant in the United States. In the 1920s the major corporations had attempted to produce a consumer society, but the Depression brought industrial activity to a halt. In the 1930s the state intervened in the economy during the New Deal, but this intervention failed to revive economic productivity and growth. With the massive intervention of the state in the war effort, however, the biggest corporations prospered from gigantic government contracts and the economy finally mobilized the labor force and the productive capacity to produce for the military struggle.[5]

Excess profits from the boom in production went into radio advertising, and radio faithfully sold war bonds, patriotic ideology, and support for the allied effort. Advertisers helped boost the patriotic spirit, used patriotism to sell their goods, and produced a positive image for firms that were primarily engaged in the production of war materials. Radio also became the most trusted source of news and a crucial medium of communication, gaining tremendous prestige in the process. The constructive contributions of the advertising and broadcasting industries helped suppress government proposals to tax advertising and to regulate broadcasting more strenuously during and after the war (Barnouw 1978, 37ff.).

Yet pressures to control broadcast monopoly continued. In 1941 the FCC followed its mandate to attack monopoly in the broadcast industry and carried out a Chain Broadcasting Investigation to explore monopoly tendencies and effects. By 1943 it had forced RCA to divest itself of one of its two networks (which became ABC). In 1946 the FCC issued a report on "Public Service Responsibility of Broadcast Licensees" (the so-called

Blue Book), which criticized both the impact on programming of an advertising-financed commercial system and the lack of adequate public affairs programming and lively discussion of controversial issues. At the same time, the report claimed that many stations had failed to fulfill the promises they had made when petitioning for licenses. The FCC proposed stricter licensing and renewal procedures, but no effective action was taken on the report's recommendations (Barnouw 1970, 227ff.).

On the eve of the introduction of television in the 1940s, the three networks—which ultimately would dominate television and serve as the oligopolistic kingpins of broadcasting—thus controlled the commercial system then in place. Within this system, the interests of the television industry guided government broadcasting regulatory agencies and advanced the television network's private interests rather than enforcing the "public interest, convenience, and necessity." Here, too, the dynamics of the broadcast industry resembled those of corporate capitalism, whereby government regulatory agencies furthered the interests of the industries supposedly under regulation (Lowi 1979; Horowitz 1989).

Indeed, government and industry frequently suppressed technologies of communication in the hopes of protecting the interests of the corporations that dominated the communications arena. These actions included the calculated abandonment in the 1930s of the facsimile technologies that would have ensured cheap delivery of print material into each home while increasing the number of news organizations and voices (Smythe 1981, 83ff.), as well as the postponement of FM radio, which would have made possible a dramatic expansion in the number of broadcasting outlets. And after encouraging the beginnings of an FM system in the early 1940s, the FCC in 1945 shifted the frequency allocation for FM, thus rendering the existing 500,000 FM radio sets obsolete and setting back the fledgling FM industry. The purported reason for this shift in frequency was technical in nature, but most experts disagreed with the recommendation that the FCC nonetheless enforced—a recommendation that once again held back development of FM radio (Mosco 1979, 50ff.). FM's inventor, Edwin Armstrong, eventually committed suicide.

The pattern was later played out when attempts were made to introduce Ultra High Fidelty (UHF), cable, pay television (Mosco 1979; Horowitz 1989), and satellite television (see section 5.4). In each case, the dominant broadcast oligopolies suppressed the new technologies, which they saw as destabilizing competitors, threatening their control over the communications field. The broadcast industries successfully manipulated Congress and governmental regulatory commissions into prohibiting implementation of the new technologies, resulting in what Horowitz calls "the sabotage of new technologies" (1989, 174ff.). The networks followed with attempts to develop, take over, and utilize the new technologies for their own interests, introducing the technologies in ways that utilized the patterns already established by the communication giants. In this manner, they strengthened corporate control of the broadcast system and the power of the dominant broadcasting interests within this system.

2.2 The Coming of Television

Network television emerged in the late 1940s from within the same framework as radio. The radio networks continued to dominate television, and many top radio stars (e.g., Jack Benny, Red Skelton, Perry Como, and Patti Page) and programs (e.g., "Gunsmoke," "Dragnet," and "Amos and Andy") migrated to television. During this transition period, beginning around 1946, the three major television networks utilized the same series formats already developed by radio and film (e.g., soap operas, situation comedies, cop and crime dramas, quiz shows, and suspense thrillers). Television thus contributed to the process of cultural homogenization decried by theorists of the so-called mass society. (For futher discussion of the "mass culture" and "mass society" debate, see Rosenberg and White 1957 and Swingewood 1977.)

Television and the Affluent Society

The advent of television and the emergence of a consumer society were part of the same historical conjuncture. At the end of World War II, corporate capitalism was geared up to produce a large variety of mass consumption goods, which needed to be sold to consumers. Corporate capital might have created a consumer society earlier, except that the Depression and war intervened (Ewen 1976); it was only during the postwar period that conditions were ripe. Industrial firms had been operating at full capacity to support the war effort, and corporations were preparing to switch from war production to consumer production. During the war, unions had gained in strength and workers had struggled for higher wages. When servicemen returned home, having accumulated large savings, they were eager to marry, raise families, and enjoy the benefits of the new age of affluence that was promised and to some extent realized.

The same period witnessed massive migrations to the suburbs. New suburban housing developments promised clean air, a wholesome environment in which to raise children, and a new mode of affluent living. Television fit smoothly into this great transformation, and its ubiquitous entertainment provided a new mode of leisure activity for suburban dwellers cut off from city culture. At the same time, television advertising and entertainment presented the new artifacts of consumer culture and promoted consumer life-styles that eventually encompassed suburban, urban, and rural life. New shopping malls provided the goods and services advertised on television, and television itself quickly became both a privileged source of advertising revenue and an important manager of consumer demand (Siepmann 1950, 328ff.; Bogart 1956, 184ff.).

As suburbanization mushroomed during the late 1940s and 1950s, the new "talking furniture" became a fixture in U.S. society. Rarely before had any new technology so rapidly and successfully taken hold in society. In 1946, when the networks were beginning to develop a regular television service, only a small number of homes had television sets. By 1950, 96 television stations were broadcasting to 3.1 million homes (Bogart 1956, 10, 12), and by 1956–1957, 500 stations were broadcasting to 40 million homes, 85 percent of which were equipped with television sets that were turned on an average of 5 hours per day (Barnouw 1975, 198). Thus, in little more than a decade, television had become a central feature of life in the United States.

At this time, transnational capitalism achieved world dominance. The United States had emerged after World War II with its economy intact, and its aggressive corporations were ready to develop a worldwide system dominated by U.S. transnational corporations. Television was a crucial element in this boom period because its advertisements promoted consumption and its programs celebrated the joys of the consumer society. Although the networks broadcast some socially critical news programs and documentaries, they tended to put their corporate interest in maximizing profit before the public interest of providing stimulating and thought-provoking information and entertainment (see Chapter 3 for documentation and further analysis).

In the late 1940s opportunities still existed to diversify television and to produce a more informative, complex, and challenging system. The new technology known as Ultra High Fidelity television (UHF) would have made it possible to greatly expand the television spectrum. But under pressure from interests in the television industry, the government in 1948 sanctioned development of a Very High Fidelity (VHF) television system, which restricted the available television spectrum to twelve channels and thus enabled the networks to dominate American television. If the UHF system had originally been mandated, however, a much more diverse and pluralistic system could have evolved (Mosco 1979).[6]

In 1948 the FCC declared a freeze on new television licenses that lasted until 1952, when a veritable television boom period began. Indeed, leisure has been organized around television watching ever since. TV henceforth became the electronic hearth in the suburbs and the city alike. The flickering TV screen was the most dazzling spectacle in the home, and the entire family was drawn to it with great fascination. In record numbers families watched the new situation comedies such as "I Love Lucy" and the variety shows put on by Ed Sullivan, Milton Berle, and Jackie Gleason. New celebrities emerged overnight and a fascinated audience viewed more than ever: In 1955, for instance, one out of every two people in the United States watched Mary Martin play Peter Pan (Bogart 1956, 1). Never before had so many people engaged in the same cultural experience at the same time. TV culture had arrived.

By the late 1940s it was clear to leaders in the industry that television would have to be an advertiser-supported medium. Its executives accordingly undertook the task of convincing corporations and advertising agencies of the virtues of television advertising. NBC President Pat Weaver led this effort and tirelessly sold television advertising, telling one group of executives:

> [T]he automated business needs a constant, dependable, unfluctuating demand for its output. . . . This and other solutions to steady demand mean a new kind of selling—a complete change in emphasis—educational selling to wean consumers from old habits into new ways of keeping with a new era. . . . The Post-War Era which created new selling problems which might have caused a recession, evened up the score by providing business with the very instrument it needed to meet the challenge and the needs of the new selling concepts and methods. That instrument—*the greatest mutation in communications history* . . . man's greatest communication invention—television. A medium that proved itself, from the first, to be also the most powerful, exciting, flexible of all advertising media. (Weaver, cited in Boddy 1987, 353; emphasis in original)

Television advertising had thus come to be the vanguard of the consumer society, educating people about the new consumer goods and services that they would need as up-to-date members of the affluent society. Television also began to emerge as a mega-business and as a major cultural and political force. The ratings system, established by the 1950s, fixed advertising revenues according to the number of people watching a particular program at a given time. So much money was involved that only popular shows with good ratings survived. From the beginning, TV became a "copy-cat" medium, repeating and imitating its own biggest successes. Consequently, successive waves of variety entertainment shows, situation comedies, westerns, action/adventure series, and quiz shows came to dominate network television in the 1950s.

Television, like radio before it, increased the power and prestige of corporations, which presented themselves as benevolent and powerful providers. The announcement "NBC presents" pegged members of the audience as the recipients of entertainment provided by the powerful TV network; the slogan "General Electric brings to you" showcased GE as a friendly benefactor whose personal "to you" suggested that the programming was specially produced for the benefit of individual viewers.

The commercial format determined the form and structure of television programming. During the first decade of television, when production was primarily live, commercials were woven into the programs in a variety of ways, ranging from "Mama's" use of Maxwell House Coffee during the broadcast of "I Remember Mama" to the various characters on "Burns and Allen" who interrupted the story line to talk about the sponsor's product (Hay 1989). These practices ended with the advent of taped television, at which time a "magazine programming" concept was adopted in which programs were regularly interrupted for advertising "breaks" or "spots." Since that time, series television programs have been edited into 30- and 60-minute segments with well-structured interruptions for advertising.

During the 1950s the sponsors literally produced the shows themselves and thus had complete control over programming form and content. Early on, they perceived that "popular entertainment" created the most favorable climate for their advertising messages. Popular shows like "Ozzie and Harriet" and "Milton Berle" made the audiences feel good, and the sponsors hoped that these good feelings would be transferred to their products. In short, the sponsors wished to eliminate unpleasant programming or programs that "confused" or "alienated" the audiences in any way. Accordingly, simple, formulaic programs quickly became the norm.

In the mid-1950s the television networks attempted to take over control of programming, either producing the programs themselves or contracting programming from production companies, thus eliminating full sponsor control. But, as Boddy argues, this move—rather than improving program-ming—was decisive in the transformation from the so-called "golden age of television" to the "vast wasteland" (1987, 347ff.). One of the first effects of this move was a switch in programming from anthology series to episodic series—a switch that, as Barnouw has argued, was influenced by commercial considerations (1978, 102ff). The individual dramas in anthology series often featured disturbing problems and controversial material, thereby creating friction between the executives, on the one hand, and producers and writers who wanted to produce more socially critical programs, on the other. Many of the anthology dramas dealt with working-class life ("Marty") and even with the underclass ("Requiem for a Heavyweight"), whereas sponsors came to prefer programs with a more up-scale ambience. In addition, some of the dramas that dealt with upper-class, corporate life (e.g., "Patterns") were critical of the business culture. Moreover, the anthology dramas, which were influenced by theater, often took place in a closed, interior space, whereas the sponsors generally preferred the open outdoors as an environment for the action and adventure spectacles that came to dominate television by the late 1950s.

From the mid- to late 1950s a shift took place from live to filmed television and from anthology drama to episodic series as the basic type of entertainment programming; meanwhile, the center of television production moved from New York to California. Commercial imperatives dictated these changes as television more aggressively reproduced the ethos and values of corporate capitalism. Later, during the 1950s and early 1960s, an ever-closer fit between television and U.S. society occurred. The famous situation comedies of the era (e.g., "Ozzie and Harriet," "Father Knows Best," "The Donna Reed Show," "Leave It to Beaver") presented idealized images of American life by portraying nuclear families and middle-class values and norms. The commercial ambience of television thus tended to replicate the commercial ambience of life in affluent society during an era when the consumer society was established as the specific form of social organization in the United States.

Sponsors also preferred fast action and quick, often violent resolution of problems. Indeed, both the situation comedies and the action/adventure programming generally followed a conflict-resolution model similar to the ads, which frequently depicted a problem and then offered a product as the solution. As sponsors seemed to prefer programming that guaranteed a resolution of problems (as did the ads), a happy ending for the program was likewise guaranteed. In addition to controlling both the format and structure of television programming, sponsors relentlessly controlled and censored program content in line with their interests (for examples, see Barnouw 1970, 3ff.; Brown 1971, 65; and Lee and Solomon, 60ff.). In a very literal sense, then, network television became the voice of corporate capitalism and the instrument of its hegemony—a hegemony firmly established in the United States during the 1950s.

Advertisers had earlier produced most radio and television entertainment and had total control over its content. In the late 1950s, however, television networks assumed control over programming in the wake of disclosures regarding quiz show "fixes" that ensured the victory of "likable" contestants (Anderson 1978). Henceforth, the networks and production companies (most of which were located in Hollywood) produced television shows, and the networks took responsibility for their content with "standard and practice" offices—a euphemism for censorship agencies, which ensured that nothing would appear on television that contradicted the interests of the corporate behemoths who controlled broadcasting. All disturbing problems such as juvenile delinquency, racism, alcoholism, and the divisive communist witch-hunts were excluded from television entertainment. Meanwhile, the cold war was presented in simplistic images in action/adventure series, thus promoting the virulent anticommunism that was sweeping the country.

Television and the Cold War

From the time of its introduction in 1946, television promoted the ethos of anticommunism that defined the cold war mentality. During the 1950s television news and talk shows were dominated by aggressively anticommunist cold war programming (MacDonald 1985, 13ff.). Even entertainment programming contained heavy doses of cold war spy dramas and dramatization of East-West struggles (Barnouw 1968, 213ff., 366ff.; MacDonald 1985, 101ff.). The Ziv television company specialized in cold war thrillers and produced such anticommunist programs as "I Led Three Lives," "Foreign Intrigue," "China Smith," and "Crusader," which dramatized the evils of communism while heroizing anticommunist intelligence agents and warriors.

The television industry also capitulated to the anticommunist witchhunts, which began with the House Un-American Activities Committee (HUAC) hearings in 1947. During these hearings, members of the film industry were attacked for their alleged communist sympathies. In 1947 a four-page pamphlet entitled "Counterattack" began appearing. In it were listed the political associations of members of both the film and television industries, and in 1950 the booklet "Red Channels" listed political associations and affiliations of 151 members of the entertainment industries who were accused of being supporters of communism. Many careers were destroyed by the adverse publicity and network blacklisting. Jean Muir, scheduled to star in the series "The Aldrich Family," found her contract canceled a week before the first telecast. In addition, actor Philip Loeb was forced off the popular series "The Goldbergs"; soon thereafter, he committed suicide when he found that he could no longer obtain employment (Barnouw 1975, 117ff.).

Some television entertainers (e.g., Ed Sullivan) actively supported the drive to blacklist alleged communist sympathizers, and the networks generally went along—especially after a Syracuse supermarket owner, Laurence Johnson, began threatening boycotts of companies that sponsored shows involving blacklisted personnel and pressuring sponsors to eliminate all politically suspicious television employees (Barnouw 1975, 127ff.). A few television executives and personalities resisted,[7] but most of the industry supported the blacklist.

Television also tended to advance the crusade of Senator Joe McCarthy, who called for elimination of all alleged communist influence from the state department, military, universities, unions, and other sectors of American life. The anticommunist cause was strengthened when Eisenhower appointed two McCarthy supporters, John Doerfer and Robert E. Lee, to the FCC (Barnouw 1975, 152). McCarthy himself frequently appeared on television talk shows, and network news programs and documentaries tended to support his aggressive anticommunist posturing (MacDonald 1985). The dramatic exception was the CBS "See It Now" team of Edward Murrow and Fred Friendly. Murrow, a prestigious and trusted journalist, agonized with his producer Friendly over the harmful effects of McCarthyism on American life. Ultimately, they began producing programming that exposed the senator's tactics and dramatized the effects of his policies.

In October 1953 Friendly and Murrow broadcast a "See It Now" program pertaining to Lieutenant Milo Radulovich, a 26-year-old Air force Reserve member who had been forced to resign his commission because his father and sister allegedly subscribed to left-wing periodicals and had "radical leanings." As none of these allegations had been proven, Radulovich and his family gave the appearance of being innocent victims of an unscrupulous political inquisition. The Air Force quickly reversed its decision and Murrow became a hero (Friendly 1967; Barnouw 1975, 172ff.).

Murrow and Friendly soon produced additional broadcasts on Mc-Carthyism and even went after McCarthy himself in a program on March 9, 1954. Most of the latter show consisted of segments of speeches and interviews with McCarthy that exposed his use of innuendo, his inconsistencies, and his bullying techniques and personality. Murrow concluded with temperate criticism of McCarthy and then allowed McCarthy to respond during a subsequent program. McCarthy attacked Murrow in his rejoinder, calling him "the leader and the cleverest of the jackal pack which is always found at the throat of anyone who dares to expose individual communists and traitors." Shortly thereafter, McCarthy's techniques were further exposed and discredited by the Army/McCarthy hearings, which were televised in their entirety by ABC and covered by the other networks as well. Following his pitiful showing, McCarthy was censored by the Senate at the end of the year. He responded by attacking Eisenhower as well as other prominent Republicans; they fought back and McCarthy was finished, dying in political eclipse two years later.[8]

The end of McCarthy did not, however, mean the end of either the blacklist or McCarthyism. Texas entertainer and folk humorist John Henry Faulk found himself blacklisted in 1956 and filed a lawsuit that took many years to win (Faulk 1964). Until Murrow's programs and the televising of the Army/McCarthy hearings, television had more or less capitulated to McCarthyism; it actually promoted the anticommunist ideology that McCarthy had so successfully packaged.

An understanding of television's role in the cold war will illuminate the specific functions that television served—and continues to serve—in U.S. society. In general, television tends to reproduce the positions of the dominant hegemonic political forces of the era simply because, in its zeal to win good ratings and big profits, it gravitates toward what it believes is popular. As a consequence, it tends to reinforce and reproduce the dominant ethos, ideology, and policies. Yet television also has a role to play in mediating social conflict, in establishing an overall ideological legitimacy for the system, and in "neutrally" depicting the major political contenders of the day. The major contending forces are Democratic liberalism versus Republican conservativism—configurations that have taken somewhat different forms from the 1940s to the present. Thus, in the event of intra-ruling-class conflict, television will tend to reproduce it.

At the end of World War II, the so-called China Lobby began to attack liberals for "losing China," and McCarthy and others began to attack their opponents as being "soft" on communism—as outright "pinkoes" or even "reds." For years, liberals had been on the defensive; but, in taking on the army and threatening investigations of the CIA, McCarthy had overstepped the boundaries of what establishment figures deemed permissible. Moreover, he had revealed himself to be a bully, a drunk, and a liar. And when someone like McCarthy, or later Nixon, goes beyond the boundaries of what arbiters of ideological legitimacy think is acceptable, television intervenes and eliminates or tempers them. From this perspective, McCarthy simply went too far and television allowed Murrow and others to criticize him—not out of liberal bias or crusading zeal, but simply because television was coming to play a central role in mediating intra-ruling-class conflict in the United States and in promoting a certain consensus and harmony. McCarthy, by contrast, was too "hot" for the "cool" TV age (McLuhan 1964) and too extreme for the centrist liberal/conservative consensus that was emerging as the dominant ideology in the 1950s. This consensus would be severely tested during the 1960s, a decade of intense conflict.

2.3 Television in the 1960s

The 1960s began with the election of John F. Kennedy as president. It is generally agreed that Kennedy was the first television president and that he manipulated the new medium better than any politician before him (Halberstam 1979, 316ff.). Moreover, it was during the Kennedy presidency that television itself became a major political force. Throughout the 1960 primaries and conventions, Kennedy successfully used television to gain the presidential nomination; furthermore, it was most likely his use of television in the campaign against Nixon—especially his superior showing in the television debates—that enabled him to win the election. Likewise, it was Kennedy who first made effective use of television news conferences, television interviews, and televised White House visits, as well as of televised political events that enhanced his image. Indeed, the drama of the Kennedy presidency was made for television: The Bay of Pigs, the visit to Berlin, the Cuban missile crisis, space shots, and the "Camelot" White House all made for great television and greatly enhanced the power and prestige of both television and the presidency.

Kennedy's good looks, his attractive wife Jacqueline, and his telegenic children also produced a positive television image. Moreover, TV seemed forgiving of his many mistakes, quickly dismissing negative stories (such as the Bay of Pigs fiasco) in favor of more positive images of Kennedy the man and president. But it was perhaps the Kennedy assassination and funeral during which television achieved its greatest triumph and prestige; indeed, it was now a central force in American political and social life. After Kennedy's assassination in Dallas in November 1963, the networks eliminated their regular programming for four days to broadcast the transition of power to Lyndon Johnson, the Kennedy funeral, and Jack Ruby's assassination of Lee Harvey Oswald. After depicting the shocking events of the day, television attempted to provide stability in an unstable world by broadcasting state rituals that served to reassure the populace that a smooth change in government was occurring. Television bound the country together in rituals of national mourning and national drama, and demonstrated that it was now a new national force.

It was during this period that Kennedy's FCC Commissioner Newton Minow made his famous "vast wasteland" speech and pushed for the development of public television. During his first speech to the National Association of Broadcasters in 1961, Minow praised what he considered good on television and then said:

But when television is bad, nothing is worse. I invite you to sit down in front of your television set when your station goes on the air and stay there without a book, magazine, newspaper, profit and loss sheet or rating book to distract you—and keep your eyes glued to that set until the station signs off. I can assure you that you will observe a vast wasteland. You will see a procession of game shows, violence, audience participation shows, formula comedies about totally unbelievable families, blood and thunder, mayhem, violence, sadism, murder, western badmen, western good men, private eyes, gangsters, more violence, and cartoons. And endlessly, commercials—many screaming, cajoling, and offending. (Minow, cited in Barnouw 1975, 300)

Early in the 1960s TV turned to the "new frontier" liberalism associated with the Kennedy administration and thus became less conservative than it had been in the 1950s. Of course, this is not surprising, given that television tends to follow the political trends and currents of the day. In fact, television became increasingly competitive during the 1960s, and the stakes were extremely high: Tens of thousands of dollars of revenue were won or lost with every ratings point, and the competition was fierce.

Accordingly, the networks constantly attempted to discern new trends, social developments, and issues to attract an audience.

As a consequence, Kennedy liberalism began to appear in 1960s television in such programs as "East Side/West Side," "The Defenders," "Ben Casey," "Dr. Kildare," and "Mr. Novak." As the United States became more interventionist and the Vietnam War escalated, more and more spy shows and anticommunist programming began appearing, including "Mission: Impossible," "I Spy," "The Man From U.N.C.L.E.," and other spy dramas. But the networks also broadcast the satire "Get Smart," which spoofed the deadly seriousness and cold war Manichaeism of the heavy-handed anticommunist dramas.

Cold war drama was the dominant mode, nevertheless: The 1960s saw more military series (in the form of both war dramas and situation comedies) than did any other epoch in TV history (MacDonald 1985, 191ff.). Such anticommunist entertainment was hardly incidental, given that this was the era of Vietnam.

At the same time, however, TV began depicting social conflicts at home to a much greater extent than previously. For one thing, the expansion of television news from 15 to 30 minutes in 1963 accelerated the amount of news coverage during a period when political struggle was intensifying. After the quiz scandals of the late 1950s and the political pressure applied by Newton Minow and other liberal FCC commissioners to improve the quality of television, the networks greatly expanded their news operations and increased not only the length and quality of the prime-time news programs but also the number of documentaries. Audiences thus began to see dramatic images of the civil rights struggle: Filling their TV screen were pictures of demonstrations, bombed churches, and blacks beaten and hosed by Southern police, chased by dogs, and brutally arrested. The 1960s also witnessed such high-quality documentaries as "Harvest of Shame," "Hunger in America," and "The Tenement," which dramatized the plight of the poor. By the mid-1960s, coverage of Vietnam had also increased and the networks began showing images of the antiwar movement and the new counterculture.

As the 1960s exploded into social conflict, television entertainment found it increasingly difficult to keep up with the unprecedented cultural change and rebellion. Television's ideological functions and conservative reluctance to embrace controversy as a consequence of its total commercialization rendered TV entertainment increasingly irrelevant to the vast process of social and cultural change that was occurring. Curiously, the only entertainment programs to portray directly the new radicalism, the experimentation with sex and drugs, and the new counterculture were cop shows like "Mod Squad" and "Dragnet"—and they generally portrayed the new ethos quite negatively. The few programs that attempted to give even a slightly positive spin to the 1960s spirit of nonconformity and rebellion were programs like "The Smothers Brothers," "Laugh-In," and "The Monkees." "The Smothers Brothers" was ultimately eliminated from television because its stars were presumably too sympathetic to 1960s radicalism and too critical of U.S. Vietnam policy; but this show appears somewhat mild and innocuous today, as do "Laugh-In" and "The Monkees."

"Star Trek" probably went to the outer limits of what was possible for network television in the 1960s. The program might be interpreted as the "starship" of Kennedy liberalism, given its theme of exploring new frontiers and going where no man (or TV program) had ever gone before. Produced by Kennedy liberal Gene Roddenberry, the series exhibited the cold war liberalist ideology associated with the Kennedy administration. The show presented allegories of the intervention in Vietnam, the cold war, U.S. imperialism, and life in the 1960s. It and other series began featuring blacks, women, and other minorities in the role of heroes, thus reflecting the integrationist liberalism and UN cosmopolitanism that became widespread in the 1960s. The series presented one of the first positive portrayals of intellectuals on network television (Dr. Spock) as well as positive images of racial integration and harmony. However, its vision of world hegemony featured a white male leader, Captain Kirk, benevolently ruling over other races and worlds, under the reign of the *U.S.S. Enterprise,* a barely disguised code for American capitalism. And although the Starship Enterprise was given the directive not to intervene in foreign cultures, Kirk and his team seemed to intervene virtually each time they encountered a culture with significantly different values.

On the whole, television's narrow vision in a period of expanding consciousness and cultural experimentation rendered it a highly retrograde culture force. Its inability to come to terms with the 1960s was evident in its coverage of one of the most divisive events in U.S. history, the Vietnam War.[9] At first, television was generally supportive of the U.S. intervention in Vietnam. Its proclivity for cold war dramas had reinforced the anticommunist ethos in which support for U.S. intervention against communism could thrive, and this mindset was evident in talk shows, news programs, and documentaries that exhibited a strong anticommunist and pro-interventionist bias (MacDonald 1985). The major news commentators of the day—Chet Huntley and Walter Cronkite—actually made films for the Defense Department that were used to warn recruits of the dangers of world communism. In short, during the first few years of the Vietnam War, network coverage was almost uniformly favorable to U.S. intervention (Hallin 1985).

Negative images of this intervention began appearing in 1965, when Morley Safer narrated a report on CBS that showed U.S. troops setting fire to a Vietnamese village. Reports during the next several years depicted growing U.S. losses and increasing protests against the war from various sectors of U.S. society, thereby promoting a national debate over Vietnam. TV's role in this debate was quite ambiguous. Until around 1968 few dissenting voices were broadcast on television. When intra-ruling-class opinion on the war became increasingly divided, television displayed this division, allowing "responsible" liberal voices to articulate the antiwar position while marginalizing the more radical antiwar movement as being communist infiltrated or "sympathetic to the enemy" (Gitlin 1980). Yet when Walter Cronkite began speaking critically about U.S. aims in Vietnam and cited the improbability of a U.S. victory, public opinion began to shift toward the antiwar position. Lyndon Johnson decided not to run for reelection in 1968 after he discerned that the antiwar forces were growing in popularity and militancy.[10]

In 1968, clearly one of the most tumultuous years in contemporary history, television was swept along with the dramatic events it was covering. Television news portrayed the vicissitudes of Vietnam and the growing antiwar movement, the antiwar campaigns of Eugene McCarthy and Robert Kennedy, the assassinations of Robert Kennedy and Martin Luther King, the black ghetto insurrections, and the bloody police riots at the 1968 Chicago Democratic Convention. As the drama intensified, television circulated images of struggle and upheaval; these images became political forces, which in turn inspired and thus circulated further struggle, as when students in one part of the country observed campus take-overs of buildings in another area and replicated the acts. Even when the network frames and commentaries attempted to contain and defuse these images, the dramatic spectacles of upheaval persisted in carrying their own meanings. But television was attracted to such spectacles, which it circulated and amplified. Television, it seemed, *might* very well televise the revolution.

It has often been remarked that television is primarily an imagistic medium, inasmuch as its images remain most vividly in the memory. Such "compelling images" present dramatic events that break with the normality of everyday life. For instance, the images of police brutality against blacks during the civil rights struggle powerfully portrayed the inhumanity of racism and oppression. Images of antiwar demonstrators chanting "The Whole World Is Watching!" as Chicago police attacked protestors during the 1968 Democratic convention presented a critical vision of the dominant culture, which was carrying out an increasingly unpopular Vietnam War while repressing its opponents on the home front. Compelling images of blacks struggling for civil rights and of antiwar protesters struggling against the Vietnam intervention legitimated and circulated the ideas behind these movements.

In particular, live events often produce images that are not subject to manipulation and control. The increasingly competitive television environment of the 1960s drove the network news divisions to seek dramatic imagery of conflict and struggle. The quest for "compelling images" resulted in pictures of contestation and opposition that helped to promote oppositional movements, even when the television discourse and framing attempted to present these movements negatively. By appearing on television, oppositional movements acquired legitimacy and attracted audiences to their struggles. Such images also inspired other oppositional groups to emulate the actions and tactics portrayed and thus circulated the messages and struggles of the antiwar movement and counterculture.

At the same time, television's proclivity for dramatic imagery often led oppositional groups to undertake spectacular, sometimes violent, actions to attract television coverage. Such tactics ultimately had the effect of deflecting attention from the antiwar movement and from the New Left critiques of the existing society; they also led some demonstrators into dangerous adventurism and violence. Thus, television's portrayal of oppositional movements was ambiguous in its effects. Although it helped to circulate contestation and to legitimate oppositional movements, it also presented negative images of these movements and sometimes undermined their attempts to develop a mass base for social change.

With the election of Richard Nixon in 1968, however, television coverage again became highly conservative, generally reproducing the administration line and only occasionally presenting more critical positions toward the Vietnam imbroglio, which continued year after year and eventually expanded into Cambodia and Laos during the early 1970s (this despite Nixon's promise of "peace with honor"). Still, the antiwar movement grew and establishment opposition to the war proliferated. Eventually it became clear to the Nixon administration that the United States could not win the war in Vietnam. A "Vietnamization" of the war was thus implemented and U.S. troops were pulled out, leading to the eventual collapse of the South Vietnamese military in 1975 and to victory by the National Liberation Front and its North Vietnamese allies.

Thus, television never really came to terms with either the Vietnam War or the tumultuous social upheavals of the 1960s. Many among the generation of the 1960s rarely watched television during this era because it had become totally irrelevant to their experience and concerns. This generation turned instead to rock music, film, and other forms of cultural expression. Television was seen as a highly conservative, culturally retrograde, and generally banal social force and institution. The Left and the counterculture mounted intense critical attacks on television, inaugurating a vigorous tradition of cultural and media criticism that continues to this day.[11] Conservative and liberal critiques of television began to proliferate at the same time. Conservatives began complaining of a liberal bias in television following Spiro Agnew's attack on the medium in 1969 (see

section 1.1). And in her book *The News Twisters*, Edith Efron (1972) argued
that television was sharply biased in favor of Hubert Humphrey and against
Richard Nixon in the 1968 election. Indeed, there may have been some
truth in the conservative critique of the media's liberal bias during this
period, but the conservatives greatly exaggerated the degree of bias.[12]

It has been argued (Hodgson 1976, 368ff.) that, following the turmoil
of the 1968 Democratic convention, the news networks reconsidered their
policies of covering demonstrations and social upheaval, and moved to a
more conservative terrain, backing off from controversy. The election of
Nixon certainly accelerated television's centrist slide, and government harassment of the media during the Nixon years clearly had a "chilling effect"
on critical news coverage (Powledge 1971; Lashner 1984). Yet even during
this period, "compelling images" of social reality circulated spectacles of
struggle and upheaval, even if the network texts and commentary were
conservative or markedly apolitical. Moreover, as the 1970s began, television
entertainment began dealing with social conflicts that the network news
divisions were trying to ignore or downplay.

2.4 Contested Terrain: Television in the 1970s

In the early 1970s television entertainment finally recognized and attempted to deal with the struggles and upheavals of the 1960s. New, and
largely unsuccessful, series featured young professionals working for change
within the system (e.g., "The Young Lawyers," "The Bold Ones"). But
these programs failed in the ratings because they pleased neither the large
(still conservative) audience who constituted the mainstay of television
viewers nor the young radicals. New comedy programs that dealt with the
conflicts of the 1960s, especially Norman Lear's "All in the Family," did
become highly popular and brought into the United States' living rooms
the sort of debates that had indeed been taking place in the real world of
struggle and conflict. These fierce, generational conflicts dramatically contradicted TV's world of harmonious resolutions of trival or unreal problems.
(For a discussion of programming in the early 1970s, see Brown 1971 and
MacDonald 1990, 191ff.)

It was as if the audiences could face the turmoil wrought by the 1960s
only in the medium of comedy, as if laughter provided both the best shield
against and the easiest access to the upheavals of the day. Indeed, television
pursued the time-honored tradition of using comedy and satire to deal
with society's most difficult and divisive problems. Interestingly, the Lear
comedies became popular with conservative, liberal, and radical constitu-
encies alike: The conservatives identified with Archie Bunker, and the
liberals and radicals identified with Archie's son-in-law Mike. In fact, the
decade of the 1970s was one of genuine contestation in the political, social,

and cultural spheres (Kellner and Ryan 1988). This decade was perhaps the most interesting period in the history of television, precisely because television reproduced in various programs the ideological struggles of the day and literally became a contested terrain—a terrain in which the competing liberal and conservative forces struggled for power and the radical position became increasingly marginalized in both the TV world and the actual political arena.

Intense struggles raged during the 1970s. The antiwar movement gained in force and influence, eventually contributing to the United States' decision to give up its Vietnam adventure. Although television arguably promoted the government intervention during the 1960s (Hallin 1985; Herman and Chomsky 1988), one might also contend that significant forces within the ruling elites eventually came around to the position that the war could not be won without great and intolerable domestic costs and that U.S. policy thus had to be abandoned. Television reflected this opposition and circulated the debate, thereby raising doubts concerning the Vietnam intervention. Moreover, although it is arguable that television rarely presented fully articulated antiwar positions, its images—whatever their ideological content—may well have contributed to the formation of a significant antiwar majority, which forced the U.S. government to give up its venture.

By the same token, it was the sheer length of the war and the sheer amount of coverage that dispirited the American public and created a negative response to the war. Saturation TV coverage of Vietnam, week after week, year after year, created the impression that Vietnam was a "downer." Even if the coverage had been more positively framed from the viewpoint of the administration, it might have contributed to the antiwar consensus. Yet, although television provides material that suggests what people should see, think, and do, it cannot determine *how* people will appropriate and use that material. There is always a distance between network intentions (the encoding of television texts) and its actual effects (the ways in which the audience decodes and uses the material). In the case of Vietnam, I would suggest that even if television did not actively contribute to promoting the aims of the antiwar movement, it eventually helped produce the antiwar consensus that led the political/military establishment to abandon the war.

The corporate establishment was obviously uncomfortable with the liberal candidacy of George McGovern during the 1972 election, and network television did little to promote his campaign, thus helping Richard Nixon win his second term as president. McGovern went beyond the boundaries allowed by consensualist centrism (which had increasingly become television's ideological stance) with his criticism of the military-industrial complex and U.S. interventionist policy, as well as with his mobilization of young and not-so-young radicals and liberals. If they had wished to, the networks could easily have done Nixon in during the 1972 campaign. The networks and other mainstream media had the essential facts concerning the Watergate break-in before the election; but, except for a two-part series on CBS, television avoided the issue until after the election, thus effectively ensuring Nixon's victory.[13] Yet after his reelection, new facts surfaced to implicate the Nixon White House in a variety of political scandals; intense conflicts broke out concerning Nixon's subversion of the democratic political process during the Watergate affair and in related activities, including dirty tricks throughout the 1972 election that went beyond the boundaries of established political rules and propriety.

Revelations of an "enemies list," which included prominent members of the television industry, also elicited widespread liberal revulsion and might have helped turn the television industry against Nixon. It was during the Watergate affair that television's rise to megapower became ratified. Television took on and then eliminated a president. It gained in prestige and legitimacy what other institutions had lost. The Watergate hearings and the Nixon impeachment hearings demonstrated that television was both a mediator of political power in the United States and the arena in which battles for hegemony took place. Of course, reporters of the *Washington Post* and other newspapers broke and stuck to the Watergate story, and congressional figures ultimately maneuvered Nixon out of office; but it was television through which the drama was eventually played out. The Watergate hearings in particular fascinated the nation and showed how television could involve its audience in complicated political drama. The process exposed scandal after scandal in the Nixon administration and portrayed television as a crucial instrument in democratic society. Ultimately, television emerged as the real winner when it eased Richard Nixon into early retirement and celebrated the ascension of Gerald Ford as his successor.

In a battle between conservatism and mild liberalism, Jimmy Carter won the 1976 presidential election. Yet Carter was a member of the centrist Trilateral Commission, and he filled his administration with key members of that organization (see the articles in Sklar 1980, especially 197ff.). His membership in the commission and consequent relationships with dominant elites may help explain the positive media coverage of Carter's campaign, which enabled him to rise from being almost unknown nationally to successfully winning his party's nomination and then the national election. Yet the center couldn't hold. After initially favorable TV coverage and popularity with the electorate, Carter became increasingly unpopular and battles between liberals and conservatives intensified in Congress and throughout the country.

For the rest of the decade, intense struggles between liberals and conservatives continued. Television mediated these contests and began producing more aggressively liberal as well as conservative programming.

It even permitted successful television producers and stars to use their series to promote their views—within certain well-defined limits, of course. Still, much programming was markedly apolitical; many producers wished to avoid all controversy and refrained from offending any segment of the audience. Nonetheless, some of the most progressive television programs ever to appear surfaced during this era.

A new "miniseries" form employed both the conventions of television melodrama and "critical realism," following the example of the British Broadcasting Corporation's presentation of dramas in a limited series form. The miniseries broke with the series form and used the expanded time frame to treat issues hitherto excluded from network television, such as class conflict, racism and anti-Semitism, imperialism, and the oppression of the working class and blacks while presenting capitalists and right wingers as oppressors and exploiters. Docudramas criticized Joe McCarthy, J. Edgar Hoover, the FBI, and other right-wing forces while vindicating Martin Luther King as well as victims of McCarthyism and FBI persecution. "Kill Me If You Can" sympathetically depicted the plight of a victim of capital punishment, Caryl Chessman, while presenting as strong a case against capital punishment as ever appeared on television.

These programs represent an important revision of idealized images of history and a reversal of conventional good guy/bad guy roles. Formerly, in programs like "The FBI" and in numerous police and spy series, the FBI, CIA, and police were portrayed as heroic saviors, whereas radicals or anyone failing to conform to the rules of the system were depicted as incarnations of evil. The U.S. economic and political system, as well as social institutions such as the family, were almost always idealized in television culture. During the mid- and late 1970s, however, television dramas exposed brutal racism in "Roots," "King," and "Roll of Thunder, Hear My Cry"; portrayed the corruption of the political system in "Washington: Behind Closed Doors" and "Blind Ambition," a fictionalized version of the Watergate scandals; displayed the evils of McCarthyism and 1950s blacklisting in "Fear on Trial" and "Tailgunner Joe"; and revealed class conflict and attacked two venerable institutions of corporate capitalism— the banks and the automobile industry—in "The Moneychangers" and "Wheels." The "critical realist" miniseries represent a form of popular culture as popular revenge (Kellner 1979). Blacks were avenged against their oppressors in "Roots," "King," and other series that portrayed racists as evil and the struggles of blacks as legitimate. "Holocaust" took revenge against Nazi oppression in its harsh portrayal of fascism and its sympathetic presentation of Jewish victims and resistance. "Fear on Trial" and other TV portrayals of McCarthyism and blacklisting gained a retrospective cultural victory for victims of political oppression by portraying the injustice, irrationality, and pettiness of right-wing oppression. And, finally, victims of FBI persecution gained revenge against J. Edgar Hoover in the representations of Hoover and the FBI in "King," "Washington: Behind Closed Doors" and in later miniseries dealing with the Kennedys. In all of these programs, the oppressed were portrayed in positive images and the oppressors in negative ones, thus providing a critical perspective on political institutions and on views previously presented positively.

A satiric form of critical television emerged in 1975 with "Saturday Night Live!" The first few seasons exhibited some of the cleverest satire in television history, focusing on television and politics. The "news" segment made great fun of political figures and policies, and Chevy Chase's stumbling and fumbling imitations of Gerald Ford helped circulate a popular image of Ford as comedic bumbler that contributed to his defeat in the 1976 presidential election.

Norman Lear's 1970s series, "Mary Hartman, Mary Hartman," subverted the forms of both the soap opera and the situation comedy while engaging in social critique and satire. Whereas soap operas generally trivialize serious problems through pathos, sentimentality, and moralistic melodrama, "Mary Hartman" approached some of the same problems more critically. Often starting with apparently common everyday problems, it used humor and self-reflective irony to suggest that something was profoundly wrong with patriarchy and consumer capitalism. Whereas situation comedy generally follows a conflict-resolution model in which problems are humorously solved in 30 or 60 minutes, the problems on "Mary Hartman" were endlessly multiplied and appeared insoluable within the present way of life. In the process, authority figures of all types were ruthlessly satirized. Such reversal of television codes and stereotypes provoked reflection on social institutions and their workings. Further, "Mary Hartman," more than any previous television show, constantly reflected on television's view of the world and its impact on American life. It confronted TV ideology with contradictory experiences and showed both the false idealizations and distortions of television by contrast to the real problems and quandaries of working-class women.

"Mary Hartman" also dealt with topics that were previously taboo, including impotence, venereal disease, union corruption, alienated industrial labor, and religious fraud. In fact, most Norman Lear series presented subjects previously eliminated from the world of television. "All in the Family," for instance, confronted bigotry and generational conflict more powerfully than ever before on television; "Maude" treated women's liberation and middle-class malaise in a provocative manner; "The Jefferson's," "Sanford and Son," and "Good Times" dealt with middle-class and working-class blacks more effectively than did previous series; "All's Fair" featured more political debates (between the conservative male and the liberal woman) than did any previous TV comedy; and Lear's syndicated comedies—

"All That Glitters," "Fernwood Tonight," "America Tonight," and "Fernwood Forever"—were imaginative shows that contained some of the most striking satires of television and American society ever broadcast.

To be sure, Lear's programs also had their limitations. "Mary Hartman" collapsed into cynicism and despair when the series ended after two years with Mary back in the kitchen, repeating her former way of life with her new lover. Evidently, the show was unable to offer any positive alternatives. Most of Lear's other situation comedies, moreover, were structured according to the standard conflict/resolution model, which manages to resolve the problems and issues confronted without serious change. "All in the Family," for instance, often implied that most problems of everyday life could be settled within the family and established society. (Of course, it also demonstrated that racism and bigotry resisted easy solutions and were serious and enduring problems.) In short, although Lear's programs presented real problems never before portrayed in the television world, they never offered solutions that transcended the limits of liberalism and the current organization of society. Individuals solved their problems through correct action, not by struggling together. Indeed, television entertainment has rarely depicted collective action and political movements as legitimate modes in which to deal with social problems.

Lear's liberalism represented the cutting edge and outmost boundary of what was permissible in 1970s network television, but it also revealed the limits of commercial television in the United States. Television liberalism does not go beyond individualism, and it rarely deals with problems of inequality, justice, poverty, or acute suffering, which arguably have their roots in the current organization of society. Television thus accepts this organization as given, and either idealizes and celebrates it in conservative forms or depicts liberal critiques and reform measures for all problems.

Nevertheless, much markedly apolitical as well as conservative programming also appeared during the 1970s. Some of the most popular programs during this decade were predominantly conservative crime dramas. In the mid-1970s another trend emerged; known as "T&A," it exploited women as sex objects. Programs like "Charlie's Angels," "The American Girls," and "Three's Company" debased women's liberation and sexual freedom, robbing these movements of their progressive elements. Silly situation comedies, mindless action/adventure shows, and vapid specials continued to dominate the network television schedules and ratings.

Yet there was probably more diversity in network television in this period than during any other in history. The decade of the 1970s was one of struggle, during which television became a contested terrain. Liberals and conservatives fought for control of U.S. society, and representatives of both groups were in the television industry. But the right wing and its prime political actor, Ronald Reagan, won the contest. Indeed, television turned sharply to the right in the Age of Reagan.

2.5 Conservative Hegemony: Television in the 1980s

The 1960s and 1970s were bad times for conservatives. Barry Goldwater, the Right's darling, suffered the most massive political defeat in history in the 1964 election against Lyndon Johnson. Soon after, the movements of the 1960s challenged all of the values in which the Right believed. But in the 1970s the Right counterattacked. It blamed liberals, Democrats, and radicals for the political and economic decline of the United States, for the growth of a cumbersome welfare state, and for the decay of morals and traditional values. Ultraconservative groups such as Jerry Falwell's "moral majority" and Richard Viguerie's New Right organization, used direct-mail campaign tactics to help elect Ronald Reagan and unseat prominent liberal senators such as George McGovern, Birch Bayh, and Frank Church in the 1980 election. The moment of the New Right had arrived.

Reaganite Entertainment

Network television wasted no time in responding to the new political hegemony of the Right. In the season after Reagan won, a set of crime drama series appeared. Such programs as "Strike Force," "McClain's Law," "Today's FBI," "Code Red," and "Magnum P.I." featured strong male heroes who represented conservative law-and-order values. They were played by long-time patriarchal movie and TV stars such as James Arness, Robert Stack, and Lorne Green, who earlier had starred in conservative TV series such as "Gunsmoke," "The Untouchables," and "Bonanza." These shows sought to tap into perceived audience needs for reassurance from strong male authority figures and a return to conservative values. Yet most of these series flopped, whereas the one new "liberal" cop show, "Hill Street Blues," became a major critical and audience success of the decade. Perhaps the public wasn't buying all of Reagan's conservative agenda after all.

Other new 1981 shows, during the first prime-time season of the Reagan era, included "Dynasty," "Falcon Crest," "Flamingo Road," and "King's Crossing," which joined "Dallas" in their depictions of wealth, greed, and power. These programs were dual edged: They can be seen as celebrating the values of wealth and power or as portraying the emptiness and corruption of upper-class life. Indeed, some people may identify with the wealthy protagonists and be reinforced in their materialist values and yearnings for the trappings of wealth. Others may perceive the corruption in a negative light and enjoy the sufferings of the wealthy. In its search for a mass audience, television does indeed often produce shows with contradictory ideological tendencies that appeal to as many people and groups as possible.

The 1982 season saw the (mercifully brief) appearance of two neo-imperialist epics, "Tales of the Golden Monkey" and "Bring 'Em Back Alive," which pastiched Indiana Jones, Frank Buck, and the white man's burden in tales depicting Third World villainy and white male heroism. Then 1983 witnessed two military soap operas, "For Love and Honor" and "Emerald Point, N.A.S." The first featured the lives and loves of young male and female recruits who, fittingly, were advertised as "Fit to Fight—Anywhere, Anytime." Both series—like the movies *Private Benjamin* (also made into a TV series), *Stripes, An Officer and a Gentleman, The Great Santini,* and *Tank,* among others—portrayed the military as an institution where love, honor, and good times were to be had, thus providing free advertisements for the free-enterprise volunteer army that Reagan and his administration were rebuilding.

The miniseries during the first years of the Reagan administration included "The Winds of War," "The Blue and the Grey," "George Washington," and, in case these past wars and their glories became boring, "World War III." Forgetting that the media are supposed to be relatively autonomous in relation to the state and economic system, network producers also presented a slew of series that advanced Reagan's political agenda. His demand for a military buildup found support in the series "From Here to Eternity," based on the popular World War II novel and film, and "Call to Glory," which dealt with military life at the time of the Cuban missile crisis. Both humanized the military at a point when the military's image needed refurbishing. Both dealt with eras during which the military either wasn't properly prepared (as in the Pearl Harbor debacle, which is the centerpiece of "From Here to Eternity") or was enjoying a moment of glory (as when U.S. military power forced Khrushchev to withdraw Soviet missiles from Cuba in 1962). The cumulative message seemed to be that without a strong military we might be subject to enemy attacks (like that at Pearl Harbor), but with a strong military we can dictate policies to the Soviets (as we did during the Cuban missile crisis); therefore, we need a strong military buildup.

Now, I am not claiming that the networks planned and orchestrated this message. Rather, they were and remain business machines seeking to maximize profits by maximizing their audiences. This policy leads them to produce programs that they believe resonate with present trends, audience desires, fears, and fantasies, and will thus be attractive to mass audiences. Obviously, the networks believed that Reagan and his policies were popular, and they attempted to capitalize (literally) on this supposed popularity by producing programs that tapped into the conservative mindset. Consequently, as Reagan built up and unleashed the CIA, series began to heroize intelligence work. In "Masquerade" (1984), for instance, ordinary Americans, like Cibyl Shepherd, were enlisted as intelligence operatives on the assumption that the KGB knew who all the American spies were. Thus ordinary members of the audience could fantasize about being spies, too—and about fighting the nasty Reds. Another short-lived spy fantasy, "Cover-Up" (1984), featured a woman fashion photographer who was accompanied by a handsome ex–Special Forces agent. The woman became an "out rider" (i.e., an undercover trouble shooter) after her intelligence agent husband was killed by a villainous French corporation hoping to steal U.S. technology and, undoubtedly, to sell it to the "evil empire."

As Reagan and his cronies contemplated and carried out military intervention in the Third World, series emerged that promoted macho interventionism or high-tech weaponry (e.g., "The A-Team," "Blue Thunder," "Airwolf," "Riptide," "Knightrider"). A series on the heroic exploits of the CIA was often announced but did not appear. In 1985, perhaps in celebration of the second Reagan administration, one miniseries portrayed Mussolini as a tragic hero and another celebrated the Russian tyrant, Peter the Great; in the meantime, Ronald Reagan's preferred class of the rich and powerful was lionized in movies and series too numerous to mention.

Analysis of episodes from some of these Reaganite fantasies reveals certain audacious revisions of history and advancements of blatantly right-wing ideology. A 1984 episode of the TV series "Blue Thunder," a spin-off of the movie, featured a high-tech surveillance helicopter, a trip to an island in the Caribbean, an American medical school, and a black population suffering under a communist dictatorship. In this rewriting of Grenada, a group of white American mercenaries, funded and directed by the KGB, plan to assassinate the black leader Maurice Priest so that a military coup led by Soviet-oriented Marxist Leninists can take over. (The Grenadan leader Maurice Bishop was evidently demoted to a priest in this episode.) The Blue Thunder team connects with democratic resistance forces and prevents the Soviet coup from taking place. On the way out, the helicopter crew disobeys orders and blows up a Soviet-Cuban arms depot (a more glamorous target than the mental institution that the U.S. forces accidently bombed during the actual Grenada invasion). Then, upon returning home, the crew learns that the Soviet-Cuban clique had taken over the government and that the U.S. president had heroically undertaken a counteraction to liberate the island—an intervention facilitated in this fantasy by the Blue Thunder bombing of the arms depot.

Historical revisionism continues in a "Call to Glory" episode of 1984. Here, after documenting the existence of Soviet missile bases in Cuba during the Cuban missile crisis, an Air Force Captain (Craig T. Williams) suddenly becomes a diplomat sent to Vietnam to investigate the Diem regime. The regime is shown to be extremely repressive and inept, thus retrospectively justifying CIA involvement in Diem's assassination so that a more effective government could be formed. (It wasn't.) The Vietnamese were, for the most part, depicted as corrupt, repressive, or ineffectual victims needing help from strong, well-meaning Americans, whereas the American hero was shown to be totally decent, strong, and heroic. To be sure, in the Vietnam episode there were questions raised as to what the United States was doing there in the first place, but the cumulative (and chauvinistic) message was that Americans are basically good and decent people who, out of misguided idealism, sometimes make minor mistakes.

I am not claiming that these series were necessarily part of a right-wing conspiracy; nor were they devastating indications of a long-term turn to the Right. Indeed, most of the right-wing series failed or, like "The A-Team," were not unambiguously conservative. One series, "The Equalizer," frequently depicted CIA types as villains, as did the highly popular "Miami Vice." In a famous episode of the latter, G. Gordon Liddy played a totally unscrupulous and unsavory representative of the U.S. intelligence service who provided illegal weapons to the Nicaruaguan Contras engaged in a dirty war to overthrow the Sandinista government. Here, the Contras were depicted as a terrorist force armed and guided by the CIA. Moreover, the action was accompanied by the musical score of Jackson Browne's "Lives in the Balance," which sharply attacks U.S. intervention in Central America. The episode thus provides a leftist critique of a central policy of the Reagan administration (Best and Kellner 1987; Kellner 1990).

In short, the Reaganite entertainment did not go uncontested. Embattled liberalism continued to be voiced in such shows as "Hill Street Blues," "St. Elsewhere," and, until it was terminated in 1983, "Lou Grant" (Gitlin 1983). Sophisticated modernism made an appearance in "Moonlighting," and Yuppie liberalism was exhibited in "L.A. Law" and "Thirtysomething." "Miami Vice" turned to the Left in the 1980s and featured episodes sharply critical of the CIA and state policy while depicting the role of the banks and capitalist financial institutions in the drug trade. Other series, such as "Frank's Place," "Cagney and Lacey," "Murphy Brown," and "Designing Women," also tended to promote a liberal view of the world, whereas "Max Headroom" promoted a left post-modernist view.

In the final analysis, Reagan never really did forge a strong and enduring conservative majority. His policies continued to be contested by liberals and radicals, and on many issues the majority of the population continued to support more liberal positions.

Deregulation and Corporate Hegemony

Meanwhile, back in Washington, in line with Reagan's attack on all regulatory agencies (Horowitz 1989), the Federal Communications Commission was doing everything possible to take apart the regulatory structure that had been built up over the past few decades.[14] FCC commissioner Mark Fowler undertook a systematic deregulation of broadcasting. By the end of 1984 Fowler's FCC had (1) increased the number of radio and television stations that a company could own nationally from seven (AM and FM) radio and TV stations to twelve of each; (2) exempted radio and television stations from government-imposed limitations on the number and extent of commercials during a given hour; (3) eliminated the requirement that broadcasters must carry a certain amount of public service broadcasting and provide a minimum amount of educational material for children; (4) extended license renewal periods from three to five years while eliminating requirements to keep either programming logs and financial records for public inspection or FCC ascertainment for license renewal, which would presumably be automatic in the future; (5) exempted broadcasters from the requirement that they own a television station three years before selling it, thus triggering mergers and take-overs among television stations; and (6) promoted the deregulation of cable. The FCC later eliminated the Fairness Doctrine, which mandated that television networks present a diversity of controversial issues of public importance. Also eliminated was the "equal-time rule," which stipulated that opposing sides would be fairly treated; that is, representatives of different positions would be allowed to express their opinions, and qualified candidates for public office would be permitted to answer opponents.[15]

NOT TRUE

Fowler's deregulation agenda attempted both to remove all major structural constraints on the broadcasting business in terms of ownerships, licenses, and business practices, and to eliminate as many restraints on programming as possible. (Fowler's FCC did, however follow the right-wing agenda of the day in attempting to regulate obscenity; and Fowler himself once sternly lectured broadcasters to "get it right" when they meekly criticized Reagan for his lax "management style".) Consequently, the Reagan FCC dramatically redefined the relation between government and television, and attempted to undo decades of regulatory guidelines and programs.

Since the late 1970s groups both in Congress and in the communications industry have been attempting to pass a new bill to update the Communications Act of 1934. Although Congress, the courts, and the FCC had amended the 1934 bill over the years, no successful effort had been made to deal with new communications systems such as cable television. Although the much-discussed new communications bill never reached the floor of Congress, both the House and the Senate, in October 1984, approved by voice vote a new cable bill after a series of compromises to resolve disputes over versions previously passed in each chamber. In November of the same year, Reagan signed the Cable Franchise Policy and the Communications Act of 1984, thus signaturing the trend toward deregulation in the communications industries that he and many of his supporters had been advocating for years.

The Senate followed the deregulation line as well. The bill it passed in 1985 (SB66) further deregulated cable television and, in effect, validated Reagan's deregulation policies. Following the trend toward deregulation, the cable television bills shifted power away from the public and cities and toward cable operations. Although the legislation allowed the cities to continue regulating cable fees, programming, and adherence to franchise agreements for two more years, the cities will have little effective power after that time to regulate rates and programming or to play a significant role in franchise renewal. Critics of the cable bill, however, described it as "an industry wish list in which Congress has given cable system owners a free hand to control every program and service they carry. Rather than establish a coherent national policy on cable television access, Congress succumbed to heavy lobbying by cable operators. The public, as usual, will be the loser" (Schmuckler and Dean 1985). Cathy Boggs, policy analyst for the Telecomunications Research and Action Center, claims that "[i]t was seen as a cities and industry battle, with consumers and third-party programmers needs not taken into account. The bill reflects the lack of input by citizens and cable users." Indeed, by now it is clear that one effect of the bill was to produce a dramatic rise in prices for cable subscription rates during the following years. For example, "Between 1986 and 1989 . . . the monthly rate for basic cable service surged sevenfold in Denver; more than threefold in Louisville, Ky., and Shreveport, La.; and nearly threefold in Gary, Ind. On average, monthly rates for basic cable service have jumped 39 percent since 1986, according to the General Accounting Office" (*New York Times*, July 14, 1990, p. 18A).

Although the 1934 Communications Act mandated that the airwaves belonged to the public as a public good and that broadcasting was to serve the "public interest, convenience, and necessity," Reagan's deregulation policies subverted the notion that broadcasters were public trustees and, in effect, stipulated that the networks were simply businesses that would allegedly benefit from deregulation.[16] The whole notion of broadcasters as public trustees who must serve the public interest was thrown out, along with accountability to the public. The result was a drastic reduction of news, documentary, and public affairs broadcasting. A Ralph Nader–affiliated public interest group, Essential Information, carried out a survey indicating that programming in 1988 carried 51 percent less local public affairs programming than that in 1979; that 15 percent of all stations carried no news at all; and that program-length commercials, prohibited until the 1980s, constituted about 2.6 percent of airtime (Donahue 1989).

Deregulation also led to dramatic conglomerate take-overs of radio stations and curtailment of radio news operations. Research in Florida revealed that

there was an average 30 percent decrease in weekday public affairs programming and a 24 percent decrease in the number of locally prepared
newscasts (Edwardson 1986). In practice, this major curtailment of local
news deprived communities lacking a local daily paper of news concerning
their area. Previously, radio was the voice of these communities, but with
the take-over of local radio stations by corporate conglomerates, local news
and public affairs programs were often cut back significantly and sometimes
even eliminated completely.

Other studies indicated an increased amount of commercial interruptions,
a dramatic deterioration of children's television, large cutbacks in the news
and public affairs programming departments at the networks, and large
increases of "reality programming" in which dramatic simulations of sensationalistic topics masqueraded as "news." Furthermore, as I shall argue
in Chapter 4, the era saw not only a sharp turn to the right in television
entertainment but also saw television actively help to forge the conservative
hegemony of the period.

The Reagan/Bush years also witnessed the merging of major networks
with giant conglomerates. (In this connection, the Reagan administration's
attack on antitrust laws was as significant as its moves toward deregulation
[Gomery 1989].) In 1985 ABC merged with Capital Cities Communications
and RCA merged with GE. The latter was a $6.3 billion dollar deal that
reconstituted the mega-conglomerate as one of the biggest corporations in
the world. (For further discussion, see section 3.3.) CBS fought off a hostile
take-over in 1985 and merged with the Tisch corporation in 1986, producing
another mega-communications giant. And in March 1989 Time Inc. proposed
a merger with Warner Communications Inc. that would form the largest
media conglomerate in the world. The combined company, Time Warner
Inc., has a total value of $18 billion and a projected yearly revenue of $10
billion from its magazine and book publishing empire, its film and television
production companies, its cable systems and networks, and its subsidiary
businesses. (See Bagdikian 1989 for documentation of the worldwide trends
toward multinational communications giants being created by this "merger
mania.")

Consequently, television networks are now entrenched as a central force
within the transnational corporate power structure and have served capitalist
interests even more directly during the 1980s (see Chapter 4). Indeed,
during this era, television and popular culture have helped produce a
climate in which a movie actor who had skillfully internalized the world
views of Hollywood film and network television could be twice elected
president of the United States. As television had shaped the world views
of the U.S. electorate, Reagan and his audience shared the common terrain
of television and film. Television helped promote Reaganism during much

of the 1980s, but it also limited Reagan by exposing the excesses of his presidency during the Iran/Contra affair (see section 4.2).

*   *   *

Reflecting on the historical and political trajectory of network television since its introduction at the end of World War II should give rise to some insights into the social and political functions of television in the United States. Television has become a central economic force that manages consumer demand and sells consumption as a way of life. The salient facts concerning network television are its blatant commercialization and its relentless promotion of the interests of capitalist corporations. Indeed, television has become a major political, social, and cultural force; its information and entertainment programming are saturated with ideologies, messages, and values that promote the interests of dominant elites and legitimate their rule. Thus, television plays a dual role; as both a business machine and an ideological apparatus, it has assumed crucial functions in the development of contemporary capitalism and the process of capital accumulation. Yet it also mediates (and is caught up in) class conflict and antagonisms as well as the contradictions between capitalism and democracy that have constituted the American experience.

During the late 1940s and 1950s television helped promote the consumer society and sold the conservative, centrist view of middle-class life that was to become the norm during the era of the consumer society. Its action/adventure series promoted anticommunism and the view that violence was justified in resolving conflict and in advancing the "good"—a view that replicated official U.S. ideology during the cold war and may have served as a defense of an increasingly interventionist foreign policy.

During the 1960s television promoted Kennedy's liberalism and then became a center of heated controversy when it began covering the turmoil and intense social conflict of the era. Television was thrust into the role of mediator of social conflict and crisis manager. At this time, the simplistic middle-class ideology that saturated its entertainment became increasingly laughable and even repugnant to many of the new generation who turned away from television and toward other cultural forms.

During the 1970s television took on a more contradictory role as it attempted to mediate the struggles between liberals and conservatives that continued throughout the decade. With the victory of Reagan and the New Right, television tentatively promoted a conservative hegemony. In a sense, then, television has been locked into a framework bound by liberalism and conservativism but has also taken on different ideological positions at various times. The ideological hegemony it has helped to create is constantly appropriating new contents—shifting and transmuting in response to changing social conditions, political struggles, and the vicissitudes of history itself.[17]

Building on these historical studies, we shall turn in the next chapter to the development of a critical-institutional theory of the role of television, which elucidates television's social functions and growing power.

Notes

1. On broadcast history, see Barnouw (1966, 1968, 1970, 1975, and 1978). I have drawn extensively on Barnouw's works, which have yet to be surpassed for their scope, depth, and critical incisiveness. I have also benefited from Waldrop and Borkin (1938), Archer (1938, 1939), Schiller (1971, 1973), Stirling and Kitross (1975), Mosco (1979), Smythe (1981), and Horowitz (1989). On the early years of broadcasting, see Douglas (1987). Archer (1938, 1939) must be consulted with caution, however, for the author's adulation of RCA President David Sarnoff and GE Chairman Owen D. Young as well as his pro-industry bias are extreme. Nevertheless, his text contains important documents released to him by RCA and GE.

2. On the development of monopoly capitalism in the 1920s, see Baran and Sweezy (1966), Ewen (1976), and Mandel (1975); Sklar (1988) describes the corporate reconstruction of American capitalism from 1890 to 1916.

3. Barnouw (1978, 34ff.) points out that "Cavalcade of America" systematically excluded references to "socialistic" government projects such as the Tennessee Valley Authority (TVA), labor, and blacks. On radio programming, see MacDonald (1979).

4. See also Waldrop and Borkin (1938, 127ff.), who document AT&T's powerful influence in the film industry and its plans to dominate broadcasting. The authors also indicate that AT&T was seen as part of the Morgan circle, whereas RCA was referred to as a "Rockefeller outfit" (p. 147), thus suggesting that broadcasting interests were allied with the most powerful sectors of finance capital in the United States.

5. As William Gibson points out in an unpublished article, "World War II: The Beginnings of the Permanent Mobilization of American Society," in 1940, 175,000 companies produced 70 percent of the total industrial product, and the 100 largest monopoly firms produced the remaining 30 percent. After three years of war, however, 100 companies accounted for 70 percent of total industrial production. Monopoly capitalism had indeed arrived. Moreover, the state financed and facilitated this transformation. Whereas in earlier stages of monopoly capitalism the state assisted monopolies in various ways, it provided capital directly during World War II. Of the $166 billion gross national product of 1945, the federal budget accounted for $100 billion. Much of this money went to the largest corporations in war contracts. Moreover, the state paid for new machines, assembly lines, and factories that were given directly to the corporations; billions of dollars worth of means of production were thus provided free of cost. Gibson also points out that the state socialized the means of production while preserving private ownership in the relations of production. War socialism thus ironically provided the basis for transnational capitalism.

6. This pattern was repeated later, when the networks and government delayed the introduction of cable and then pay television (Mosco 1979). By the mid-1980s dominant corporate interests, once again supported by the government, were able to hamper the development of satellite television by allowing HBO and other cable networks to scramble signals. In so doing, they precluded the development of a direct-broadcast system from satellites to home owners, instead forcing consumers to pay for each channel, ensuring corporate control of the satellite system, and maximizing exploitation of consumers. (For further discussion, see section 5.4.)

7. ABC resisted the blacklisting pressures, however, and in 1951 received a Peabody Award for taking "a firm stand at a time when stations and networks were firing or refusing to hire writers and actors on the basis of 'unsupported innuendoes' in the publication *Red Channels*" (cited in MacDonald 1985, 25).

8. Emile de Antonio's brilliant documentary "Point of Order" (1963) incisively portrays McCarthy's hubris, recklessness, and aggressiveness. De Antonio argues that the Army/McCarthy hearings were the last relatively open congressional hearings and that television was the hero of the proceedings. (This information was recorded during interviews in Austin in October 1989.)

9. For differing positions on television's role in Vietnam, see Arlen (1969); Braestrup (1978); Hallin (1985); Gibson (1986); and Herman and Chomsky (1988).

10. On the impact of television coverage of Vietnam on Johnson's decision not to seek reelection, see Halberstam (1979) and Gibson (1986).

11. Television was at the center of the Left's cultural critique. Former SDS President Todd Gitlin (1972) wrote a provocative article entitled "Sixteen Notes on Television and the Movement," while more radical and theoretically sophisticated works from Europe were translated and disseminated during the 1970s. Discussed in these latter works were the theory of the cultural industries of Horkheimer and Adorno (1972 [orig. 1947]), the theory of radical intervention and reconstruction of the media of Brecht (1967) and Benjamin (1969), and the media theory of Enzensberger (1974), who attempted to synthesize these positions. A group of radical media critics based at Columbia University, collectively called The Network Project, published a series of pamphlets criticizing corporate control over the broadcast media and the lack of adequate alternative broadcast media (see The Network Project's Notebooks 1–11 [1972–1975]).

12. Efron's analysis was criticized by Stevenson et al. (1973). The conservative critique began in the 1950s, when William Buckley (1951) and others began attacking the "liberal bias" in the media—a trend that accelerated with the founding of the conservative *National Review*. In the 1960s conservatives became angry over television's depiction of Nixon and then of Goldwater in his 1964 race for the presidency. The "liberal bias" position became the official stance of the Nixon administration and was religiously taken up by conservative commentators of the era. Conservatives became increasingly hysterical in their attacks on television during the period in which Nixon was driven out of office and Jimmy Carter defeated Gerald Ford. For instance, Efron, Phillips, Buchanan, and others who were published in *TV Guide*, owned by Ronald Reagan's good friend Walter Annenberg, claimed that television was promoting the agenda of "new class" ultraliberals and the New Left. The deep conservative hatred for television was also apparent in remarks by Oliver North

and Richard Secord during the Iran/Contra hearings and in Reagan's 1988 "Iron Triangle" speech in which he attacked the media, the government, and the intellectual elite.

13. On television's role during the Watergate affair, see Halberstam (1979) as well as Lang and Lang (1983). The Langs argue that although key aspects of the story were initially published in newspapers, television more adequately covered the Watergate story than the press.

14. Reagan's deregulation policies provided an impetus for liberals to criticize conservative free-market ideology and to express outrage at the dismantling of decades of regulatory structures. See Brown (1981, 1982, 1984).

15. On the Fairness Doctrine, see Simmons (1978) and Rowan (1984).

16. For further discussion of television and the FCC under Reagan and Bush, see Chapters 4 and 5.

17. J. Fred MacDonald's (1990) history of television and Martin Lee and Norman Solomon's (1990) "guide to detecting bias in news media" reached me only as I was correcting page proofs, so I was not able to draw upon their research, though I referenced the books a couple of times; on the whole, they support many of the positions that I argue for in this book. MacDonald, however, suggests that an era of network television is coming to an end and that the reign of the three major networks is over. I would argue in response that although the hegemony of the "big three" is declining, nonetheless, the system of network television is still intact and that the new networks emulate the older ones in their programming, operations, ends, and effects—an argument that I shall elaborate in the succeeding chapters.

3

Television, Government, and Business: Toward a Critical/Institutional Theory

The only really fundamental approach to the problem is to inquire concerning the necessary effect of the present economic system upon the whole system of publicity; upon the judgment of what news is, upon the selection and elimination of matter that is published, upon the treatment of news in both editorial and news columns. The question, under this mode of approach, is not how many specific abuses there are and how they may be remedied, but how far genuine intellectual freedom and social responsibility are possible on any large scale under the existing economic regime.
—John Dewey

The United States is the only Western nation relying so exclusively upon advertising effectiveness as the gatekeeper of its broadcasting activities. The consequences of using the public spectrum primarily for commercial purposes are numerous, and increasingly disturbing. The idea of broadcasting as a force in the public interest, a display case for the best of America's creative arts, a forum of public debate—advancing the democratic conversation and enhancing the public imagination—has receded before the inexorable force of audience maximization.
—William McGill et al., for the Carnegie Commission

Studies of the history of television reveal that the broadcast media have been constituted by the twin forces of democracy and capitalism in the United States. As part of the capitalist economic system, network television is a business enterprise governed by the dual imperatives of maximizing profit and legitimating the system of capitalist democracy established in the United States. The democratic imperatives of television include the establishment of broadcasting as part of the public sector, as a public utility to be governed by the public interest. The broadcast media are protected by the First Amendment right to free speech mandated by the Bill of Rights and, hence, are established as a vital part of the democratic social order. Their democratic functions—established variously by law, governmental regulatory bodies, and the judicial system—include providing the information vital for a functioning democracy, the stricture to be impartial in political contests and debates, and a tradition of independence with responsibility for exposing corruption, abuses of power, and illegal or destructive behavior in the social and political system.

Television has overwhelmingly served capitalist interests, but it has also had its democratic moments. As we saw in the last chapter, television eventually helped eliminate Joseph McCarthy from political life through the Murrow exposures and, especially, the Army/McCarthy hearings; it promoted the civil rights movement by exposing the evils of a brutal system of segregation; it has furthered environmentalism and women's rights by depicting pollution and injustice toward women; it raised questions about the U.S. intervention in Vietnam and helped circulate opinions critical of the war; it helped bring down the corrupt administration of Richard Nixon through its exposures during the Watergate hearings; and it criticized abuses of the CIA, corporate malpractice, and governmental corruption in the 1970s. In all cases, it carried out these democratic functions primarily as an effect of intra-ruling-class controversies in these areas and/or as a response to popular movements. Furthermore, the democratic demands and criticisms of the system involved in these controversial issues were in all cases constrained, narrowed, and managed through their media presentations to the extent that the democratic functions of the media have been severely curtailed during the short history of television in the United States.

Capitalist interests and control of the media grew stronger in the 1980s, whereas its democratic moments diminished (see section 2.5 and Chapter 4 for discussions of television's "right turn" in the 1980s). Yet it would be a mistake to generalize from the 1980s conservative hegemony within the media, state, and society to assume an instrumentalist model of the media in which the media are conceptualized merely as an instrument of capitalist domination, or solely as a mouthpiece of capitalist and state propaganda. In the subsequent chapters, I shall attempt to demonstrate the superiority of the hegemony model over the liberal pluralist, or instrumentalist, model by arguing that the hegemony model more accurately theorizes (1) the nature and effects of corporate control of television; (2) the contradictory relations among television, government, and business; and (3) the antagonisms between capitalism and democracy that constitute the system of broadcasting established in the United States. In addition, I argue that the hegemony model more accurately theorizes the extent of intra-ruling-class rivalry, social antagonisms and struggle, and the ways in which the capitalist class has actually tightened control over television during the 1980s.

The hegemony model theorizes the current configuration of power and domination in a society in terms of historical processes, which are subject to change and transformation. Thus it provides openings for political intervention and struggle. Whereas the instrumentalist model provides an ahistorical picture of capitalist domination in which the society is completely controlled by the logic of capital, the hegemony model portrays capitalist strategies as a response to crisis tendencies, social struggles, and the fundamental antagonisms of a social order governed by class divisions and the often-contradictory imperatives of capitalism and democracy. The instrumentalist and propaganda models assume a historical continuity, an identity of societal configurations from the 1950s through the present, that obscures the differences among the 1950s, 1960s, 1970s, and 1980s in terms of the various social functions and effects of television during these eras. The latter models are thus homogenizing and continuous, whereas the hegemony model focuses on discontinuities, ruptures, and changes in the social order in different eras and situations, while also theorizing major continuities.

To enlarge on this perspective, we shall explore some of the institutional structures of television and study its key social functions and contradictory imperatives and effects. This chapter thus develops a critical-institutional theory of television, which conceptualizes the multifaceted functions of television within U.S. society and attempts to specify its complex relations with the other major centers of power—the state and business.

3.1 Toward a Theory of Network Television

Network television provides the structure for the commercial system of television dominant in the United States. From a technical standpoint, this system is a web of cables, satellites, and microwave relay stations radiating from centers in New York to affiliates all over the United States and throughout the world. From an institutional perspective, the network structure is the aggregate of institutions, practices, rules, and personnel that makes up the commercial broadcasting system. As a system of production and distribution, the dominant networks (ABC, CBS, and NBC) pay studios to produce programs and then pay affiliates (i.e., individual stations belonging to the networks) to broadcast them.[1] Affiliates in turn agree to broadcast a certain amount of network programming, while advertisers pay the networks a fee based on the number of viewers watching at a particular time according to Nielsen and Arbitron ratings. The networks thus play the role of "television overlords," whereas the affiliates are their sometimes docile, sometimes restive, vassals. Conceived as a whole, network television is a system of powerful centralized corporations, local broadcasting outlets, advertisers, production studios, and ratings research companies that provide the numbers that shape advertising rates and incomes.

By 1990 each of the three major networks had roughly 205 affiliates. Each affiliate holds an exclusive contract with its network that is periodically renewed. The Reagan deregulation program allowed each network to own up to 12 affiliate stations, as long as their total viewership does not represent more than 25 percent of the total U.S. audience. The profitability of the networks was greatly increased, as they derived large profits from owning affiliate stations. The three networks spend roughly $450 million dollars a year on the "compensation" they pay affiliates for broadcasting their programs; network advertising revenue, in turn, approached $10 billion in 1989, a twelve-fold increase over such revenue in 1960 (*Variety*, October 11, 1989, p. 95).

The theory of network television presupposes a distinction between *network television* as a system of commercial broadcasting and *a specific network* such as CBS or NBC. According to Gaye Tuchman, "A network is a corporation that seeks stations as affiliates. It leases airtime from its affiliated stations and sells portions of that leased time to commercial advertisers. Networks also own and operate stations" (1974, 7). Yet in focusing on specific corporations one fails to grasp the fact that the network system encompasses commercial broadcasting corporations and their affiliates, production studios, a star-publicity system, advertising agencies, sponsors, ratings agencies, trade magazines, journals, and popular magazines such as *TV Guide*. The network system was once constituted by the three major networks (which Bunce [1977] calls ABCBSNBC to call attention to their similar structures and interchangeable personnel and programming), but with the emergence of the "Age of Cable" in the 1980s, many other networks have appeared (CNN, A&E, ESPN, etc.). Despite the increase in diversity, however, the structure, programming, and effects of television have remained much the same. Thus, the theory of network television assumes that despite competition and differences between the specific networks, each is like the others in its operations, its goals, and its interchangeable personnel and programs.

Indeed, the absorption of cable into the network system reveals the power of the commercial system of television in the United States. During the early 1980s, when cable television was being widely introduced into the United States, Les Brown's journal, *Channels of Communication*, declared a communications revolution and coined the term *Television II* to conceptualize what its editor and some contributors considered to be the fundamental difference between the "old" broadcast television and the "new" cable television. However, the fact that the new cable networks are still largely commercially supported operations has ensured that they will be pretty much like the old networks in programming, personnel, and operation.

Commercial imperatives have dictated frequent advertising breaks, selection of familiar programming to gain a predictable share of the audience, and continued economic domination by ratings and advertisers of all aspects of cable. In short, it appears that cable has thus far brought merely more of the same rather than a qualitatively different type of television.

At the same time, cable and satellite television (along with home video recorders, remote-control devices, and other new technological devices) potentially gives viewers more control over their communications environment and thus potentially empowers them. Individuals can now "program" their television environment, recording which programs they most want to see and viewing them at a time of their own choice. Remote-control devices make it possible to mute or skip over advertisements while providing the opportunity to "graze," whereby one quickly moves from one channel to another, observing what is taking place from moment to moment on the different channels. Yet the increase in range of channels and viewer control may actually strengthen the hold of television over leisure and consciousness, and it is certainly profitable for the corporations that viewers must pay for the use of cable or satellite programming.

Most important, network television follows the pattern of other giant corporate enterprises—a pattern in which oligarchical corporations in the same sector of capitalism produce similar products in a similar way within the same corporate and market structure. Another analogy would be the concept of "Hollywood," which has come to refer to the system of American film as a distinguishable mode of production and product. Unlike broadcasting systems in many other capitalist and socialist societies, where government finances, regulates, and sometimes controls television, no other alternative but a "free-market" system of broadcasting has ever been seriously considered in the United States. From the beginning network television has been the creation of private enterprise, and only in the United States is television so free from accountability to the public and government.

Defenders of the network system contend that advertising-supported television is "free" television and that competition guarantees diversity and a variety of programming. But this claim is a myth. By attracting the audience with the lure of "free entertainment," television generates immense profits and gains enormous sociocultural power. Eventually, however, the audience pays for its "free lunch." Advertisers pay the television networks for time-spots purchased according to the number of people supposedly watching at a given time, and these advertising expenses are in turn passed down to the consumer. Thus, even in the privacy of one's home, one is exploited by corporate capital. Not only is leisure "colonized" (Aronowitz 1972) and "industrialized" (Enzensberger 1974), but it has also become an indirect form of exploitation in which audiences surrender their time and consciousness to the ideological productions of the entertainment industry, which trains them as consumers and citizens (Smythe 1981).

In the commercial system, the networks derive enormous profits from the aggregate size of the audience, whereas advertisers not only attempt to manage consumer demand but also force the audience to pay higher prices for its commodities as the cost of viewing "free" TV. Television viewing thus increases the power both of capital and of the broadcasting industry. In addition, the imperatives of commercial television produce a rather homogeneous system in which all programming is fundamentally the same. In the pursuit of megaprofits, the networks broadcast whatever they think will attract the largest audience: Indeed, one rating-point difference can cost a network more than $100 million a year in advertising revenue. Thus the networks follow established formulas, loading their prime-time viewing schedule with situation comedies, action/adventure shows, and often mindless specials. Network insiders have confessed that the programmers seem to adhere to the "lowest common denominator" scheduling philosophy of alienating the fewest possible viewers by avoiding controversial, complex, and innovative programs (Klein 1972, 43). The result is the familiar mediascape of silly sitcom families, violent battles between good and evil, simplistic morality tales, and so-called specials that hype the network's "personalities" or other entertainment-industry players.

In effect, commercial control of network television means that the corporations that own the broadcast media incorporate their values in programming that establishes a suitable atmosphere for commercial advertising messages (see section 2.2). The process of ideological control and production of capitalist hegemony does not take place in the process of watching a given program or series of programs. Rather, the communications environment as a whole produces an ambience for the promotion of consumer capitalism. Television pervasively projects an ethos of materialism through its programming as well as its advertising. Images of happiness through material well-being pervade television, and the conflict-resolution structure characterizes both programming and advertising. Both imply that all problems can be resolved either through purchase of the correct commodity (advertising) or through the proper social behavior (TV programming). Commodities, affluence, and conformity thus constitute the value system of television.

It is a myth to hold that television entertainment is a harmless diversion that has nothing to do with education or the transmission of values and ideologies. In fact, television entertainment is coded into ideological forms, generally utilizing the format of conflict/resolution, which projects the illusion that all problems can be easily solved (in thirty or sixty minutes) within the parameters of the existing system. Television entertainment projects models for proper and improper gender and social behavior. It rewards certain actions and punishes others, thus reinforcing dominant moralities. TV entertainment is full of myths, symbols, and values and thus is a potent force that shapes individuals' values, ways of looking at the world, and behavior.

In addition, television constantly affirms in both subtle and not so subtle ways that the system of capitalist democracy is the greatest system in the world. Visions of U.S. society as free and democratic are projected both in advertising (which affirms freedom of choice and the possibility of purchasing a wealth of consumer items) and in news programming (which celebrates the system of "freely" choosing candidates in elections). Although television often voices fundamental criticism of other social systems (e.g., the Soviet Union and other communist societies, Japan, Korea, and any number of Third World countries), it never carries out systematic criticism of capitalist democracy in the United States (Cohen 1989, 13–14).

Television also obscures class and class relations. Although social class is arguably still a major determinant of U.S. society, it is almost invisible on TV. Indeed, television portrays a fundamentally classless society. There are few entertainment programs that deal with working-class life, and viewers are more likely to hear obscene language and see nude bodies than to hear the word *class* or to see images of class struggle. The same is true of news programs and documentaries. As Goldman and Rajagopal (1990) argue, class relations and capital are invisible on TV news. During major strikes, television may exhibit frequent images of strikers and short clips from labor spokespersons but few, if any, images of the corporation against which the workers are striking or of the corporate executives themselves. TV news often frames the strikes in terms of conflict between strikers and consumers, beginning strike reports with discussions of how the action will affect consumers. Then it usually cuts to images of strikers and perhaps to brief sound-bites quoting labor spokespersons. More often than not, the network correspondents themselves will articulate the company point of view or quote a PR spokesperson, whereas top executives only rarely appear on camera.

In addition, network news coverage of strikes rarely contextualizes the events by explaining them in terms of class relations, class struggle, and the broader context of relations of production. In their study of CBS news texts of a coal strike in 1977–1978, Goldman and Rajagopal concluded that

CBS contributed to the hegemony of dominant interests by *fragmenting* conceptual thought and discourse. Fractured discourse resulted from lack of attention to background context, partial and selective reporting, a persistent tendency toward abbreviation and reduction, and decontextualizing discourses from social, economic and political experiences. Fragmented sequences of this sort produce incoherency, and thereby act as an obstacle to popular public debate of issues—encouraging instead apathy and passivity. . . . Though miners appeared on screen more than operators, CBS's method of presenting them did not permit articulation of oppositional attitudes or ways of seeing. Brevity of interviews and intimate camera distances emphasized workers' emotions, and not their rational arguments. While capital remained invisible, labor was fractured into a hundred abbreviated voices and systematically denied opportunities for discursive speech—hence, though a dominant ideological agenda was not ratified, alternative narratives and ways of seeing could not be articulated. In conjunction with restrictions on discursive speech aimed at rational critique, CBS's narrative strategies reproduced the hegemony of dominant class interests by blocking development of any explanatory accounts of institutional relations. (1990, 6–7)

In the 1980s particularly, labor was almost invisible on network television. There were few news stories regarding the government attacks on or the decline of unions, and little coverage of capital-labor relations (other than some airtime spent on the Eastern airline strike and less on the Hormel strike and the Pittson mining strike). The networks have business reporters but no labor reporters. Prime-time news programs report the stock market figures every night but not the figures on inflation or unemployment that might interest workers rather than investors. Indeed, the preferred network mode is to ignore the discourse of class altogether, in favor of portrayals of a middle-class utopia of consumption and democracy. This is the image and message of most advertising, most entertainment, and much news. The world of the networks is thus a projection of the ideological vision of the culture industries that glosses over class and class relations.

In a sense, then, television programming attempts to create spectator consumers and citizens who conform to the hegemony of corporate capitalism. It tries to produce audiences for advertisers. In turn, advertising and a commercial ambience produce consumers; news and information produce systems legitimacy and citizens; and sports, entertainment, and a flow of programming produce passive, docile spectators. Of course, television may not bring about precisely the effects that it wishes, especially when viewers "zap" (by means of remote-control devices) advertisements or programming that bores them. Viewers may also fail to respond to commercial or political messages, or become confused or frustrated by the programming. In such cases, inertia and apathy, rather than productive consumer and citizen behavior, are the result. Television may also end up angering or alienating people and predisposing them toward oppositional behavior. As I shall argue later, the effects of television are indeed contradictory and difficult to specify.

Yet the system is organized in such a way as to encourage the hegemony of capital over the population. Far from providing a "free" service to audiences, television insidiously reinforces precisely those ideologies and behaviors that strengthen the power of capital. In the words of one industry insider:

> The lords of the television business, who are in a favorable position to promulgate their message, miss few opportunities to tell us that their industry is a fine example of American free enterprise. "Free enterprise" in this case is a euphemism for what is the most powerful, most effective, and most impregnable monopoly in the history of the United States: the television-network monopoly. The fact that the monster has three heads—NBC, CBS, and ABC—makes television competitive only within the most limited of terms; the three heads snap and bite at each other while fighting for an identical, virtually agreed-upon audience. (Reel 1979, x)

The networks not only reap multimillion-dollar profits by running the television industry; they also garner megaprofits by controlling a large number of network affiliates in local markets. They are purchasing and merging with more and more other businesses as well. It is thus highly accurate to describe the networks as business media, as the voices and instruments of big business run by and for big business. In their very commercial operation, the networks advance their business agenda by advertising massively and projecting ubiquitous images of affluence and happiness through consumption. They also promote a commercial ethos through their programming by promoting the consumer society, the family, law and order, dominant institutions, and the values of the mainstream (Gerbner 1977; Gerbner et al. 1982). When conflicts occur in network programming, they are played out primarily between important sectors of the ruling groups or within the broader society over controversial social issues such as drugs and abortion. Yet, as I shall argue later, the TV networks are also forced to respond to the ideas and struggles of oppositional social movements.

Indeed, as serious conflicts *have* occurred from the 1960s to the present over U.S. intervention and the role of the military, women's rights and abortion, sexuality, the environment, civil liberties, and other issues, these conflicts have naturally been played out in the media, which have the role of mediating between dominant social groups in the interests of social integration and stabilization. In this environment it is television that frames the controversies, presents various positions, and sometimes privileges one position or another. But it often does so in contradictory and arbitrary ways, by mediating the structural conflicts and tensions between democracy and capitalism that constitute the system of broadcasting in the United States.

3.2 Capitalism, Democracy, and Television

A variety of books in the past decade have analyzed the contradictions between capitalism and democracy that have been instrumental in shaping the history and institutional structure of the United States.[2] Whereas most conservative and liberal theories claim that there is a basic kinship and harmony between capitalism and democracy, radical approaches see contradictions between these forces in the contemporary era. As television is a crucial sector of both the democratic and capitalist systems in the United States, it is useful to study the ways in which democracy and capitalism contribute to the system of network television, either together or in conflict with each other. I shall argue that, by amassing tremendous concentrations of wealth and power, major corporate institutions in the capitalist system have come to control the state, the media, and other dominant institutions, to the point where the system of democracy in the United States is in peril. To better understand this situation, we shall first examine how television fits into the corporate power structure in the United States; then we shall explore some of the problems created by commercial ownership and control of the media as well as the ensuing conflicts between capitalistic and democratic imperatives.

Television in the Corporate Power Structure

Studies of the political economy of television have demonstrated the degree to which the TV industry is embedded in the structure of corporate capitalism.[3] The broadcasting networks were initially owned and controlled by individual entrepreneurs who ran their businesses as competitive firms in the communications market. Early on, the older broadcast networks (CBS and NBC) merged with record companies, publishing, electronics, and other sectors of the entertainment and consumer industries. Later, in the 1950s, the broadcasting industries began merging more aggressively with other major corporate interests and became an important sector of transnational capitalism. By the 1960s the networks were being run by individuals whose specialties were corporate management and maximization of profits, rather than by individuals who were primarily interested in entertainment or communications.

It was also in the 1950s that the entertainment industries began empire building and became communications giants. ABC, for instance, allied itself with major movie studios and established a transnational television empire called "Worldvision" (Bunce 1977, 76ff.). ABC actually set up television industries in countries throughout the world, and CBS concentrated on providing programming. Two critics of transnational corporations pointed to CBS's extensive media empire in the 1970s, noting that CBS distributes its programs to 100 countries. Its news-film service, according to its 1968 annual report, is now received by satellite "in 95 percent of the free world's households." The leading U.S. TV shows, such as *I Love Lucy, Gomer Pyle, Hogan's Heroes, Mary Tyler Moore,* and *Perry Mason,* are distributed throughout the continent. *Hawaii Five-O* was dubbed into six languages and sold in 47 countries. *Bonanza* is seen in 60 countries, with an estimated weekly audience of 350 million. In 1970 and 1971 both CBS and NBC sold more than a half billion dollars' worth of "cultural emissions" overseas. In 1968 ABC International had controlling interest in 16 foreign companies that operated 67 TV stations in 27 countries around the world. (In Latin America ABC affiliates reach roughly 80 million spectators.) (Barnet and Müller 1974, 144–145)

On the whole, however, U.S. television companies have not been successful in taking over and running foreign broadcasting systems. National demands for sovereignty and the preservation of national cultures have led most nation-states to take over and run their own industries or to allow national broadcast corporations to control the broadcasting industry in their countries (Read 1976). This has led the U.S. television industry to concentrate on distribution, on maximizing the penetration of foreign markets with U.S. products. Yet here, too, the U.S. television industry has faced barriers, as many countries impose quotas on the amount of U.S. or foreign television allowed into their country. These limitations, however, are starting to erode as cable and satellite television penetrate new markets and as governments weaken quota restrictions in response to conservative governments or outside pressures.

Over time, cultural imperialism and the exporting of American television intensified. Developing countries fought in the United Nations and elsewhere for a "new world information order" that would permit them to control the information and entertainment flowing into their countries (see the Report of the International Commission for the Study of Communication Problems 1980, often referred to as the "MacBride Report"). The United States, however, fought for "freedom of information," encouraging and supporting commercial television enterprises throughout the world that would be open to U.S. programming and advertising.

During the 1980s U.S. domination of the world television market dramatically increased. In 1984 U.S. programs accounted for 75 percent of the $400 million international marketplace (*Television/Radio Age,* May 14, 1984, p. 12). By the end of the decade, U.S. television program distributors were taking in more than $1.3 billion from program sales; and it has been predicted that, by 1992, U.S. distributors will be taking in more than $3.6 billion, with $2.7 billion coming from Western Europe (*Television/Radio Age,* November 14, 1988, p. 53). There was also increased investment by the U.S. networks in foreign television systems and the beginning of foreign co-productions between the networks and other television systems. NBC, for instance, has an option on a 15 percent stake in Quintex Australian Ltd. and a 5 percent investment in New Zealand's TV3 (*Hollywood Reporter*, February 10, 1989, p. 85).

As a consequence, the U.S. broadcasting industry today has a truly "global reach" and is now a major component of transnational capitalism. It has followed not only the corporate trends toward global expansion but also the current trends toward mergers and expansion into corporate conglomerates aligned with the central sectors of capital. Although the Justice Department blocked a merger between ABC and communications giant IT&T in 1966, all three networks were allowed to merge with giant corporations in the 1980s (see section 2.5). The communications industry was indeed marked by growing concentration during the 1970s and 1980s; as Ben Bagdikian (1987) has documented, 29 major communications corporations dominated the market in 1986 (down from the 50 that dominated it when he surveyed the field for the first edition of his book in 1983). This corporate control of information and entertainment has resulted in what Bagdikian (1987) calls "a new Private Ministry of Information and Culture."

The television networks are part of this conglomerate structure, which has ties to the other major entertainment and information industries (film, publishing, music, radio, cable TV, etc.) as well as to other major corporate and financial powers. (NBC's ties to the defense industry are particularly close.) The networks are also connected with the space and satellite industry, health care and management concerns, housing, crime and surveillance, education, and manufacturing (Bunce 1977). In addition, the networks are tied to banks and major financial institutions, and interlocking ownership and shared boards of directors link them with other major corporations as well (Morrow 1985; Herman and Chomsky 1988, 10ff.; Henwood [*Left Business Observer*, April 1989]). For instance, by the early 1970s Rockefeller-Morgan banks had "voting rights to 23.1 percent of the stock of CBS, to 24.6 percent of ABC, and to 6.7 percent of NBC" (Barnet and Müller 1974, 235). Analysis of the board of directors and holdings of the television networks over the last two decades discloses the extent to which the broadcasting industry was deeply interconnected with other major corporations, as Tables 3.1 and 3.2 make clear (see also Network Project 1973a, and 1973b).

The merger between GE and RCA/NBC allied NBC with one of the major transnational conglomerates and pointed up the centrality of communications within the transnational corporate power structure. RCA and GE had been among the largest defense contractors, and their merger made them the second largest contractor to sell electronics to the Defense Department (*Business Week*, January 27, 1986, p. 117). GE produces crucial components of nuclear weapons, airplane engines, and guidance systems

TABLE 3.1 The Board of Directors at GE

GE's board is a conservative cross-section of the power elite—corporate executives, bankers, retired cabinet members and generals, an Ivy League president and several Ivy boardmembers. There are multiple ties with the Morgan bank, Citicorp, Manufacturers Hanover. GE boardmembers also serve on several media industry boards—Harper & Row, Reuters, the Washington Post. They are well-represented in the branches of the permanent government, too: according to INFACT, three (Preston, Welch, and Sigler) belong to the Business Roundtable; three (Preston, Welch, Wriston) to the Council on Foreign Relations; two (Michelson, Wriston) to the Rand Corp. Six (Hood, Jones, Sigler, Smith, Welch, Wriston) either belong to or visit the all-male Bohemian Club, which owns the California retreat where a naked George Shultz might be seen pissing on a tree next to an equally naked Harold Brown.

OUTSIDE (not GE employees)

H. Brewster Atwater, Jr. Chair and CEO, General Mills. *Other boards/memberships:* Norwest, Sun Co. [Boardmember since 1989]

Richard T. Baker. Consultant to Ernst & Whinney (accountants). High-profile Clevelandite. *Other boards/memberships:* International Paper, Louisiana Land & Exploration, Pacific Construction. [1977]

Charles D. Dickey. Retired Chair and director, Scott Paper. *Other boards/memberships:* J.P. Morgan/Morgan Guaranty Trust. [1972]

Lawrence E. Fouraker. Business educator and fellow, Kennedy School of Government, Harvard. *Other boards/memberships:* Citicorp, Gilette, R.H. Macy, The New England, Texas Eastern; Museum of Fine Arts, Boston. [1981]

Henry H. Henley, Jr. Retired chair and CEO, director, Cluett, Peabody & Co. (apparel). *Other boards/memberships:* Bristol-Meyers, Manufacturers Hanover, Home Life, Olin, West Point-Pepperell). [1972]

Henry L. Hillman. Chair, Hillman Company ("diversified operations and investments"). *Other boards/memberships:* Chemical Bank, Cummins Engine, PNC Financial; Business Council. [1972]

Gen. David C. Jones (Ret.). Retired Air Force general and former chair, Joint Chiefs of Staff. Criticized the Carter/Brown military budget as inadequate; strident promoter of the Soviet Threat. *Other Boards/memberships:* U.S. Air, USX. [1986]

Robert E. Mercer. Chair, Goodyear Tire & Rubber. *Other boards/memberships:* CPC Intl., Manufacturers Hanover. [1984]

Gertrude G. Michelson. Senior vice president, External Affairs, R.H. Macy & Co. (retailers). *Other boards/memberships:* Chubb, Goodyear, Harper & Row, Irving Trust, Quaker Oats, Stanley Works; Columbia University, Federal Reserve Bank of New York; Markle Foundation, Helena Rubenstein Foundation, Rand Corp. [1976]

Barbara Scott Preiskel. Attorney, New York. *Other boards/memberships:* R.H. Macy & Co., Massachusetts Mutual, Textron, Washington Post; American Women's Economic Development, Ford Foundation, New York City Board of Ethics, Yale Univ. [1982]

Lewis T. Preston. Chair, J.P. Morgan & Co./Morgan Guaranty Trust. *Other boards/memberships:* Business Roundtable, Council on Foreign Relations, Federal Reserve Bank of New York. [1976]

Frank H.T. Rhodes. Geologist and President, Cornell Univ. *Other boards/memberships:* Carnegie Foundation for the Advancement of Teaching, Committee for Economic Development, Gannett Foundation, Mellon Foundation, Memorial–Sloan Kettering Cancer Center. [1984]

Andrew C. Sigler. Chair and CEO, Champion International (paper and forest products). Famed for denouncing corporate raiders. *Other boards/memberships:* AMF, Bristol-Meyers, Chemical Bank; Business Roundtable. [1984]

William French Smith. Former Attorney General and partner, Gibson, Dunn & Crutcher (L.A. law firm). Former lawyer to Ronald Reagan. The Sunbelt seat—Smith is well-connected in Southern California. *Other boards/memberships:* American International Group, Fisher Scientific, H.F. Ahmanson, Earle M. Jorgenson Cos., Pacific Lighting, Pacific Telephone, Weintraub Entertainment; Center for Strategic and International Studies (Georgetown), Kennedy School of Government (Harvard), National Symphony, Ronald Reagan Presidential Library, University of California. [1986]

Walter B. Wriston. Retired chair and director, Citibank. One of the pioneers of modern, aggressive banking style. Former economic adviser to Ronald Reagan. *Other boards/memberships:* Bechtel, Chubb, J.C. Penney, Pan Am, Pfizer, Reuters, Tandem; American Enterprise Institute, Council on Foreign Relations, Fletcher School (Tufts), Manhattan Institute, Rand Corp. [1962]

INSIDE (GE employees)

Lawrence A. Bossidy. Vice-chair and Executive Officer. [1984]

Edward E. Hood, Jr. Vice-chair and Executive Officer. *Other boards/memberships:* Aerospace Industries Association, National Academy of Engineering. [1980]

John F. Welch, Jr. Chair and CEO. *Other boards/memberships:* Natl. Acad. of Engineering; Business Roundtable, Council on Foreign Relations [1980]

Source: Doug Henwood, *Left Business Observer,* April 1989, No. 27, p. 5. Reprinted with permission.

TABLE 3.2   The Board of Directors at CBS

INSIDE (CBS employees)

Walter Cronkite. Consultant to CBS.

William S. Paley. Acting chairman; ran CBS from 1928–1983. ⅓ interest in *International Herald Tribune.* Worked with FBI in 1940s and 1950s. Allowed CIA to use CBS as cover for agents and to funnel contributions through his personal foundation. *Other boards/memberships:* Columbia Univ., Harriman Inst. (Soviet studies), Museum of Modern Art. 1988 compensation: $700,000.

Laurence A. Tisch. President and CEO. Militant supporter of Israel. Once denounced Peter Jennings as pro-Arab. *Other boards/memberships:* ADP, Bulova, CNA, Loews, Petrie Stores, R.H. Macy, N.Y. Stock Exch.; Carnegie Corp., Council on Foreign Relations, Metropolitan Museum of Art, N.Y. Public Library, NYU. 1988 pay: $1.25 million.

OUTSIDE (not CBS employees)

Michael C. Bergerac. Private investor. Former chair, Revlon; former executive, ITT. *Other boards/memberships:* ICN Pharmaceuticals, Manufacturers Hanover, Topps; Cornell Medical Coll., N.Y. Zool. Soc.

Harold Brown. Consultant and chair, Foreign Policy Inst., Johns Hopkins. Secy. of Defense, 1977–81; Secy. of the Air Force, 1965–69. Pres., Cal Tech, 1969–77. *Other boards/memberships:* AMAX, Cummins Engine, IBM, Philip Morris, Synergen; Atlantic Council, Cal Tech, Council on Foreign Relations, Natl. Acad. of Sciences, Rand Corp., Rockefeller Fdn., Trilateral Commission.

Roswell L. Gilpatric. Retired partner, Cravath, Swaine & Moore. *Other boards/memberships:* Corning Glass, Eastern Air Lines; Metropolitan Museum, N.Y. Public Library.

James R. Houghton. Chair and CEO, Corning Glass. *Other boards/memberships:* Dow Corning, Metropolitan Life, J.P. Morgan & Co.; Metropolitan Museum, Pierpont Morgan Library.

Newton N. Minow. Chicago lawyer and former chair, FCC. *Other boards/memberships:* Aetna, Encyclopaedia Britannica, Foote Cone & Belding, Sara Lee; Carnegie Corp., Carnegie Endowment, Northwestern Univ., Notre Dame, Rand Corp.

Henry B. Schacht. Chair and CEO, Cummins Engine. *Other boards/memberships:* AT&T, Chase Manhattan; Brookings Inst., Business Council, Cmte. for Econ. Devel., Ford Fdn., Yale Univ.

Edson W. Spencer. Chair, Ford Fdn. Retired chair, Honeywell. *Other boards/memberships:* Carnegie Endowment, Mayo Clinic.

Franklin A. Thomas. President and CEO. Ford Fdn. *Other boards/memberships:* AT&T, Alcoa, Citibank, Cummins Engine.

Preston R. Tisch. President and co-CEO of Loews Corp. Brother of Laurence. Postmaster General, 1986–88. *Other boards/memberships:* Bulova, CNA, Hasbro, Rite-Aid; NYU.

Marietta Tree. Architect, consultant, and city planner. *Other boards/memberships:* Pan Am, U.S. Trust; Citizens Cmte. for NYC, Cooper-Hewitt, Winston Churchill Fdn.

James D. Wolfensohn. Investment banker and business partner of Paul Volcker. Friend of Teddy Kennedy and David Rockefeller. *Other boards/memberships:* Brookings Inst., Carnegie Hall, Institute for Advanced Study (Princeton), Joint Center for Political Studies, Metropolitan Opera, Rockefeller Univ.

Source: Doug Henwood, *Left Business Observer,* August 1989, No. 31, p. 5. Reprinted with permission.

for ICBMs and has close relations with the air force. RCA specializes in advanced radar, satellites, and electronic equipment for missile-launching cruisers and has close relations with the navy. Together, they have been heavily involved in the development of the Star Wars technology proposed by the Reagan administration. GE also plays a key role in the nuclear power industry and the manufacturing sector. Both GE and RCA have a diverse portfolio of businesses in electronics, advertising, financial services, transportation, and a variety of other enterprises. Together, the corporations "would rank seventh on the Fortune 500, just behind IBM" (*Fortune,* January 6, 1986, p. 6).

Since the merger, GE/RCA has consolidated its holdings in broadcasting, with GE capital "providing more than $2.7 billion for 19 deals spread across cable, broadcast TV, radio and publishing" (*Channels*, October 1988, p. 65). In 1988 GE/RCA became part of the cable industry by purchasing Cablevision's sports, news, and entertainment programming (*Broadcasting*, December 26, 1988, pp. 27ff.; *Variety*, December 28, 1988, pp. 1–2). This enabled the conglomerate to acquire six sports channel networks as well as the Rainbow Network, which includes Bravo, American Movie Classics, Long Island News 12, and the Consumer News and Business Channel. It also entered the world of entertainment production by contributing to a restructuring of New World Entertainment.

The mid-1980s network mergers have thus contributed mightily to trends toward concentration in the broadcasting industry and toward merger of the television networks with other major corporate enterprises. ABC, for instance, owns eight TV stations, eighteen radio stations, a Satellite Music Network, several cable channels, many newspapers and magazines, and various data-base concerns (see Table 3.3). Hence the television networks can be considered big businesses interconnected in significant ways with other big businesses in the system of transnational capitalism. As Herbert Schiller (1971, 1973, 1976) and others (Mattelart and Siegelaub 1979; Mattelart 1983) have documented, the networks are also an intrinsic part of the U.S. economic empire and are closely linked with the capitalist state. Schiller notes that

> [m]ass communications are now a pillar of the emergent imperial society. Messages "made in America" radiate across the globe and serve as the ganglia of national power and expansionism. The ideological images of "have-not" states are increasingly in the custody of American informational media. National authority over attitude creation and opinion formation has weakened and is being relinquished to powerful external forces. The facilities and hardware of international information control are being grasped by a highly centralized communications complex, centralized in the United States. (1971, 107)

The U.S. government has encouraged ABC to build a television empire in Latin America and now supplies free programs to countries all over the world through the U.S. Information Agency (USIA) (Schiller 1971; Bunce 1977). Moreover, in 1959

> the United States agreed to finance construction of the entire United Arab Republic (Egypt and Syria) TV system, which began telecasting the following year. With the financing of additional stations, Jordanian audiences were brought into the project. Following the fulfillment of U.S. government commitments, ABC International announced the formation of the Arab Middle East network. It consisted of TV stations serving Syria and Jordan as well

TABLE 3.3   ABC's Lines of Business and Board of Directors

Lines of Business

Broadcasting ABC Television Network • 8 TV stations • 18 radio stations (11 AM, 7 FM) • Satellite Music Network (supplies music to radio stations)

Cable Arts & Entertainment (38%-owned) • ESPN (sports channel, 80%-owned) • Lifetime (women's lifestyle and health programming, 33%-owned)

Newspapers 9 daily papers including *Kansas City Times/Star* • *Fort Worth Star–Telegram* • *Wilkes-Barre Times Leader* • 33 weekly papers in 5 states • 19 shopping guides in 6 states

Magazines over 60 consumer and trade publications, including: *American Metal Market** • *Daily News Record** • *Dairy Herd Management* • *Electronic Component News** • *Family Practice News* • *Financial Services Week** • *Institutional Investor* • *Internal Medicine News* • *MIS Week** • *Motor Age* • *M, The Civilized Man** • *Prairie Farmer* • *W** • *Women's Wear Daily** (*Fairchild Publications title)

Miscellaneous NLIS Publishing Co. (insurance database) • National Price Service (building supply database) • Word, Inc. ("bible products" and "inspirational communications")

Board of Directors

Chair Thomas S. Murphy was a member of the group that started Capital Cities in 1957, when it was a rag-tag collection of small TV stations; among his colleagues was late CIA director William Casey. Casey was counsel to the firm and member of its board from 1976 until he became chief spook in 1981. Casey's failure to disclose his holdings in Cap Cities caused a mild furor when it was revealed by *Newsday* in 1985. Casey was, and Murphy and fellow boardmember Thomas Macioce are, members of the Knights of Malta, a secretive international club of right-wing ruling class Catholics whose U.S. members include Bill Buckley, Alexander Haig, Lee Iacocca, William Simon, and J. Peter Grace, chair of W.R. Grace & Co., whose board is full of Knights.

INSIDE (Cap Cities/ABC employees)

Daniel B. Burke. President. Former head, Jell-O division, General Foods, brother of just-retired Johnson & Johnson chair James Burke. *Other boards/memberships:* Conrail, Rohm & Haas; American Film Institute, American Women's Economic Development Corp., National Urban League, N.Y. Botanical Gardens, Ohio Wesleyan Univ.; Conference Board, Council on Foreign Relations. 1988 salary: $969,286.

Thomas S. Murphy. Chair. *Other boards/memberships:* General Housewares, IBM, Johnson & Johnson, Texaco. Member of legendary class of '49, Harvard Business School. Member, Knights of Malta. 1988 salary: $1,030,501.

John B. Sias. Executive vice president, ABC Television Network Group and veteran of Cap Cities' publishing division. Sias has a reputation as a cut-up—the kind of guy who wears a Captain Marvel T-shirt under his white business shirt. 1988 salary: $815,286.

OUTSIDE (not Cap Cities/ABC employees)

Robert P. Bauman. Chair, Beecham Group (British drug company that will merge with SmithKline Beckman). Harvard Business School classmate of Daniel Burke. Former General Foods exec and former vice chair of Avco and Textron.

Warren E. Buffett. Legendary billionaire investor based in Omaha, with major holdings in Cap Cities, Salomon Bros., Washington Post Co. Owner, *Buffalo News,* several insurance companies and retailers. Close friend of *Post* publisher Katharine Graham and CBS head Laurence Tisch. Promoter of population control, nuclear nonproliferation, rhino preservation, and U.S.–Soviet friendship. *Other boards/memberships (partial list):* Berkshire–Hathaway (Buffett's investment vehicle), *Omaha World-Herald,* Salomon Bros.; Boys Clubs of Omaha, Grinnell College, Urban Inst.

Frank T. Cary. Retired chair, IBM. *Other boards/memberships:* Hospital Corp. of America, J.P. Morgan, Merck, New York Stock Exchange (whose chair and vice-chair are members of the Knights of Malta), PepsiCo, Texaco; Business Council, MIT.

Leonard H. Goldenson. Retired chair, ABC.

Leon Hess. Chair, Amerada Hess; owner, New York Jets. *Other boards/memberships:* Mutual Benefit Life.

George P. Jenkins. Consultant to W.R. Grace & Co.; retired chair, Metropolitan Life. *Other boards/memberships:* Bethlehem Steel, Chicago Pacific, Trammel Crow.

Frank S. Jones. Professor of urban studies, MIT.

(continues)

Table 3.3 *(continued)*

Source: Doug Henwood, *Left Business Observer*, June 1989, No. 29, p. 5.

as Kuwait (largely the work of American engineers), Iraq (constructed in part by American technicians), and Lebanon (where the Ford Foundation, Time-Life and ABC had each been active building stations). (Bunce 1977, 86)

The U.S. government has also been active in building a global satellite network that is partially owned and financed by private corporations, thus calling attention to the merger between the capitalist state and transnational corporations. As Schiller has pointed out, more than half of the broadcasting spectrum is assigned to government and much of this portion is given over to the military (1971, 34). Indeed, government-military communications networks are hidden from the public who are unaware of the extent to which communications technology is used for surveillance, counterinsurgency, and economic, military, and government functions serving the private interests and policies of small ruling groups. From this perspective, communications technology is an important part of a new system of neoimperialism in which powerful corporations, aided by the capitalist state, affect the destinies of individuals and countries throughout the world. As Schiller comments: "What lends sophistication to the still-youthful American imperial structure is its dependence on a marriage of economics and electronics, which substitutes in part, though not entirely, for the earlier, 'blood and iron' foundations of more primitive conquerors" (1971, 5).

The penetration of foreign countries by U.S., or other imported, television constitutes a new form of cultural imperialism. Although there is some extraction of profit from television sales, many European countries give so-called underdeveloped countries free television, and the United States charges very low rates in order to acclimate the country to consumer capitalist media forms and ideology. This form of imperialism destroys traditional culture and values (under the code of "modernization") and imposes a new kind of transnational, global consumer culture on the entire world.

By the mid-1970s the USIA had 115 transmitters and a staff of more than 800 people in 100 foreign countries; it was also broadcasting in 35 languages to an audience estimated by the agency at 200 million people. "Over its 25 year history, the USIA has spent more than $3.5 billion developing its arsenal for 'the information war' " (Network Project 1974, 5). Pat Aufderheide reports that by the mid-1980s, the Reagan administration had doubled the agency's budget since 1979—"with a whopping 20 percent increase from 1984, bringing the bill to $796.4 million" (*In These Times*, November 13, 1985, p. 12).

During the 1980s the USIA was taken over by hardcore anticommunist rightists who used the substantial government communications network— which is perhaps as large as CBS and NBC together—for state propaganda. In addition to "Voice of America" and other radio broadcasts, U.S.-sponsored films, and documentaries, USIA developed a regular news video service called Worldnet, which it provided free of cost to any broadcast facility that would take it (ibid.). Thus both state-sponsored television and U.S. commercial TV have penetrated the world, producing a new type of cultural imperialism.

Cumulative developments within the television industry in the 1980s contributed greatly to the restructuring of capitalism and to the development of a new technocapitalist order. The restructuring of capitalism has been a response (1) to the struggles of the 1960s for more democracy and a more responsive state; (2) to the economic crises, energy shortages, and economic instability of the 1970s; and (3) to the development of new technologies. As noted, the corporate response to the "democratic distemper" of the 1960s has been less democracy through tightened corporate control over the state and media. Corporate capital won more control over the state by supporting the pro-business Republican candidates in the 1980s and thus experienced fewer constraints from the state. Corporate conglomerates also assumed firmer control over the media through mergers and buyouts of the top three television networks. This increased control was, of course, made possible by a compliant state that overlooked antitrust laws, carried out a frenzied deregulation of broadcasting and other major industries, and championed an unrestrained "market" as the solution to all problems and as a model for all types of economic activity.

To the economic instability and crises of the previous decade, capital responded with more conglomerate mergers and increased control of markets, as well as with additional corporate planning and centralization. Television participated in this centralization of the economy and encouraged the atmosphere of deregulation, speculation, and mergers. The television industry followed the 1980s trend toward economic concentration whereby fewer broadcast corporations controlled more television outlets. It also followed the trend toward increasing conglomerization as the TV networks merged with other major corporations.

The television industry thus became part of a new communications and information sector. The expanding world capitalist economic order has required information in order to function, and satellites, data bases, and communication technologies have become essential components of the new technocapitalist order. In this environment, information processing and transmission have become an important economic sector. In some ways, television is a vanguard of the new technocapitalism: It is allied with the advertising, public relations, market research, opinion polling, management consulting, and computer industries and is interconnected with the cable and satellite industries as well as with various other information and entertainment concerns. The 1980s witnessed not only the widespread introduction of computers into everyday life in the United States but also the expansion of cable television and new technologies such as video games, video recorders, and video cameras. Television screens are now used to watch broadcast (or cablecast) programs and to play recorded or rented videocassettes as well as video games. In the homes of the future, the television set will probably be even more centrally linked to information data bases, home entertainment, and both work and leisure activities.

The media, information, and entertainment industries are indeed becoming more and more central to the new formation of technocapitalism. Since the 1950s there has been a steady movement in the United States away from industrial production and manufacturing toward the service, entertainment, and information industries. As Luke and White have noted:

> By the late 1960s, the primary information sector of the economy—computer manufacturing, telecommunications, mass media, advertising, publishing, accounting, education, research, and development as well as risk management in finance, banking, and insurance—produced 25.1 percent of the national income. The secondary information sector—work performed by information workers in government and goods-producing and service-producing firms for internal consumption—produced 21.1 percent of the national income. Already by the late 1960s, prior to widespread computerization of the 1970s, informational activities produced 46 percent of the U.S. national income and earned 53 percent of total national wages. By the mid-1970s the primary information sector's overall share of national income production alone rose from 25 to 30 percent, and all information workers in both sectors surpassed noninformation workers in number. . . . Current projections hold that 40 percent of all economic productivity can be improved by microprocessing technology. Data-intensive production could mean that at least 50 percent of the current shopfloor workers will be replaced by highly skilled technicians and robots by 1990. (1985, 33)

Furthermore, a 1988 Office of Technology Assessment study indicates that "about 40% of all new investment in the United States now goes to purchase information technology—computers, telecommunication devices and the like. Just 10 years ago the share was only 20%" (cited in Schiller 1989, 4). Accordingly, the new video, information, and entertainment technologies have rendered the television networks ever more central and powerful economic forces. Their economic power in particular has been strongly reinforced by the important informational, educational, and political functions of television. Thus television and the broadcasting industries are best conceptualized as the cultural arms of a technocapitalist economic system in which new technologies are used to promote private profit and to strengthen the hegemony of the capitalist system in the United States and throughout the world. It is important to note that technology is never neutral or independent of the social system in which it is introduced and developed. From the beginning, the system of broadcasting in the United States has been structured by the imperatives of corporate capitalism, and the media are primarily capitalist media. The important roles of the media in contemporary capitalist society and their control by giant corporations point to the centrality of technology and communications in the current stage of capitalism. Moreover, analysis of television reveals the new alliances being forged among transnational corporations, the capitalist state, and communications technologies in the era of technocapitalism. In the next section, I shall explore the consequences for democracy of this new and threatening situation.

Television and Democracy

A free press was one of the pillars of the democratic order developed in the United States (Emery 1972; Tebbel 1974; Schiller 1983). Although the "Alien and Sedition Acts" passed in 1798 provided for government control over the press, extension of the acts was defeated in 1801, after several attempts at prosecution and much public debate over the issue (Emery 1972, 120–126). Consequently, the press was largely freed from government censorship, but many debates emerged concerning the regulation of the press and the types and limitations of government regulation. This issue was rendered more acute with the advent of the broadcasting media, with millions of people receiving messages from a relatively small number of sources. Henceforth, a combination of presidential decrees and initiatives, congressional actions, the development of a federal communications regulatory system, and judicial decisions helped establish the relationship between the media and the government.

With the rise of the broadcast media, however, other problems emerged such as corporate control of the media, media concentration and monopoly, and media abuses. The latter resulted when commercial enterprises put private profit over public responsibility and blatantly used the powerful broadcast media to promote specific political interests and agendas. The government had declared that broadcasting was a public resource, like air and water, and that broadcasting performance should be judged on the basis of whether it served the "public interest, convenience, and necessity." But how can these be measured? What should government do to ensure that the media are serving the public interest? What *is* the public interest, anyway? Although the broadcasting corporations themselves opposed any and all regulation on the First Amendment grounds that it infringed on their freedom of speech, most commentators and judicial authorities declared that the media had important responsibilities in a free democracy and that broadcasting was subject to regulation and should maintain an informed citizenry and a healthy polity.

Summing up the philosophy behind the functioning of a commercial press in a democracy, Fred Siebert writes that it "is the right and duty of the press to serve as an extralegal check on government. The press was to keep officers of the state from abusing or exceeding their authority. It was to be the watchdog over the workings of democracy, ever vigilant to spot and expose any arbitrary or authoritarian practice" (1956, 56).[4] Siebert went on to say that

> [t]he media were envisaged as the principal instruments for adult education. They were to be the avenues by which the general public received information and discussion on matters of public importance. The federal postal system was no sooner set up than reduced rates were authorized to encourage the growth of newspapers and periodicals. The success of democracy was posited upon an intelligent and informed electorate, and the mass media along with public schools were charged with providing the public with educational materials. The media were to contribute to the development of arts and sciences, to the elevation of public tastes, and to improvements in the practical business of daily living. (1956, 56–57)

Theories concerning the social responsibility of the press gradually emerged as the media matured, as new media appeared, and as public debate over the role of media in society established certain ideas and positions. The media themselves adopted professional codes and guidelines: The press established the "Canons of Journalism" in 1923, the film industry adopted a Production Code in the early 1930s, the radio industry adopted a Broadcasting Code in 1937, and the television industry adopted a Television Code in 1952. As these attempts at self-regulation through establishment of industry standards and practices were often part of an effort to avoid government regulation, they never adequately defined the responsibilities of the media in a democratic society. Furthermore, government and the courts were forced to step in and provide legislation to curb abuses in the broadcasting and entertainment industries.

Yet despite a series of governmental decrees, court decisions, and industry attempts to define the social responsibilities of the media, neither consensus nor established code has defined their responsibilities in a free and democratic society. Instead, the fact that the dominant media are commercial enterprises has led some of their spokespersons to claim that they have no social responsibilities whatsoever. In 1946 the head of the National Association of Broadcasters, Justin Miller, declared the idea that the people owned the airwaves (an idea central to the 1934 Federal Communications Act) to be "hooey and nonsense" (Barnouw 1968, 221–222). During the Reagan/Bush years, the notion of the media as private businesses subject only to the laws of the marketplace and competition became commonplace (see section 2.5). Reagan's FCC Commissioner Mark Fowler stated that "broadcast regulation is shrouded in myths, myths about service to the community. . . . The FCC must deal with the reality of broadcasting, a reality that begins with the fact that broadcasting is a business" (Fowler, cited in Brown 1981, 21).

In Fowler's view, the broadcast industry knows best how to serve its audiences, and thus extreme deregulation best serves the public interest. Indeed, Fowler pursued deregulation with religious fervor and provided the broadcast industry with almost undreamed-of favors. At one point, he stated: "I pledge myself to take deregulation to the limits of existing law. No renewal filings, no ascertainment exercises, no content regulation, no ownership restrictions beyond those that apply to media generally, free resale of properties, no petitions to deny, no brownie points for doing this right, no finger-wagging for doing that wrong" (Fowler, cited in Brown 1982, 27).

For Fowler, the regulatory apparatus of the FCC was "the last of the New Deal dinosaurs" and television was "just an appliance, like the toaster," that required no special regulatory attention (Fowler, cited in Black 1984, 53). This attitude—which Fowler put into practice by carrying through most of his pledges—ignores the fact that the broadcast media, in comparison to newspapers, *were* officially ordained in the Federal Communications Act of 1934 to serve the public interest. Moreover, the entire history of broadcasting had previously conceived of broadcasting as a public good subject to government regulation. In fact, as noted in section 2.1, even as business-oriented a figure as Herbert Hoover originally conceived of broadcasting as a noncommercial medium in the 1920s. In 1922 Hoover stated that radio was one of the few cases in behalf of which the public was unanimously in favor of an extension of federal government regulation. Both Hoover and Coolidge supported a public utility attitude toward broadcasting, seeing broadcasting as a public resource to be administered according to the public interest (Fly et al. 1959, 10). And the 1934 Federal Communications Act—which still provides the basis for existing communications law and regulation—stipulates that broadcasting is part of the public sector, that it is a public utility subject to government regulation.

Yet by the 1940s commerce had obviously come to dominate the form and content of the broadcast media. The FCC commissioned a study, *Public Service Responsibility of Broadcast Licensees* (the so-called Blue Book), which reaffirmed the public, democratic, and noncommercial principles that were to govern the broadcast media (anthologized in Kahn 1978, 132ff.). During the same period, a Commission on Freedom of the Press attempted to spell out the functions and responsibilities of the press in a democratic society. Both the Blue Book and the Commission mandated that the government assume responsibility for the establishment and maintenance of a democratic system of media and mass communication. Over the years, a variety of court and FCC decisions reaffirmed the democratic principles of communication for the broadcast media. These principles and decisions specify to some extent what is meant by broadcasting serving the "public interest." They include (1) a 1944 Supreme Court decision that affirms the First Amendment right of people to receive information from the most diverse and antagonistic sources; (2) a 1949 FCC decision that affirms the right of people to be informed and to hear competing sides of an issue; and (3) a court decision that affirms the right to reply to one-sided or distorted discourse (cf. the Fairness Doctrine in the 1967 Red Lion case).[5]

After the Watergate Affair, during which many claimed that the news media had unfairly driven president Nixon from office, Justice Potter Stewart stated that, the media had in fact carried out their constitutional responsibilities, as the First Amendment, which guaranteed a free press, was meant "to create a fourth institution outside government as an additional check on the three official branches" (Stewart, cited in Barnouw 1975, 463). Furthermore, the FCC itself has decreed that the "basic purpose" of broadcasting is "the development of an informed public opinion through the public dissemination of news and ideas concerning the vital public issues of the day. . . . [The] foundation stone of the American system of broadcasting [is] . . . the right of the public to be informed, rather than any right on the part of the government, any broadcast licenses or any individual members of the public to broadcast his own particular views on any matter" (cited in Epstein 1973, 48).

Consequently, there is a contradiction among the democratic principles of broadcasting (as interpreted by Congress, the FCC, the courts) and the broadcast practices that limit the spectrum of opinion and constrain communication. More specifically, we have here a typical example of the contradiction between capitalism and democracy that is central to the

American experience. A democratic social order would engage in popular debate of the central issues in a society and allow expression of various sides of a given issue by individuals who would have an opportunity to make their case. Democracy presupposes the existence of a public sphere in which vigorous debate on issues of public importance takes place so that decisions can be made on complex and controversial issues. In a commercial system of broadcasting, however, profit imperatives limit the amount of time given to political debate. Indeed, the three major networks tend to broadcast programming that pulls in the biggest audiences, thus maximizing ratings and profits. Commerce has predominated over communication to the point where CBS president William Paley regretted the day that CBS issued corporate stock, telling Bill Moyers that CBS simply could not afford to produce quality documentary or discussion shows regularly because "the minute is worth too much now" (Paley, cited in Halberstam 1979, 734).

Democracy has thus clearly become subordinate to capitalism in the current system of commercial broadcasting. In an advanced industrial/ technological order, access to the means of public communication is necessary to ensure that adequate presentation of various points of view and debate can take place. However, in a capitalist society where the means of communication are concentrated in powerful corporations, the access of minority, oppositional, or alternative views is denied or limited. Indeed, studies have shown that the opinion spectrum presented is severely limited, and that many groups and individuals are denied access to broadcast media (Schiller 1973; Morrow 1985). And restriction of access to the media and limitations on public debate contradict the need for an informed public that can participate in democratic politics.

There are also contradictions between the nature and purpose of commercial television, on the one hand, and a democratic social order, on the other. Paul Klein claims that network television maximizes its audience by offering noncontroversial programs to keep from offending people and by utilizing a "least objectionable program" philosophy (1972, 43). This situation leads to "lowest common denominator" programming, which, in seeking a mass audience, avoids challenging that audience. From this perspective, television is perceived as a commercial medium that seeks to attract, entertain, and pacify its audience while selling commercial goods and ideology. Accordingly, those who call television a "democratic" or "populist" art fail both to understand the nature of democracy and to see how television has been diminishing democratic participation by replacing political struggles with "photo opportunities" and spectacles, and reducing elections to a manipulation of political images (see Chapter 4).[6]

In addition, there are contradictions between democracy and the advertising that sustains network operations. Advertising seeks to show that people can resolve their problems by purchasing something. It contains images that celebrate the society as it is, rather than stirring people to political action or social participation. It suggests that happiness and value are located in the private sphere, thus encouraging a privatized, consumer existence. Democracy, however, thrives on controversy and requires participation in social processes; it presupposes that people are motivated enough to want to get involved in public life. Democracy thus requires a degree of "civic virtue" and a lively public sphere in which discussion, debate, and participation combine in collective public decisionmaking.

Thus the conflicts between commerce and communication are built into the system of commercial broadcasting developed in the United States—a system that represents a series of compromises between its conflicting imperatives, where the interests of commerce and private profit almost always triumph over democracy and the public interest. In a commercial broadcasting system, therefore, commerce predominates over communication and the private interests of advertisers and broadcasters systematically prevail over the public interest and democracy. Control of television by giant corporations thus precludes its vigorous "watchdog" or adversary role as an independent "fourth estate," separate from the other dominant societal institutions. Television in the United States today is, instead, more of a corporate and political "lapdog" that faithfully obeys and serves its powerful masters.

Hence corporate control severely compromises the democratic functions of television and renders it, first and foremost, an instrument of social control and legitimation rather than a medium of information and democratic debate. Increasing control of network television by giant corporations therefore means that television is becoming a tool of capitalist hegemony and is sacrificing its functions as a critic of government and business. In short, commercial television is unable in principle to fulfill its mandate to develop "an informed public opinion through the public dissemination of news and ideas concerning the vital public issues of the day." (In chapter 4 and the Appendixes, I shall document the failure of television to assume its democratic mandate, from the 1980s to the present.)

Nonetheless, given the conflictual nature of contemporary capitalism, intense conflicts often emerge among television, business, and government, as well as between the capitalist system and the underlying population. In the next section, I shall explore some of these conflicts in an attempt to conceptualize the relations among some of the major institutions of capitalist democracy in the United States.

3.3 A Critical/Institutional Theory

As an institution, television stands beside and between the state and business as a major institutional force within contemporary U.S. society. By the 1980s network television had become one of the most powerful social and political forces in the United States; it had also assumed a central role in the social reproduction and defense of the existing economic and political system. Today, network television confronts government and business as a major player in the established power structure, as a key institution that helps to control the direction of U.S. society. Conceptualization of the relationships among network television, government, and business is rendered complex, however, by the fact that the television networks are both businesses and parts of a democratic/public sphere mandated to fulfill certain crucial democratic functions. Television is thus part of capitalism, and its networks have become major corporate conglomerates. These conglomerates constitute a powerful economic force as well as part of a democratic public sphere with mandates to provide adequate information and all sides of controversial issues.

Moreover, television serves as a conduit for state policies, as an instrument of governance for state personnel, and as an occasional check against excessive state power, corruption, illegality, and incompetency. Television is thus simultaneously part of the state apparatus and subject to government regulation, and yet separate from the state, able to topple heads of state and those it deems adequate targets for its powerful scrutiny. For analytical purposes, one can nevertheless distinguish among network television, government, and business as key institutional forces in contemporary U.S. society. In this connection, a critical/institutional theory of television attempts to analyze the complex and contradictory matrix within which television relates to and intersects with the state and business.

It is possible to make a distinction between business and the television networks because, although television functions according to the imperatives of profit maximization and capital accumulation, it also has social functions and effects that go far beyond those of any other business organization. Network television must turn over profits to retain its viability as a business enterprise, but it must also maintain a certain amount of ideological legitimacy for the system as a whole and support at least a certain level of apparent democracy. Accordingly, television must function as a crisis manager, as a mediator of social conflict, as a manager of consciousness, and as a force of systems maintenance.

Although the state has regulatory power over television, television has such enormous cultural power that it can often exert influence over state policy and determine the fortune of major and minor political players. Thus, network television is best conceptualized as an integral part of the capitalist system, deeply embedded in the corporate economic structure and closely linked to the capitalist state. Nonetheless, as there are certain conflicts among network television, government, and business, a critical theory of television must conceptualize both the conflicts and the connections, and interactions between them.

Structural Conflicts and Tensions: Legitimation and Air War

One of network television's key political functions is to legitimate the system of democracy established in the United States as the best possible political system. It does so by promoting elections, by attacking nondemocratic (mostly communist) systems, and by celebrating state rituals such as elections, inaugurations, State of the Union and other presidential addresses, and special events sponsored by the state. Presidential elections dominate news and public affairs programming during the entire year in which they take place, through tremendous amounts of news coverage, saturation discussions on talk shows, and special programs covering various aspects of the process. The message is that these events are particularly important, that a fair and open contest is going on, and that this form of democratic government (i.e., regularly scheduled elections) is the greatest form of government on earth. Other forms of democracy such as participatory democracy, workers' democracy, and socialist democracy are rarely presented, however, and violations of electoral democracy in other countries tend to be prominently featured in news reports (unless the violators are special allies of the United States).[7]

Television thus engages in system-maintenance legitimation that sanctions the basic institutions in the United States. Although it often criticizes specific governmental regimes, policies, and personalities, it never criticizes the form of the democratic state established in the United States itself. When television does criticize specific government targets, its critical remarks are usually articulated by prominent establishment spokespersons who point to failed or controversial programs that are themselves the subject of intra-elite conflicts or are contested by significant masses of people. The media have a certain responsibility for ensuring both the stability and the legitimacy of the established system; hence they are permitted to go after individuals or policies that violate the rules of the game, that are highly ineffective, or that fail to fulfill the interests or follow the agenda of ruling elites. Accordingly, television frequently does intervene in key conflicts and has become a major player in constituting the political agenda, managing social conflict, and arbitrating severe and protracted differences among ruling elites.

Initially, at least, the broadcast media commonly publicize and mobilize support for new government programs. Roosevelt's New Deal, Kennedy's

New Frontier, Johnson's Great Society programs, various Vietnam policies, Nixon's Watergate defense, Carter's Middle East diplomacy and his responses to the Iran and Afghanistan events, Reagan's tax cut and economic policies—all were initially promoted by the media, which explained and to some extent legitimated them. In the early stages of new policies and programs, network television tends to be a sympathetic amplifier of government policies and programs and to interpret them in a favorable light. However, as soon as criticisms and failures of government policies develop, network television articulates opposition and raises doubts about them. If the failures become too obvious, television focuses on the deficiencies of those policies and, in this way, subverts governmental policy efforts. These "exposures" are often popular, for audiences (often justifiably) distrust government and enjoy seeing it come under attack.

For instance, in 1989, when Bush announced his program to bail out the savings and loan (S&L) industry, which was facing a massive series of failures and bankruptcies, television featured government spokespersons who outlined the program with charts and graphs. The news coverage rarely, if at all, presented opposing programs or positions; nor did it allow criticism of Bush's program. If (as appears to be the case) its failure is massive and significant opposition emerges, then television will probably articulate criticisms of the program and alternatives to Bush's bailout scheme. Thus television tends to initially support state policies; but if they fail or there is serious opposition, they will reproduce the conflict.

Network television is sometimes a mouthpiece for particular government policies and personnel and, at other times, a critic. In turn, various administrations have criticized and attempted to regulate television. Although most administrations try to curry favor with the powerful television networks, they occasionally threaten or act against television as did the Nixon administration (see Lashner 1984). Indeed, the relationship between broadcasting and government has been fraught with conflicts and contradictions. Most FCC commissioners have been network allies, although a few have challenged various aspects of network practice.[8] In these ways, serious conflicts often emerge between government and television.

Indeed, over the last several decades, the major conflicts in U.S. society have been played out in television air wars. Competing sides have fought to gain access to television and to make their views and positions known. In addition, there have been at least occasional battles between television and government. Consequently, the relationships among television, government, and contemporary politics have been complex and conflictual.

Instrumentalist Versus Hegemony Theory. Many radical theories of the media have failed to note the contradictions and tensions between television and government. Claus Mueller (1973), for example, assumes in *The Politics of Communication* that the media are simply a mouthpiece for state propaganda. Louis Althusser (1971), Parenti (1986), and Herman and Chomsky (1988) would tend to agree.[9] These theorists assume an instrumentalist theory of the state whereby the state is simply a tool of the ruling class used to assert its interests. Against instrumentalist theory, hegemony theory maintains that the state is relatively autonomous and independent from capital, but also that it is a prize that corporate elites frequently win and use to advance their interests. On the whole, the capitalist state has both steering and management functions as well as legitimation functions (Habermas 1975). The capitalist system legitimates itself as democratic and thus must maintain at least a facade of democratic competition. Occasionally, the state genuinely mediates between competing groups and also responds to popular struggles for civil and women's rights, protection of the environment, curtailment of aggressive foreign interventions, and so on. It often carries out compromises between different sectors of the ruling class and public interest movements and thus, like the media, assumes contradictory functions and effects.

During the 1980s conservatives directly seized control of the state with the election of Reagan and Bush. Indeed, they used the state to advance the interests of the capitalist class. As corporate capital also seized control of the media, there was an especially tight fit among the state, media, and business (as is frequently the case in contemporary capitalist societies). In general, however, instrumentalist theory overlooks not only the conflicts between different ruling elites and policies that are played out in the media, but also the contradictions in the media's alternating criticism and promotion of government. In addition, instrumentalist theory fails to distinguish between the state (as the institutional political structures, institutions, and practices of a given social order) and government (as the administration currently in place). The media rarely criticize state forms (e.g., constitutional democracy, the balance of powers, the bill of rights), but they frequently criticize specific government policies and personnel.

Instrumentalist theory also obscures the oscillation between state regulation of the media (which may contradict capitalist interests) and complete capitalist control of the state and the media. Part of the problem derives from the limitations of the instrumentalist model, which mechanistically posits the state as the exclusive tool of a unified ruling class and interprets network television as the mouthpiece of the ruling class. In short, instrumentalist theory fails to perceive the conflicts between government and the media, the contradictions and struggles within the dominant economic class, and the contradictory government and media positions that reproduce actual conflicts within the society.

In the most dramatic instances, conflicts between government and network television take the form of media exposure of the worst failures of specific policies, practices, and personnel. For example, television presentations of

Vietnam, Watergate, the Iran/Contra affair, and the crimes of the CIA, FBI, and other state agencies seriously delegitimated state practice. Whereas early television coverage of the Vietnam War defended government policy, coverage after the Tet offensive raised serious doubts about the war policy (see section 2.3). Soon after, Lyndon Johnson announced that he would not seek reelection, and more attention was given to the antiwar movement. Network television tended to present uncritically Nixon's view that U.S. involvement in Vietnam was scaling down, but it also exposed various scandals such as the Calley affair at My Lai, troop insubordination and the shooting of officers, the murder of white American students at Kent State, and corruption in the South Vietnamese government. Although network television defined Vietnam as a "tragic mistake," and never really analyzed why the United States had intervened in the first place (Gibson 1986), the coverage of the fall of Saigon, capped by incredible pictures of helicopter flights from the U.S. Embassy and their destruction at sea, made it clear that Vietnam represented not merely the defeat but the rout of government policy. In a three-hour documentary, shown soon after the fall of Saigon, CBS tried to present itself as the enlightened critic of the war whose coverage and exposure of the failures of state policy helped the United States out of a morass into which it should never have fallen. Aside from its obvious self-promotion, the program exhibited the conflict potential between government and television as well as television's attempt to gain some of the prestige and cultural power lost by the state.

Probably the most dramatic conflict between the government and media took place during the Watergate affair. Although network coverage of Watergate initially accepted the Nixon administration's explanation of the Watergate affair as a "third-rate burglary," television played a crucial role in the downfall of the Nixon presidency as the scandal escalated. Although the administration had carried out a systematic program to intimidate and control the media, and had established an "enemies list" that contained prominent media personnel, the networks decided to televise the Watergate hearings, which involved a fascinated nation in one of the great passion plays of the era. Network television processed the Watergate affair as the drama of a Bad Man against the Good System—a typical trope that fit in well with the formulas of popular culture. So much corruption was exposed, and public opinion was so firmly mobilized against Nixon, however, that he was forced to resign—thus providing a dramatic example of how the media air wars could act against the interests of those who occupy power within government.

Indeed, those theorists who maintain that, in an era of "presidential television," TV fundamentally aids government (i.e., by serving as a powerful instrument of governance and control) must account for the fact that several presidents in succession—Johnson, Nixon, Ford, and Carter—were forced to renounce a further term, to resign, or to lose an election largely because of negative television presentation of their policies and personal flaws. This phenomenon can be partially explained by television's need to mediate between severe ruling-class contradictions and to eliminate policies and personnel that are either harmful to the ruling elite or simply ineffective. One could argue that this series of presidents either engaged in unpopular and ineffectual policies or were poor state managers of corporate interests. To the extent that politicians or policies do not serve the interests of ruling elites, they are fair game for media critique. However, if other presidents (such as Reagan) are perceived as protecting and advancing the interests of ruling elites, they will probably be subject to very little criticism or adversarial coverage unless specific policies come to contradict the interests or views of the ruling elites—as did Reagan's policies in the Iran/Contra affair (see Chapter 4).

The intra-capitalist rivalries and power struggles visible on network television suggest that there is no one, unified ruling class with a unitary strategy, goals, and a "politics of control." As Enzensberger argues, "The degree to which the power struggles within the ruling class are extroverted by Western television is without precedent in history, and all current theories of manipulation only serve to obscure this fact" (1977, 249). Against the neoconservatives, Enzensberger is also probably correct in saying that television has the overall effect of stabilizing the social order and containing opposition:

> Like Congress, only much more so, it can therefore be seen as a sort of homeostatic machine expressing, and at the same time containing, the contradictions which arise within the ruling class. The in-fights of this minority are acted out symbolically on the screen, as a kind of strategic simulations game which tends to prevent open clashes from occurring in reality. On balance, television thus works as a servo-mechanism increasing the overall stability of a given social system. Obviously, such a setup is much more sophisticated than a simple switch, and far more effective as a means of controlling complex and fluid situations. (ibid., 250)

Air War and Social Struggle. Although television serves functions of system maintenance, it also reproduces social struggles and circulates images of conflict and upheaval. Although it attempts to manage and gloss over these struggles, it occasionally reinforces them by providing models and inspiration for groups bent on change. Precisely because the networks are to some extent competitive businesses, television news often focuses attention on severe conflicts, or government scandals, in which the audience is interested. For instance, television's proclivities toward drama, conflict, and violence naturally led it to focus on the dramatic civil rights movement, and its images of white brutality and black courage advanced the interests of the movement against white racism and the racist power structure. The images of struggle and oppression during the civil rights era inspired groups to intensify their struggles and to emulate the actions of previous groups, as did TV images of the antiwar movement during the Vietnam War (see section 2.3). Images of prison revolt prompted a cycle of revolts in the mid-1980s, leading television producers to decide against covering them any further: They were literally providing models for prisoners throughout the country. Similar stories have circulated concerning network decisions to play down representations of the antiwar movement following the tumult of the 1968 Democratic Convention in Chicago (Hodgson 1976).

Television also responded to pressures from the environmental, women's, gay, black, Chicano, and other new social movements, especially in the early 1970s (Montgomery 1989). Network entertainment divisions were pressured to portray more positive images of blacks, women, Hispanics, gays, and other minorities, and to hire members of some of these groups for the news and entertainment divisions as well. Some television producers, such as Norman Lear, created programs that exhibited controversial issues and sometimes took distinctly liberal positions. Likewise, television movies took on more controversial themes and in turn became the subject of growing controversies.

In fact, it is often remarked that television is primarily a visual medium that seeks dramatic images for its news and information programming. As such, television is attracted to conflicts. Indeed, during the 1970s and 1980s television showed a world in turmoil: In the 1970s it dramatized the Nicaraguan and Iranian revolutionary movements, and in the 1980s it emphasized the upheaval in the communist countries. Even during the conservative 1980s images of struggle against imperialist domination continued to appear. There was heavy coverage of the movements in the Philippines and Haiti, where dictorial regimes were being overthrown, and of the struggle in Panama to oust a thoroughly corrupt dictator who was a close ally of U.S. ruling circles and was eventually thrown out by his own sponsors when he turned against them. In South Africa, as well, the struggle against apartheid was frequently and sympathetically portrayed. In short, television images may at times privilege democratic movements and people in struggle.

During the summer of 1989 television broadcast image after image of the heroic fight for democracy in China. Although such coverage fits into the frames of traditional anticommunism, the images conveyed the impression that only people's movements, only militant and resolute struggles, can bring about progressive change. These positive images of rebellion tend to promote democratic and social values, which are significantly at odds with the individualist and consumerist values of the capitalist system. Furthermore, when the Chinese government moved to violently repress the demonstrations, network news coverage continued to be strongly sympathetic to the struggles for democracy and sharply critical of the state repression, thus promoting popular democracy against state authority.

In the fall of 1989 television focused intently on the struggles for democracy going on in the Soviet Union and Eastern Europe. This coverage, too, was congruent with anticommunist ideology; yet it portrayed democratic struggle as the appropriate vehicle for social change and refuted the right-wing position that communist governments would never allow change or reform. The portrayals of change in the communist world also undermined conservative arguments for gigantic defense budgets and intervention against the Soviet Union or its perceived allies. In general, portrayals of the changing communist world undermined the cold war ideology of a dangerous and thoroughly vicious enemy that justified tremendous arms expenditures as well as tremendous investment in the military occupation of Europe and elsewhere in the world. Thus television not only helped reduce cold war tensions but also brought into question the further maintenance of a military-industrial complex that is arguably superfluous in a world without a dangerous, totalitarian communist adversary.

It is also clear that television circulated struggles from one country in Eastern Europe to another. East Germans watched with astonishment as Poland elected a noncommunist government and Solidarity candidates handily won a free election. Czech citizens watched with fascination as massive East German demonstrations eventually surfaced on television and drove out a corrupt communist government, paving the way for the elimination of the Berlin Wall and future free elections. Romanian citizens watched as masses of Czechs demonstrated for democracy, forcing out the Stalinist puppet government imposed by the Soviet Union after its 1968 invasion. In turn, the Romanians provided lessons in mass struggle and armed insurrection for their neighbors; mass agitation subsequently increased in Bulgaria and Yugoslavia. In this explosive matrix, television became a major force as it circulated mass struggle and, in Eastern Europe, served as a powerful force of democratization—a function that it could conceivably serve in the United States when its citizens, too, decide that they want genuine democracy.

Yet television could also serve as an instrument of pacification and control in the communist countries. A *Wall Street Journal* article on Gorbachev's use of television in the Soviet Union suggests that his circle may be the first ruling group in the USSR to understand how television might be used to pacify and contain its citizens (June 7, 1989, p. 1). The article describes a fascinated Soviet citizenry watching for the first time debates in the new Soviet parliament: "In a society where saying what you think is still a novelty, the stormy inaugural session of the new Soviet parliament has galvanized the public. The deputies have discarded all the old rules of Soviet parliamentary behavior. They have argued, heckled and insulted one another in an outpouring of long-suppressed grievances, abandoning the formal agenda, the principle of unanimity and any pretense of courtesy. Television cameras have beamed their antics live into millions of Soviet homes and offices." The article then indicates that the Russian population watched the proceedings in great fascination rather than demonstrating in the streets as the Chinese were doing. Some weeks later, however, economic difficulties prompted some Russian workers to strike and demonstrate as well—actions legitimated by the positive Soviet images of *perestroika*. And in the succeeding Soviet parliamentary meeting, proceedings were broadcast only at night, as production had dropped dramatically during the previous televised proceedings!

TV images can thus serve to stabilize or destabilize a ruling party or system in both the capitalist and the communist worlds. The view that television takes different positions in different historical conjunctures is indeed confirmed by the changes in portrayal of the Soviet Union in the 1980s. For decades, television served cold war ideology by presenting negative images of the Soviet Union and repeating declarations that communist societies were totalitarian and resistant to any democratic reform whatsoever. The television images of struggles for reform in communist countries that began appearing in the 1980s revealed communist societies as more open to change and pluralistic than the previous wholly negative images had suggested. This surprising turn in network frames began intensifying in late 1987, when television broke with its long-standing negative representation of the Soviet Union to present positive images of Gorbachev and his policies of *glasnost* and *perestroika*. Indeed, when Gorbachev came to the United States (and to Europe), he was accorded superstar status by the American media, which had been less negative toward the Soviet Union in recent years. Thus detente was promoted, and the rationale for an insanely expensive and destructive arms race was undercut.

In fact, even when the turmoil in the communist world is framed in terms of anticommunist ideologies, it circulates positive, indeed compelling, images of mass demonstration and struggle, thus broadcasting the message that to change society, mass struggle is necessary. Television's images are always double-edged, subject to audience decoding, and available for uses not anticipated by network programmers. Consequently, even ideological discourse can encourage oppositional readings and action, and television images can always be "read against the grain" and used to promote enlightenment and social change.

And yet it seems that, in capitalist countries, television primarily promotes a depoliticization of the audience. For instance, television elections in the United States have arguably decreased participation in the political process:

Fewer than half of the registered voters even bother to vote in presidential elections. In short, television in the United States generally produces a privatized, consumer culture but rarely promotes civic life and the public sphere. News and information focus largely on establishment authorities, not on groups or individuals struggling for social change. Entertainment usually focuses on private dramas or professional authority figures but rarely features political activists, movements, or civic activity. Television's ubiquitous advertising promotes commodity solutions to social problems, and the unrealistic conflict/solution models of both its ads and its entertainment are in opposition to the long and difficult political work needed to carry through social change. Indeed, the sheer amount of time spent watching television mitigates against an active civic and public life.

Television and State Power. Television can serve as a check on excessive state power, but it also provides government with an incredibly powerful instrument of governance and social control. To begin with, television provides the president with the power to address millions of people whenever she or he wishes (Minow, Martin, and Mitchell 1973). News formats privilege administration policies by presenting their positions in all debates. Since almost everything a president does is news, the opportunity exists for daily manipulation of the media by government—a practice developed into a fine art during the Reagan administration. This theory of "presidential television" holds that TV provides a powerful instrument of governance and state power, serving as a cultural arm of state capitalism.

Indeed, heated debates have emerged over the last two decades concerning whether television is—or is not—an instrument of state power and the presidency. Neoconservatives claim that television has undermined the president's ability to govern by submitting every policy and action to intense media scrutiny and debate. They also argue that television has promoted a "democratic distemper" by publicizing the efforts of various groups to make demands on government (see section 1.1). Meyrowitz (1985) argues that television has played a key role in destroying several presidencies by publicizing opposition to their policies and by dramatizing their weaknesses and failures. He claims that television demystifies political leaders and thus undermines their authority, making it more difficult to govern in the television age. Finally, Robinson argues that overexposure of the president and his policies inevitably produces a negative response from viewers (1975, 117ff.).

I would argue, however, that it is only when government administrators or personnel are ineffective, or are perceived by key ruling elites as not serving their interests, that they are subject to systematic criticism by the media. Moreover, Walter Karp (1989) has argued that members of Congress and other government personnel largely set the media agenda. As news reporters depend on government sources to "break" or fill out stories, these sources play a fundamental role in shaping the media agenda and in slanting their stories. Karp (1989) provides several examples whereby the media slavishly followed the congressional agenda and discourse in presenting the conflict in Central America, the *Challenger* disaster, the Iran/Contra hearings, and the debates over the competency of Ronald Reagan. Karp suggests, for example, that although it was known that NASA engineers had warned that it was unsafe to launch the *Challenger*, NASA officials approved the launch because of pressure from the Reagan administration; the night of the launch, Reagan had planned to deliver a State of the Union paean to "America moving ahead" and the administration wanted the *Challenger* mission to serve as his prime example. Karp argues that because a presidential panel investigating the disaster failed to dramatize the reason behind the catastrophe, the media joined ranks and did not publicize the scandalous evidence that NASA had succumbed to political pressures (ibid., 63).

Karp cites reporters such as Tom Wicker who point out that inside government sources are essential to a reporter's career, and that the media must cultivate their sources by releasing stories and information that government officials want released while holding back information that might prove embarrassing to their sources. Karp concludes that "[i]t is a bitter irony of source journalism that the most esteemed journalists are actually the most servile. For it is by making themselves useful to the powerful that they gain access to their 'best' sources" (ibid., 62). Moreover, the journalistic code of "objectivity" holds that nothing can be said "unless some official-enough spokesman could be found to say so" (Wicker, cited in Karp 1989, 63). In these ways, Karp suggests, government officials play a key role in determining what is and what is not legitimate news. Thus, in an era when congressional opposition is muted or absent, critical discourse in the media is unlikely.

Accordingly, the media serve the interests of the state by privileging the president and Congress as sources of news; by favorably presenting, at least initially, new government programs; and by generally supporting government foreign policy initiatives. Herman and Chomsky (1988) and Chomsky (1989) document the ways that the media have supported administration efforts in Indochina, Central America, the Middle East, and other parts of the world over the last few decades. Finally, the media can also support the administrations and policies they favor—as they did with the Reagan administration in the 1980s (see Chapter 4).

Yet the media can also oppose specific policies, personnel, or administrations, producing the sense that they are feisty watchdogs, while provoking the ire of policy supporters or people targeted by their criticisms. Inadvertently or not, television circulates struggle and may inspire oppositional attitudes and action. It has thus served government interests in some cases

Book Reviews

Richard Harding Davis: Royal portrait of an ego

The Reporter Who Would Be King: A biography of Richard Harding Davis. Arthur Lubow. (Scribner's, 866 Third Ave., New York, N.Y. 10022). 438 pages. $25.

Foreign correspondents can be found weighted down with portable transmission equipment and other paraphernalia, but the goods today hardly compare to the essentials of that most dashing, most handsome of reporters in the early part of the century, Richard Harding Davis.

When Davis covered the Boer War in South Africa, "he acquired a beautiful tent with window panes, ventilators, clothes lines," says Lubow in this definitive biography of Davis. "His equipage during that campaign included two tables, two chairs, a bathtub, a folding bed, two lanterns, and a Cape cart; and his staff of three black boys featured one who did noth-

War I. He chronicled the entry of German troops into Brussels: "For three days and three nights the column of gray, with fifty thousand bayonets and fifty thousand lances, with gray transport wagons, gray ambulances, gray ammunition-carts, gray cannon, like a river of steel cut Brussels in two."

He has an exciting brush with death at the hands of the Germans, who want to take him out and shoot him. You meet some of his early comrades, such as writers Jack London and Stephen Crane. You also meet the dominant personalities in his personal life, his famous author mother, and his two wives, the second a vaudeville actress.

His encounters with censorship and lack of access to information ring familiar today.

Lubow, who lives in New York, writes for *Vanity Fair* and other magazines.

Unsilent Revolution: Television News and American Public Life, 1948-1991. Robert J. Donovan, Ray Scherer. (Cambridge University Press, 40 W. 40th St. New York, N.Y. 10011-4211). 357 pages. $17.95.

in the airing of debates.

The book is an enlightening narrative history of tv in politics from the first use of tv in the White House covering a speech by Harry Truman in October 1947 to the current administration.

The first 12 chapters are case history studies of tv coverage "when television news changed the course of events and built or destroyed the careers of public figures." Among the subjects are the death and funeral of President Kennedy, the Vietnam War, the Army-McCarthy hearings, and the rise and fall of Nixon.

Donovan was the chief of the Washington bureau of the *Los Angeles Times*; Scherer is a former NBC White House correspondent.

Radio and Television Pioneers: A Patent Bibliography. David W. Kraeuter. (Scarecrow Press, P.O. Box 4167, Metuchen, N.J. 08840). 329 pages. $35.

Who invented and developed radio and television? You will not settle for a few names with this book. Here is a

officer. After he married at 53, his wife accompanied him to battle areas in the Far East and the Congo.

Always dandily dressed, he lost one of his first jobs because he would not follow an order to take off his gloves when he sat down to work in the newsroom. When a new member of a newspaper staff once asked him his first name, he replied simply, "Mister."

His career in newspapers in Philadelphia and New York, and as a special reporter for syndicates and magazines, found him assigned to the Johnstown, Pa., flood disaster and the first electrocution in the electric chair. Lubow goes on in great detail over this long-delayed and botched execution, although Davis was off someplace else at the final moment.

Davis is remembered in anthologies for a number of stories, among them the execution of a young rebel in Cuba in 1897. Davis was a poetic writer, careful to include significant detail. As the young rebel, who was smoking a cigarette, snapped back from the firing-squad volley, Davis noted "the cigarette still burned, a tiny ring of living fire, at the place where the figure had first stood."

The sense of detail came through in his reporting of his last war, World history of tv in politics, from Truman to Bush, and venture some of the lessons learned. For one thing, "deplorable as they may be, commercials that attack an opponent have proved too effective for politicians to abandon."

They point out the effectiveness of a negative or sleazy ad, even if it be withdrawn and denounced. Case in point is an ad of the Democrats on the candidacy of Barry Goldwater. The tv spot shows a little girl picking daisies, threatened by references to the destruction caused by nuclear fallout. Goldwater had objected to a test ban treaty. Reacting to criticism of the ad as unfair, Democrats pulled the ad, but not until it had had its effect.

The authors cite a turn in the use of tv following Richard Nixon's disastrous debate with John Kennedy. Nixon in the 1968 campaign decided that appearance was more important than substance on tv and began to manipulate tv, foreshadowing, they say, the electronic strategies of Ronald Reagan and George Bush.

The book's thesis is hardly a surprise: tv changed the political process from top to bottom, sometimes for the worse, with its preoccupation with sound bites; sometimes for the better, ventors. They range alphabetically from the inventions of Ernest Alexanderson (1878-1975)—alternating-current generator, voltage-regulator, etc.—to Vladimir Zworykin (1889-1982)—electric high-frequency signaling apparatus, etc. The book should be a comprehensive guide for those interested in the history of broadcasting.

Kraeuter is a reference librarian at Washington and Jefferson College, Washington, Pa.

—Hiley Ward

Cowles dividend

Cowles Media Co. of Minneapolis has declared a dividend of 73¢ per share, payable Sept. 7 to shareholders of record on Aug. 21.

In a meeting Aug. 3, the board also authorized the company to purchase up to 15,000 shares of its stock from time to time in the open market. Shares will be used primarily for certain employee compensation and benefit plans.

Cowles publishes the Minneapolis Star Tribune, the Scottsdale (Ariz.) Progress, and special- and general-interest magazines and books.

and opposed dominant policies in others. It has reinforced sexism and racism through its images and representations of women and people of color, while at other times undermining racism and sexism and promoting civil liberties. Consequently, the media have complex, often contradictory relations with government as well as contradictory political functions and effects.

Television and Business

Television may be one of the strongest ideological and commercial arms of the capitalist system, but one also notes occasional conflicts between network television and business, or at least between television and specific corporations, business practices, and businesspeople. In the 1970s television news, documentaries, and special-events programs began to call attention to business malpractice, environmental pollution, and corporate greed and disdain for the public.

As advertisers generally flock to television to hawk their wares in a lopsided seller's market, television has little to fear from business pressure and threats. Because of widespread hostility toward big business and corporate ripoffs, shows such as "60 Minutes" win big ratings with their exposés of corruption and their practical advice on how to avoid being cheated by business malpractice. Although "60 Minutes" provides morality plays that expose individual corruption, rather than critical analyses of the system as a whole, and although it reduces the issue to individual cases of corruption, it may also tap into and reinforce suspicion and mistrust of business in general.

Despite its critical moments, however, network television never calls fundamental political or economic structures and institutions into question. As an integral part of the capitalist system, television has clear limits beyond which its adversary functions will not pass. This "logic of exclusion" precludes raising questions about the viability of the capitalist system, or about such matters as the social and economic effects of giant corporate conglomerates, an advertising-dominated media system, government bailouts of corporations and financial institutions, corporate tax breaks, or whether socialism might be a superior alternative in some circumstances (see section 1.2). In addition, the networks rarely cover or raise questions about their own business operations, programming, or treatment of labor.

Nonetheless, television news sometimes presents business failures and scandals in ways that could raise serious questions about corporate practices. TV news often covers product-liability stories such as the ones about the Pinto automobile, whose rear-end gas tank was said to explode upon impact, and the Firestone radial tires that frequently burst, causing serious injury. Television also regularly broadcasts government studies on dangerous food

additives, pesticides, herbicides, and unsafe products; it reveals, often graph-
ically, pollution and environmental destruction by profit-pursuing industries;
and it shows the failures of the energy system and, especially after Three-
Mile Island and Chernobyl, the dangers and madness of nuclear energy.

Indeed, portrayals of threats to the environment and human health posed
by corporate products have become a standard part of television news, thus
attesting to the strength of the antinuclear and environmental movements.
Yet the networks rarely present the movements themselves as political
actors, even though they often convey the messages of these movements.
And, by nature, these messages would be antibusiness given that businesses
are polluting and threatening the environment and producing unsafe
products.

Furthermore, the trials and tribulations of the economy are daily broadcast
in tales of stagflation, rising interest rates, exorbitant mortgage rates, wildly
fluctuating gold prices, and a jittery stock market. During the 1987 stock
market crash, television once again pointed to the irrationality of the
capitalist system with dramatic coverage of the biggest decline on the stock
market in history, including special night-time features and many talk
shows. Yet, soon enough, the television discourse evolved into one of calm
and optimism—a discourse that was repeated in October 1989, when it
appeared that another big fall might be in the making.

Even during the conservative 1980s, almost nightly presentations of the
plight of the homeless, the difficulties of buying a new house, and the
mistreatment of the elderly starkly exposed the downside of life in the
United States. Because of such "negative coverage," specific corporations
and corporate executives became increasingly vocal in their criticisms of
network television in the late 1970s and 1980s, repeatedly claiming that
television is biased against business. James L. Ferguson, chairman of General
Foods, accused the media of an "underlying hostility toward the business
community and all its works," while another top industrialist claimed that
"the press is biased in favor of the public interest groups" (Simons and
Califano 1979, xii–xiii). Oil corporations have been intensely critical of the
way in which television news presents oil company profits and policies, and
have bought ads in top newspapers attacking the networks when barred
from buying network time to present their own point of view.[10] Walter
Winston, chairman of Citibank, argues that the media are hypercritical of
all American institutions and are eroding public confidence: "[T]he accent
today is not on the evidence of progress in a multitude of fields; the
heaviest emphasis is upon failure. The media, supported by some academic
'liberals,' would have us believe that things are not just going badly, they
are growing progressively worse. The dominant theme is the new American
way of failure. No one wins; we always lose. Jack Armstrong and Tom
Swift are dead" (ibid.).

More documentation of conflicts between business and the media can be found in A. Kent MacDougall's series of articles in the *Los Angeles Times* during February 3–5, 1980. His first article, "Flaws in Press Coverage Plus Business Sensitivity Stirs Bitter Debate," begins as follows: "Businessmen who rank journalists with bureaucrats and environmentalists as their most irksome tormentors are starting to strike back at newspaper and television news coverage they consider biased against them" (February 3, 1980). MacDougall then documents a series of criticisms and lawsuits by major corporations against the networks and some newspapers. In a later article, MacDougall focuses on TV coverage of business, claiming that

> Mobil's low opinion of TV news is shared by other oil producers and by big business in general. While regarding most newspapers and news magazines as neutral-to-sympathetic, the oil industry looks on television as often un-friendly, inaccurate and superficial—and at least partly responsible for turning public opinion against it. Large corporations especially resent TV for biting the hand that feeds it. Television has no income other than what it gets from corporate advertisers, who poured more than $10 billion into TV last year. As Leonard S. Matthews, president of the American Association of Advertising Agencies, warned: "To expect private companies to go on supporting a medium that is attacking them is like taking up a collection among the Christians for money to buy more lions." (February 5, 1980)

In 1989 the networks provided detailed coverage of Exxon's complicity in the Alaskan oil spill of that year, thereby dramatizing its failure to provide adequate safety provisions and its inadequate efforts to clean up the mess. The cumulative message of the coverage pointed to the need to provide stronger environmental protection and to curb the self-interest of big corporations. The coverage was consistent and repetitive enough to evoke widespread indignation against Exxon (the second largest corporation in the world) and to promote boycotts of its products. Ironically, to win back its market share and prestige, Exxon was forced to buy more ads from television to relegitimate itself; for once, an oil corporation did not publicly complain about adverse network coverage.

Television coverage not only annoys particular corporations, but it may also be dysfunctional for certain recurrent capitalist stabilization strategies, inasmuch as the networks continue to provide images of abundance, hedonism, and good times when certain sectors of the business system attempt to impose a regime of scarcity. One of the contradictions of capitalism is that between the emphasis on high consumption as a means to happiness and business's attempt to keep wages and inflation down as a means to profit. During periods of scarcity and downturns in the economy, it is in the interests of the capitalist class to scale down expectations—but television's perpetual emphasis on consumption as the way to happiness may be dysfunctional for the capitalist system. As the editors of *Business Week* wrote in October 1974: "It will be a hard pill for many Americans to swallow the idea of doing with less so that big business can have more. . . . [N]othing compares in difficulty with the selling job that must now be done to make people accept the new reality" (emphasis in original). Whereas significant sectors of big business want to halt the growing state sector, dismantle or contain the social welfare complex, enforce a lower standard of living, discipline labor, and impose a reign of scarcity, TV advertising and entertainment continue to promote individual fulfillment, economic progress, and consumer gratification. During the 1970s when members of the Trilateral Commission and others wanted to curtail democracy and political struggle (Huntington et al. 1975), TV news occasionally focused on intense labor unrest, as municipal workers, schoolteachers, firemen, police, air-traffic controllers, meat-packing workers, or airline maintenance workers and pilots went on strike to gain higher wages and better working conditions—or at least to protect what they already had.

TV news programs continued to sell a version of corporate liberalism during the 1970s, when significant sectors of business and their political allies wanted to dismantle the welfare state and return to an unregulated "free-market" economy; yet TV was showing the benefits of government regulation when sectors of business wanted to do away with it. TV news has broadcast antinuclear struggles and exposed the dangers, excessive costs, and irrationality of nuclear energy, just as the energy corporations tried to promote and sell nuclear energy to the public. Indeed, television often reports stories and focuses on issues that run counter to the interests of dominant political and economic elites. During situations of economic and political crisis, in fact, television tends to intensify the crisis, ultimately proving dysfunctional for the system. Television naturally gravitates toward drama and excitement; the bigger the crisis, the greater the excitement—and the more that television will cover it.

Television also tends to pursue short-term interests by gaining audiences and profits at the expense of long-term systems maintenance. Upon occasion, the short-range economic interests of a network may therefore lead it to broadcast news that brings into question received ideas and corporate or political practices, thus undermining corporate and state long-range interests in increasing their power and hegemony. In order to gain maximum ratings and profits, the networks must deal with the crucial problems, scandals, and crises in society that attract the attention of the audience. Their corporate interests may lead them to sacrifice their more general interest in legitimating the capitalist system as a whole. Likewise, if the audience is attracted to entertainment programs dealing with current social problems and issues, the networks are likely to air these more controversial shows, even if they are critical of established society. Consequently, the imperatives to maximize profits and yet defend the established power structure, of which television is a significant part, are conducive to producing conflicts and tensions within the television industry and between television and other institutions in U.S. society.

At the same time, television is often a crisis manager par excellence. During hurricanes, earthquakes, and natural disasters, it is television that portrays the disaster and then calms, reassures, and pacifies the audience. Television has also frequently explained away or defused negative aspects of events such as the U.S. military defeat in Vietnam, Watergate, or the Iran/Contra affair. Let us now turn to a discussion of how television news and information reproduces and mediates social conflicts, thus providing ideological discourses on current events, crisis management, and systems maintenance legitimation.

TV News, Ideology, and Media Mediation

Critics of television news argue that although television attempts to present itself as a "mirror" of or "window" on the world, it is really an ideological construct.[11] TV news follows an aesthetic of realism, attempting to convey the impression that it is showing what is really happening, that it is telling the truth. It creates a realist effect by its live reports, its on-the-spot reporting, its coverage of special events, and its interviews with the movers and shakers of the capitalist state. For years, Walter Cronkite revealed the code of TV news by signing off his headline service with, "And that's the way it is."

In fact, television news is a symbolic construct, produced according to professional, ideological, and narrative codes. There is first of all a heavy element of selectivity as to what the networks consider newsworthy. The fundamental contradictions of television, however, produce tensions within the newsroom between the journalistic values of "hard news" and the entertainment values of news stories that will appeal to a large audience. As noted, television is torn between the contradiction of providing public information necessary for a democratic polity and selling breakfast food and headache remedies. On one hand, therefore, TV news attempts to provide significant public information, while, on the other hand, it attempts to attract an audience for its advertisers. The latter imperative has led in the 1980s to increasingly sensationalistic, entertaining "human interest" stories that will titillate a mass audience.

By definition, news deals with what is new, with current events, with the present. News constructs an image of the present that is always changing. The ephemeral and contemporaneous nature of news constitutes part of its fascination and appeal. News is thus a construct of modernity that presents the modern age as constantly changing and developing.

But things are not always what they seem. Although television news prides itself on its actuality, its presentation of what is new, and its immediacy, much TV news is in fact delayed and consists of carefully constructed packages that symbolically represent events and issues. Although apologists of TV news claim that it presents the extraordinary, much of it in fact presents events that are planned, that are expected, that are part of the routine of government. And although the dominant journalistic ethic is that of objectivity, of presenting fair and balanced pictures of events without personal commentary or interpretation, TV news, like all television, is a symbolic construct fraught with structural, professional, and ideological biases.

Structurally speaking, television news is organized as entertainment, as a series of carefully constructed narratives that follow the codes of TV story telling. Epstein cites a memo by NBC News executive producer Reuven Frank, who stated that "[e]very news story should, without any sacrifice of probity or responsibility, display the attributes of fiction, of drama. It should have structure and conflict, problem and denouement, rising action and falling action, a beginning, a middle and an end. These are not only the essentials of drama; they are the essentials of narrative" (1973, 4–5). Because of time constraints, television is attracted to the short-story form; the last half or so of each prime-time newscast tends to be taken up with little stories having thematic unity and a beginning, middle, and end. Thus, the structural format of television news follows narrative conventions that reduce complex events to stories with a clear narrative line; television narrative, in turn, tends toward closure and happy endings. Indeed, television news stories often impose misleading narrative closure on events or issues that in actuality are complex, open-ended, and perhaps difficult or impossible to resolve. Or they simply drop stories that do not allow for closure or successful resolution.

Furthermore, as television news is highly visual, it tends to be drawn toward compelling images and dramatic events. Dramatic images are a prime requisite for TV news, which is highly imagistic in nature. News programs thus lean toward the sensational, dramatic, and pictorial. They often omit detailed analysis or interpretation that would situate the news in the context of the vicissitudes of corporate capitalism, and they simplify presentations and ignore material that is not suited to packaged news formats. Television discourse is akin to headline services, which package complex stories in reductive frames. Since television is a visual medium, news stories gravitate toward events with dramatic pictures, using images to convey meaning.

TV news is by nature superficial because its stories are packed into a 22-minute nightly news format that calls for telescoping of meaning, lack of in-depth interpretation and contextualization, and simplistic rendering of complex events. In addition, the interspersing of news with commercials—

which dramatize the tribulations of the individual body, abstracted from social life—blunts responses to the significance of the events portrayed. Moreover, critics have indicated that during the 1980s there was an increase in entertaining stories, "happy talk" news, and superficial vignettes that reassure the viewer (Hallin 1987; Hertsgaard 1988). Competitive pressures for viewers and ratings have thus diminished serious news, and the news programs strive to attract audiences with reassurance and entertainment rather than seeking to disturb them with highly critical reports.

Moreover, *professional codes* contain certain biases. Codes of "fairness" and "balance" require that both sides of a story must be told and that the news must not exhibit a subjective point of view. Television news codes require presentation of its reports and commentary as factual, objective current events: The appearance and vocal inflections of the anchor-people and correspondents, the apparent objectivity of "balanced reports," and the instantaneous reports and images from the entire world must create the impression that "that's the way it is," that television is the Institutional Voice of Truth and Objectivity (Gibson 1980). TV news apologists repeatedly claim that they are just reporting the "facts" rather than setting agendas. But it is journalistic codes and biases that determine what constitutes a "fact" and which "facts" are significant enough to appear in the highly selective world of TV news. Professional codes ensure that what is considered important is that which is said and done by important people. And important people are people in power. TV news thus privileges holders of power, especially those in Washington and New York who are accessible to the network news bureaus. The president, above all, is considered the most significant voice of the news, with hardly a day going by without presidential coverage.

TV codes of objectivity also promulgate an objectivist/instrumentalist view of the world that is functional for technocratic capitalism (Hallin 1985). Such codes make it appear that TV news is presenting "facts" and thus supports the positivistic view that only solid, objective "facts" count as legitimate knowledge (thereby ruling out values, norms, aesthetics, and so on, from the realm of knowledge). The use of polls, statistics, and graphs on TV also reflects the objectivist ideology and mentality. Election coverage, in particular, is oriented toward numbers and the "horse race" aspects of elections, which often take precedence over substantive issues and the competencies of candidates.

TV news also privileges instrumental action and takes an instrumentalist view of politics. Foreign policies are usually evaluated in terms of instrumental goals and their success or failure in achieving these goals. Coverage of the 1989 Panama invasion, for instance, focused constantly on the administration goal of eliminating and capturing Noriega. When he fled, the invasion was deemed a partial success; and when he surrendered and was returned to the United States, the invasion was presented as a total success. Such instrumentalist coverage downplayed normative issues, such as the morality, legality, and political effects of the intervention. The toll in human life and property lost was also played down in deference to instrumental ends. In these ways, TV news privileges objectivist and instrumentalist values as well as surrender to facts, success, and achievement.

Journalistic codes also dictate what is and is not permissible to depict, and the competition for ratings ensures that TV news will not be excessively upsetting. Television news usually reinforces existing opinions; it is not a forum for new ideas or critical perceptions. Gerbner (1977) is therefore correct in stressing the "mainstreaming" functions of television, which aim at a mass audience and tap into and reinforce what the consciousness industry perceives as dominant beliefs, values, behavior, and trends.

Nonetheless, because U.S. society (and the world at large) is riven with conflict and struggle, television news portrays these conflicts, albeit within frames that attempt to harmonize and smooth over their rough edges and challenges to the existing order. In these cases, television news attempts to mediate between the opposing factions on different issues, policies, and ideologies and to promote a middle-of-the-road consensus, flattening out differences and managing conflicts. Thus, in an important sense, television news is ideological in that it attempts to legitimate existing institutions and the system of capitalist democracy.

It is important to note, however, that both the form and the content of television programming are ideological, that television is saturated with *ideological bias*. Its focus on individual authority figures as privileged spokespersons reflects the ideologies of individualism and elite authority. Its focus on the resolution of conflict, or on winning, advances the ideology of success. In addition, the format of television news often blunts its potentially radical messages, serving as a headline service that presents fragments of social events abstracted from their sociohistorical context. The paucity of contextualization and interpretation that characterizes TV news lends itself to ideological ends whereby the images and narratives of TV news stories legitimate existing policies and distort or exclude disturbing aspects or interpretations that would portray events in a different light. Detailed presentation of the overwhelmingly negative world reaction to the Panama invasion, or detailed dwelling on the loss of Panamanian life and property, would raise disturbing questions about the invasion; but such questions were excluded from the quick news summaries, dramatic pictures, and focus on Noriega that framed the actual TV news accounts.

The ideological content of TV news and information ranges from outright lies, distortions, and omissions to a "greying of reality." The codes of TV news often downplay, or blur, sensational events; one news program described the murder of Chilean President Salvador Allende by stating that "Allende died in a coup against his government." Network coverage omitted reports that the CIA was involved in this coup, that the CIA had been systematically attempting to destabilize and overthrow his government for months; and the word *died* "greys over" the fact that Allende was murdered. In similar fashion, U.S. military invasions are often described as "incursions" (Cambodia) or "interventions" (Panama) and puffed up with ideological names (e.g., "Operation Just Cause" for the unjust and criminal invasion of Panama) dutifully repeated by the media.

Television news often serves as an ideological conduit for disinformation, as when the media became a vehicle for a right-wing campaign to make the Bulgarians (and Soviets) responsible for the attempted assassination of the pope (Parenti 1986; Herman and Chomsky 1988); when yellow bee feces were taken as "evidence" of communist chemical warfare in Southeast Asia (Parenti 1986); and when reports during the 1984 U.S. presidential election claimed that Soviet MIGs were being delivered to Nicaragua (Chomsky 1989). Much television "information" is therefore sheer propaganda that merely repeats the distortions and lies of government spokespersons, intelligence agencies, and their ideological supporters within the media industries (Parenti 1986; Herman and Chomsky 1988; Chomsky 1989).

For decades, television was a key instrument in manufacturing a cold war, anticommunist ideology. In the service of this crusade, it neglected to report on the worst crimes of U.S. imperialism and its allies while magnifying the misdeeds and crimes of communist regimes. During the 1980s bogus reports of an alleged communist plot to assassinate the Pope and of a Libyan plot to assassinate the U.S. president were widely promulgated by gullible, or complicit, network media—as were uncritical accounts of Reagan's invasion of Grenada, his bombing of Libya, and his administration's support for the Nicaraguan Contras. The networks generally took the side of the U.S. administration in controversial issues such as the Russian shooting down of a civilian Korean jet, the U.S. shooting down of a civilian Iranian airplane, Middle-East terrorism, and U.S. support for counterrevolutionary forces throughout the world.

Against Herman and Chomsky (1988), however, I would argue that the hegemony model is superior to the "propaganda" model. The former model stresses that personnel working for capitalist corporations assimilate certain views of the world, frames, codes, and practices that they "naturally" reproduce. Although the network news personnel probably do not see themselves as purveyors of ruling-class ideology, in fact their belief systems, values, and codes conform to the dominant ideologies of democratic capitalist societies—ideologies that legitimate the right to accumulate unlimited amounts of property and private capital, the superiority of capitalism over socialism, the belief that U.S. democracy is a model political system, and so on. Ideology refers to ideas that reproduce the ideas of the ruling elites and that legitimate an established system of domination. A hegemonic ideology is thus one that is assimilated as "common sense," as "natural," as the way things are (Kellner 1978).

The propaganda hypothesis, by contrast, presupposes a conscious intent to deceive and manipulate—to explain why the news media advance the views and interests of ruling groups. Network television is part of the corporate structure and naturally adopts the positions of the forces with which it identifies. In Chapter 4 and the Appendixes I will present some examples of how the logic of exclusion leads to omission of many stories that would be damaging to the interests of those who control the corporations and the state. Indeed, exclusion is as important a part of the ideological nature of television news as are disinformation, distortions, and the greying of reality.

Yet for all its limitations and failings, television news does often provide vivid representations of events and occasionally exhibits real understanding and insight. My close television monitoring of the events in China was interrupted in the summer of 1989 by a six-week trip to Europe. Following the events in the newspaper, I discovered the extent to which television at its best provided access to events through live coverage that encouraged more vivid empathy and understanding than did abstract and fragmented newspaper accounts. But it is precisely this illusion of immediacy and direct participation that creates splendid opportunities for distortion and manipulation. Indeed, television provides not immediate access to the real but a highly mediated, symbolic construct of events and the world that must be critically decoded by its audiences.

One could also argue that the network coverage of China following suppression of the democracy movement was in some ways scandalous. In talk shows, Henry Kissinger and others with close business interests in China urged "understanding" for the Chinese government's actions and argued against the imposition of economic boycotts or pressure.[12] Network news eventually dropped the story and made little effort to follow up on the future fate of the democracy movement. In effect, it followed the political line of the Bush administration, which called for "normalization" of relations with China after its brutal and shocking suppression of the democracy movement, thus demonstrating, once again, how network television follows the line of established government policy and the economic interests of the major corporations, many of which were building connections with China.

In any case, the contradictory messages of network television preclude the simplistic view that TV news and information carry unambiguous and monolithic social meanings and functions. Moreover, socially critical moments do often appear in news reports. During the 1960s and 1970s television journalism made possible the presentation of views critical of established economic and political forces. Such critical moments are an ever-present possibility because television news does gravitate to some extent toward the dramatic, sensational, and novel. When compelling scandals arise, television is often there. When dramatic social upheavals occur, television is often there, attempting to manage crisis but also circulating images of struggle. When new social movements attract widespread attention, television eventually discovers them.

In short, although television provides ideological legitimation for the capitalist system and serves the interests of dominant economic and political elites, it does have some socially critical and democratic moments. Its primary functions are systems maintenance and legitimation, mediation between conflicting ruling groups and social movements, and stabilization of the system as a whole; but it must also depict the conflicts and crises that it attempts to mediate and manage in order to maintain credibility. As the images of struggle and crisis are often more compelling than those of resolution, socially critical effects are created despite the conservative coding of television. For example, network coverage of the invasion of Panama in 1989 focused on the U.S. military triumph and the successful search for Noriega. Although it downplayed the widespread destruction of neighborhoods, occasional images of looting and dead bodies slipped through and may have raised critical questions concerning the invasion.

The portrayal of intense conflict, corruption, and privilege may subvert the ideologies and policies of certain groups and spread confusion, cynicism, and even critical consciousness. And the resonant and compelling images of television may promote development of critical consciousness and circulate oppositional ideas. Television is an inherently conflictual medium, and, as we shall see in the next section, its conflicts are rooted in the internal structure of the institution as well in its sometimes conflictual relationships with business and government.

Yet television's conflictual images may also promote confusion, apathy, and indifference. As Michael Robinson (1976) argued in the mid-1970s, the then frequent images of social conflict and reports critical of U.S. society created a sense of helplessness and cynicism that he termed "videomalaise." Indeed, we do not know what effects even socially critical television will have, nor can we be certain that socially critical television will raise political consciousness. And as many people do not closely watch television news, we cannot be certain as to what discursive effects it has; critical viewers can read against the grain, and aberrant reading is always possible. We shall take up the thorny issue of appraising and interpreting these effects at the end of this chapter. In the meantime, however, we shall continue our analysis of television's contradictory images and social effects.

3.4 Internal Conflicts and
Television's Contradictory Images and Effects

There are conflicts inherent in the operations of broadcast media in a capitalist society that help explain the occasional adversary relations among television, government, and business. Most critical theories of television fail to perceive the frequent tensions and conflicts among television's drive toward profit-maximization, its creation of hegemonic ideology to engineer social consent, and its production of news and entertainment according to professional codes. There is a parallel here to the contradictions that James O'Conner (1973) finds in the capitalist state between its accumulation and legitimation functions. Both network television and the state are concerned (albeit in different ways) with the accumulation of capital and with legitimating the system as a whole. In both institutions, these functions are often in conflict with each other and attest to contradictions at the center of contemporary capitalist societies.

To maximize profit, network television must produce programs that appeal to the audience and must hire people who can produce appealing programs. These individuals may have strong political ideas, although the networks attempt to hire and groom producers and news correspondents who do not exhibit "bias." Contradictions therefore emerge in news production between professional codes of objectivity, investigative reporting, and the democratic requirement that news and information serve the public interest, on the one hand, and pressures to gain ratings and turn over a profit, on the other. Tensions also develop between reporters and correspondents and their corporate managers. Conflicts often emerge, according to much testimony, between production of a news product that affirms and legitimates the existing society, and professional news codes that call for objectivity, neutrality, and adversarial or investigative reporting. Although many studies reveal that network news organizations, codes, and personnel policies restrict oppositional views and criticism,[13] professional codes and organizational imperatives have often led to news productions that contradict the interests of the network managers and the power structure to which they and their corporations belong. Fred Friendly, Daniel Schorr, Leslie Stahl, and others have written or told of the struggles waged with network executives over criticisms of Joseph McCarthy, various corporations, the Vietnam War, Richard Nixon, the CIA, Ronald Reagan, and other evils of the times.

Although top management often exerts heavy-handed control over news production, many news personnel see themselves as journalists with professional codes and responsibilities. These codes may lead them to broadcast news that criticizes existing practices, politics, and even institutions within the society. Moreover, during periods when "investigative journalism" is celebrated, the adversary functions of the press may intensify conflicts within the broadcast media as well as between network and other dominant institutions.

Conflicts between news production groups and corporate management are reproduced in television entertainment in the contradictions between the "cultural apparatus" of producers, directors, writers, and actors and the "consciousness industry" in New York with its corporate executives, managers, and censors.[14] Here we see the emergence of conflicts between business and culture. Producers in the cultural apparatus are often interested in producing original, realistic, or controversial works. Interviews with television cultural workers indicate that many people working within television do not want to produce bland, conformist programming and constantly struggle against network censorship in an attempt to create more provocative shows.[15] The network executives and managers, however, are primarily concerned with profits and ratings and thus desire programs that will not offend their massive audiences, corporate sponsors, special-interest groups, or government regulators.

Yet network television also depends on people with "creative talent," who may not share traditional values or capitalist ideology and may be quite critical of some aspects of U.S. society. Corporate managers must therefore make some concessions to the cultural apparatus, which may occasionally produce critical-realist, satirical, or nonconformist works that subvert hegemonic ideology and criticize the established society. For instance, certain topical and controversial shows of the 1970s, such as "All in the Family," "Maude," "Mary Hartman," and other Norman Lear comedies, broke previous television taboos and opened new space for social critique and satire. Then miniseries such as "Roots," "Washington: Behind Closed Doors," "Wheels," and "Holocaust" broke new ground for historical drama dealing with oppression, political corruption, and class conflict, while offering a more realistic picture of the central problems of life in the United States and its history (see section 2.4). Beyond making concessions to the cultural apparatus, however, network television must hold an audience. It cannot simply reproduce the old formulas; rather, it must produce new programs that may well subvert traditional ideology. Hence, as the race for ratings and profits intensifies, and as new communications technologies are introduced, the television networks may be forced to expand the limits of censorship and to broadcast programs that may sacrifice previous ideologies and idealizations of life in the United States.

In a similar way, network television may promote social change. Although 1960s television portrayed the counterculture, new values, and life-styles negatively, or tried to ignore or co-opt them, it nonetheless showed dramatic changes taking place. Even if these changes were represented negatively, TV might have inadvertently advanced countercultural and radical values. For even negative images of student antiwar demonstrators or of young people taking drugs might have circulated positive images of countercultural opposition and life-styles. Yet the adversary functions of television and the media rarely, if ever, go beyond the boundaries of liberalism. At times, television does promote a liberal agenda and thus incurs the wrath of conservatives. As liberals believe in the possibility and desirability of significant reform within the present organization of society, they are often brought up against conservative agendas and positions. Members of the cultural apparatus tend to be liberal and thus come into conflict with their more conservative industry managers. Yet when liberalism is on the defensive and prominent liberals are not active, television serves as a mouthpiece for hegemonic conservative views and furthers conservative policies and ideals.

This is not always the case, however, for network television is subject to a variety of social pressures from women, people of color, and gays, as well as from varied political, educational, labor, and religious groups (Montgomery 1989). Over the last three decades, network television was pushed to make concessions to the civil rights movement, the women's movement, the gay movement, the sexual revolution, and other struggles and movements of the 1960s. Consequently, by the late 1960s and early 1970s images of women, blacks, gays, and other minorities had become relatively progressive in contrast to the racism and sexism that prevailed, and still prevails, in large parts of the country. Indeed, it was precisely the tendency of the television networks to go for a mass audience and to mediate among conflicting social groups that rendered the medium an instrument of integration and inclusion rather than one of exclusion. Television executives discerned that there was a large black audience and were thus willing to broadcast a few programs with likable blacks such as Flip Wilson and Bill Cosby. In addition, as TV demographics targeted women between 18 and 49 as the most desirable television audience (because of their consumer roles), it is not surprising that more positive images of women emerged in the 1970s and 1980s. Therefore, both its marketing functions and its integrating functions render television more likely to promote civil rights and integration rather than sexism, racism, and segregation.

Yet there are discernible limits to television's promotion of minority and women's rights. Hispanics have been almost completely neglected in prime-time television programming, despite the fact that they constitute more than 10 percent of the population. And although a large number of blacks have been featured in prime-time series, they tend to resemble white, middle-class models and therefore fail to promote serious probes into racial discrimination, poverty, or ethnic and racial subcultures. Women, too, tend to be underrepresented or subject to sexist stereotypes or male-oriented models that portray them as competitive and aggressive. Few positive portrayals of sisterhood or assertive female sexuality have emerged, and lesbianism and the women's movement have been almost entirely avoided by prime-time television.

One should note, however, the different dynamics involved in the changing representations of women, blacks and other people of color, gays and lesbians, and various minority groups. Changing portrayals of blacks were influenced by the massive civil rights movements of the 1950s and 1960s through which blacks struggled to become integrated into U.S. society. Advertisers saw blacks as an unexploited market, and by the late 1960s, after some resistance by Southern affiliates to featuring blacks in regular TV series, blacks were a regular feature of network television, although black groups struggled to eliminate lingering racist stereotypes and to produce more positive images of black Americans (see Montgomery 1989).

Representations of women were influenced by feminist critiques of sexist stereotypes of women and struggles for more positive images. Women had, of course, long been incorporated into television entertainment but usually in secondary and supportive roles as wives, sex objects, secretaries, or handmaidens to male heroes. As a result of feminist struggles and critiques, and because advertisers and television executives began to perceive women as an important target due to their roles as consumers, images of independent women began appearing in the early 1970s (such as "The Mary Tyler Moore Show," "Police Woman," and "Rhoda," although series like "Charlie's Angles" continued to exploit its active and independent women as sex objects).

Representations of the working class were arguably influenced by a combination of working class power and self-assertion and network marketing perceptions. In the 1950s, after some working class comedies such as "The Life of Riley" and "The Honeymooners," the working class disappeared from regular television series. TV was trying to sell an upscale, consumer life and chose typical middle-class families, professionals, and the wealthy as their favored topics. The intense generational conflicts of the 1960s enabled Norman Lear to present a working class milieu in "All in the Family," but few working class dramas appeared in the 1970s ("Skag" is an exception). In the 1980s, the Reagan administration turned on unions and celebrated wealth and power; television almost completely ignored the working class during this period, though the popular "Roseanne" appeared near the end of the Reagan era, featuring stories of how hard economic times produced problems for working class families. Thus, the series portrayed the negative impact of the conservative economic policies of the 1980s that had greatly increased class divisions and inflicted hardships on the poor.

Consequently, a variety of economic, political, and cultural factors help determine the trajectory of how various groups are represented in television entertainment. These include how advertisers and the television networks perceive the consumer power of various groups; the extent to which groups like blacks, women, and workers are organized and force media attention on their demands through political struggle; and the extent to which representatives of these groups are active in media production and are able to articulate their experiences and perceptions. Whether images of specific groups are present or absent, positive or negative, is thus the result of a complex set of factors and influences.

In addition, television often succumbs to pressures by conservative and liberal groups to curtail portrayals of sex and violence and to defend traditional values such as the family and religion. Yet tensions and contradictory images have emerged in this context as well. During the 1980s a right-wing movement attempted to curtail television portrayals of sex, while the AIDS epidemic led to pressures from gays and liberals to advertise condoms and to discuss "safe sex." The abolition of "standards and practices" (i.e., censorship) departments as a result of budget-cutting measures in the 1980s led to more explicit language and sexual portrayals, but the reaction by right-wing groups, which carried out sponsor and network boycotts, forced the networks to return to more conservative programming. Television is often caught between conservative and liberal segments of U.S. society, and it is subject to pressures from competing groups concerning their programming and its effects. Hence network television is either full of political contradictions and tensions, or (in the majority of cases) it is bland, middle-of-the-road pap that attempts to avoid all controversy whatsoever.

In general, television entertainment belatedly portrays social change after the turmoil has abated. Hence it is often out of synchrony with social experience, such that the Today of its news is dissonant with the Yesterday of its entertainment programs or the Tomorrow of its advertisements. After the tumultuous civil rights struggles in the early 1960s, for example, blacks finally began to be accepted in the television world. After the agitation of the women's liberation movement and the sexual rebellions of the 1960s, television increasingly portrayed independent working women, unmarried couples, broken families, singles living together, and gays—in contrast to the previous decade, when nuclear middle-class families were the television norm. These changes should not be exaggerated, however, for representatives of women's and other oppressed groups continue to complain that television has not actually broken with sexist and racist stereotypes in favor of realistic complex portraits of women and minorities.[16]

When television portrays social change or oppositional movements, it often blunts the radical edge of new social forces, values, or changes. Moreover, it tries to absorb, co-opt, and defuse any challenges to the existing organization of society. Nonetheless, because the United States is made up of various regions, groups, and individuals with different values, ideologies, and cultures, television presents changes that have taken place in certain regions and groups to individuals in other regions and groups. Thus programs about premarital sex, drugs, the breakdown of the family, political-economic scandal, and corruption may be unsettling to traditionalist groups. Television may help some groups adjust to social changes they have not yet experienced, but it can also challenge others with new ideas and experiences to which they are resistant.

This analysis of network television's contradictory images and social effects helps explain, I believe, the inadequacies of the dominant and conflicting positions on television today. The theories that focus solely on television's hegemonic-legitimating images and homogenizing social effects are one-sided and limited, as are those conservative theories that postulate primarily "liberal," or "subversive," effects. Both positions fail to see the contradictions within television and its contradictory social effects. Both tend to overlook the specific ways in which television influences its spectators through discourse, images, genres, and types of information and entertainment. Both lack adequate historical contextualization, inasmuch as they assume recurrent effects of television rather than postulating different social functions with different effects in different historical contexts. Both also neglect the fact that audiences decode television in particular ways and that there is always a potential distance between television encoding and audience decoding. In the next chapter, accordingly, I shall specify some of the ways in which recent media politics and image battles have transformed the nature of politics in the United States. I shall also indicate how, during the 1980s, television favored the conservative side and became a major force of conservative hegemony. First, however, I wish to conclude this chapter with some comments about cultural hegemony.

3.5 New Modes of Cultural Hegemony

Previously, cultural hegemony was largely produced by schools, churches, and the family, which were the instruments by which individuals were integrated into society. With the introduction of broadcasting and, especially, the rise of television to the center of culture and leisure during the 1950s, new modes of hegemony produced new types of experience, culture, and social control. Of course, television is more accessible to its audience than were previous forms of culture; the print media, for example, required complex skills of literacy and were thus accessible only to those with sufficient schooling and motivation. Television, by contrast, is a visual and aural medium that is accessible to anyone who can see and hear; it requires no specialized training or skills. Television is also an especially fascinating cultural form, given its use of bright and shining moving images to capture and involve the audience in its programs and spectacles. The moving images provide a certain dynamism, while the brightness captures attention through its intensity and color. Indeed, there is an element of magic in the experience of television, whereby images, sounds, and pictures are mysteriously transmitted into one's home from faraway places, allowing one to participate in the sights and sounds of the entire world.

Television transforms space and time and the very modality of experience itself, introducing its audience into a high-tech capitalist modernity. The simultaneity between television and events or scenes creates an impression of speed and immediacy that is reinforced by rapid editing and cutting. Viewers become attracted to the glitzy images and fast pace, and grow impatient with slower sequences of images and experiences. The fragmentation of television into different programs, segments, and images also creates more atomized, disconnected experience, thus acclimating viewers to social fragmentation and differentiation.

Thus television initiates its spectators into the forms of hypermodernity— spectators who become acclimated to a fast, fragmented, high-tech world. As a cultural form, it produces a privatized, spectator culture in which individuals are positioned comfortably in front of the tube, usually in their homes. Television increases trends toward privization and helps destroy a more participatory public sphere by keeping its viewers in their own homes, away from other people. TV is also an atomized form of culture: Individuals watch alone or alongside other individuals who are staring at the same screen, watching the same images. Its transmission is a form of one-way communication that does not allow response or interaction. Unlike the telephone, short-wave and CB radio, and face-to-face communication, television transmits images and messages to an audience that is reduced to passivity and spectatorship.

It is widely argued that the visual culture of television undercuts and subverts the previously dominant mode of rationality and linear thinking fostered by print media (McLuhan 1964, Gouldner 1976, Schwartz 1983, Postman 1985). Whereas McLuhan believes that this new mode of culture provides positive sensory experiences and a new global, ecumenical culture, critics such as Postman contend that it constitutes a dangerous decline of rationality, literacy, and sociality.

Some critics have argued that television culture tends to be homogeneous and conventional, following dominant codes and formulas. As Adorno (1957) points out, television exhibits a "fake realism" and is organized around the standardization, predictability, and repetitiveness of mass culture conventions and stereotypes. For Adorno, "this rigid institutionalization transforms modern mass culture into a medium of undreamed of psychological control. The repetitiveness, the selfsameness, and the ubiquity of modern mass culture tend to make for automatized reactions and to weaken the forces of individual resistance" (ibid., 476).

In the transition from an individualist to a conformist, administered society, Adorno argues, mass culture devalues the inwardness and internal psychological conflicts prevalent in older cultural forms and instead encourages conformity, other-directedness, and extroversion. The culture industries aid in this process by eliminating genuine suspense and unresolvable conflicts from culture, and by making fun of "introverts," and by celebrating the noisy and happy conformity of well-adjusted (or resigned) character types. The constant repetition of the same values and messages assumes an increasingly authoritarian ring, he claims, and operates in a way similar to "psychoanalysis in reverse" (ibid., 480). For whereas psychoanalysis attempts to break down repetition compulsions, defense mechanisms, infantile regression, and rigid behavior, the culture industries encourage precisely these character traits by repeating the same formulas, stereotypes, and messages, and by frightening viewers into submitting to social conventions through portrayals of the painful consequences of deviating from established paths. Reversing the psychoanalytic aim of enlightenment, the culture industries manipulate their audiences into surrendering to the conservative status quo by imposing symbols, hidden messages, and ideology on them under the guise of fun and entertainment.

Thus, as a mode of socialization, television tends to inculcate individuals into conventional patterns of thought, behavior, and feeling. Of all the arms of the culture industries, television is perhaps the most centralized, given that its three major networks in the United States produce highly similar types of programming watched by millions of people. TV has thus helped create a mass society by homogenizing culture and experience and by drawing masses of individuals into more or less the same type of programming, spectacles, and experience. Moreover, the specific type of commercial television that has come to dominate the United States is especially nonreflective, eschewing complex or disturbing material that might require thought or action and encouraging instead a consumerist hedonism and conformity.

Whereas critics such as Adorno argue that television is a cultural homogenizer that imposes its mainstream culture on the entire country, more recent critics contend that these homogenizing effects are exaggerated and that television is currently presenting more diversity and is even "demassifying" society (Toffler 1980). Their argument is that new technologies such as cable, satellite television, video recorders, video cameras, and remote-control devices have provided viewers with many more options and much more control over their communications and media environment. Indeed, some critics are beginning to worry that the diversity in proliferating media channels might destroy the identity and unity of U.S. culture and lead to fragmentation and ungovernability (see Barber 1982 and the critique in Karp 1983).

Against such visions of diversification and "de-massification," I maintain that the growth in media sources has not produced significant diversity. On the contrary, the current trend toward media mergers and conglomerates has given fewer corporations control over the images, information, and entertainment received by the vast majority of viewers. Although Toffler predicted that by the end of the 1980s the network television audience share would fall beow 50 percent (1980, 150), as of this writing in 1990, the major network audience share is around 70 percent. That figure is slowly dropping, but the networks still control the television experience and continue to be a force of cultural homogenization and blandness.

By its very ubiquity, then, television enforces a new kind of cultural hegemony—one that serves as a powerful instrument of socialization and social control. Nonetheless, theories of socialization during the 1950s and 1960s, when television was playing a growing role in social life, tended to ignore or downplay the process through which individuals are shaped in their thought and behavior to think and behave as required by a given society. For example, in their influential book *The Social Construction of Reality*, Peter Berger and Thomas Luckmann (1972) fail to mention the mass media in the process of socialization. And the influential theorist of social linguistics, Basil Bernstein, writes that "[t]he basic agencies of socialization in contemporary societies are the family, the peer group, school and work" (Bernstein, cited in Berger and Luckmann 1972, 172).

Some mainstream theories of socialization maintain a distinction between primary and secondary socialization, attributing to the family the role of primary socialization while claiming that the church, school, media, and peer groups function merely as instruments of secondary socialization (Danziger 1971). But this distinction between primary and secondary socialization seems highly dubious in the age of television. Children are exposed to television at an extremely early age (Goldsen 1978). TV is used as an electronic baby sitter for large numbers of families, and it has arguably become the nation's first collectivized kindergarten. In many families, television also plays an important role in family life, particularly if most of the time spent together passes in front of the TV set. Children, on the average, have spent more time watching television by the time they enter school than they will spend during their entire lives in the classroom. In addition, television stories, with their dramatic and emotive force, might have a stronger impact on children's behavior and view of the world than the more intellectual aspects of primary education in the school. Moreover, TV trains children for consumption by selling them specific toys and products (Engelhardt 1987, 68ff.). Much peer-group activity among children involves playing with toys or games promoted on television, and the television personalities who provide role and gender models for young children and teenagers have a powerful impact on their fantasy lives and actual behavior.

I have argued elsewhere that television has replaced fairy tales and myths as the primary producer of childrens' tales, and that it is one of the most important producers of myths and symbols in the society (Kellner 1982).

Indeed, television has become the nation's teacher and entertainer of choice. Furthermore, both television entertainment and information may well gain in power precisely because individuals are not aware that their thoughts and behaviors are being shaped by the ubiquitous idea and image machines in their homes. In a sense, television provides continuous education throughout life, offering a popular day and night school for the nation. One could therefore argue that television has taken on such a powerful role in the process of socialization that the distinction between primary and secondary socialization has broken down, and that television thus plays a central role in socialization from cradle to the grave.

Yet there is no real consensus concerning television's socializing functions, and we don't really know the extent to which television shapes beliefs, attitudes, values, and behavior. Whereas earlier accounts favored the "two-step flow" model, which gave more weight to "opinion leaders" than to the media, more recent analysts have conceded that the media may be playing a more direct role in influencing thought and behavior.[17] Indeed, the issue of "media effects"—especially the effects of television—is still being hotly debated; hence a definitive position would be premature.

Still, I believe that the debates discussed in this chapter are relevant to the controversy surrounding media effects. It seems reasonable to assume that television sometimes has strong effects on thoughts and behavior and, at other times, little discernible impact. In some cases, it might promote prosocial behavior; in other cases, antisocial behavior. These contradictory effects result from television's contradictory images and the fact that different members of the audience choose different programming depending on their prior inclinations and personality structures. And, as I have stressed, individuals may read television against the grain such that its effects are opposite to those that might be inferred from analysis of the explicit message or discursive position in question. For example, although Norman Lear intended to fight bigotry with "All in the Family," the viewers who identified with Archie Bunker may have been *reinforced* in their bigotry.

Television does tend to reinforce existing beliefs, values, and personality structures; but because its audience is "preformed" by early exposure, its cumulative effects on socialization may be greater than many theories allow. In other cases, contradictions between the television world and individual experience, or between TV encoding and audience decoding, may render television a vehicle of cultural homogeneity and social control that is less powerful than many claim. Despite television's attempt in the 1950s and early 1960s to idealize and celebrate American life, a decade of social conflict did take place. Likewise, in the mid-1970s and early 1980s, despite television's mild portrayal of women's liberation and liberalism in general, a traditionalist conservative revolt occurred that was often critical of television. And although conservatives achieved political and cultural hegemony in the

1980s through their control of the state and the right turn of the media
(see Chapter 4), the majority of the population never completely bought
into the conservative agenda (Ferguson and Rogers 1986; King and Schudson
1987).

Indeed, both conservatives and radicals—and some critical liberals—have
been attacking television with equal vehemence and often in similar terms,
thus suggesting that many people are not pacified or being homogenized
by the tube. It is my position that the conflict between radicals who view
television as a hegemonic tool of the established society and stress its
integrating-stabilizing effects, and conservatives who decry its disintegrating-
destabilizing effects, exhibit the opposing poles of the contradictory and
ambiguous social effects of network television. Television *does* have different
effects on different audiences and can even have contradictory effects on
a given individual. Some viewers may be frightened and made passive by
television violence, as Gerbner and Gross (1976) argue, whereas others may
be led to carry out aggressive or violent acts (see the studies in Feshbach
and Singer 1971 and in Comstock et al. 1972). Because audiences select
the shows to which they are attracted, television probably reinforces
preexisting dispositions; but its ubiquity also contributes to the shaping of
basic attitudes, beliefs, values, and behavior.

And yet we cannot be sure. Television's social and political effects are
extremely difficult to specify. Most theories of media effects are too
rationalistic, given their focus on television's discursive positions and ideologies to the exclusion of its form, image, and subliminal effects. Television
not only mobilizes and channels desire but also organizes and manages
consciousness. A critical theory of television must therefore analyze the
ways in which TV images organize experience and then attempt to specify
their effects. In this study, I have attempted to argue that television discourse
includes images and codes as well as linguistic discursive positions; but I
also contend that these positions are potentially ambiguous because specific
audiences might well decode the same images and messages in very different
ways (Hall 1980; Kellner 1980b).[18]

Moreover, although we can never be certain about the effects of television,
we do know that it has assumed different functions and had different effects
in various historical eras. In the 1930s broadcasting served as an instrument
of diversion that distracted people from the troubles of the day. During
the 1940s broadcasting continued in its escapist function but served also
as a voice of patriotism and unification in the war effort. During the 1950s
television celebrated the consumer society and became a ubiquitous center
of leisure. During the 1960s and 1970s television attempted to mediate and
manage the conflicts of the times and thus entered a storm of controversy
within which it is still embedded. And in the 1980s (as I shall argue in

the next chapter) television became a powerful force for conservative hegemony.

At certain times, then, a liberal bias may be detectable; at others, it is predominantly conservative or apolitical; at still others, it is so saturated with contradictions as to be without a discernible slant. It follows that a general theory of media effects would be rather empty and that one would need to study the specific effects of specific programs on specific audiences in order to reach any definite conclusions. On the whole, however, it is safe to conclude that television has been highly functional for capital. Though occasionally critical of a specific corporation or government policy, it is for the most part a powerful instrument of state capitalist hegemony.

Because of its contradictory images and effects as well as its ubiquity and centrality in everyday life, television has become a prize sought by competing parties and interests struggling to gain positive images in the TV media. Many critics of television have studied the various frames into which events and personalities are organized into readable texts. In the 1960s, for instance, the media framed radicals as violent threats to law and order while promoting more moderate liberal opposition to U.S. policy (Gitlin 1980). Parenti (1986) has noted the negative ways in which the media have framed labor and oppositional social movements, emphasizing the recurrent anticommunism that has permeated the press and broadcast media over the past decades. Women and minorities have struggled for more than two decades now to advance better images of themselves in television and the media. And by the 1970s both right-wing and progressive advocacy groups were struggling to get their messages into the mainstream media and to eliminate images and subject matter that they found offensive (Montgomery 1989).

Consequently, television stands today at the center of new modes of image production and cultural hegemony, the political struggles of various groups, and the restructuring of capitalist society. In the next chapter, I shall discuss the ways in which the new forms of cultural hegemony served the interests of conservative forces in the 1980s.

Notes

1. On the business of television, see Brown (1971), Mayer (1972), Reel (1979), Bedell (1981), and Gitlin (1983).

2. On the contradictions between capitalism and democracy in the American experience, see Wolfe (1973, 1977), Cohen and Rogers (1983), and Bowles and Gintis (1986).

3. On the political economy of television, see Network Project (1973a, 1973b), Bunce (1977), Compaine (1979), Bagdikian (1987), Herman (1988), and the analyses by Henson in the *Left Business Observer*, Vols. 27, 29, and 31 (1988–89).

4. Siebert and his colleagues (1956) admirably explicate the democratic philosophy of a free press, but they fail to analyze the constraints on the media from business, all the while attacking communist restrictions on the press in cold war rhetoric. In so doing, they reveal the limits of cold war liberalism by defending a democratic polity but failing to see how capitalism systematically undermines democracy.

5. For further discussion of the Commission on the Freedom of the Press, see Commission (1947), Hocking (1947), and Peterson (1956). And for further discussion of the debates over free speech, government regulation, and the role of government in the media system, see Barron (1973), Friendly (1977), and Horowitz (1989).

6. An employee of the Castelli Ad Agency once stated that television is "the democratic process in action, the viewer voting with his (sic) knob" ("60 Minutes," October 11, 1981). For ideological claims by network television and academic apologists that television is a democratic and populist medium, see the texts of almost any network television executive and Marc (1984).

7. Herman and Chomsky (1988) and Chomsky (1989) criticize the "double standard" in mainstream U.S. media, which focus attention on the crimes of communist regimes and their allies while downplaying the atrocities of U.S. foreign policy and its allies.

8. Researchers have noted that "21 of 33 commissioners leaving the Federal Communications Commission (FCC) between 1945 and 1970 became affiliated with the communications industry as employees or as lawyers and engineers who were practicing before the FCC. The so-called 'revolving door' is also widely prevalent at the staff level" (cited in Herman 1981, 179). The heroes of Eric Barnouw's epic history of American broadcasting are the FCC commissioners such as Fly, Durr, Minow, and Johnson who stood up to the network titans and seriously tried to regulate broadcasting in the public interest, attacking monopoly, banal programming, and overly restrictive network control of the communications spectrum. These commissioners were frequently targets of vicious attacks by Congress, whose members had become increasingly dependent on broadcasting for political advertising and publicity. On the whole, Congress has a woefully pathetic record in communications legislation. For a discussion of government regulation of broadcasting, see Fly et al. (1959), Johnson (1970), Cole and Oettinger (1978), and Horowitz (1989).

9. Instrumentalist theories see the media as nothing more than the instruments of the state or corporations. Althusser describes the media as an "ideological State apparatus" and argues: "1. All ideological State apparatuses, whatever they are, contribute to the same result: the reproduction of the relations of production, i.e., of the capitalist relations of exploitation. 2. Each of them contributes towards this single result in the way proper to it. The political apparatus by subjecting individuals to the political State ideology, the 'indirect' (parliamentary) or 'direct' (plebiscitary or fascist) 'democratic' ideology. The communications apparatus by cramming every 'citizen' with daily doses of nationalism, chauvinism, liberalism, moralism, etc., by means of the press, the radio and television" (1971, 154). Althusser's one-dimensional articulation of the instrumentalist position is odd because in his earlier writings he argued for the "relative autonomy of the superstructures," "overdetermination," and thus institutions that had some relative autonomy from control of the dominant class.

Parenti, too, takes an instrumentalist perspective, writing: "While seen as something apart from business, they actually *are* a big business. But like the 'nonprofit' churches, universities, law, schools, professional associations, arts and political parties, the media also are an institution geared for ideological control. Their role is to reproduce the conditions of social and class stability, to carry out the monopoly management of image and information, *but in such a way as to engineer an appearance of class neutrality and an appearance of independence from the corporate class that owns them*" (1986, 32). Such an instrumentalist theory obscures the contradictory imperatives that help shape the system of television resulting from the combination of private ownership and public interest and covers over ("monopoly management") the actual contradictions and conflicts within the corporate class as well as the changing configurations of media power. It also denies the relative autonomy of the media, thus obscuring the times that the media actually criticize ruling elites or institutions.

10. Mobil Oil's attacks on the CBS News presentation of its profit increases was published, among other places, in *Broadcasting*, November 12, 1979, pp. 76–77. Earlier, Mobil published an attack on ABC's "20/20" for its coverage of the issue of oil deregulation in the *Wall Street Journal*, August 31, 1978, p. 7. Mobil, Kaiser, and other major corporations, irritated by the fact that the networks refuse to sell them time for "public service" advertising (i.e., corporate propaganda), have placed ads in print attacking network coverage of various issues while presenting their own points of view (see *Broadcasting*, June 25, 1979, p. 72). If the networks sold time to the corporations to promote their positions, public interest groups could demand time to rebut the corporations under the Fairness Doctrine—and the networks presumably fear "clutter" of airtime with political messages. On the desirability of pressuring the networks to present "public service" spot advertising, see Phil Jacklin's article, "Access to the Attention System," in *Access*, May 17, 1976, pp. 9–10.

11. For critiques of the format of television news, see Epstein (1973), Gibson (1980), Hallin (1987), and Goldman and Rajagopal (1990). Insider histories of television news are also worth consulting; see, among many others, the sources cited in Note 13. See also the studies of TV news production by Epstein (1973) and Gans (1979).

12. Henry Kissinger is a frequent guest on ABC's "Nightline" and other talk shows despite the fact that he is a consultant for firms that have economic interests in the issues under discussion. His conflict of interest surfaced during the aftermath of the brutal suppression of Chinese students in Tiananmen Square: When he called for "understanding" and "restraint," he was serving the interests of his corporate clients—that is, by supporting "normalized" relations to stabilize U.S. business. (There was no indication by the networks utilizing him that they were hearing the views of a highly paid PR man.)

13. See Friendly (1967), Kendrick (1969), and Schorr (1977).

14. On the contradictions between the "cultural apparatus" (a term introduced by C. Wright Mills in 1959) and the "consciousness industry" (coined by Enzensberger in 1974), see Gouldner (1976).

15. For some vivid examples of network censorship and repression of dissidents, see Ellison (1975), the discussion in "View from the Typewriter" in *TV Guide*,

August 3, 1974, and the 1977 PBS documentary "You Should See What You're Missing," based on David Rintel's testimony before the Senate Subcommittee on Constitutional Rights (February 8, 1972).

16. See United States Commission on Civil Rights (1977). On images of women in television and the mass media, see Modlesky (1982) and Baehr and Dyer (1987).

17. For a discussion of the "two-step flow" model, see Katz and Lazarsfeld (1955) and the critique of this position in Gitlin (1978) and Schiller (1989).

18. An emerging dogma in both television studies and certain circles of postmodern theory celebrates the active audience, arguing that audiences create the messages and meanings and thus determine the effects of television (see Ang's summary of this position in Downing et al., 1990, 155ff.). In fact, viewers may be either active or passive, and it seems a mistake to posit either position dogmatically. Structurally, television positions the audience as passive receivers of meanings and messages, though audiences may resist proffered meanings and "read against the grain." Although there is clearly an important distinction between television's encoding of media texts and audience decoding, it is a mistake to focus attention solely on the latter, though it will certainly be useful to have more concrete studies of how audiences actually use and receive television.

4

Television, Politics, and the Making of Conservative Hegemony

This is the beginning of a whole new concept. This is it. This is the way they'll be elected forevermore. The next guys will have to be performers.
—Roger Ailes, 1968

Every moment of every public appearance was scheduled, every word was scripted, every place where Reagan was expected to stand was chalked with toe marks.
—Donald Regan, 1988

He looked presidential. It created the image he needs as he goes into the campaign.
—Walter Cronkite after Bush's 1988
Republican Convention acceptance speech

The simple story of this election is that the Bush commercials have worked and the Dukakis commercials have not.
—Pollster Lou Harris on the 1988 presidential campaign

[Media power derives] not only from what is said, but more significantly from what is not said. For these media not only continue to affirm the status quo but, in the same measure, they fail to raise essential questions about the structure of society.
—Paul Lazarsfeld and Robert Merton

In this chapter, I shall argue that television played an essential role in the creation of a conservative hegemony during the 1980s. This book opened with an epigraph by James Madison, who wrote that "a popular government without popular information or the means of acquiring it, is but a prologue to a Farce or a Tragedy; or perhaps both." Democracy can

133

work only if the citizenry is informed and if there is a balance of power between competing forces. In the Age of Television, this means that the media must serve as a check on excessive governmental power; they must provide information critical of government. The failure of television and the liberal opposition to adequately criticize the major conservative figures and their agenda led in the 1980s to the farce of Reagan and the tragedy of Bush. My argument here will be that television did not provide the information necessary to produce an informed electorate and that the media actively helped forge a conservative hegemony rather than impartially mediating among competing social forces.

I first explore how the media helped elect an ex-movie and television actor, Ronald Reagan, as president of the United States, and then I discuss how television helped him govern and survive one of the most explosive political scandals of the century, retiring as the most popular president in recent times (see section 4.1). Next I examine the 1988 presidential election and discuss the ways in which television and the transformation of politics into a battle of images helped George Bush win the presidency (see section 4.2). I argue that television and the media were key factors in protecting the Reagan administration from complete collapse after the Iran/Contra affair in 1986–1987 and in electing Bush president in 1988, thus preserving the conservative hegemony that the media had helped construct during the first half of the decade. I also argue that this "hegemony" argument is more illuminating than the "postmodern" image analysis, which claims that television's most important effects are to replace "reality" with images. I conclude by criticizing the claim that television has a "liberal bias" and specify how and why television helped forge a conservative hegemony (see section 4.3).

4.1   The Simulated Presidency

It is generally agreed that Reagan and his media managers fine-tuned the politics of the image to a highly sophisticated art.[1] In the 1980 election, the Reagan team mobilized images of patriotism, anticommunism, and fear of decline under the Democrats to sell the majority of the public on the virtue of electing a highly conservative candidate who had never before held national office as president of the United States. Reagan acted the role of the presidential candidate effectively and managed to defeat Jimmy Carter, whose symbolic fortunes were at a low point. Other machinations, too, were going on behind the scenes to ensure the Reagan victory (see Appendix A).

Indeed, television helped prepare the way for the coming of Reagan through its negative coverage of the Carter administration, especially toward its end. Night after night, television portrayed the Iranians holding Americans hostage and Carter's seeming inability to do anything about it. Television news harped on energy shortages and crises, the decline of U.S. power, economic instability, moral decline, and other themes which made it appear that matters were growing ever worse and that the Democrats were part of the problem. Moreover, Reagan's program of a stronger defense, the reassertion of U.S. power and pride, and conservative economic management provided seeming solutions to the problems that television news was dramatizing.

In addition, powerful economic forces stood behind the Republican candidate, who was able to finance an expensive television election (Ferguson and Rogers 1986). Reagan could afford the best available image managers, and his ads and media politics skillfully presented him as a real alternative to the faltering Democrats. The corporate forces behind Reagan were disturbed about the amount of wealth and power that had been transferred to the state sector and wanted to strengthen the corporate sector at the expense of the state. They saw social welfare programs as a threat to capital accumulation and government regulation as an intolerable drag on profits. Important corporate leaders saw Carter as an ineffectual manager and turned against him, cutting back on investment and allowing interest rates and inflation to soar. In effect, capital went on strike against the Democrats during the 1970s, in what was a typical strategy of corporate forces against social democratic and liberal governments.

Thus, both economic forces and the media helped elect Reagan. Major corporations wanted to restructure the capitalist system after the economic crises of the 1970s and the turmoil of the 1960s. This required a pliant state, friendly to business interests, that would allow corporate mergers and free up the requisite capital to develop new technologies and corporate structures. Corporate capital bet on Reagan, and he complied with tremendous tax breaks, deregulation, a loosening of antitrust laws, and a blatantly pro-business agenda.

Reagan's Media Politics

One of the first priorities of the television presidency was to sell Reagan as a friendly, positive, likable fellow who was also strong, efficient, and in control. This required isolating Reagan from the press because he frequently botched his facts. Indeed, the line between fantasy and reality was extremely thin in Reagan's mindset, and fantasy often took over altogether, as when he told Israeli politicians that he had been present at the concentration camps in Europe when they were liberated (mistaking his viewing of newsreels as an actual event), and when he recounted events from Hollywood films as if they had really happened. An especially unkind "60 Minutes" show once juxtaposed scenes from his movies with references in his speeches, policies, and actions; and Michael Rogin (1987) detailed how many of Reagan's "ideas" such as his "Star Wars" nuclear-umbrella fantasy, had analogues in his films.

Yet Reagan maintained a generally high level of popularity, despite polls that showed public opposition to most of his policies, such as his support for a Nicaraguan counterrevolutionary force and his stubborn reluctance to negotiate arms reductions with the Soviet Union until late in his presidency. Was his alleged popularity due in large part to positive images of Reagan smiling, waving at reporters, and acting "presidential"? In fact (media myth to the contrary), Reagan was not particularly popular during his early years in office. Studies of press coverage during the first two years of his administration indicate that the media constantly assumed the existence of a popularity that was belied by actual figures in the polls. Media commentators and politicians alike constantly proclaimed Reagan's great popularity when, in fact, his approval ratings—first, after two months and, then, after two years in office—were well below those of Eisenhower, Kennedy, Johnson, Nixon, and Carter at similar stages of their presidency (King and Schudson 1987, 37).

The media myth of Reagan's popularity became a self-fulfilling prophecy that helped him govern, win reelection, and survive one of the greatest scandals in U.S. political history. The media also promoted the myth of Reagan as "great communicator," as if he were a master of political communication. From the beginning, media commentators from the networks to PBS's "Washington Week in Review" praised his ability as communicator (Nimmo and Combs 1983, 154ff.). Granted, Reagan was competent at making a speech with a tele-prompter, and he could adequately memorize and perform short speeches and statements from cue cards. But he routinely misspoke, contradicted himself, and often became incoherent during press conferences or spontaneous conversations. Indeed, without his cue cards he was hopeless, so his aides were forced to give him cards to read for events from telephone calls to interventions in important summit meetings. To say that this simple-minded raconteur of folksy and corny stories is a "great communicator" is to reduce communication to simulation—precisely the process to which television itself was reducing politics and public communication.

Yet Ronald Reagan was the United States' ideal made-for-television president. His training as a professional actor enabled him to deliver highly effective speeches and to project a pleasing and strong image—and his media managers fully exploited these talents. Each night, Reagan was given cue cards to memorize, and most of his official day was devoted to performance in which he would act out the prefabricated script (Mayer and McManus 1988, 25ff.). His daily performance was so tightly scripted that even his small-talk, jokes, and telephone calls were written out in advance and memorized while diagrams and arrows pointed to where Reagan should stand, to whom he should speak, and so on. The Reagan administration thus developed a simulated presidency that carried out largely symbolic politics, devoting much of its time to image production and using television to govern and to sell the figurehead and his conservative policies.

Of course, media politics began before the Reagan era. In *The Selling of the President*, author Joe McGinniss (1969 and 1988) claims that during the 1968 presidential campaign one of Nixon's media advisers, Roger Ailes, stated: "This is the beginning of a whole new concept. This is it. This is the way they'll be elected forevermore. The next guys will have to be performers" (Ailes, cited in McGinniss 1969, 155). McGinniss reports that there were frequent battles in the Nixon campaign team between old-style politicos like John Mitchell and Nixon himself concerning the role of the media (especially television) in the election, and that Ailes and the media specialists were frequently overruled by the politicians. By 1980, with the ascendancy of Reagan to the presidency, media "handlers" and managers became central to both political campaigns and daily governing. Consequently, public relations specialists, advertising experts, and media managers permeated the Reagan administration, and the art of governing became centered on producing positive images for prime-time news and on managing and manipulating the media to promote the administration's goals.

The public relations blitz began early each morning, when key officials decided on the "line of the day." This was then sent throughout the White House via computer terminals (Hertsgaard 1988, 32ff.). In encounters with the press, the Reagan team would have their script in hand and the day's party line on their tongues. In this way, the administration attempted to focus the media on whatever theme or message they desired to have broadcast on the daily news. Next, Reagan's media manager, Michael Deaver, orchestrated a daily "photo opportunity" to produce positive images for television news. Deaver and his team sought to provide attractive images through appropriate settings, background, and framing. In order to effectively promote the images and message of the day, they devoted detailed attention to placement, camera angles, lighting, color coordination, and sound (Hertsgaard 1988; Deaver 1987).

As Reagan's chief of staff, Donald Regan, was later to write:

> Deaver was a master of his craft. He saw—designed—each Presidential action as a one-minute or two-minute spot on the evening network news, or a picture on page one of the *Washington Post* or the *New York Times*, and conceived every Presidential appearance in terms of camera angles.
>
> If the President was scheduled to make a ceremonial appearance in the Rose Garden, he could be sure that he and the recipients of whatever greeting or award was involved would be looking into the sun so that the cameras

would have the light behind them. . . . His position was always chosen with the idea of keeping him as far away as possible from the reporters who hovered at the edge of these events with the intention of shouting questions. Every moment of every public appearance was scheduled, every word was scripted, every place where Reagan was expected to stand was chalked with toe marks. The President was always being prepared for a performance, and this had the inevitable effect of preserving him from confrontation and the genuine interplay of opinion, question, and argument that form the basis of decision. (Regan 1988, 248)

This effort at manipulating the day's media agenda was supplemented by periodic media events to dramatize the larger issues and to present Reagan's policies and Reagan himself in a positive light. Such events included televised "pseudo-events" such as foreign travels, Fourth of July spectacles, a spectacular D-Day celebration in Europe celebrating the victory in World War II, appearances at the 1984 Summer Olympics, and Reagan's less successful Bitburg speech at a cemetery in Germany in which former Nazi SS officers were buried.[2]

Major military interventions were also packaged as special events. Reagan's April 1986 bombing of Libya, for instance, was orchestrated as a media event: The bombing was carried out in the middle of the night, coordinated to coincide with the beginning of the evening news in the United States. Secret government opinion polls had shown that Libyan leader Muammar Qaddafi was the most disliked political figure in the United States and that the people polled would strongly support the bombing of Libya (Mayer and McManus 1988, 221). Reagan's popularity had been falling in the polls, he was losing ground in his Contra war and in other foreign policy initiatives, and his team wanted to replicate the public relations success of his Grenada invasion with a spectacular (and relatively unrisky) military event. The ploy worked, winning strong approval in the polls. Reagan's overall approval rating jumped to 68 percent, an all-time high for the simulated president (ibid., 223).

Television presented the Libyan bombing as a "special event," interrupting regular programming with periodic news bulletins and dramatizing the actions with special late-night talk shows. As no live footage was immediately available, television used previous combat footage of Libyan planes interspersed with other combat footage, to dramatize the event. Such footage contained a positive charge, inasmuch as it was associated with films featuring high-tech combat action. (The then-popular movie *Top Gun* also featured a dog fight with Libyan planes.) Such resonant images tend to marshal emotions around the excitement of dramatic action while mobilizing the patriotic sentiments that often emerge during times of war or national crisis. In this way, the Reagan team employed the images and codes of television to bolster the fortunes of the president—that is, by manufacturing a crisis with Libya and carrying out a carefully managed spectacle to mobilize public opinion around him. Such was the fate of politics in the Age of Television.

Reagan and Television

Television thus promoted Reagan by allowing itself to be manipulated by his media politics and by failing to call attention to his flaws and limitations. Mark Hertsgaard (1988) documents the press's reluctance to criticize Reagan and his policies, and details the ways in which the media helped promote a "right turn" in U.S. politics. From the beginning, television failed to raise critical questions concerning Reagan's economic policies; it also failed to indicate who would benefit and who would suffer from his tax program. After the failed attempt to assassinate Reagan in 1981, TV became increasingly positive toward Reagan himself and only sporadically criticized his policies when the economy turned sour in 1982. With economic recovery and patriotic fervor over the Grenada invasion in 1983, television became overwhelmingly positive toward Reagan, all the while perpetuating the myth that he could not be beaten in the 1984 election.

The lack of significant television criticism of Reagan was in part due to the lack of significant Democratic opposition and criticism—at least at the level of leadership with access to the media. Generally speaking, television does not spontaneously articulate critiques of an administration's policies or of the personality of a president or other prominent political figures. Rather, it broadcasts the criticisms or opposite views of official spokespersons within an oppositional party or group. (In the case of a Republican president, top Democratic leaders would be the official spokespersons for oppositional views.) Consequently, although many politicians, members of public interest groups, and others had sharp criticisms of Reagan, they were rarely broadcast because of the extremely limited spectrum of opinion circulated on television—a spectrum articulated mostly by prominent (and safe) members of the opposition party in Washington.

During Reagan's first term, the media was naturally favorable to his aggressively pro-business agenda. As a rich and powerful part of the business establishment itself, network television had much to gain from Reagan's tax "reforms," which gave it windfall profits. The media were also favorably inclined toward his rollback of government regulation (television hated regulation) and had no problems with his attacks on unions (the television industry was frequently harassed by militant unions). There was also widespread support in the corporate sector, of which the television industry is an essential component, for Reagan's attempts to rebuild the military, to present a more positive image of the United States, and to assert a more aggressive and effective role in managing world politics.

At bottom, corporate/conglomerate mergers integrated the major television networks more centrally into the economic power structure of transnational capitalism during the Reagan years (see section 3.2), and television responded by taking a conservative turn that was generally supportive of Reagan's economic policies. Reagan's program of deregulation allowed the television networks to greatly increase their power and profitability. They were allowed to own more affiliate television stations, to broadcast more advertising and less news and public affairs programming, and, basically, to expand into any field that they wished. Furthermore, television's celebration of consumerism in advertising and of society through happy endings on its entertainment programs went hand in hand with Reagan's sunny optimism and idealization of the United States: The commercial environment of television thrives on the feeling that all is in order, and Reagan was just the man to sell the belief that the accumulation of wealth, commodities, and luxury was the key to the good life—hence the perfect fit between Reaganism and TV ideology.

Hertsgaard argues that during the 1984 presidential race the media played into the Reagan campaign's hands in at least three ways: (1) by promoting horse-race journalism, which focused coverage on polls that invariably announced that Reagan was ahead, rather than by focusing on issues; (2) by broadcasting every night the flattering pictures that the photo opportunity of the day was designed to produce; and (3) by promoting the "America Is Back" ideology of the Reagan campaign, upon which Reagan successfully ran and governed (1988, 238ff.). But the media failed to present critical information that could have raised serious questions about Reagan's presidency, including such issues as Reagan's disastrous Central American policy, his failed Middle East policy, his secret wars throughout the world, the astronomical proliferation of the federal deficit, the rapidly growing gap between rich and poor, the widespread corruption and scandals in his administration, his "Star Wars" nuclear umbrella, and the dangers inherent in his escalation of the arms race and hostility toward the Soviet Union.

Television also failed to raise questions concerning Reagan's age and his competency; it failed to ask who was really running the show behind the scenes. Indeed, during his second term, it was clear that Reagan's lax "management style" and distance from the details of running the government had allowed his subordinates a clear field in which to pursue their own aims. Yet television failed to adequately criticize his policies or to raise questions concerning his competency during the entire first term of Reagan's administration, and it did little to discuss such problems critically during the election. Its timidity was shared by the hapless Democratic candidate, Walter Mondale, who also failed to articulate sharp criticisms of Reagan or his policies.

But I believe there are other reasons for Reagan's popularity—reasons that have to do with the tight and successful fit between the Reagan presidency and the television world. For a habitual TV viewer, the Reagan era was an extended prime-time miniseries replete with action/adventure excitement, melodramas, situation comedies, special events, and a highly entertaining cast of characters. Even Reagan's political failures and the scandals of his administration made for amusing and exciting television. Who can forget Oliver North's thrilling Iran/Contra testimony and the fervent response of the television audience to the "average guy" caught up in bureaucratic crossfire, Fawn Hall's tales of shredding, Ed Meese's assurances that he was not a crook, and so on. During the Reagan years, the country was treated to the incomparable spectacle of the Iran/Contra scandal, to the juicy scandals involving scores of his administration officials prosecuted for corruption and criminal behavior, to insider gossip concerning Reagan's lax management style and Nancy's reliance on astrology, and to hilarious images of Reagan sleeping at major economic summits, being awakened and handed a note to read by George Shultz at one such meeting or being suckered into offering to barter away the country's entire nuclear arsenal by the wily Gorbachev at the Iceland summit in 1987 (Schieffer and Gates 1989, 278ff.).

Yes, Reagan was a highly entertaining fellow. The butt of European and sophisticated American humor, he provided the television audience with sitcom amusement and action/adventure drama. Given an audience addicted to television and movies, the fact that the Reagan years were highly entertaining might have been sufficient to maintain his popularity with the television audience. Above all, the Reagan team was able to turn politics into images, spectacles, and stories, by producing narrative frames for its policies and figurehead. Drawing on his experience as a master of illusion and narrative, Reagan was able to dramatize political issues as simple conflicts between evil and good (bad government and good people, the Evil Empire and the City on the Hill, spend-and-tax Democrats and frugal Republicans). He was also able to identify himself and his policies with the "good." Indeed, Reagan's own mindset was molded by his Hollywood and network television experience, and he translated this mindset into a political vision in which the United States became the embodiment of pristine goodness and its "enemies" became absolutely evil adversaries who would destroy "us" if we didn't destroy "them." Reagan's Manichaean view of the world thus reflected the mythologies of Hollywood genre films (i.e., westerns, war movies, and adventure films) as well as the television entertainment molded on this format. Reagan himself took great delight in telling little stories that dramatized his views, and his handlers provided a full repertoire of narratives for their chief actor to recite.[3]

From the beginning, Reagan excelled in creating often imaginary enemies against which he could define himself. In his successful 1980 campaign he promised to get government "off your back," and during the first years of his administration he inveighed against the "Evil Empire," the "totalitarian Marxist Sandinistas," the "tax-and-spend" Congress, criminal drug dealers, welfare cheats, and other demons and villains of the conservative mind. Reagan also provided real action/adventure scenarios to support his narrative: the Grenada invasion, the bombing of Libya, the Contra war, and countless other secret wars all over the world. It was Reagan's good fortune to be able to insert his fantasies into a television world view that for decades had promoted anticommunism as its dominant ideology (Parenti 1986; Herman and Chomsky 1988). Consequently, Reaganism fit into the world of television, which in turn promoted Reagan, selling his policies and personality in its nightly news images and entertainment programs. Up until the Iran/Contra scandal of 1986–1987, the media promoted the myth of Reagan's popularity and success with the electorate, despite continued opposition to his policies by the majority of the people in the United States. The Reagan presidency was thus the United States' most highly realized administration produced for and scripted according to television codes and frames—that is, the first fully simulated presidency—and Ronald Reagan was clearly the most highly developed television president.

Reagan provided the same sort of reassurance and security as that supplied by the predictable and upbeat mass entertainment of Hollywood and the networks. His light-hearted banter, optimism, and good cheer pleased the audience greatly. Each day, Reagan delivered a smile and a shrug—signs that everything was "A-OK in the U.S.A." Instead of giving lectures on greed and moral sloth à la Jimmy Carter, Reagan assured the country that wealth and privilege were as American as cherry pie and provided frequent circuses and spectacles when the bread supply and private housing became scarce or unaffordable. In these ways, the "great communicator" simulated the presidency in a seemingly effective manner and provided sufficient spectacles to keep the audiences entertained.

Then a serious crisis erupted: the Revenge of the Real, the Iran/Contra affair. The Reagan presidency was out of control (Cockburn 1988); yet Reagan, Bush, and others survived the crisis. How was this possible, and what role did television play in this most exciting and thrilling episode of "The Reagan Years"?

The Iran/Contra Scandal

During the winter of 1986–1987, the television networks played a key role in uncovering, dramatizing, and eventually containing one of the most extraordinary political scandals in U.S. history: the Iran/Contra affair. On

November 5, the day after the Democrats regained control of Congress in the 1986 elections, the *New York Times* featured a front-page story reporting that Robert McFarlane and other members of the Reagan White House had traveled to Iran to negotiate illegal arms sales to the Iranians, who were embroiled in a long and protracted war with neighboring Iraq.[4] Soon the story had become the sensation of the Reagan era.

The uproar over the scandal forced Reagan to appear on television on November 13. He denied that the arms had been sent in exchange for hostages and that they were offensive weapons; he also claimed (falsely) that only a small amount of arms had been sent, a quantity that could be fit into a "single cargo plane." Media attention dramatically escalated on November 25, when Ed Meese held a news conference and announced that funds generated from the (illegal) sale of arms to Iran had been diverted to the Nicaraguan Contras. U.S. military and CIA aid to the Contras had been cut off in 1984 by the Boland Amendment, when Congress, tired of the secret and dirty war fought by the Contras and the CIA, prohibited U.S. funding and CIA support. The Reagan administration immediately set into motion an illegal supply operation and used funds from the Iranian arms sales, among many other sources, to support the venture.

A fascinated media reacted immediately with saturation coverage, and new details of the story were broadcast night after night. The networks devoted most of their prime-time news programs to the story for the next several weeks; special reports and talk shows were also dominated by the scandal. The Cable News Network (CNN) broadcast live all the major press conferences and speeches pertaining to the affair, and Iran/Contra became the media event of the season. Commentators began comparing the scandals to Watergate, and thought naturally turned to impeachment and the destruction of the Reagan presidency. The networks engaged in some genuine investigative reporting to uncover the details of both the Iranian arms sales and the diversion of funds to the Contras. Reports detailed the use of the CIA-controlled airline Southern Airways to ship the arms to Iran and illegal supplies to the Contras. The media uncovered the roles of Oliver North, Richard Secord, Albert Hakim, and others. Television reports noted that "Max Gomez" was in charge of the arms drops to the Contras, operating out of Ilopango, El Salvador, and that "Max Gomez" (the *nomme du guerre* of long-time CIA operative Felix Rodriguez) was linked to Donald Gregg, one of Vice-President George Bush's deputies (see Appendix C.2).

One might wonder why the media turned on Reagan, if, as I argued earlier in this chapter, they shared certain ideological frames with him and appreciated his aggressive defense of business interests. Reflection on the sudden and intense television criticism of Reagan reveals both how the media respond to scandal and crisis, and how they eventually function as crisis managers. Television news cannot ignore a really sensational scandal because intense competition for ratings and profit drives the networks to scoop their competitors. A sort of "pack mentality" also drives television news to the "big story," and journalists appear competent or incompetent according to how well they provide either insights into the story or new facts and angles. In the case of the Iran/Contra story, the scandalous aspects of the affair provided justification for reporters who might have had doubts about Reagan, or Reaganism, and desired to provide a more critical perspective on him and his policies; such reporters had been restrained by their corporations for the past five years and, in some cases, may well have been eager to uncover details of incompetency, scandal, or criminality. For example, Hertsgaard documents battles during the previous years between CBS reporters who wanted to broadcast more critical reports on Reagan and managers who toned down or "killed" such reports (1988, 161ff).

But there are perhaps deeper reasons, rooted in the intensifying absorption of television into the corporate power structure and linked with the growing power and importance of television in organizing public opinion, that explain why the mainstream media suddenly assumed a more critical posture toward the Reagan administration. By nature, television is a centrist, "middle of the road" medium that seeks mass audiences and attempts to avoid offending them. Indeed, one reason television was not more critical of Reagan earlier on had to do with his perceived popularity and the need not to offend, with critical reporting, viewers who liked Reagan. But during the second term of the Reagan administration, there was a sharp turn to the right, toward more extremist positions and policies. The "centrist Troika" that had managed the White House and the actor president during Reagan's first term had broken up: Michael Deaver went into private business; James Baker, now in charge of the economy, was less concerned with overall policy and foreign affairs; and Ed Meese had moved to the Justice Department. The new, dictatorial chief of staff, Donald Regan, wanted to "let Reagan be Reagan," and he too encouraged more conservative policies (Regan 1988, 223ff.).

But it was especially in the field of foreign affairs that a dramatic turn to the right had taken place. Whereas George Shultz attempted to carry out relatively "moderate" policies, hardline right wingers took over the direction of foreign policy. The ambitious but deeply flawed Robert McFarlane took over as national security adviser and unleashed Oliver North and his zealous colleagues, who blundered into the Iran/Contra scandal. Behind the scenes, activist spymaster William Casey encouraged and perhaps directed the more aggressive covert actions, and former CIA chief George Bush tacitly approved and perhaps actively supported the more aggressive initiatives (see Appendixes B and C for additional details).

The right-wing cabal that took over the White House aggressively carried out the illegal Contra war, and Oliver North bragged that he was the "point man" in the forthcoming Nicaragua invasion (a rumor that portended another Vietnam with all its social division and turmoil). The hardline right wingers in the administration had thus far blocked any significant arms control measures and continued to push for a massive arms buildup centering on Reagan's "Star Wars"—a program that would militarize space and cost billions of dollars, although few qualified scientists believed it could actually work. Others in the administration were beginning to push for aggressively conservative social changes; Ed Meese, for instance, started waging a war on pornography and drugs, and called for overturning Supreme Court decisions that had legalized abortion and outlawed school prayers. The extreme Right had obviously taken over the Reagan White House and was aggressively pursuing an extremist agenda.

Some members of Congress began to get alarmed at the sharp turn to the Right during Reagan's second term, but the president continued to dominate the legislative and ideological agenda. At this juncture, only television was powerful enough to block the Right and move the Reagan administration back to the center. There were good reasons why such action would be in accord with the interests of the television industry. The corporations that controlled television would not be served by the turmoil that would accompany a Nicaraguan invasion or protracted turmoil over domestic and foreign policy. Significant individuals within the power structure—both leading Democrats and some Republicans—for the first time in years appeared to be aggressively criticizing Reagan's policies. The Democrats had recently gained control of Congress and, for the first time, were beginning to fight these policies. In this heated situation, television reversed its previous policy of squelching criticism of the Reagan administration and allowed limited criticism to take place.

During intense battles between significant forces in the U.S. power structure, television usually does not take sides, or only gradually moves toward one side or another—and such was the case with the Iran/Contra scandal. Television allowed the Reagan administration an opportunity to present its case and to attempt to "manage" the crisis, but it also allowed the critics a voice. Consequently, the policy to go easy on Reagan and his administration was dropped. The media briefly opened the windows in the House of Reagan and peeked inside at the shadowy and bizarre affairs of the administration. Intense scrutiny was focused on the National Security Agency, out of which Oliver North operated. Attention was also given to the CIA and its director, William Casey, although the media to this day have neither delved deeply into Casey's role in the affair nor revealed the full magnitude of the scandal.[5] Friends and critics of the Reagan administration appeared on the evening news and talk shows to reveal the shocking details of its conduct of foreign and domestic affairs. Reports that funds solicited from private sources to support the Contras had been used by the Reagan administration in a concerted campaign to defeat anti-Contra congressional figures in the 1986 election especially outraged Congress. The media responded by intensifying comparisons to Watergate, which had also involved domestic political subversion.

During such revelatory periods, the media tend to appear as the Voice of Truth as they briefly open the window looking into the political (or economic) establishment and reveal shocking information previously withheld from public view. They focus attention on scandals, dramatize them, and bring them to public attention. If the scandals are sufficiently threatening to and de-legitimating for the entire political-economic system, however, the media tend to deflect attention from the deeper causes of the scandals and desist from uncovering the more shocking elements involved. Such was clearly the case in the Iran/Contra affair. The media immediately began looking for scapegoats, focusing during November 1986 on the question of whether National Security Agency employees John Poindexter and Oliver North, or White House Chief of Staff Donald Regan or other higher-ups, were ultimately responsible. As a result of this focus, Poindexter and North were fired and Regan was eventually forced to resign.

Having aired the scandal, found scapegoats, and created the illusion of thoroughly investigating the crisis, the media then turned to the *cover-up* phase of their crisis-management. This began in early 1987, when the media shifted their focus away from the failings of the Reagan administration and eventually restored his legitimacy. Although the Reagan administration had clearly gone beyond the limits of what is acceptable in a system that purports to be governed by rule of law and constitutional government, the media and the power elite in the corporate and political sectors appeared resolved to avoid another scandal of the magnitude of Watergate, which involved the resignation of a president along with revelations of unending scandals and criminal activity. Severe criticism was directed against the "teflon president" in November and December 1986, and questions were raised concerning Reagan's possible criminal involvement in Iran/Contra and his fitness to govern, but these criticisms were put aside in 1987.

The "re-teflonization" of Reagan began after his State of the Union address in January 1987. Some critics had raised the question as to whether Reagan was still capable of acting out the role of president. Reagan had just undergone surgery, was reportedly ill and depressed, and had been performing poorly at press conferences and during televised speeches. After his State of the Union speech, however, the television pundits pronounced that there was no real cause for alarm. Dan Rather stated on CBS that "[i]t was—whatever one may think of the substance of the address—a good address with notation that he had some trouble with his voice about ¾ of the way through." And Bill Plante of CBS observed that "[t]his is one which he had to *perform* well on, Dan, and the first consideration of the people who advised the president and wrote that speech was that he *look good*" (emphasis added). Indeed, the network commentators all seemed to agree that Reagan did "look good" and had performed well, thus explicitly revealing the extent to which a president is judged according to the politics of the image. Had he failed to adequately simulate the presidency, questions concerning impeachment or resignation would have intensified.

In the spring of 1987 the cover-up of the Iran/Contra scandal continued with the Tower Commission Report. The report accused Reagan of a lax "management style," but it also exonerated him and his White House of any legal wrongdoing and shut the door on the specter of impeachment and constitutional crisis. The media focused a tremendous amount of attention on the report, some of which was unflattering to Reagan and his associates. In retrospect, however, the report and its aftermath can be seen as a cathartic attempt to assure the public that the worst was over, that the president was innocent, that there would be no impeachment or further laundering of dirty linen.

The Tower Commission Report was a typical government cover-up—similar to the Warren Commission Report and other attempts to defuse major scandals—whereby individuals deeply involved in the power structure were called upon to investigate their cronies and to obscure their more disturbing activities. The media tend to be complicit in major cover-ups, not questioning the reports issued or the individuals participating in the inquiries. Yet there was one final chapter in the Reagan era scandals to be played out: the Iran/Contra hearings held in the summer of 1987. Amidst the immediate outcry over the Iran/Contra revelations, congressional committees were established to uncover the "truth" behind the scandals. In particular, a forum was needed to get Oliver North and John Poindexter to testify, inasmuch as they had refused to testify to Congress unless they received immunity. A deal was cut and they were provided with "use immunity," which guaranteed that nothing that had appeared during the televised hearings could be used against them in court.

In the months preceding the hearings, the media more or less ignored the Iran/Contra story. Few, if any, serious attempts were made by the mainstream media to uncover the incredible scandals connected with the main event, nor were the media or Congress inclined to go after Reagan as they had gone after Nixon. Media spokespersons claimed that the public was not really interested in the affair and that there was no need to delve into it further; only the investigative press continued to pursue the story (see Appendix B).

Nonetheless, the televised Iran/Contra hearings, which began in May 1987, recreated the excitement of the Watergate hearings and raised expectations that new elements of the story might surface—as had occurred during the Watergate affair. Richard Secord, Oliver North, and others revealed some fascinating details of the Iran/Contra affair, but their revelations were overshadowed by the celebration of North as a national hero. North's self-righteous defense of his actions and his appearance as a martyr, as a "little guy" who was being persecuted by the system and was struggling for his life, went over well with television viewers, many of whom perceived the committee members to be bullies. The Democrats went along with the cover-up, failing to probe into the more sordid aspects of the illegal arms/drugs network with which the Contras were involved, or into North's efforts to set up a Federal Emergency Management Administration (FEMA) that would suspend constitutional freedoms in times of crisis and allow the government to round up and jail its opponents in concentration camps (see Appendix B).

After North's testimony, the rest of the hearings were anticlimactic and the networks eventually abandoned the story. During the 1988 presidential campaign, the story dropped from sight almost completely—despite George Bush's alleged involvement in several aspects of the scandal (see Appendix C). Unlike Watergate, Iran/Contra scapegoated middle- and high-level officials without bringing about a dramatic shift in ruling elites. Thus, the whole affair constituted an excellent example of television's role as an instrument of containment and crisis management for system-threatening scandals and crises, and for the media's role as instruments of conservative hegemony during the 1980s.

Ultimately, however, the story of Iran/Contra was too complex, delegitimating, and threatening; it involved too many people, as well as the viability of the entire intelligence apparatus of the National Security State, and therefore had to be eventually contained and covered up. The scandal was of such complexity and magnitude that it did not allow for a happy resolution (à la Watergate) whereby a few unpopular politicians and their underlings could be sent to jail. Preservation of the National Security State demanded covering up the full extent of the Iran/Contra scandals. This cover-up clearly aided the candidacy of George Bush in the 1988 election and helped him win the presidency.[6] Reflection on this event should clarify the extent to which television has become a central player in U.S. politics, as well as the extent to which the media helped implement "centrist" conservative ideological hegemony during the 1980s.

4.2 The 1988 Election

Elections have long been rituals that maintain order and legitimate the system of government in the United States as a democratic one (Nimmo and Combs 1983). Almost all observers commenting on the 1988 election agree that television has become the dominant force in U.S. politics, that presidential campaigns are now exercises in media politics, and that elections are won and lost via television. Most observers also agree that the 1988 presidential election was the most dispiriting in recent history. It attracted barely 50 percent of all eligible voters, resulting in one of the lowest voter-participation levels among Western democracies. It is safe to conclude that the dismal quality of the election and the low turnout were related in fundamental ways to the growing role of television in U.S. politics and to the transformation of elections into a battle of images determined by money and media strategy.

Primaries and Conventions

U.S. presidential elections are long media events in which television is assuming an ever more important and central role. In pre-primary election coverage, television producers decide who to cover and who to ignore, thus highlighting certain candidates at the expense of others. Once the primaries begin, television is there to elevate winners of early primaries into front-runners and to call attention to itself as the primary arbiter of the electoral process. Indeed, throughout the primaries, television ads, TV coverage, and television debates are usually the key events that determine the outcome of the primary race; thus elections are oriented more and more toward television, and well-financed and televisual candidates tend to be privileged in this situation. In fact, during some of the most intense primary races, candidates fly from airport to airport, holding press conferences and doing interviews with local television personalities, rather than actually speaking to or meeting with live voters. Such television primaries tend to favor candidates with the money to mount such television campaigns and to hire media specialists and "handlers" who know how to manipulate the media.

In the 1988 primaries, after a shaky start in Iowa, George Bush's media team, his well-financed organization and campaign, and the lack of a convincing challenger assured him an easy victory. A large number of democratic candidates were effectively whittled down to two, Michael Dukakis and Jesse Jackson, after the first couple months of the primaries. Dukakis had a well-financed and relatively competent organization that was able to effectively use television to promote its candidate, whereas Jackson depended on charisma and popularity to attract large crowds and some television coverage. Although Jackson surged ahead at one point, his politics, his race, his lack of funds to buy television advertising, and his unfavorable media coverage in the Pennsylvania and New York primaries helped Dukakis win an eventual victory.

Televisual candidates are also helped by TV election coverage, which invariably focuses on the "horse race" aspects of who wins particular primaries and who's ahead in the race as a whole. This focus deflects attention from the actual issues and competencies of the candidates, and helps mediocre candidates who are able to buy and project a TV image at the expense of more substantial individuals. Almost invariably, network commentators discuss the numbers in the delegate and vote counts; they also tend to focus interview questions on the "horse race" aspects rather than questioning candidates about their positions on political issues or their visions of the future.

The summer conventions were largely media events whose results were determined in advance. The candidates' media teams were able to orchestrate these conventions to produce positive images for each candidate. In both cases, the candidates depended on a convention speech to ratify their credentials. Fittingly, it seems that, in the television age, one's ability to deliver on television becomes a prime criterion for one's fitness as president. Both candidates trained and rehearsed for the Big Event, and both delivered performances that were deemed successful.

Interestingly, the network television commentators judged the candidates' speeches in terms of their televisual qualities. In a revealing discussion among the CBS pundits after Dukakis's speech, Dan Rather judged the speech to have been well delivered but lacking in striking "sound bites" that could be packaged for television news; in other words, he appraised the speech according to its ability to play on TV! Network commentators judged that George Bush's speech was the best of his life and that the usually clumsy Bush had performed quite well. Walter Cronkite commented to Dan Rather that "[h]e looked presidential. It created the image he needs as he goes into the campaign."

And so television itself establishes the criteria upon which a nation is to judge its presidential candidates. Elections have become televisual events.

Ads, Photo-Opportunities, and Television Debates

The Bush campaign in particular mobilized itself around the production of negative and positive images, projecting in ubiquitous television ads a view of Michael Dukakis as soft on criminals, weak on patriotism and defense, lax on environmental protection, and too "liberal" for a supposedly conservative country. In a meeting in Maine at the end of May, the Bush team perceived that it was behind and required aggressive attack strategies and image management to turn the election around (Schieffer and Gates 1989, 358ff.). "Focus-group testing" among a group of Democrats, who had voted for Reagan and now declared that they were for Dukakis, indicated that those interviewed were shocked that a convicted murderer, Willie Horton, had brutally beaten a Maryland couple and raped the woman while out on a pass from prison during a Massachusetts prison furlough program while Dukakis was governor. The Bush team organized a series of TV ads around this theme to make it appear that Dukakis was soft on crime.

As *Village Voice* commentator Leslie Savan noted (October 21, 1988, p. 24), the Bush ads were mobilized around the gut emotion of fear and aversion to dirt—meaning the sludge of Boston Harbor or the human scum whom Dukakis supposedly wanted to let out of prison: "The issues raised by the ads are carefully chosen for their lack of substance, in order to leave a clear field for the imagery." Savan failed to note, however, that these ads (which were repeatedly telecast) also incorporated a strategy whereby the Big Lie was repeated until it passed for truth. In fact, the Bush team's contempt for truth was quite striking. After Bush's 1984 vice-presidential debate with Geraldine Ferraro, his press secretary, Peter Teeley, told reporters: "You can say anything you want in a debate, and 80 million people will hear it. If reporters then document that a candidate spoke untruthfully, so what? Maybe 200 people read it, or 2,000 or 20,000" (cited in Holly Sklar, *Zeta Magazine*, December 1988, p. 8).

This "pragmatic" attitude toward truth was the touchstone of Bush's 1988 campaign. Taking a successful tactic from Hitler's media manager Goebbels, the Reagan/Bush media manager Roger Ailes perceived that image was becoming more important than substance or fact, and that endless repetition of any lie supported by a reinforcing image could sell any policy or person. Too late, Dukakis's campaigners complained that their candidate had a good record on environmentalism, that he had tried to clean up Boston Harbor, that the Reagan-Bush administration had provided the biggest obstacle to his effort, refusing to release Federal Clean-Water funds, and that Bush—trying to foist himself off as an environmentalist— had a totally deplorable environmental record. Eventually, the Dukakis team also responded to the Willie Horton ad, arguing that the prison furlough program had been initiated by his successor, a Republican governor, and that most states in the country had a similar program. Nonetheless, the Bush team continued to run the ad and to argue that Dukakis was a weak, "bleeding-heart" liberal on crime and other issues.

It is, indeed, generally concluded that television advertising played a crucial role in the election and that Bush's ads were more effective than Dukakis's. In a *New York Times* article "TV's Role in '88: The Medium Is the Election," (October 30, 1988), Michael Oreskes states that the "next President will have been chosen in a campaign dominated as never before by television. In this television election, more voters are telling pollsters that ads matter, more money is being spent on them than ever before and it is the dictates of television, campaign officials contend, that have led the candidates to attack each other from the stump with uncommon frequency for a modern Presidential race." The article also cites Pollster Louis Harris, who says: " 'The simple story of this election is that the Bush commercials have worked and the Dukakis commercials have not. . . . As a result of this continuous pounding on TV commercials, Dukakis's rating as a leader has declined.' " What also declined was his image as a crime fighter and as someone qualified to handle world affairs (ibid.).

In the television age, politicians are thus packaged as commercial products sold to voters. Voters in turn are seen as commodities that politicians attempt to purchase through TV ads or by constructing images on news programs that induce the viewer to "choose" their candidate in polls or in the voting booth. In such commodified politics, the candidates must use the techniques of marketing and advertising to sell themselves in a competitive marketplace to the audience, who in turn must be sold on the virtue of voting and of "participating" in the "democratic" process of elections. Television has come to play an important role in both processes, given its incessant hyping of the importance of presidential elections and its ubiquitous presence within the electoral process itself.

In their (successful) TV ads, the Bush team combined negative packages with positive ones showing George Bush eye-balling Gorbachev and kindly and gently embedding himself in the sign-system of Reaganite imagery of a happy America. One Bush ad presents George cavorting with his children and grandchildren while cooking up a big stew to ladle out to his constituency. The ad uses slow-motion imagery, gentle "musak," soft-pastel images, and smooth cutting to convey an image of George Bush as a nice guy/family man eager to provide nurturance to a country wanting reassurance. Barbara Bush stood by her man in this case, reporting that her husband was supported by a "great big family, thousands of friends."

For voters who needed stronger medicine and more reassurance that George was "the One," another "I am That Man!" ad centered on Bush with, in the words of one observer, "index finger pointing to the heavens. Now the music is louder, more Presidential, as the Vice President fades into the White House in a somewhat ghostly manner. 'This is my mission and I will complete!' declares the candidate, promising that America will never be weak again. Thus the tough George Bush, the Extra-Strength Tylenol of politicians" (Walter Goodman, New York Times, October 23, 1988, p. H-27). Yet, "these buy-me commercials are short of reasons why anybody should choose the product. When a reason is advanced, it seems hyperbolic even by advertising standards. There is the candidate, pushing a baby on a swing in slow motion while an authoritative voice informs us that 'it was George Bush who led the way' to the disarmament agreements with the Soviet Union" (ibid.). In fact, as these ads are shorthand symbolic texts that present positive political images, they indicate the extent to which the politics of image has replaced substantive discourse, coherent positions, or political arguments of any sort.

Indeed, the Bush campaign reveals the extent to which symbolic politics now employs images, narrative scenes, and subliminal messages to attract voters to its product. The Dukakis campaign desperately attempted to compete in the image realm with early ads replicating the imagistic format of the Bush formula. In one example, a hand chops the air in slow motion and its owner, Michael Dukakis, greets two helmeted police officers while the voice-over intones: "Leadership—it's meeting the tough problems head-on. That's how Mike Dukakis fought crime in Massachusetts." Statistics then demonstrate his crime-fighting success, and the ad fades out with the Duke's firm and earnest countenance framed by an American flag.

Dukakis's later, more distinctive ads fell into two categories. One set contained meta-ads about the Bush TV ads and campaign. This multipart "Packaging of George Bush" series featured a heavy-set fellow, resembling Roger Ailes, who oozed out proposals for anti-Dukakis ads ("Well, I think we need another TV commercial on the furlough thing"), countered by a worried Yuppie who replies, "They're beginning to write about Dukakis's real crime record." "Nobody reads anymore," the Ailes character chortles. "But Dukakis changed that furlough program," the earnest adviser responds; and he then rattles off the ways in which Dukakis actually dealt with crime in Massachusetts. The ad concludes: "They'd like to sell you a package. Wouldn't you rather choose a president?"

This series exhibited enough critical reflection on the construction of TV ads and the packaging of TV campaigns to please a moderate modernist or Brechtian. But they were apparently too complex and confusing for audiences, and they were rated ineffective by experts. Dukakis eventually turned from the aesthetic of modernism to that of stark naturalism, stepping in front of the camera, usually in rolled-up shirt-sleeves, to tell the audience why they should vote for him for president. These uninspired occasions of naturalistic didacticism also suggested that the Dukakis group had failed to understand the dynamics of image politics.

Of course, the election was not won through TV ads alone. Closely following Reagan's governing strategy, the Bush campaign produced a daily photo-opportunity to illustrate a daily theme: showing Bush in a flag factory, talking to small-town folks, hanging out with country-music singers, lecturing police about law and order (a big favorite), or appearing in a heavily polluted Boston Harbor to sound off on environmentalism. The Bush team carefully selected backdrops (such as flags and balloons) and emphasized visual images; it also tried to manufacture a "quotable quote" for the day. In these ways, it followed the successful Reagan governing strategy whereby one image package per day was produced for broadcast on the prime-time television news. More often than not, the television networks cheerfully played along.

The process of manufacturing positive images by the campaigns for news broadcasts is analyzed by William Boot, who provides an example of the Republican strategy:

> *Labor Day, September 5. NBC's Lisa Myers reports on Bush campaigning in Disneyland. We see Bush surrounded by U.S. Olympic athletes and folks dressed up like Disney cartoon characters. He awards gold medals in the shape of Mickey Mouse heads to the Seoul-bound athletes. Cut to scene of Bush at lectern, with Mickey Mouse dressed in red-white-and-blue Uncle Sam garb standing beside him.*
>
> *Myers (voice-over): "Sometimes it pays to be vice-president!"*
>
> *Bush (to athletes): "You're representing the country of the little guy. No matter what the circumstances of your birth and background, you can go anywhere and do anything."*
>
> *Cut to the Andover-Yale-Skull-and-Bones man, sleeves rolled up, unloading fish at a San Diego cannery. (Myers: "To identify with the little guy"). Then cut to Bush at lectern, San Diego Harbor as a backdrop, firing a salvo at Dukakis: "I wouldn't be surprised if he thinks that a naval exercise is something you find in Jane Fonda's workout book."*
>
> Note: No press conference, no access, yet Bush images compliantly mongered, along with the scripted messages: Bush is no elitist but Dukakis is an exotic lefty. (Boot 1989, 24; emphasis in original)

The photo-opportunities were orchestrated to produce effective sound-bites for the evening news, and, sure enough, the three networks, almost every evening, produced just about the same images and sounds as those the Bush campaign had so carefully orchestrated. In addition, the Bush team coordinated the ads with the photo-opportunities: The sludge-in-Boston-Harbor ads were released when Bush made a speech there, and Bush appeared in a flag factory when his ads were attacking Dukakis's patriotism. Total media management was the name of the game in this age of media politics.

One might note here that the so-called photo-opportunities were really what Daniel Boorstin (1962) calls "pseudo-events." Staged solely for the media, these events were packaged into highly condensed sights and sounds that project a certain positive image. Daily campaigning was reduced in this election to the manufacturing of attractive images for the nightly news. One event featured George Bush in middle America: He is shown with three women country music singers (Loretta Lynn and her sisters), who, on Bush's campaign bus, sing "Stand by George Bush!" with George and Barbara beaming on. These masterpieces of image construction began with close-ups of the three singers, panned to Bush when the tag "Stand by George Bush" appeared, faded out with another pan to a smiling Barbara, and ended with a two-shot of George and his wife. The same vignette and productivity. Pressured assignment desk editors and re-porters go for what's quick and easy—the stuff crackling on the scanner or something they can "hose down" in a hurry.

Do viewers want hosed-downed news? The evidence suggests they'll reach for their remote controls, searching for something else on those 55-plus channels. And local news will be left in a spiral of collapse—quick fixes, screeching teases, dazzling graphics—while their viewers look in vain for a report on what matters to them.

Stevens, who has worked in television news since 1966, was the first woman television news director in the United States. She has also worked as a reporter, anchor, managing editor, executive producer and associate news director. She is cur-rently managing editor for the 15 stations that make up Conus Communications' Rocky Mountain region.

Todd Gitlin ■ Money talks

The scandal of local news is twofold. First, it "works": It makes financial officers hum with delight. Second, it isn't considered scandalous by the responsi-ble parties. That is, in the light, or dark, of their degraded standards, a wave of the hand toward big numbers is the beginning and end of the conversation.

When I say local news "works," I mean, of course, that it does what its pro-prietors want and expect it to do: It delivers big audiences. It does this via the recipes dreamed up by consultants—the standard issue Mr. and Ms. weightless anchors indistin-guishable from coast to coast, able to look concerned, chip-per, urgent and cheerful—in rapid succession ("*Now this...*"); the state-of-the-art technology, the videocams and uplinks; the logos, the jaunty theme music, the hairdos and color combos. The resulting numbers please advertisers, which in turn pleases management.

The local news personifies this

more analytical, more risky sort of coverage might, given enough time, make money? But in television, the point is not to make money but to make more money—more than the other guy, more than you used to make, more than you feared you might make. And this is the real scandal: There are no sufficiently powerful countervailing motives. That is why "the system works."

In television, as in football, "Winning isn't everything, it's the only thing." That this is the rule in local television is a comment not only on the power of the idea of winning but on the weakness of other passions in American culture.

I had a visit once from a former student who'd been one of the sharpest I'd known. As a college senior, he had dis-played every interest in critical thought. Now he found him-self the assistant news director at a network affiliate in a major city, and he confessed to me, with some embarrass-ment, that he hadn't read a serious book in years. (His shame was the most touching and impressive thing about him.) The reason, he said, was that he "didn't have time"—a

winning formula except in a formulaic way. "Dope busts tonight." "Celebrity trapped in fire donates liver." "Cheers" bloopers. Weather giggles. Happy talk. Rule One: Never be at a loss for pictures. Rule Two: Never be at a loss for words. Mindlessness abhors dead air and loves video wallpaper. (Just what kind of pictoral jolt is supplied by the flames of the 1,001st fire anyway?)

Sure, there are exceptions. For example, I've heard excellent reports from San Francisco-Oakland's Fox affiliate, KTVU. I recollect vividly the moment when the anchor segued from a report on President Reagan's Bitburg visit to a report on who the SS were. ("History!" as George Bush would have said.) In some major metropolitan areas, there's a bit of a market niche, to use the repellent term of the business, for stories that last more than a minute-fifteen, and periodically one of the franchises sucks in its collective breath and goes for a walk—usually short—along the high road. But that reliable strumpet commerce is invariably strutting her stuff at the next crossroads.

Television journalists will say, with a wring of the hands followed by a knowing look and a roll of the eyes, that they themselves would prefer to go down in history as the local version of Edward R. Murrow. But, alas and alack, there's no commercial alternative to the quick and the lurid, because, let's face it, sufficient numbers of masses keep offering up their delectable eyeballs for the rental of advertisers.

Who knows if the more probing,

The last track is no place for reflection. Stand still and think, and somebody gains on you.

A friend of mine has spent more than two decades in local television news. His career is considered distinguished. He's won awards. But if he weren't there, personable and "believable," wearing lightly his knowledge of the world of cops and criminals, someone else—most likely someone less knowledgeable—would happily substitute.

Naturally, I trust my friend to "get a story right" more than I trust someone I don't know. But he observes that the longer he works there, the faster he talks and the shorter his attention span gets. He doesn't trust his mind anymore, and rightly so. What he has come to value in a story, now, is a look on a hostage's face or the face of a bereaved mother. He knows there is something limited about the "flash 'n' trash" that is his bread and butter.

The thousands of wannabes who would "kill" for his job are waiting in line to leapfrog over his hard-earned knowledge of how institutions work and jump directly to his savoring of the moments of pain. In my experience, they don't particularly care what he has given up to "get" what's "real." They can't wait for the chance to go for the gold.

Gitlin, professor of sociology and director of the mass communications program at the University of California at Berkeley, wrote about media coverage of President Clinton in our April issue. He is the author of "The Sixties: Years of Hope, Days of Rage."

was played on at least two evening news shows (CBS and ABC on September 28, 1988) and was obviously packaged by the Bush campaign and fed to the networks. (One of the reports stated that no reporters were on the bus, but, in fact, the two networks in question played identical images of the Bush bus pulling into a small Illinois town lined with cheering crowds. I was thus led to wonder whether this image, too, had been concocted by the Bush media team, fed to the networks, and dutifully broadcast.)

These photo-opportunities were so blatant in their manipulations of the media that even certain media voices became critical of the daily campaign process. On September 21, 1988, CBS News telecast a highly disingenuous attack on the image campaigns (though without really probing the role of television itself in the process). Reporters complained about the lack of substance and threatened to boycott meaningless image events (New York Times, October 4, 1988, p. 1) but continued to play along. The term sound-bite entered the conventional political vocabulary, referring to short fragments of image and sound reproduced in the nightly news. Whereas many commentators deplored the reduction of a political campaign to the production of daily sound-bites, image apologist Dan Quayle defended the practice by stating that "[o]ne-liners say a lot. There are a lot of subtleties communicated with a sound bite. . . . Voters can receive a complex message from a simple one-liner, especially when body language is added in" (NBC Weekend News, October 23, 1988).

The third key ingredient in the mix of media politics—along with TV ads and daily photo-opportunities on the campaign trail—were the television "debates." These manufactured-for-television events had played a key (perhaps even decisive) role in the 1960, 1976, and 1980 elections, and it was here that Dukakis had perhaps his best chance to score some points and perhaps even a knock-out. Like Reagan, Bush frequently makes major blunders in his speeches and spontaneous remarks. Moreover, he has difficulty producing a coherent sentence when he is without a script, and the transcripts of his debates with Dukakis often exhibit incoherent fragments of sentences. Yet, despite his arguably superior performance during the debates, Dukakis failed to gain in the polls that followed. Here, too, image came to dominate substance, and the networks arbitrated political reality.

After the first debate, commentators immediately praised both candidates and the consensus emerged that neither was a big winner. As Christopher Hitchens points out:

Having observed George Bush in the first debate on September 25, some members of the punditocracy were moved to remark that he looked and sounded quite "presidential." In that Bush babbled and bluffed and lied, he can at least be said to have been presidential in the 1980s sense of the term. Toward the end of his ninety minutes of evasion and innuendo he slipped in a breathtaking claim: "And I have long said that I supported the President on this other matter [the Iran arms sales], and I've said mistakes were made. Clearly, nobody's going to think the President started out thinking he was going to trade arms for hostages. That is a very serious charge against the President, and that has been thoroughly looked into." (Hitchens, The Nation, October 17, 1988, p. 333)

Hitchens then documents the magnitude of this lie and notes that neither the network commentators nor the press picked up on this theme, thus continuing to erase the Iran/Contra scandal from popular memory.

After the network commentators' highly dubious opening remarks following the first debate, the country was treated to Bush's "spin doctors." They appeared during the post-debate discussions to proclaim that their man had won, but also that the public had clearly seen the difference between the "nice man and the ice man" (a message dutifully reiterated by Dan Quayle the next day and obligingly taken up as sound-bite by ABC News). The CBS and CNN polls declared Bush the winner, and the commentators (with the exception of William Schneider of the American Enterprise Institute, who on CNN ridiculed Bush's poor performance) made "balanced" comments and thus eliminated the debates as a decisive factor in the election. (The second debate was generally appraised as a draw or slight win for Bush; Dukakis appeared listless and dispirited, whereas Bush appeared breezy and buoyant, if not brilliant.)

Network commentary following the Bentsen/Quayle vice-president debate also favored the Republicans. Much attention has been focused on Quayle's mediocrity and lack of qualifications for the presidency. Indeed, if his performance in the debate had been perceived to be highly incompetent, the Bush campaign would have been in trouble. But the network pundits stepped in yet another time to defuse a potentially damaging situation for the Bush campaign, once again showing the media in the role of conservative consensus management and damage control. Although an ABC poll after the debate declared Quayle the loser (about half the respondents stated that he was unfit to assume the presidency), the network commentators put a positive gloss on Quayle's performance. Jeff Greenfield of ABC claimed that "[h]e did a credible job. . . . Most of the time he performed well." Dan Rather of CBS had this to say: "The bar over which Senator Dan Quayle had to get was pretty low. It seemed to me that he did that. He was calm. He marshalled his arguments rather well." Tom Brokaw of NBC concluded that "[n]o one scored a decisive victory," and John Chancellor of NBC commented in response to Brokaw: "No, but I think Dan Quayle did himself a little bit of good. . . . If you were undecided . . . I think you might feel that Dan Quayle is not the kind of hopeless lightweight the Democrats have said he is" (cited in Boot 1989, 23). The Bush/Quayle "spin doctors" could hardly have spun what many viewers and critics took to be an extremely bad performance into a more positive plus for the Bush campaign.[7]

Then again, perhaps the debates don't really have an impact one way or the other *unless* the networks pull out choice segments to ridicule or clearly declare one candidate the big winner. The claim has been made that Gerald Ford lost the election in 1976 because of his gaffe that Eastern Europe was not dominated by the Soviet Union; however, as some commentators have indicated, the gaffe was not picked up by most viewers until it had been repeated over and over and commented upon for days. TV critics have plausibly argued that a story or point must be continually repeated for at least three full days before it has any real effect on public perception of issues and personalities. The fact remains that television has enormous power to frame issues, to make or break candidates, and to create political reality by selecting stories, events, and images to be highlighted, repeated, and thus impressed upon the national psyche.

But television may have an even deeper, more subtle, and perhaps more insidious power in shaping our perceptions and expectations of political candidates. Indeed, it might be that Bush's personality and physical appearance fit into the television format better than did those of Dukakis and that the debate format (actually a stand-up news conference format) helped Bush. Certainly his easy-going, glib answers segued better into TV talk show and light entertainment formats than did Dukakis's crisp articulation and recitation of facts. In other words, Bush was a resonant TV image whereas Dukakis appeared foreign to the images of the TV world.

Commentators suggested that the "likability factor" became an important factor in the 1988 election (see John Buckley's September 16 *New York Times* op-ed piece). Apparently, there is a certain television model of "likability," and television predetermines what the audience considers "likable." It is precisely those familiar people from TV entertainment programming who provide models of "likability": talk show hosts, celebrity guests, situation comedy characters, TV game show contestants, and so on. Thus a candidate who fits in with standard TV images and fare is likely to come out ahead. Reagan's professional training as an actor enabled him to adapt to the conventional frames and images of popular culture and to project the sort of likability already associated with the characters he had played. And Bush was simply fortunate that his personality type was more compatible with television frames than was the technocratic and distant Dukakis.

In addition, political managers attempt to discern what people consider "likable" and try to get their candidates to ape these characteristics, thus once again employing popular television behavior as a model for politicians to emulate. Dukakis clearly fell into a trap during the second debate, when he attempted to fake an occasional smile, tried to verbally convince the audience that "I'm a likable guy," and backed away from sharply criticizing Bush or the Reagan administration. This emulation of "likable" personality traits thus creates a situation whereby bland television-like personalities become the norm and television images arbitrate what the audience will accept and vote for *and* what it will reject because it does not fit into familiar television frames.

In these ways, the fabricated images in TV ads and "free TV" images in the nightly news became the key components of the 1988 campaign. While the candidates tried to fine-tune their images and manage the sound bites, their campaigns increasingly isolated them from the press and from the public. Whereas Dukakis was initially accessible to the press and attempted to provide substantive positions in his speeches, Bush aggressively attacked his opponent and Dukakis was besieged by reporters asking him to comment on Bush's charges. Dukakis was put on the defensive, and his advisers insulated him from the press as his lead vanished (William Greider, *The Rolling Stone*, November 3, 1988, p. 39). Likewise, Dukakis's team perceived that the news sound-bites were failing to articulate his positions and were presenting him as boring and didactic. Consequently, Dukakis also began to attempt to produce sellable images. In September, for instance, he traveled to Yellowstone Park to be shown in a natural habitat with a lumber jacket. Then, in the campaign's biggest flop, he even allowed himself to be telecast in a tank wearing a helmet, to the great amusement of onlooking reporters. As more and more flags and balloons appeared as backdrops to his appearances, it became clear that the era of image politics had arrived with a vengeance and was perhaps here to stay.

Meanwhile, Ailes, in Leslie Savan's words, had taught "Bush to quit gesturing like a clothesline in the wind, to lower his voice and slow his delivery, to growl from deep within his diaphragm with simulated righteous indignation" (*Village Voice*, October 21, 1988, p. 24). These lessons came in handy when he defended Dan Quayle against media attacks and snarled that the governor of Massachusetts had compared his president to a "rotten fish." And he learned to effectively sneer everytime he used the "L" word, referred to his opponent as a "card-carrying member of the ACLU," and whipped gullible crowds into a frenzy when he implored them to "Read my lips. No-o neww taxes!" These demagogic scenes were complemented by an affable smile as Bush appealed to "values," "a thousand points of light," and "a kinder, gentler nation." The media encouraged this type of empty rhetoric as well as the battle of images, given its own zeal for pictures, its love of spectacles, and its predilection for narrative forms.

Postmodernism and the Politics of the Image

A successful strategy of media politics thus helped George Bush become president. The acceleration of media politics seems to support the postmodern media theory of Jean Baudrillard and others who claim that image has replaced reality in a contemporary media society and that the incessant proliferation of images ("radical semiurgy") has produced a state of affairs whereby individuals can no longer distinguish between the image and the real. In short, they contend, the image has come to constitute a new mass-mediated reality.[8] Baudrillard's postmodern theory rests on the key assumption that the media, simulations, and codes have produced a new realm of experience, a new stage of history, and a new type of society. For Baudrillard, modernity is characterized by production and industrial capitalism, whereas postmodernity is characterized by new technologies, media, and simulations. The postmodern turn thus involves "passage out of a *metallurgic* into a *semiurgic* society" (Baudrillard 1978, 185), and postmodern society is marked by the proliferation of images that define and replace "reality."

In *Simulations*, Baudrillard (1983a) characterizes postmodern society as a social order in which simulation models and codes have come to constitute our architecture, our interior design, our sexual practices, our fashion, and our politics. For Baudrillard, "implosion" is another chief category of postmodern society. This term, taken from Marshall McLuhan's (1964) media theory, signifies a collapse of boundaries between previously separated phenomena—between television and politics, for instance, or between politics and entertainment. In fact, as Reagan's one-time media adviser Michael Deaver has noted in television interviews, because television is primarily concerned with entertainment, television politics must fit into television entertainment codes, just as TV news itself is increasingly structured by entertainment codes (see sections 3.3 and 4.2).

Simulation politics also suggests an implosion between images and reality. Historically, philosophical theories of truth and representation assessed the degree to which images, or ideas, accurately corresponded to reality. According to Baudrillard, however, this situation is reversed in a media society, where "reality" is judged in terms of whether it measures up to media images. For instance, we judge political candidates according to whether they correspond to the image, or model, that the media world has propagated and made familiar. In other words, images have come to define what is real and have obliterated previous distinctions between image and reality. A number of commentators have, in fact, reflected on the 1988 election and our current image politics in these terms. In a *Time* magazine commentary, Lance Morrow remarks that "the candidates perform simulations of encounters with the real world, but the exercise is principally a series of television visuals, of staged events created for TV cameras. The issues have become as weightless as clouds of electrons, and the candidates mere actors in commercials" (October 24, 1988, p. 21).

Consequently, both theorists and journalists now claim that television has become the key factor in politics today.[9] As earlier noted the claims of postmodern media theory are insightful but also seriously limited. First of all, although postmodern cultural critique is often taken as the avant-garde of radical theory, the popular critique of the media based on postmodern theory does not go that far beyond the liberal approach in a film like *Broadcast News*. This critique settles for mild complaints that television news elevates personality over professional competency, image over discourse, style over substance, and simplicity over complexity. Moreover, the excessive rhetoric of much postmodern media theory tends to reduce reality to image and projects a one-dimensional vision of a society completely determined and controlled by image, code, simulations, and cybernetic mechanisms (Baudrillard 1983a, 1983b; Kellner 1989b).

Postmodern media and social theory, however, completely ignores economics and the role of material interests, focusing instead on signs, images, or technologies. A residual idealism and technological determinism thus inform postmodern theory, which claims that the form of media determines the trajectory of contemporary politics and society. For example, postmodern analysis of television and politics ignores the role of money and economic forces, thus obscuring the extent to which corporate interests drive the battle of images in our political marathons. Indeed, the costs of modern elections have skyrocketed because of the need to purchase not only various forms of media but also campaign image "managers." Bush's media guru Roger Ailes, for instance, allegedly received $25,000 a month for his services and took in a $3 million commission for his ads (*Newsweek*, September 26, 1988, p. 19). Television ad spots, in turn, sell for anywhere between $100,000 and $300,000 per minute depending on the specific program, time-slot, ratings, and so on. The high costs of elections thus give big business and political action committees (PACs)—which themselves are largely the products of business and corporate interests—undue influence and power in the U.S. political system.

Such postmodern image fetishism also obscures the importance of structural institutional formations and imperatives in contemporary society. In Chapter 3, I argued that television can best be analyzed in terms of its relations with business and the state, and in terms of the contradictions between capitalism and democracy, commerce and communication. But such structural institutional constituents and contradictions are disregarded by postmodern theory, which attributes exaggerated power and influence to images and, à la McLuhan, to the formal effects of media. Accordingly, although a postmodern media theory such as that of Baudrillard accurately portrays a society fascinated by media images and politics, the issue is not merely that television has reduced politics to a battle of images, substituting image for reality. Rather, media content and effects have more to do with the institutional structure and commercial organization of network television and its position in the U.S. corporate power structure. Thus, although a postmodern critique provides some insights into television, politics, and the current crisis of democracy, it illuminates only part of the problem; indeed, it obscures what I take to be key factors in our current configuration of politics and society.

4.3 Scandals, Omissions, and Capitalist Hegemony

In this section, I shall argue that what does not get on television is as significant as what does get on. As Paul Lazarsfeld and Robert Merton once noted, media power derives "not only from what is said, but more significantly from what is not said. For these media not only continue to affirm the status quo but, in the same measure, they fail to raise essential questions about the structure of society" (Lazarsfeld and Merton: cited in Gitlin 1972, 345). I would add that in serving the status quo, the media fail to pursue some stories while dwelling on others. Constant coverage of Jesse Jackson's off-the-cuff reference to "Hymie town" in the 1984 election produced a negative image of Jackson that cost him credibility and alienated him from many people who perceived him as anti-Semitic; moreover, constant reiteration of this image day after day fixed the event in the public memory. Yet significant scandals concerning other political candidates have been ignored or briefly noted and then dropped.

In regard to the 1988 election, omission of adequate coverage of a series of scandals involving Bush, Quayle, and the Reagan administration was as significant to the final outcome as was the transformation of politics into a battle of images. More specifically, I would argue that George Bush was elected president largely due to the failure of the mainstream broadcast media to report in any detail on the many scandals in which he was implicated during the Reagan years—including involvement with Panamanian dictator and drug dealer Manuel Noriega, connections to an illegal Contra supply operation also involved in drug dealing, and participation in the illegal arms-for-hostages deal with the Iranian ayatollahs (see Appendixes A through C for details and documentation).

The Reagan/Bush group's illegal deals with the Iranians allegedly date back to the fall of 1980, when Reagan was involved in a close race for the presidency with Jimmy Carter. According to stories widely reported in the investigative press but generally ignored in the mainstream media, the Reagan election team cut a deal with the Iranian ayatollahs to hold the Americans hostage in Iran until after the 1980 presidential election, so that Carter would not benefit from an "October Surprise" (i.e., patriotism and relief from the release of the hostages) that might secure him the presidency. According to widespread reports, the Reagan team successfully cut a deal with the Iranians to the effect that the hostages would not be released until the day of Reagan's inauguration. Thereafter, it is alleged, the Reagan administration began sending (via Israel) arms shipments to Iran, thus enabling the Iranians to carry through their war with Iraq. It has also been claimed that George Bush, who was head of the CIA in 1976 and Reagan's vice-presidential candidate in 1980, played a significant role in the negotiations (see Appendixes A and C.3).

The "October Surprise" story was ignored totally by network television. The mainstream media also failed to investigate either Bush's record as head of the CIA or well-documented allegations that he was in the CIA as early as 1962—a claim denied by Bush's team but argued in *The Nation* and other print media sources (see Appendix C.1). Persistent charges that Bush was deeply involved in the illegal arms sales to Iran were ignored, as were charges that the illegal arms network to the Contras was run out of Bush's office by his assistant Donald Gregg, before Oliver North took over as frontman for the operation. There was also no real television investigation of the claims that this illegal Contra arms-supply operation was involved with Noriega, who used the operation to bring illegal drugs back into the United States (see Appendix C.3).

Indeed, none of these potentially explosive scandals were investigated and aired. The mainstream broadcast media generally ignored Bush's past record in their coverage of the 1988 election—even though it was reported and developed by the investigative press, including *The Nation, In These Times, Mother Jones, The Progressive, Village Voice, Playboy, Rolling Stone,* and a variety of other publications. I maintain that the failure of television and the other mainstream media to investigate these stories reveals the extent of media corruption in the United States. By extension, I would also argue that the mainstream media neither went down on "bended knee" to the Reagan administration, as Hertsgaard (1988) argues, nor simply "bellied up." Rather, they were an active force in negotiating and establishing an ultimately centrist conservative hegemony in the 1980s.

In a sense, the disgraceful role of the mainstream media in actively serving the Reagan and Bush administrations demonstrates the steady erosion of investigative reporting and honest journalism since the days of Edward R. Murrow and Fred Friendly at CBS, or since the Watergate investigations conducted by Carl Bernstein, Bob Woodward, and others in the 1970s. It seems that the mainstream media—especially television—have managed over the years to eliminate all the mavericks, forcing out independent journalists such as Murrow, Friendly, and Daniel Schorr while cultivating the more docile and malleable media personalities who read and present the "news" to the nation. A more conservative atmosphere was also present in the television industry during the 1980s, and television—despite its enormous power—seemed less inclined to critically report on the failings of the Reagan administration and on Bush's involvement in many scandals of the era. Why is this so, and what do these trends portend for journalism and democracy in the United States? Analysis of these questions should lay to rest the persistent conservative claims that the media have a "liberal bias."

Antiliberal Bias?

Since Spiro Agnew's assault on network television in 1969, a legion of conservative pundits, researchers, and writers have claimed that there is a liberal bias in television news and entertainment (see section 1.1). Radical critics, by contrast, contend that television manifests a conservative bias, that it serves as a powerful ideological tool for reproducing the status quo, and that it is governed solely by the logic of capital. Although I generally concur with the radical position, I have argued that at some historical junctures the media have sided with certain sectors of the ruling class while occasionally making concessions to public interest groups and progressive political movements. In addition, I have argued that when the audience has seemed to be on the left or liberal side of the spectrum, as in the late 1960s and early 1970s, television has exhibited what appears to be a "liberal bias" (see section 2.3). But I have also argued that television during the 1980s clearly exhibited an antiliberal bias and that it helped forge a moderate conservative hegemony, eventually delegitimating the more extreme right-wing views of many in the Reagan administration—views to which the media gave some legitimacy in the early to mid-1980s. When Reagan and key members of his administration went too far to the right during the mid-1980s, the media exposed the scandals of the Iran/Contra affair and helped eliminate the extreme right wing (see section 4.1). But since George Bush fit in with a more centrist conservative ideology, the mainstream media had no problem supporting him.

Reagan's deregulation program had given the networks almost everything they wanted—deregulation, tax breaks, the possibility of corporate mergers, and the ability to expand their operations. Yet they were denied one goal—namely, permission to own and syndicate their own programming. In the early 1970s the networks had signed consent decrees with the Justice Department antitrust division that prevented them from producing their own television entertainment series. The government argued that the networks had unfairly extracted financial concessions from independent producers in negotiating contracts for TV series such as situation comedies and police dramas. Thus the networks were forced to buy their series programming from Hollywood production studios that they did not own or control. This system prevented the networks from selling programs to local affiliates for re-runs. Throughout the 1980s the networks sought to have these rules rescinded, but Reagan—because of his close ties to the Hollywood production community—refused to grant this wish.[10] Consequently, the networks hoped that Bush would do so.

Rescindment of the production/syndication rules would be a multibillion-dollar bonanza for the networks. Programming costs are growing by nearly 8 percent a year and, as of 1990, top $4.5 billion; if the networks produced their own programs, they could cut back on programming costs. Syndication rights range from $100 million for a moderately successful situation comedy to more than $600 million for a blockbuster success like "The Cosby Show" (*Business Week*, November 13, 1989, pp. 92–93); thus, if the networks could produce their own series, they could enter the highly profitable syndication market. In addition, the networks could gain additional millions of dollars if they could produce programming and sell it to the lucrative foreign market, which is expected to reach $3.7 billion for U.S. distributors by 1992 (see section 3.2). This tremendous expansion of the profit potential has led the networks to put heavy pressure on the Bush administration to rescind the "financial interest" (i.e., in producing programming) and syndication rules (labeled the "fin-syn" rules by the networks). The networks' desires to expand into production would naturally lead them to support more conservative candidates who favored deregulation and were friendly to network interests. Accordingly, when Robert Wright became president of NBC in 1986, one of his first acts was to establish a Political Action Committee for NBC employees that would be used to support conservative candidates; however, opposition to this plan within the organization and the leaking of the story to the press forced Wright to abandon the project (*Broadcasting*, December 15, 1986, p. 58).

Did the hopes of gaining rescindment of the production/syndication rules lead the networks to favor Bush in the 1988 election? In the previous section, I argued that television aided Bush's election by refusing to air a series of controversial stories that implicated him in a wide-ranging number of scandals and questionable activities. By contrast, the networks broadcast many rumors concerning Dukakis, including the story planted by the extremist Lyndon LaRouche group that he had undergone treatment for severe mental problems, the rumor that his wife Kitty had burned a U.S. flag in an antiwar demonstration, and the rumor that some of his top campaign officials used drugs.[11] Yet the mainstream media did not broadcast much of anything concerning the "October Surprise" story, the Contra guns/drug story, Bush's CIA record and connections, the extent of Bush's involvement with Noriega, or rumors that Bush had had a long-time affair with his appointments secretary Jennifer Fitzgerald, as well as affairs with other women.[12]

More generally, during the 1988 election the mainstream media neglected to probe into what might be called the "sleaze factor" and the corruption that permeated the Reagan administration and the Bush team. The Reagan administration was one of the most corrupt in history, with more than 100 officials accused of illegal activities and many top officials resigning in disgrace or being indicted after leaving the government.[13] Establishment media also failed to delve into the corruption in which top officials of the Bush campaign were implicated. One of Bush's key managers, Lee Atwater, had recently worked for a public relations firm that was under contract to promote the image of the government of the Bahamas, which in turn was under attack because of allegations of drug-dealing. Furthermore, Stuart Spencer, who was in charge of Quayle's campaign, worked for a PR firm that was employed by Noriega to improve the dictator's image (*Time*, September 19, 1988, p. 21). There was little reporting on the anti-Semitic and fascist groups that supported Bush—groups with which he frequently associated at rallies, in the White House, and elsewhere (John Judis, *In These Times*, September 28, 1988, pp. 6–7).

Various other subtle and not-so-subtle biases against Dukakis and in favor of Bush emerged in the daily broadcast coverage of the campaign. The networks bought into the Bush "photo-opportunity" strategy, presenting nightly images beneficial to Bush; but this was not the case in their coverage of Dukakis. Indeed, when the Dukakis campaign picked up momentum in the aftermath of Dukakis and Bentsen's effective debate performances, the networks highlighted a blunder in the Dukakis campaign (the candidate had made a chauvinistic buy-American speech at a factory owned by an Italian company).

Careful scrutiny of the campaign coverage in 1988 discloses many examples of such negative coverage of the Dukakis campaign, a bias even more blatantly evident in CNN's daily coverage of the election. CNN could count on conservative ideologues Patrick Buchanan and Robert Novak to savage the Democrats in their frequent talk shows and commentary; "liberal" commentator Stephen Hess from the Brookings Institution could be counted on to smilingly ratify the conservative position, with "liberal" Tom Braden limited to ineffective bluster; and CNN anchorperson Bernard Shaw opened the final debate with the question of whether the Democratic candidate would favor the death penalty for someone who raped and killed his wife Kitty. More subtle bias was evident in the CNN nightly news coverage, which frequently used flattering images of Bush and Quayle while highlighting more negatively coded images of Dukakis and Bentsen. For instance, in the flush of victory following Bentsen's debate with Quayle, most of the networks showed Dukakis and Bensen enjoying a (quite temporary) rush in popularity and enthusiasm among their crowds. On the same night that the three networks showed generally positive images of Bentsen on the offensive (October 6, 1988), CNN alternated images of a mean Bentsen beating on Quayle in the debate with images of an old, tired Bentsen dragging on the campaign trail.

Indeed, the use of selective images, camera angles, lighting, editing, juxtaposition of images, commentary, and so on, can code a nightly news blip as positive or negative. For example, on October 7, 1988, the CNN nightly news report opened with Bush speaking out on crime. The visuals, which included the by-now familiar mugshot of Willie Horton, showed Bush surrounded by adoring police officials while he gave his speech. They also zeroed in on a *Reader's Digest* article, being circulated by the Bush team, that detailed how Dukakis's prison furlough program had gone sour. The visuals then cut (rather gratuitously, one might say) to Bush and Dukakis coming out to shake hands at the first debate, with Bush towering over Dukakis; and then to a news conference with relatives of some of the victims of criminals released on Dukakis's furlough program, complaining about Dukakis's complete lack of sensitivity toward victims of crime— precisely the point that CNN showed Bush making in his speech. In these ways, CNN provided dramatic and obviously well-orchestrated confirmation of Bush's points concerning Dukakis's failed crime program—allegations that Dukakis later denied.

After this long and positive Bush report, CNN cut to an image of Dukakis, looking somewhat sinister in dark glasses as he visited an automobile factory. As earlier noted, it focused on his gaffe concerning the "buy America" speech he had given in a factory owned by Italians. This negative report was followed by a quick clip of Bentsen, shot at a distance and looking away from the camera, who, rather nastily, called Quayle an "incredible misfit." This was consistent with CNN's theme of old man Bentsen attacking nice young Dan. The report ended with the omnipresent CNN poll, which showed the Republicans ahead 49 percent to 40 percent. (In fact, CNN repeatedly showed the Republicans as being 10 points ahead during the last month, whereas the other polls usually depicted a 3 to 5 point spread.)

A more subtle example on network bias against the Democrats is found in this analysis by William Boot:

> October 19. We see the governor [Dukakis] in shirt sleeves speaking to an outdoor rally in Illinois. He denounces the Bush people for purveying "garbage . . . political garbage"—referring to a brochure declaring that criminals such as the notorious Massachusetts rapist-on-furlough Willie Horton would be voting for Dukakis.
>
> Cut to scene on a campaign motorcade bus, where we see Dukakis struggling ineffectually to close his window. It seems that Sam Donaldson and crew have been given access to the candidate's own bus. (That alone would have constituted news had it occurred on the Bush campaign.) Donaldson: "Did you see in the paper that Willie Horton said if he could vote he would vote for you?" Dukakis (face impassive, eyes averted from Donaldson, still struggling with window): "He can't vote, Sam." (Boot 1989, 25; emphasis in original)

The visuals in this report replicated precisely those images (of Willie Horton) that the Bush team wished to circulate; they also portrayed an ineffectual Dukakis unable to open the window. Still other network biases occurred as a result of pseudo-objectivity and rigged attempts to "balance" criticism. That is, almost every report concerning negative advertising and the rather low level of the campaign made equal criticisms of the Bush and Dukakis teams, even though the Dukakis ads rarely attacked Bush personally or distorted his record. Thus the attempt at "balance" made it appear that both candidates were equally involved in misrepresenting the other's record, mud-slinging, and negative campaigning.

Probably the most blatant media bias in the 1988 campaign was present in their treatment of Jesse Jackson. During the primary season, the mainstream media neglected Jackson almost completely, devoting much more coverage to such also-rans as Bruce Babbit, Dick Gebhardt, Albert Gore, and Robert Dole. When Jackson won the Super Tuesday primary elections and then briefly surged ahead of Dukakis by winning the Michigan primary, the media suddenly turned attention to Jackson—but the result was not pretty. The television networks labeled him a "spoiler" and widely reported the claims concerning his alleged anti-Semitism made during the Pennsylvania and New York primaries. *Time* magazine kicked in with a grotesquely racist article, incisively dissected by Susan Douglas in *In These Times* (April 20, 1988, p. 16).

Douglas points out that the *Time* story on Jackson of April 11, 1988, uses the word *passion* repeatedly to associate the candidate with violent and uncontrollable emotions. He is also referred to twice as the "illegitimate son of a teen-age mother." In Douglas's words, "Adjectives used to describe him include 'provocative,' 'beguiling,' 'fiery' and 'impetuous.' As a candidate, Jackson 'arouses Democratic passions.' His relationship to his supporters is really a 'love affair.' But this is not some innocent, romantic puppy love: his devotees are consumed by a 'fever.' 'Hundreds of supporters chased their champion down a dark street after nightfall.' Jackson, 'infused with a frontrunner's frenzy,' has 'unleashed primordial Democratic passions' " (ibid.).

As the 1988 Democratic convention approached, the media presented Jackson as a "spoiler" who might destroy Democratic unity. During the convention, Jackson was linked to "special interests" and presented as a force of disunity who was "causing trouble" because of his challenges to Democratic platform planks (Lee and Solomon 1990, 156f.). The media did give him a moment in the spotlight when he presented a stirring convention speech, but after the convention, however, Jackson once again disappeared almost completely from television's coverage of the election—despite his almost daily campaign trips on behalf of Dukakis. Obviously, the media did not want to give credence to a left populist political program, such as

Jackson's, that attempted to mobilize the poor and oppressed who had been left out of the conservative celebration of the 1980s. The negative and often nonexistent coverage of Jackson also, I believe, attests to the "right turn" taken by the media during the 1980s.

But this conservative hegemony can also be attributed to the collapse and bankruptcy of liberalism. Congressional liberals submitted to this hegemony by failing either to oppose Reagan or to offer alternative programs and visions. The 1984 and 1988 presidential campaigns of Mondale and Dukakis were especially pathetic, with Dukakis failing to embrace liberalism until late in the campaign. Establishment liberals appeared in the 1980s to be totally bereft of ideas, vision, courage, and leadership. The failure of liberals to articulate sharp critiques of and alternative policies to Reaganism contributed to the conservative hegemony because the form of television requires a "balanced" presentation, with top Democratic party spokespeople called upon to comment on the conservative policies. If they fail to articulate sharp opposition and alternatives, the conservative policies will dominate. The collapse of liberalism thus contributed significantly to the conservative hegemony of the 1980s.

Capitalist Media

As noted, television significantly aided Bush in his election effort and promoted Reagan during his reign by deflecting or diminishing the most serious criticisms while simply glossing over the worst crimes and scandals. Thus, it is safe to conclude that the media took a "right turn" during the 1980s.[14] I am not, however, claiming that the media's undeniable move to the right in the 1980s was a conspiratorial action on the part of a small group of individuals who plotted out successive moves in the making of a conservative hegemony. The media are both active and reactive; on the whole, they tend to be opportunistic and timid. They are also in complicity with the interests of the dominant ruling elites—whoever they are. Above all, the media are businesses that are governed by the "bottom line" and must get good ratings to keep up profits. In a highly competitive market situation, such as the television business, the networks play to what they perceive as the prevailing ideological currents. Such events as the election of a conservative president and the defeat of key liberal senators in the 1980 election impressed the media, and they played to what they consider to be the new ideological trends (see the related discussion in sections 2.5 and 3.4). Furthermore, there were reports by various news personnel during the 1980s to the effect that, when the media were too critical of Reagan there was a strong negative audience response. In this climate, ratings-conscious media managers—or reporters wishing to keep their jobs—no doubt softened their criticism.

Indeed, there were also reports that a significant shift in news operations took place in the 1980s—a shift related to increased competition for ratings and profits.[15] Hertsgaard reports, for instance, on the impact of Van Gordon Sauter on CBS news (1988, 172ff.). With its evening news rating falling, CBS brought in Sauter from CBS sports to run the news division. Sauter's primary concern was to boost the ratings, and in the process he cut back on national political news, increased human interest stories, and eliminated many of the "old guard" at CBS News who resisted such changes. Budget cuts helped legitimate his revamping of the news operation, and the result was a marked decline in investigative journalism, political coverage, and criticism of the Reagan administration.

Sauter advanced the rather novel philosophical view that the function of the network news was to establish "a national agenda of aspirations, of apprehension, of joy and purpose" (ibid., 174). As Hertsgaard notes, such a conception of journalism is inconsistent with the position that its function is to provide adversarial coverage and to present issues of public concern in a balanced fashion (ibid.). Indeed, positive coverage of the British royal family dramatically increased under Sauter's reign, and the Reagans themselves were often presented as royalty. Sauter's "innovations" worked, however, and CBS News returned to the top of the evening news ratings. The lesson was not lost on other networks, which also revamped the format of their news programs; NBC, for instance, eventually (albeit temporarily) topped CBS in the ratings by bringing in a former PR man as news division president, increasing the percentage of tabloid-style news, and heavily promoting Tom Brokaw and the NBC news team in saturation advertising (ibid., 177–178).

The corporate conglomerate take-overs in the 1980s also had a serious impact on network news operations (see sections 2.5 and 3.2). All three networks severely cut back on news personnel and thus had fewer investigative reporters at their disposal. The new corporate climate was increasingly conservative, and news personnel who wished to survive the cuts no doubt moderated critical reports that went against the interests and views of the new corporate managers. The threat of a take-over of the "liberal" network CBS by Ted Turner, Jesse Helms, and other rightist groups in the mid-1980s probably helped curtail reporting critical of the Reagan administration; and when the Tisch group eventually took over CBS in 1986, its first act was to drastically cut back on the news operation, thus further intimidating any "liberals" left at CBS and producing the clear message that people could lose their jobs at any time if they didn't toe the corporate line.

Furthermore, right-wing pressure groups used a variety of strategies to push and keep network news coverage on the right track. For instance, the "Accuracy in Media" group carried out campaigns against programs with a "liberal bias" and demanded, and sometimes received, free time to "answer" supposedly liberal programs (see section 5.2). Lawsuits by General William Westmoreland against a CBS Vietnam documentary, and by Israeli General Ariel Sharon against *Time* magazine, pressured the media against criticizing right-wing politicians who were taking up libel lawsuits to keep the media in check. Both Westmoreland and Sharon lost their lawsuits, but these highly publicized media events had a chilling effect on the mainstream media, no doubt checking critical discourse.

The relentless commercialism of network television also led to a dramatic decrease in documentaries during the 1980s. As Hertsgaard reports, whereas each network broadcast around twenty documentaries a year during the 1960s, by 1985 all three networks together were broadcasting a mere fourteen hours worth. Instead, news magazines such as ABC's "20/20" and CBS's "West 57th" appeared, along with "reality programming" (sensationalistic tabloid journalism of the sort found in the New York *Daily News* or *Post*), including Geraldo Rivera's "exposés" of satanism and live drug busts. In this way, political journalism turned toward tabloid journalism and away from political analysis and criticism.

The competition for ratings and profits thus led inexorably to cutbacks on political reporting and to increases in sensationalistic and "positive" news stories. Thus, it is clear that there was more corporate control over news in the 1980s and, as I have argued, a distinctive conservative bias. Indeed, the notion of a liberal bias in the news is no longer convincing. Well-organized and well-financed right-wing media watchdog groups and other conservative organizations applied a firm and steady pressure on television to avoid any "liberal bias" during the 1980s. Conservative groups vocally and aggressively attacked the media every time they criticized Reagan or policies favored by conservatives, and the media were seemingly sensitive to these charges of "liberal bias."

In their concerted attempt not to appear too liberal, media liberals ended up helping to create a conservative hegemony. As Mark Miller put it in a *New York Times* op-ed piece (November 16, 1988), "Telejournalists, finally, are also burdened by their own convictions—for, by and large, they are indeed a bunch of liberals. But this ideological slant has worked *against* any 'liberal bias' by the TV news, as reporters bend over backwards not to seem at all critical of Republicans. Eager to evince his 'objectivity,' the edgy liberal reporter ends up just as useful to the right as any ultra-rightist hack." Although Miller's psychologistic analysis has some value, I believe it has been the actual pressure from corporate managers, right-wing groups, and the government that made the networks so edgy about the prospect of alienating the Right. Such pressures connect with the fact that the networks are businesses, obsessively concerned with rating points, and thus eager not to alienate any major constituency that would be likely to tune out and tune in to another channel. This indeed helps explain why the

concern w/ profits + not offending

establishment media went so easy on Reagan: Every time they criticized him sharply, there was such a conservative outcry that they feared losing viewers or readers if they came down too hard on him.

In addition, the Reagan administration had set up a national propaganda ministry to sell its highly unpopular Central America policies to the public— a "program" that was centered on manipulating the media and public opinion (Parry and Kornbluh 1988). Organized around the model of a domestic CIA operation, this government project specialized in disinformation and intimidation of the administration's critics. It is highly possible that fear of government harassment prevented some individuals in the mainstream media from more overtly exposing and attacking the secret (and not so secret) wars and many scandals of the Reagan and Bush administrations. Indeed, mainstream reporters depend on government contacts to get "scoops" and "insider" information that might give them an edge on their competitors. Consequently, such journalists are unlikely to be overly critical of a government in office for fear of losing their "sources" and access to government officials and information.

This dependence on government sources has also helped the government to manipulate the network news and to plant stories and "disinformation" that aids its policies. There are many examples of such government manipulation of the networks during the Reagan administration. Hertsgaard tells in detail how some ABC reporters discovered that the Grenada invasion was under way and how the network held back on the story because their chief Pentagon correspondent, John McWethy, was assured by his government contacts that there was no invasion forthcoming at all (1988, 206ff.). Mayer and McManus (1988, 222) recount how McWethy and another government informant dissuaded ABC from breaking the story of the impending bombing of Libya (1988, 222). Carlisle (1988) tells of how McWethy served as the vehicle for a false story concerning the attempted assassination of Contra leader Eden Pastora, which might have been part of a disinformation project to justify an invasion of Nicaragua (see Appendix B). McWethy also broke the "story" that Russian MIGs were being sent to Nicaragua on the day of the 1984 election—a story that turned out to be totally untrue. McWethy was awarded for his (ideological) service with recognition by his peers as the top "diplomatic" correspondent of the networks (*TV Guide*, July 15, 1989, p. 5).

Indeed, many major media commentators and correspondents are, like McWethy, blatantly conservative. ABC commentator George Will helped Reagan rehearse for his debate with Carter in 1980 with a debate book stolen from the Carter campaign; in his commentary for ABC, not surprisingly, he praised Reagan's debate performance. As a mark of absent journalist integrity during the 1980s, Will was allowed to remain with ABC, even after the story of his involvement with the stolen debate book was revealed; thus he was allowed to support Reagan's policies and even to call for an invasion of Nicaragua. Reporter Diane Sawyer, who has held positions with both CBS and ABC, had worked for the Nixon White House, had helped Nixon write his memoirs, and was a conservative activist; but this background did not disqualify her as a network correspondent. Thus, claims of a "liberal bias" in television news are hardly credible.

On the contrary, there is much evidence to indicate that during the 1980s the networks actively engaged in the forging of a conservative hegemony: Television constantly served as a vehicle for Reagan/Bush dis-information, and it was heavily biased toward Republicans. Hence I conclude that it is because of the control of media institutions by multinational capital (big business) that the media have been biased toward conservativism, thus furthering what they perceive as their own economic interests. Increased corporate control, cutbacks of news departments, and a more conservative working environment helped push the networks toward privileging conservative positions during the 1980s—whatever the political proclivities of the journalists themselves might have been. NBC—the biggest and probably most conservative network conglomerate (which was taken over by General Electric)—failed to investigate any of the scandals mentioned in this chapter and discussed in detail in the Appendixes. As other media critics have shown, NBC has been a conduit for the most outrageous anticommunist propaganda (Parenti 1986; Herman and Chomsky 1988), and on the domestic front it has most blatantly ignored the scandals and failings in the corporate capitalist system.[16]

Immediately after NBC's merger with GE, a major producer in the nuclear energy industry, NBC broadcast a documentary touting the benefits of nuclear energy by focusing on France's nuclear power industry. This came during a time when it appeared that the Chernobyl nuclear accident in the Soviet Union had conclusively demonstrated the insanity of nuclear power. As noted, NBC president Robert Wright attempted to form a company PAC, continuing the GE policy of staunchly supporting conservative candidates (recall that Ronald Reagan was a GE employee during the 1950s and 1960s). The fact that this corporation—one of the major producers of nuclear weapons and energy, a top defense contractor, and a key player in the military-industrial complex (INFACT 1988)—was allowed to take over a major television network and use it to advance its corporate goals makes a mockery of the antitrust laws, the public utility status of broadcasting, and the federal regulatory apparatus.

ABC, CBS, and CNN are also guilty of extreme bias toward the Reagan and Bush administrations and, hence, of furthering centrist conservativism. In a story about the reasons for which ABC spiked controversial stories concerning close friends of Ronald Reagan in 1984, Mark Dowdie suggests that ABC was interested in a lucrative merger it was negotiating and, because of its business interests, might have killed stories that could have endangered Reagan's reelection or angered him (*Mother Jones*, November–December 1985, pp. 33ff.). GE/NBC and the other networks are currently interested in having the Bush FCC rescind rules that prevent the networks from producing programming and syndicating popular series. The networks see a lucrative future in entertainment and information enterprises, and want to maximize their intervention in these areas. Consequently, it is unlikely they will be excessively critical of the Bush administration with so much at stake in gaining a favorable ruling.

Mainstream commercial broadcast media in the United States are therefore best interpreted at this juncture in history as *capitalist media,* as ideological mouthpieces for the corporate capitalist system. The broadcast media during the 1980s were captured (and corrupted) by the same conservative economic interests that captured the state, and they constitute essential elements of the conservative hegemony of the 1980s. It is thus incorrect to conceptualize today's media (especially network television) as a "fourth estate" (i.e., as an autonomous journalistic force), for they willingly serve their capitalist masters and the dominant conservative forces. In short, network television is the shame of the nation today—a complacent, compliant servant of power. Rather than promoting democracy, robust public debate, and an informed public opinion, the networks diminish and weaken U.S. democracy. They also promote the conservative interests that own and control them, thus precipitating a massive crisis of democracy and journalism in the United States today.

I conclude, therefore, that a severe imbalance between capitalism and democracy, between commerce and journalism, has occurred, such that capital and commerce dominate democracy and journalism. While at some junctures in U.S. history democracy was threatened by state control or state censorship of the media, the main dangers to democracy and journalism now result from excessive capitalist control of the media. Accordingly, the future of American journalism and democracy is in dire peril. Unless the media become responsible, investigative, and critical of the powers that be, there is no hope that a functioning, viable, and genuine democracy might someday exist in the United States.

In fact, there has never been fully participatory democracy in the United States. The U.S. Constitution was developed by property owners who organized the system of government to defend their own economic interests and to guarantee control of the political system by the wealthy, propertied classes (Beard 1965 [orig. 1913]). Only property-holding white men had the vote, while black men were refused the vote until after the Civil War, and women did not receive voting rights until 1920. In addition, the inauguration of poll taxes and literacy tests in the 1890s reduced the United States from having one of the highest percentages of individuals voting in elections to a rather low percentage, which has dropped sharply in recent years. Further, "democracy" in the United States has generally been limited to choice of candidates from parties and groups who serve the ruling powers. This sort of "formal democracy" limits democracy to periodic voting rituals, while more robust, participatory democracy, in which individuals would participate in actual debate, decisionmaking, and political activity, has been severely curtailed. Moreover, there has been little economic democracy instituted in the United States, and most major institutions are ruled hierarchically with little substantive democratic participation.

And yet even the minimal, formal democracy operative in the United States has provided more or less fair political contests with the broadcast media being at least somewhat neutral until the 1980s when, as I have argued, they came to support the conservative, Republican agenda (newspapers, by contrast, have traditionally been heavily Republican-owned and sharply partisan toward conservative Republican candidates). Elsewhere in the world, however, democracy has become a vibrant and powerful ideology that has motivated struggle and upheaval. The United States has proclaimed its superiority over communist regimes by virtue of its commitments to democracy, and its declared foreign policy is to promote democracy throughout the world.

Running counter to this worldwide trend toward democratization, the right turn of the television industry and its takeover by conservative corporations have severely undermined even formal democracy in the United States by the television networks' partisan support of the conservative agenda. Thus, I argue that during the Reagan/Bush years, powerful corporations took over the major television networks and transformed them into blatant corporate tools to advance corporate interests. In this situation, the television networks siding with conservative administrations, which were advancing the business agenda, have eroded the balance of power in the U.S. constitutional system. During the 1980s and early 1990s, the networks have largely failed to criticize the corruption and crimes of the ruling conservative administration, while promoting its shamelessly pro-business economic policies and interventionist foreign policy. Their failure to broadcast stories that would raise serious questions about the competency and suitability for public office of Reagan, Bush, and others threatens the very lifeblood of democracy, which requires an informed electorate to make intelligent decisions concerning governing elites. The takeover of television networks by giant corporate conglomerates and the decline of the federal regulatory apparatus have compromised the media, which are supposed to be a public utility serving the public interest, separate from and critical of the policies of the state and business.

The crisis of democracy thus involves a dramatic shift in the balance of power between major institutions, with the television networks ever more firmly entrenched within the heart of transnational capital. It involves a right turn by the television industry that has made it an accomplice of the conservative economic and political forces that were hegemonic in the 1980s. And it raises questions as to whether there will be fair and free elections in the United States in the future. What, then, are the chances that noncommercial media such as public television, public access television, and new video technologies might promote democracy in the United States? What are the prospects for an alternative system of broadcasting in the United States?

Notes

1. On the media and politics in the contemporary era, see Nimmo and Combs (1983), Hertsgaard (1988), and Luke (1989). On Reagan and the media, see Deaver (1987), Mayer and McManus (1988), Regan (1988), and Schieffer and Gates (1989).

2. On "pseudo-events" see Boorstin (1962), and on media spectacle see Debord (1975). On media spectacles of the Reagan years, see Luke (1989) and Schulte-Sasse (1987–1988).

3. For a discussion of how Reagan's films and the Hollywood mindset influenced his world view, see Rogin (1987) and Ducat (1988). On the dominant ideological frames of U.S. popular culture and the extent to which Reagan's mindset is in accord with these frames, see Jewett and Lawrence (1988).

4. On the previous day, the *New York Times* reported that a Middle Eastern magazine had stated that McFarlane and others were exchanging arms with the Iranians for the release of the American hostages held by radical Islamic groups in the Middle East that supposedly had close ties with Iran. On November 6, the *Los Angeles Times* and the *Washington Post* published fuller versions of the story, and the television networks picked up on it.

5. On the Iran/Contra scandal, see Cockburn (1988), Marshall, Scott, and Hunter (1987), Woodward (1988), and Appendix B.

6. Several reports in 1987 and 1988 indicated that Bush's involvement in Iran/Contra would destroy his chances for winning the presidency. See the accounts that detail his involvement in the scandal in *Newsweek,* February 8, 1988; *Newsweek,* May 23, 1988; and the *Christian Science Monitor,* May 19, 1988. See, especially, the references cited in the Appendixes. In May 1988 there was a flurry of reports linking Bush to the illegal Contra arms/drug ring, as well as articles linking him to Noriega (see Appendix C.2). Suddenly, such stories were dropped completely, and television, the mainstream media, and the timid Democrats failed to pursue the stories during the election campaign.

7. Curiously, a Dan Quayle gaffe similar to Ford's went unnoticed by the commentators, who were presumably looking for such signs of his ignorance and incompetence. In response to a question concerning the Central America policy of the Reagan administration and the Bush/Quayle team, Quayle responded: "There's another issue that Michael Dukakis is wrong on in Central America. And that's

Grenada." None of the pundits managed to note that Grenada is not in Central America. The network commentators let him get away with this, as did later reporters. One wonders what the results would have been if the networks had cited and repeatedly replayed such misstatements. The mainstream media also did not pursue allegations that Dan Quayle was a regular drug consumer during the 1960s and that his alleged drug dealer was put in solitary confinement at the orders of federal prison officials when, right before the 1988 election, he began to tell reporters details of his drug sales to Quayle; see Lee and Solomon 1990, 162ff. and Joel Bleifuss, *In These Times* (Aug. 15–28, 1990, pp. 4–5).

8. On postmodern theory, see Baudrillard (1978, 1983a, 1983b) and the critiques in Kellner (1987, 1989b).

9. A journalistic version of the postmodern image critique is found in a critical analysis by William Boot (1989). Although Boot presents a good analysis of how the media were manipulated by (or in complicity with) the Bush campaign, the analysis centers on the politics of the image and fails to penetrate into the deeper reasons for network support of Bush and the conservative hegemony of the 1980s. In addition, Boot fails to mention any of the damning stories concerning the Reagan administration and Bush that were circulated in the investigative press and yet were ignored in the mainstream media—stories on which I shall focus in the next section. Boot thus reveals the limits of liberal media critique and disregards the more distressing aspects of the media's function in the 1988 election and beyond. An academic version of the popularized postmodern media critique is found in the articles collected in Gitlin (1987) and criticized in Best and Kellner (1987). There are thus two versions of the postmodern media theory: the more extreme version advanced by Baudrillard and his followers, and the popularized version found in much political journalism and in some academic studies of the media and contemporary culture.

10. For evidence indicating that the networks had been keenly interested in rescinding the production/syndication rules since the early 1980s, see *Broadcasting,* December 6, 1982, pp. 71–72. For indications of current interest, see *Forbes,* April 17, 1989, p. 127; *Broadcasting,* January 22, 1990, p. 32; and *Business Week,* November 13, 1989, p. 88.

11. The LaRouche group circulated a press release at the 1988 Democratic convention to the effect that Dukakis had undergone psychiatric treatment for a nervous breakdown. The story surfaced in the mainstream media during a press conference in late July. When Ronald Reagan was asked to comment on the report, he smugly joked that he "was not going to pick on an invalid." The *Columbia Journalism Review* criticized "*The Washington Times,* for not letting the facts get in the way of a juicy anti-Dukakis story. The paper's August 4 follow-up on all those ugly rumors that the Democratic candidate had undergone psychiatric treatment for depression quoted Dukakis's sister-in-law as saying, 'It's possible, but I doubt it. It may have been on a friendly basis, one friend to another in private. I don't know. . . . I wasn't with him all the time'; the distorting headling read DUKAKIS KIN HINTS AT SESSIONS." The mainstream media also repeated the charge while ignoring completely all the more serious and well-grounded accusations leveled at Bush. Schieffer and Gates (1989, 363ff.) point to the widespread circulation of the story and suggest that it damaged Dukakis even though it was purely fabricated.

12. Documentation for these stories is provided in the Appendixes.

13. On corruption in the Reagan administration, see notes 1–8 in Appendixes for sources and Schieffer and Gates (1989, 308), who describe what they call the "sleaze epidemic" in the Reagan years: "Toward the end of Reagan's presidency, some zealous reporter compiled a list of transgressors. The final tally revealed that more than a hundred members of the administration had been accused of either criminal or ethical misdeeds. That record invites comparison not with Watergate— which was essentially an exercise in the abuse of power—but with the excesses of the Teapot Dome scandal that occurred during the term of Warren G. Harding."

14. The term *right turn* is borrowed from Ferguson and Rogers (1986), whose book by that title documents the corporate shift toward support of right-wing agendas in the 1980s and analyzes the economic forces and sectors of corporate capital behind Reaganism. My study, by contrast, assumes a shift to the right within corporate capital and analyzes its manifestations within the television media.

15. On network news cutbacks following the conglomerate take-overs of the 1980s, see Hertsgaard (1988) and Boyer (1988).

16. On the failure of NBC to note the connection between its new parent company GE and a major scandal, see Appendix D and *New York Times*, December 3, 1989, p. 14 and Lee and Solomon 1990, 77f.

5

Alternatives

With television, an event is broadcast or it is ignored: either it is in enormous headlines or it is nowhere at all. This power to choose what the great mass of people shall see . . . is altogether too great to be left to the judgement of a few television companies and to private arrangements made by committees and commercial sponsors.

—Walter Lippmann

What is logical and good ought to be expressed even if it appears inachievable at the moment.

—Ben Bagdikian

A community will evolve only when a people control their own communications.

—Frantz Fanon

The question is: how are freedom and democracy in the long run possible at all under the domination of highly developed capitalism? Freedom and democracy are only possible where the resolute will of a nation not to allow itself to be ruled like sheep is permanently alive. We are "individualists" and partisans of "democratic" institutions "against the stream" of material constellations.

—Max Weber

If you think that this is utopian then I would ask you to reflect upon why you think this is utopian.

—Bertolt Brecht

Structural conflicts and tensions between democratic and capitalist imperatives continue to exist in the television system. On the whole, however, the 1980s exhibited the defeat of democracy by capitalism in the United States. At present, big corporations control TV news, information, and entertainment in accordance with their economic and political interests. The commercial system of television sells television advertising to corporations and political candidates who can afford to purchase highly expensive

179

airtime, thus ensuring control of the economic and political system by the wealthy and powerful. It is precisely this system of corporate-controlled and television-mediated elections that has "turned off" the electorate, giving the United States the lowest rate of participation in major elections among major capitalist democracies. And it is the paucity of information provided by commercial television that renders the electorate highly uninformed and thus incapable of intelligently participating in the political process.

Control of television by powerful groups ensures that certain issues will not be adequately covered and that certain points of view will not be articulated. Can one seriously expect GE/NBC to critically cover nuclear energy and the military-industrial complex when it is one of the nation's largest defense contractors and producers of nuclear energy plants? Can one expect CBS to adequately cover Israeli/Palestinian relations given that CBS owner Laurence Tisch has declared that he is passionately pro-Israel? Can one expect ABC to provide critical coverage of the Pentagon or U.S. military interventions considering that its correspondent John McWethy is strongly pro-military and depends on inside sources for his "scoops?" Can one expect any of the three major networks to be sharply critical of the Bush administration when they are hoping for new FCC rules that will allow them to enter the immensely lucrative area of television production and syndication? Can one expect any of these capitalist corporations to criticize the capitalist system and offer alternative perspectives?[1]

The problem with television is not television itself; it is not the technology and medium of television per se (Mander 1978). Television can be used for or against democracy (Raboy and Bruck 1989), and democracy itself is a contested terrain, subject to definition and structuration by competing groups and ideologies. My point is that television in the United States is being used more and more against democracy in order to secure the interests of the groups that control both the media and the state. In this chapter, however, I shall discuss the ways in which the system of television can be democratized and work *for* democracy. The system of commercial broadcasting has resulted in a situation whereby the three major networks control the entertainment and information watched by the majority of people in the United States. In this commercial system, ratings and private profit determine what sorts of programs are broadcast and which information is heard and seen. More innovative, complex, and challenging television is precluded in favor of "lowest-common-denominator programming" that offends the fewest people while garnering the largest ratings. Also precluded are articulation and discussion of a wide range of views in favor of a limited range of official and safe establishment perspectives.

Commercial ownership and control result in a broadcasting system biased toward the class that owns and controls it, thus excluding oppositional voices and criticism. The argument of this book is that capitalism and democracy inevitably come into conflict with each other and that it is now necessary to reinvigorate a rapidly deteriorating public sphere to preserve democracy in the United States. My study suggests that Horkheimer and Adorno's (1972) analyses of the culture industries, whatever their limitations, illuminate salient aspects of the current system of commercial media in which capitalist corporations control the system of mass communications. Entertainment and information in this system are predominantly ideological and serve the interests of maintaining a capitalist system. My study also confirms Habermas's (1989 [orig. 1962]) theory of the decline of the public sphere under the influence of mass-mediated institutions controlled by the capitalist class. Indeed, I am suggesting that the crisis of the public sphere and democracy is even worse than that analyzed by Habermas.

I have attempted in this book to show that the worst aspects of the commercial system of broadcasting intensified during the 1980s, when the television networks merged with other corporate conglomerates and thus fell into the hands of blatantly commercial and conservative interests. As a result, the amount of advertising has increased, commercial pressures for ratings have greatly diminished the number of documentaries and public affairs broadcasts, and the amount of innovative, challenging programming has declined. At present, therefore, commercial imperatives determine the nature, format, and structure of television, and the commercial networks are more obviously serving the interests of the transnational conglomerates that own and control them.

Yet the crisis of democracy is not caused solely by the commercialization and deregulation of television. Deregulation (i.e., unrestrained capitalism) has created havoc in several fields—banking, transportation, housing, health care, and broadcasting—and must be deemed a catastrophic demonstration of the destructiveness of a market economy not subject to rational regulation and social control. Although such conclusions may go against conventional wisdom, impartial scrutiny of the banking, transportation, housing, and communications systems certainly reveals the failure and destructiveness of the Reagan/Bush deregulatory programs.[2] Other crises in health care, education, urban centers, and housing are also contributing to the growing crisis of democracy in the United States, as are the growing divisions between classes, accelerating poverty, and a mushrooming underclass of people condemned to lives of drug addiction, disease, and decaying urban ghettoes.

From the 1980s to the present, a sort of Wizard of Oz irreality has reigned in the United States. Like the Scarecrow in the popular fable, the president appears to have no ideas. Like the Tin Man, the Congress functions only when it is liberally oiled with corporate funds; otherwise it creaks along, unable to address the immense problems of the country. Like the Lion of the tale, the media are cowardly, although they occasionally roar at harmless "enemies" or hapless villains. Like the denizens of Oz, U.S. citizens either submit to domination by spectacle and political manipulation or they tune out, lost in private concerns. The machinery of government often appears powerful, particularly when the wizardly apparatus of the media puffs up its image; when the veil is lifted, however, our "rulers" are shown to be inept, corrupt, and enmeshed in fantasy, in the never-never land of the contemporary United States. The homeless die in the streets; thousands die of AIDS and cancer; millions are addicted to drugs; and for diversion the dying empire invades small and defenseless countries while waging secret wars all over the world.[3]

Deregulation and the growing squalor of public life under the Reagan and Bush administrations have produced the need for a radical reconstruction of the polity. Part of this democratic reconstruction and new politics calls for a new communications politics and the democratization of television. In this chapter, accordingly, I shall discuss what can be done to democratize television and sketch some alternatives to the system of commercial broadcasting that has served the United States and the world so poorly. In particular, I shall argue that the alternatives to commercial broadcasting are (1) an enlarged, strengthened, and revitalized system of public television and radio; (2) an expanded system of public access television; and (3) development of a people's satellite network, complemented by people's communication centers and a people's information network that would use new technologies to broaden and diversify information sources and services. Although some of these proposals inevitably have a utopian dimension, they are all based on existing technological, organizational, and financial capabilities. For just as contemporary U.S. society is characterized by an immense concentration of wealth and power, and by corporate control of the mainstream media, so too is the contemporary scene characterized by a wealth of prefigurative social movements, alternative modes of communication and culture, and political activism and struggle.[4] New technologies are being used by a growing number of citizens, and public interest groups are intervening in the policy vacuum created by a paralyzed government that is bereft of new ideas or initiatives with genuine public support.

To be sure, capitalism is predominant over democracy in the United States, and the existing alternatives are sometimes neither seen nor heard in the mainstream media. But they are there, and they prefigure the possibilities for a future democratic society. A critical theory of television must therefore conceptualize both sides of the existing society and culture—namely, the forces of domination and those that prefigure and struggle for a better society. This process involves both criticizing the existing capitalist media and proposing democratic alternatives for a more progressive system of communication and culture in the United States today. Such a project will initially require a new philosophy of democratic communications, accompanied by proposals for a new democratic communications system.

5.1 Toward a Democratic Broadcasting System

During the 1980s a capitalist communications philosophy ruled in the United States. It was promulgated by Mark Fowler and the FCC, and it guided the most radical deregulation of broadcasting in the history of the United States. Although it was occasionally challenged, no new alternative democratic communications philosophy has appeared to systematically crit-icize and replace it. The capitalist communications philosophy is simple: It holds that complete deregulation and an unrestricted marketplace will provide the best communications system for the people of the United States (see sections 2.5 and 3.2).

In implementing deregulation, the FCC in 1984 abolished the 5-5-10 guideline, which mandated that television stations affiliated with the networks or independents on the VHF frequency must carry 5 percent local, 5 percent informational (news plus public affairs), and 10 percent nonenter-tainment programming between 6:00 A.M. and midnight. Then, in 1987 the FCC repealed the Fairness Doctrine, which required that broadcasters air controversial issues of public concern and provide a fair presentation of opposing views. The FCC argued that replacing the Fairness Doctrine would eliminate an "impediment to the broadcasting of controversial issues of public importance," as broadcasters might fear that opposing groups would demand free air time to counter controversial programming. What actual impact, then, did the FCC revolution have on programming?

A study undertaken by Jim Donahue for "Essential Information," a public interest group affiliated with Ralph Nader, indicated that the results of FCC policy changes have been detrimental to public affairs programming and that deregulation has been a distinct failure in this regard. Donahue claims that

"[c]omparing the results of this study to a 1979 study by the FCC shows a 51 percent decrease in the average percentage of issue-oriented public affairs programming between 6:00 A.M. and midnight on commercial television in the markets studied. This study also shows that compared to a 1978 study . . . more network affiliates and VHF independent stations neglected to meet the minimum programming levels of the 5-5-10 guideline. Thus, the FCC's theory that market forces propel broadcasters to air public interest programming has not [been] borne out. (1989, 1)

The new Fox Broadcasting Network was the most delinquent in presenting public interest programming, in that 40 percent of its affiliates neglected to present a public affairs program at any time during the week and 87 percent neglected to present any newscasts at all; in addition, almost 33 percent of the local stations affiliated with the major networks failed to present a local public affairs program and 15 percent of all stations carried no news at all. Furthermore, there was not only a drastic decline in public affairs programming during the Reagan/Fowler regime, but program commercials (entire programs devoted to commercial goals) constituted 2.6 percent of the total broadcast time. (Such programming did not even exist earlier.) Moreover, the amount of advertising increased during the 1980s. Previously, industry/government guidelines stipulated that advertising during a prime-time hour could not exceed 12 minutes. But Fowler's FCC rescinded this agreement and advertising time generally increased. The most dramatic increases occurred in advertising on children's programs. Deregulation and elimination of all programming requirements thus led to a demonstrable decline in public affairs programming and an increase in blatantly commercial fare and advertising time.

In fact, with respect to broadcasting, the marketplace/commercial philosophy of the Reagan/Bush era is incredibly simplistic and one-sided. From the beginning, broadcasting in the United States combined commercial and democratic criteria, mixing private ownership and competition with government regulation and mandates to serve the public interest. Broadcasting in the United States is both a privilege and a responsibility. The U.S. government licenses stations, which are protected from censorship by the First Amendment and are allowed to make as much profit as the market allows; in practice, a television license is a "license to make money," as one pundit put it. Yet broadcasting is also mandated to serve the public interest. As I argued earlier, the communications law implemented by Congress, the FCC, and the courts has defended and articulated, however inadequately, the public interest philosophy.

The problem, however, is that the "public interest" has never been adequately defined and spelled out; nor does a democratic communications philosophy exist to guide public policy and regulate broadcasting. Adding to the dilemma is the communications explosion of recent years. The rapid expansion of cable, public access and satellite television, new informational uses of cable wires and telephone lines, and the impact of computerization on all aspects of information and communications require a new philosophy of democratic communications. But the entire history of broadcast regulation cannot simply be thrown out and replaced with an unrestricted marketplace philosophy. As noted, deregulation has not demonstrably improved the broadcast system in any agreed-upon way, and it violates the delicate balance between the governmental and economic forces that have thus far structured the U.S. system of broadcasting. Broadcast policy in the 1980s created a sharp imbalance between capitalism and democracy, between the private interest and the public interest at the expense of democracy and the public. What, however, would constitute a viable alternative democratic broadcasting philosophy?

Television in a Democratic Society: Accountability, Access, and Adequacy

A new democratic broadcasting philosophy should begin by defining and concretizing the elusive concept of the public interest. On the one hand, although this concept has guided communications law and public policy for five decades (despite its abuse by the Reagan FCC), it has never been adequately clarified or specified by official FCC policy or rulings, or by presidential and congressional policy and statements. It has become an easy target for critics who can legitimately point to the vagueness and imprecision of the concept. On the other hand, the 1934 Communications Act, of which the public interest concept is a key aspect, clearly mandated that broadcasting be treated as a public good (like air, water, and other elements that belong to everyone, or like parks and highways that can be used by all people). Even before the 1934 act, broadcasting was treated as an industry subject to government regulation, much like highways, commerce, trade, and other commercial activities. From this regulatory perspective, the public interest thus referred to an understanding that broadcasting was a public good that should serve goals of benefit to the public.

As Herbert Schiller has pointed out, however, the difficulty of articulating a public interest in a badly divided society had become apparent by the 1960s (1969, 62ff.). For the ruling class and the wealthy, Schiller noted, the public interest involved maintaining law and order and affluence. For the poor and oppressed, by contrast, the public interest involved social restructuring and a redistribution of wealth and power. Indeed, in a democratic and pluralistic society there is bound to be a variety of publics with different interests—as is certainly the case in the United States. Yet it is possible to articulate a concept of the public interest in this context if one assumes that in a democratic society the public's interest is to further democracy. Toward this end, each individual would have to be provided with an equal opportunity to participate in the political process and to advance economically and socially.

This version of the public interest requires equal access to education, information, and the media of public debate. Although the country pays lip service to these ideals, in fact a large number of people are uneducated, uninformed, and deprived of all means of public participation and expression. Achieving democracy, even in a minimal sense, thus requires greater access to education, to diverse sources of information, and to participation in social and political processes. From this vantage point, one could appraise the extent to which television is serving the democratic public interest by measuring the extent to which it provides the wide and diverse range of ideas and essential information necessary for participation in politics and social life.

I believe that this notion of the public interest is compatible with the views of all of those who genuinely support democracy, whether they are liberals or conservatives, democratic socialists or feminists, civil libertarians or minority rights advocates. The relevant questions regarding broadcasting, then, are these: What is the role of broadcasting in a democratic society? How can broadcasting serve the public interest in promoting democracy and creating a freer, more egalitarian, more participatory, and hence more democratic society? As noted, an era of new communications technologies and new industries such as cable and satellite television obviously requires new reflection on broadcasting, democracy, and the public interest in terms of existing technological, political, and economic capabilities. In the following discussion, I contend that notions of accountability, access, and adequacy provide clarification of the articulations between democracy and the public interest, and thus can serve as heuristic concepts underlying a democratic broadcasting theory and practice.

Accountability, which has always been implied in the notion that broadcasting should serve the public interest, acquires even more importance and urgency during an era when the mass media—especially television—are of central importance in our politics, society, and everyday life. With television so powerful and influential, broadcasting should be all the more accountable to the public for the effects of its programming. Providing adequate news, information, and public affairs programming is thus a civic responsibility; for if the public is not well educated and informed, a vital, robust, functioning democracy is not possible. In a democratic public sphere, the citizenry are informed and able to debate and participate in public decisions (Habermas 1989).

From this perspective, one thus has to raise the question of whether the public interest is served by the current 22-minute evening news broadcasts by the three networks. Although many individuals in the television industry have called for expanded evening newscasts, advertisers, network affiliates (which make a higher profit on syndicated game shows and reruns than on TV news), and the bottom-line magnates who control the industry have always resisted such pressure. But the current news is barely a "headline" service, allowing little or no time for in-depth discussion, contextualization, or analysis. One might also raise the question of whether the public interest is served by the current network practice of drastically cutting back (almost to the point of elimination) the production and broadcasting of documentaries and public affairs programming during prime-time hours.

Furthermore, political discussion and debate on the three major networks are almost exclusively limited to Sunday morning talk shows and ABC's "Nightline," which features late-night debates of topical interest. But one wonders whether the public interest is served by the composition of these network talk shows, which are generally limited to mainstream representatives of the two major political parties or to other white, male, establishment figures. A study of "Nightline," for example, indicates that over a six-month period host Ted Koppel's guests were almost always white, male, conservative spokespersons. Indeed, Henry Kissinger, Alexander Haig, Jerry Falwell, and Elliot Abrams were the most frequent guests (FAIR 1989).

In a follow-up investigation, FAIR compared the guest list of Koppel's "Nightline" with public television's "The MacNeil/Lehrer News Hour" and found that during the 6-month period from February 6 to August 4, 1989, "Nightline" slightly broadened its panel of experts, "while public TV's Newshour is narrower, whiter, more male-dominated, more government-oriented and more conservative than "Nightline." MacNeil/Lehrer's virtual exclusion of public interest leaders is a sad commentary on public TV" (FAIR Press Release, May 21, 1990; see the full report published in *Extra*, Vol. 3, No. 4, 1990).

According to the report, MacNeil/Lehrer's most frequent guests included nine U.S. government officials (six of whom are conservative) and four "experts," two of whom are from conservative think tanks. Further, the conservative Center for Strategic and International Studies provided the show's resident experts on foreign policy, and the conservative American Enterprise Institute provided its resident experts for domestic political issues. "Experts from progressive think tanks such as the Institute for Policy Studies and the World Policy Institute never appeared." Ninety percent of MacNeil/Lehrer's guests were white, and 87 percent were male; 89 percent were current, or former, government officials, professionals, and corporate representatives, and only 6 percent of its guests represented public interest, labor, or racial/ethnic groups.

FAIR's case studies involved the environment and Central America. Of the seventeen guests on MacNeil/Lehrer who discussed the environment, only one guest was an environmentalist. The Exxon Valdez oil spill was the major environmental story during the period under investigation, and MacNeil/Lehrer had seven segments on the spill, but not one included an environmental representative! On MacNeil/Lehrer's seven Central America segments, all twenty-two of the guests were either U.S. officials or officials of U.S. allies in the region; all were male. There were no members of the massive U.S. anti-interventionist or Central American Solidarity movements. FAIR's report was given to MacNeil/Lehrer and the PBS President with a cover note which stated: "MacNeil/Lehrer's narrow, pro-establishment guest list mocks the original mandate of public television. The Carnegie Commission Report that gave birth to PBS urged that public television 'be a forum for debate and controversy' and 'provide a voice for groups in the community that may otherwise be unheard' and 'help us see America whole, in all its diversity." On these points, public TV's News Hour has utterly failed. Much of MacNeil/Lehrer's coverage—its selection of news-makers and experts—is even narrower than commercial TV" (ibid.).

Broadcasting interests always use First Amendment protection to resist pressures toward regulation that would affect program content in any way. But the Founding Fathers were more interested in individual rights of freedom of speech than in corporate rights; it would have been impossible to imagine during the 1770s and 1780s that a handful of giant corporations would one day control the dominant medium of communications. Expanding and guaranteeing freedom of speech thus require consideration of the right of individuals to *access* in broadcasting, which in turn requires more diversity, a broader spectrum of opinions and points of view, and a reversal of current policies that restrict access to establishment spokespersons.

One government policy that promoted such access was the 1972 FCC ruling that the then-emerging cable systems must provide at least three public access channels for community, local government, and educational use. This ruling would make possible local public access systems as alternatives to the commercial networks. But the Supreme Court threw out this ruling in 1979, on the grounds that the FCC did not have the authority to make such a decree. Nonetheless, many access systems were already in place, and several cities have been able to negotiate access channels in bidding processes with cable companies during franchise award procedures. In short, there is now an important public access movement that provides a genuine alternative to commercial television and an important example of com-munications in the public interest. (This topic is discussed in detail in section 5.3.)

Yet another access issue has emerged concerning the right of the public to gain access to broadcasting material, especially news and information programming (on this issue, see Saldich 1979 and Kellner 1980a). During the first two decades of broadcasting, most television networks simply destroyed their evening news programs and reused the videotapes. In the 1960s they began forming their own news archives, and in 1968 the first television news archive was established at Vanderbilt University. CBS, however, attempted to block the formation of this archive and the use of its materials by scholars and the public (Saldich 1979, 106ff.). The networks have tended to treat their programming as a private commodity and have refused either to provide access to the public to their archives or to allow citation and quotation of actual broadcast material—except in special circumstances. Yet because television is having such an important impact on our society and politics, it is obviously in the public interest to allow scholars "fair use" of media material so that they can cite and quote media images, texts, and sequences in articles, documentaries, and other examinations of broadcast materials. (For further discussion of these issues, see Lawrence and Timberg 1989.)

To be sure, television archives have been formed despite CBS's pressures, and PBS documentaries and other programs regularly quote clips from network news and other shows for critical purposes. Still, some educators and educational facilities are reluctant to tape or allow classroom viewing of network programming because of copyright considerations. The concept of "fair use" of media materials thus remains to be adequately specified and translated into law. In any case, it is important to perceive access to study and quotation of media materials as part of the broader issue of increasing citizens' access to the media.

This issue thus involves both the right of individuals to have access to media materials for study and criticism, and the right to access in the media. Obviously, as the national networks are not able to allow all individuals access to their facilities, development of a public access system becomes a key element in promoting television democracy. Yet on the national level, the Fairness Doctrine, which allowed individuals access to reply to unfair criticisms, would seem to be an essential component of a fair and democratic television system. The Reagan FCC eliminated this doctrine, and Reagan vetoed congressional bills that attempted to reinstate it. A democratic communications policy, by contrast, would attempt to resurrect and strengthen a fairness doctrine that would increase the access of citizens, corporations, and public organizations to the broadcast media.

A democratic communications policy might also consider criteria of *adequacy* in the assessment of whether programming serves the public interest and make recommendations on how it might improve. A democratic broadcasting philosophy would hold that broadcasting in a democratic society should help make possible an informed citizenry by airing controversial issues of public importance from a variety of positions; it should facilitate access to citizens and public interest groups; and the public interest should be determined by the extent to which broadcasting promotes a robust democracy and helps produce a democratic public sphere. Thus there are obvious connections among accountability, access, and adequacy; only the realization of all three goals would produce a genuinely democratic system that was accountable to the public, provided better and more access, and offered more adequate programming to meet its democratic responsibilities.

More adequate programming, in turn, would require that steps be taken to increase programming diversity and to ensure that all significant groups and tendencies are allowed access to the media. The United States is generally agreed to be a pluralist society with great ethnic, racial, regional, and political diversity. A pluralist broadcasting system would represent a diversity of voices and cultures, and would provide access to the dominant political philosophies, ethnic groups and cultures, and regional experiences in the country. Public interest advocates argue that market forces diminish market choices and that the commercial system of broadcasting, which aims for mass audiences, does not really provide for diversity and access to different voices in the broadcasting spectrum. Development of a broadcasting system that genuinely serves the public interest requires the establishment of a robust, vital, and open system of national public broadcasting as well as the creation of local public access systems. (These issues will be taken up in sections 5.2 and 5.3.)

As noted, a certain quantity of news, public affairs, and nonentertainment programming was mandated previously by the FCC. During the Reagan years, however, these requirements were dropped, the amount of public affairs programming was reduced by more than 50 percent, and documentaries almost disappeared altogether on network television. As a democratic society requires news and information in order to function adequately, as most people get their news and information from television, and as most people watch network prime-time television (more than two-thirds of the country is watching prime-time television on any given evening!), a free flow of news, information, and public affairs programming should obviously be available during the prime-time hours. Accordingly, it seems reasonable to argue that the FCC requirements mandating a certain percentage of news and public affairs programming should be reinstated, perhaps with the additional stipulation that a certain amount of prime time should be devoted to public affairs programming as well.

Furthermore, to ensure adequate coverage of key issues and events, the media must subject themselves and be subjected by others to critical public scrutiny. As of now, with the exception of an occasional ABC "Viewpoint" special (which is usually dominated by conservatives or carefully chosen "critics"), there exists no regular feedback mechanism by which network news performance can be criticized. Given the immense power of the media, it seems necessary to produce more responsible media watchdog mechanisms that would criticize the media for inadequate performance and attempt to correct their failures and biases.

In order to adequately monitor, criticize, and correct network news practices it would be useful to resurrect the institution of a National News Council that would be a forum for receiving and studying complaints against news practices of the mainstream media. The National News Council was established in 1973 to monitor press coverage in the United States. Its founding committee announced selection of nine council members from the public and six from news organizations. It met regularly from 1973 to 1975 and undertook investigations of 59 complaints made against the mainstream press; 23 of the complaints were against the television networks. The council investigated the charges, found 33 to be unwarranted, 5 to be warranted, and 21 beyond the council's competency or resolved by the parties in question during deliberations. In 1975, the National News Council published a report on the complaints and their investigations.

Such a news council could provide a watchdog agency against the sorts of abuses by the television networks documented in this book. It would provide a useful corrective to their failure to engage in self-criticism and to provide the public with alternative versions of political and social reality. It would, in short, help reinvigorate democratic politics in the United States.

Before sketching some democratic alternatives to the existing system of commercial broadcasting, I wish to comment on the need for direct and immediate reform in certain areas of the current broadcasting system. I am indeed convinced that a politics of information and media reform is crucial for the development of a democratic/progressive political agenda of the future, as information and media become even more central to all aspects of contemporary life.

Media Politics: Some Necessary Reforms

I have linked a democratic broadcasting philosophy with the project of strengthening democracy in the United States. From this perspective, changes in the broadcasting system that strengthen democracy could be said to be in the public interest, whereas those aspects of the current system that weaken democracy are not. I assume that democracy is strengthened when the public is informed on issues of current importance and is able to participate in political controversies through debate, input, and voting power. The current low rate of political participation and the failure of the commercial networks to cover many issues of political importance (see the Appendixes for examples) suggest that network television is not acting in the public interest and that dramatic reforms are needed to resolve the current crisis of democracy.

Let us first examine the role of television and TV advertising in elections. In recent years, there has been much discussion of the extent to which television advertising and debates have been harmful to the democratic electoral process. In this regard, I wish to propose some important reforms. In Chapter 4, I discussed the role of political advertising in the 1988 election and noted the growing consensus to the effect that it is becoming increasingly central to the electoral process. Most commentators agree that political advertising is extremely harmful in its effects and that expensive, negative, and predominantly imagistic advertising will continue to play a central role in the political campaigns of the future; some even believe that such negative advertising will undermine the democratic foundations of the country.

The current form of political advertising arguably pollutes the political process and constitutes a clear and present danger to the political health of the nation; but it also contributes to the domination of the electoral process by big business and thus is highly antidemocratic in character. Indeed, most commentators agree that the dramatic increase in expensive, high-tech political advertising is a major factor in accelerating the cost of elections. Candidates are thereby forced to raise astronomical amounts of money in order to be viable—thus, of course, giving their donors influence over them and opening the doors to greater political corruption (as was obvious in the savings and loan scandals of the 1980s and 1990s). This process favors conservative politicians who are able to raise the money needed for expensive elections; it also provides those able to help finance elections with political clout and influence denied to the average citizen.

What is needed, then, is systematic reform of campaign spending practices, which might involve elimination of the political action committees that arose to circumvent previous election reform, but also systematic reform of the function of television in elections. This could take the form of rules forbidding both the prediction of winners from exit polls and computer projections of election results until all polling stations in relevant elections have closed throughout the country.

Reform of political advertising, debates, and television coverage of elections should also be undertaken. Indeed, significant reforms of current political advertising practices could be implemented quite simply if the public demanded them and Congress took decisive action. It would be quite easy to eliminate the current 30- and 60-second paid political advertising spots, as Britain and other countries have done. One could argue that such political ads do not contribute to political dialogue or enlightenment but have contributed mightily to the replacement of a politics of discourse by a politics of image. Moreover, during primary seasons, free time could be allotted to candidates running in primaries according to the number of signatures they received on a petition.

To increase political discourse during the main election, both the commercial and public broadcasting networks should be mandated to provide blocks of 5- and 30-minute spots to each major candidate free of charge, so that they could present their views and qualifications in some detail to the electorate. The two major party candidates should receive an equal amount of time, and alternative candidates should be allotted time according to the number of votes they received in primary elections.

As a second step, the candidates could be required to use this time to address issues or their own qualifications for office. They could also be required to speak directly to the audience rather than using high-tech gimmickry and slick images to manipulate the viewers. In other words, the free political blocks would be shot in studios, where the candidates themselves would face the camera and address specific issues. Allowing the use of free political ads alone would merely increase the sort of nonsubstantive image manipulation that currently dominates TV advertising and campaigns. By contrast, serious discussion of issues would promote a politics of discourse that in itself would constitute a major reform of the political system of the United States. It would help revitalize democracy by providing information that would allow voters to make intelligent choices based on the candidates and the issues rather than on slick advertising images.

In addition, stations could be mandated to provide a certain amount of time for substantive political debates in which political candidates genuinely debate the issues. Of course, this measure would involve changes in the television debate process in national presidential elections. Many major critics and commentators have agreed that the debate format utilized since 1976 is extremely cumbersome and not conducive to genuine discussion or debate. In this format, selected news personalities pose questions to the two major candidates, who in turn are allowed two minutes to answer and then a minute to rebut without any genuine dialogue or interaction. In several other countries—such as Canada, Great Britain, and France— interactive debate formats provide a much better forum for genuine debate than does the stand-up news conference format of U.S. presidential debates.

In primary and local elections, candidates could face community leaders who would pose questions that they would discuss among themselves and with their interrogators; time could also be allowed for questions from the audience. This practice is often used in Austin, Texas, for City Council elections; Austin Community Television and, occasionally, local stations provide the time and resources to make such political dialogue possible. Such a system could easily be implemented on the local level more generally; it could also accommodate races for the House of Representatives and the Senate at the district and state levels.

Teledemocracy? A more controversial proposal involves the use of a television/computer system to record citizens' votes and reactions to issues. In 1970 Robert Paul Wolff proposed such a system of television democracy, arguing that it would make political participation accessible to more voters. Genuinely democratic implementation of such a system would require that citizens be genuinely informed on the issues and have access to information; that questions posed in polls or referenda not be rigged or slanted; and that every citizen have a television and computer to participate in the television democracy (low-income people would have to be given these instruments free of charge). As Wolff writes:

I propose that in order to overcome the obstacles to direct democracy, a system of in-the-home voting machines be set up. In each dwelling, a device would be attached to the television set which would electronically record votes and transmit them to a computer in Washington. (Those homes without sets would be supplied by a federal subsidy. In practice this would not be very expensive, since only the very poor and the very intelligent lack sets at present.) In order to avoid fraudulent voting, the device could be rigged to record thumbprints. In that manner, each person would be able to vote only once, since the computer would automatically reject a duplicate vote. Each evening, at the time which is now devoted to news programs, there would be a nationwide all-stations show devoted to debate on the issues before the nation. Whatever bills were "before the Congress" (as we would now describe it) would be debated by representatives of alternative points of view. There would be background briefings on technically complex questions, as well as formal debates, question periods, and so forth. Committees of experts would be commissioned to gather data, make recommendations for new measures, and do the work of drafting legislation. One could institute the position of Public Dissenter in order to guarantee that dissident and unusual points of view would be heard. Each Friday, after a week of debate and discussion, a voting session would be held. The measures would be put to the public, one by one, and the nation would record its preferences instantaneously by means of the machines. Special arrangements might have to be made for those who could not be at their sets during the voting. (Perhaps voting sessions at various times during the preceding day and nights.) Simple majority rule would prevail, as is now the case in Congress. (1970, 34–35)

Critics, however, charge that *all* polling and technologically administered elections would be inherently manipulative, and that they raise questions concerning privacy and surveillance (Ginsberg 1986). Obviously these concerns would have to be addressed, but it is possible that a fair computer voting system could be devised. Since Wolff's proposal, there have been many experiments with "teledemocracy," ranging from the use of television and telephones to allow participation in electronic town meetings to the use of television as instruments of voting in elections and referenda.[5] Both fervent advocates and sharp critics of teledemocracy have spoken out (Atherton 1987, 18ff.). Clearly, future discussions of the implementation of genuine democracy in the United States will need to sort out both the dangerous and promising potentials of the use of television in democracy.

Benjamin Barber is probably correct in saying that a system of teledemocracy is certain to be abused if it is not supplemented by other measures to promote democracy, such as neighborhood town meetings, electronic city and regional meetings open to citizens' input, changes in mailing rates facilitating the dissemination of political literature, citizen access to information and data bases, and so on (1984, 261ff.). But he also urges that voting in elections must take place in a public space to preserve the symbolism of the public sphere—with the proviso that arrangements be made for those with physical disabilities to vote at home (1984, 290).

Probably a mixture of the Wolff and Barber models would best serve the construction of democracy in the United States. It is surely the case that, if genuine democracy is to flourish, teledemocracy must be supplemented by local, participatory democracy. Perhaps major elections *should* take place in public spaces. Yet certain referenda could be carried out at home, and surely more experiments with teledemocracy in the home should be undertaken. Such a system might, at the least, provide a superior alternative to the current use of polling and manufacture of public opinion. Even though instant telepolling could be manipulated and used to support repugnant and illegal actions such as the invasion of Panama, expansion of the data base in public opinion polls seems potentially preferable to the current system of polling, which uses a small sample of individuals to generate "public opinion." On issues such as abortion rights, environmental protection, urban development, workers' safety, and the like, expanded polling would probably serve progressive ends. And in light of the manipulative politics and political apathy of the 1980s, television elections are preferable to the current system of elections in which only one-half of the registered voters even bother to show up to vote in major national elections, while large numbers do not even bother to register.

Indeed, nationally mandated and automatic voters' registration should also be implemented, with required registration at the age of 18. This procedure could be carried out in high schools and colleges, and individuals could be required by law to register to vote, much as individuals are required to register for selective service or to get a social security number before they seek employment. In short, all possible means must be undertaken to promote political participation and to carry out political education— and the media, along with the schools, are an important part of this process.

Overcoming the Effects of Deregulation. Yet reform of the media system does not involve merely reform of its use in the political arena. A progressive agenda should also take up the issue of curtailing advertising and developing a revitalized federal regulatory system. One obvious candidate for regulation would be children's television, which was radically deregulated during the Reagan administration. In 1969 the FCC ruled that toy companies such as Mattel could not create shows that aimed at selling products modeled after characters in the show. Later, in 1974, the FCC adopted rules limiting advertising on children's television to 12 minutes per hour on weekdays and 9.5 minutes per hour on weekends; once again, they required the "adequate separation [between program content and the commercial message] on programs designed for children." In 1979 the FCC reaffirmed and strengthened the guidelines. The FCC's reasoning in the 1974 ruling was that "very young children cannot distinguish conceptually between programming and advertising." Since children are exposed to advertising at an especially young and impressionable age, "special safeguards may be required to insure that the advertising privilege is not abused" (above quotations and figures cited in John Judis, *In These Times*, July 22, 1987: p. 2).

The pre-Reagan FCC was also concerned about the quality and type of children's television programming and encouraged educational television for children. During the Reagan/Bush years, by contrast, the FCC regularly took the side of business against public interest groups that attempted to defend children against commercial manipulation. In 1983 a group known as Action for Children's Television (ACT) argued that the program "He-Man and the Masters of the Universe," based on Mattel toys, violated the FCC rule. The FCC dismissed the complaint and opened the door to a slew of programs based on children's toys such as "Rainbow Brite," "My Little Pony 'n' Friends," and "Gummi Bears"; thirteen such programs existed by the end of 1983, and by 1989 there were seventy children's television programs based on toys. (See Aufderheide 1989 and the systematic analysis of these programs by Engelhardt in Gitlin 1987.) These programs constitute advertising gimmicks that attempt to induce children to buy their little TV friends; they also utilize uninspired cartooning techniques and extremely conventional gender models.

In 1983 the FCC also moved to eliminate all restrictions on TV advertising, including children's television. The result was that a fifth of the stations in the top fifty markets averaged more than the former maximum of 12 minutes per hour of commercials, with commercials on children's television totaling as many as 20 minutes and 48 seconds in a single 30-minute program, if one considers the promotion of the series characters/toys as commercials (Aufderheide 1989). Furthermore, "some advertising tells kids to hold the phone up to the TV—so the beep sounds can 'dial' a number for the child. Unsuspecting kids calling the 'Slime Line' or the 'Freddy Pumpkin Horror Line' have spent hundreds of dollars of the family budget before dad and mom got the bill" (ibid.). And most educators agree that little or no innovative children's programming appeared during the Reagan orgy of deregulation.

The deregulation of the Reagan years proved to be extremely harmful, and Congress in 1989 began considering a children's television bill that would re-regulate children's television. If this bill is to be effective, however, restrictions on advertising must also be considered. For instance, limits could be placed, as before, on the number of advertisements permitted during a given hour. In addition, advertising could be taxed and more strictly regulated. Currently, corporations are permitted to write off advertising as a legitimate business expense and thus, in effect, steal billions of dollars from the federal treasury each year. Indeed, fully 2 percent of the gross national product ($110 billion a year) is expended on advertising.[6] Consumers may think they are getting free TV as a result of this corporate largesse but, in fact, they are paying higher prices for products to support the advertising infrastructure. In addition, devoting tremendous amounts of resources to advertising and exempting it from taxation contributes to increased public squalor by depriving the government of a tax base from tax-fee advertising expenses and write-offs. In an era of sky-rocketing federal deficits, it thus makes perfect sense to call for limiting tax write-offs for television advertising and for more strenuous taxation of television and other advertising revenues.

Indeed, certain types of advertising should be banned outright, following the lead of the ban on cigarette advertising in the 1970s. This ban could perhaps be extended to advertising for alcohol, firearms, and other products of dubious social value, such as war toys for children. In short, more and better regulation is needed to curb the dangerous excesses of the commercial system of broadcasting. Rich and powerful corporations are certainly not going to reform themselves, and without political action the abuses of the commercial system of broadcasting will only get worse.

Many more elements of the Reagan/Bush FCC deregulation program must be addressed if the public interest is to guide a democratic communications policy, including deeper limitations on the number of TV stations that networks and individual corporations can own, restrictions on corporate mergers, restrictions on the number of ads that can be run during a given hour, requirements to run a certain amount of public affairs programming, stricter licensing and renewal policies, and, finally, the return of the Fairness Doctrine.

The results of deregulation on the economic front have been an increase of communications monopolies as well as concentration of media ownership and the growth of conglomerate communications giants. The unrestricted merger movement of the 1980s has already brought about less diversity, more ads, and potentially high profits and greater power for media conglomerates. As the mergers and new conglomerate giants are already in place, Congress could undertake a study of the effects of mergers and of the concentration of ownership both on the system of broadcasting and on society as a whole. Earlier, Congressman Wright Patman (D-Tex.) undertook one such study of the banking industry, and a bill to study concentration in industries like the media was introduced by Morris Udall (R-Ariz.) in 1977. (The latter, however, never got out of committee.)

Such a study, especially one detailing the effects of media concentration of ownership, would be extremely healthy for democratizing the broadcasting system. Thus Congress and the FCC should be encouraged to begin such a study. Establishment of an independent foundation might also be encouraged to promote an inquiry into the rapidly increasing concentration of media ownership. If it could be shown that such concentration of power in the communications industries was detrimental to democracy and to the agreed-upon values for a democratic broadcasting system, then Congress and the appropriate regulatory agencies should take action to break up media conglomerates and to reinstate stricter ownership requirements. In fact, Ben Bagdikian recommends that instead of the 12/12/12 Reagan FCC ruling that allows corporations, including the television networks, to own twelve television stations, FM radio stations, and AM stations, a given company should be allowed to own only *one* of each (1987, 228). Bagdikian also calls for severe limits on cross-ownership of the media, for "[m]edia that truly compete with each other produce more variety and innovation and they monitor their competitors' business practices more closely" (ibid.).

Systematic study might also be undertaken of the effects of Reagan-era policies of deregulation and the loosening of antitrust laws. Such an analysis might document the impact on broadcasting and the public sphere of these policies; and if the impact was deemed to be harmful, then remedial action should be taken to reverse deregulatory practices that are in the interests of business but not of the public. For instance, it might be necessary to force the networks to divest themselves of other nonbroadcasting interests and to concentrate solely on television production and distribution. In particular, broadcast conglomerates such as GE/NBC/RCA might be broken up to avoid the obvious conflicts of interest involved. It might also be necessary to require that publicly responsible and responsive broadcast companies have boards of directors representing different segments of the society rather than just corporate elites. In any case, the effects of deregulation and the corporate conglomerate takeovers of the television networks need to be studied carefully and appropriate action should be taken.

The "Reagan revolution" attempted to undo fifty years of regulatory practices and government programs that, at their best, had attempted to balance the power relations between capitalism and democracy and to give the people institutional power to defend themselves against predatory business practices. The irony of deregulation under Reagan and Bush is that regulation historically tended to rationalize markets and to serve the interests of the industries regulated; moreover, according to Horowitz (1989), the industries most radically deregulated were those that had come to accept a certain level of regulation. In any case, the Reagan/Bush program attempted to weaken government immensely and to transfer wealth and power to business, especially the corporate sector. If the resulting imbalances between capitalism and democracy, the private and public sectors, and commerce and communication are to be addressed, however, the Reagan/Bush policies must be decisively repudiated and efforts must be undertaken to strengthen U.S. democracy and the public sphere against domination by corporate capital.

Yet the history of broadcast legislation and regulation makes it clear that neither Congress nor the system of commercial media is going to implement any of these reforms in the immediate future. Congress, in fact, is woefully ignorant regarding communications/broadcasting issues, and it is subject to manipulation through the power of the broadcasting corporations. Some members of Congress have broadcasting interests themselves, and all are dependent on broadcasting media for reelection. Furthermore, they are all aware that the media, especially television, can easily destroy them if they turn against it or act in ways deemed undesirable by the industry. Likewise, the FCC has historically been dominated by broadcasting interests and has never systematically reformed the broadcasting system, despite several comprehensive studies and reasonable recommendations.

If such reforms are to be possible, the citizens reform groups that emerged in the late 1960s and early 1970s will have to be reinvigorated (Montgomery 1989). Such groups could monitor television programming and practices, and struggle for further reform. In addition, licensing policies would have to be reinstated such that stations delinquent in meeting public service requirements would risk losing their licenses. Such a citizens reform movement would also have to reform the FCC and impress upon Congress the importance of democratic communications reforms.

Indeed, both Congress and the FCC must be dramatically reformed if there is to be any democratic reform of the communications system. To begin with, members of Congress should be required to sell broadcasting holdings so as to avoid conflicts of interest, and rules should be passed forbidding FCC commissioners to work for broadcasting corporations within a certain number of years following their tenure. Moreover, arrangements should be made to form a depoliticized FCC with a nonpartisan independent body recommending its members, who would be subject to review and public scrutiny. Given the importance of broadcasting in contemporary society, the cabinet post of Secretary of Communications should be instituted, parallel to posts in the Department of Health, Education, and Welfare and the Department of Education. In this way, trained and experienced professionals in government could act intelligently and independently as official trustees of the public interest in broadcasting.

As neither government nor the television industry is likely to initiate such reforms, however, it is up to interested individuals and groups to save our politics and consciousness from image pollution, to restore democracy, and to struggle for a democratic communication system. Watchdog groups are needed to monitor the media and to disseminate information on their abuses. (The group FAIR, for instance, with its newsletter *Extra!* and its many interventions into contemporary media politics, has undertaken such a role since the mid-1980s in exemplary fashion.) Individuals and groups should become more concerned with the politics of information and the media, and become more involved in the struggle for a democratic system of communication. They should attempt to educate Congress and the public on communications issues, and struggle for immediate reforms and systematic renovation of the broadcasting system. Although such reforms are unlikely at present, "what is logical and good ought to be expressed even if it appears inachievable at the moment" (Bagdikian 1987, 225).

Television today is a key element of the public sector and should provide a crucial dimension of the public sphere of genuine debate. Here a diversity of views can be expressed in a truly democratic marketplace of ideas, thus informing the public of policy options with respect to important issues under consideration. Yet the broadcast media have thus far done little to foster democracy in the United States—as evidenced by the diminishing percentage of voters in national elections and the limited space for genuine debate or public affairs programming in the commercial system. Part of the problem is that capitalism and commercial values have overwhelmingly dominated democracy in the system of broadcasting in the United States. Although defenders of the commercial television system pay lip service to democratic ideals and continually argue that the conjunction of capitalism and democracy provides the most democratic system of broadcasting, capitalist control of the communications media have, in fact, produced a mind-numbing system of commercial broadcasting controlled by powerful economic interests that have undermined democracy in the United States to a dangerous extent. Accordingly, all efforts should be made to limit the power of capital, to liberate communication and all other spheres of life from domination by business interests that are in conflict with democracy.

Although media reform would in itself constitute only a small part of the process of genuine democratization, given the power of television and the media stressed throughout this book, it is nevertheless essential that a democratic media politics be part of any progressive agenda. Unfortunately, however, media politics has been a neglected dimension of post-1960s progressive political movements in the United States.[7] Unless progressives are able to actively intervene in the communications system, they will become increasingly marginalized and ineffectual in the current political arena. Indeed, the New Right was able to win and hold cultural and political hegemony in the late 1970s and 1980s precisely because of its effective media politics and use of new technologies of communication. If the Left wants to be a player in the politics of the future, it too must devise an effective media and communication politics. Such an agenda would involve consideration of an alternative system of public broadcasting as well as alternative public access systems, and it is to discussion of these alternatives that I shall now turn.

5.2 Public Broadcasting: Promises and Failures

From the beginning, public broadcasting was conceived as an alternative to commercial network television. Although the FCC established the foundation for an educational television system as early as 1952, the development of a genuine public broadcasting system took many years. The Ford Foundation provided grants for building stations and producing some programming, but many regions of the country—including the largest television centers—were unable to raise matching funds, and public television was erratic at best. Ford's National Educational Television (NET) system began providing stations with programs, but the system had no cable or satellite linkage until the 1960s; thus films and then videotapes were initially shipped by mail and relayed from station to station.

The public broadcasting system slowly evolved and the federal government gradually and hesitantly began contributing, such that by 1966 there were 100 stations and some notable programming achievements.[8] In 1966 a Carnegie Commission on Educational Television issued a report recommending increased government support and suggested that the term *public television* be used to encompass "all that is of human interest and importance which is not at the moment appropriate or available for support by advertising" (cited in Barnouw 1978, 64). The commission explicitly recognized that public broadcasting needs could not be met by a commercial-based system and urged that public financing be arranged, whereby public broadcasting could evolve. Through such broadcasting, the American people could come to "know themselves, their communities, and their world in richer ways." Such a system would be a "civilized voice in a civilized community" (cited in Barnouw 1978, 179).

The Carnegie report urged the development of a Corporation for Public Broadcasting (CPB), which would use public funds to produce and distribute quality television programming via cable and satellite. President Johnson—an owner of broadcasting stations himself, and desirous of maintaining consensus during the Vietnam period—approved the Carnegie plan and helped provide congressional support and funding for the project. Yet the new public broadcasting bill rejected the Carnegie Commission's recommendation to finance the system through a tax on television sets and through fees levied on commercial uses of the system in order to insulate it from the congressional pressures inevitably involved in gaining annual appropriations. Instead, the system was launched with a minimal first-year appropriation of $4,500,000 and thereafter was funded by annual appropriations from Congress—a procedure that makes the system highly vulnerable to political pressures and the changing forces of hegemony.

Despite its dependence on congressional generosity for continued funding, the new Public Broadcasting Service (PBS) began regular national broadcasting in 1970 and produced some genuinely alternative programming that was critical of U.S. Vietnam policy and engaged in occasional social satire and critique. The integrity of the system was soon threatened, however, when in 1972 Richard Nixon vetoed a two-year federal appropriation, thus signaling that public broadcasting would have to get other funding and should reorganize along the lines of "grass-roots localism." Nixon administration officials also made it clear that public television had to steer clear of public affairs programming and that it would be carefully scrutinized by the state (Stone 1985).

The public broadcasting system was "saved" from financial crisis by the oil corporations, which were taking in record profits from the 1973-1974 energy crisis and skyrocketing energy costs. Their support of public broadcasting enabled the oil corporations both to gain a hefty tax write-off and to buy some favorable publicity during an era when they were coming under attack by many social forces. The de facto economic control of public broadcasting by the big oil companies inspired critics to mock the "Petroleum Broadcasting System." Nevertheless, with the growing participation of other corporate sponsors who began funding programs, their influence was eventually diluted—even though corporate influence on the whole was obviously expanding.

Under the presidency of Ronald Reagan, the FCC led the way in carrying through deregulation. Meanwhile, the PBS system became subject to attacks from the Right. Indeed, PBS took a sharp "right turn" during the Reagan/ Bush years and continues to be dominated by conservative political talk shows and pro-business programs. In 1988, however, viewers and critics began attacking the blatantly conservative and pro-corporate tilt of public broadcasting, chastising the network and its affiliates with phone calls and letters protesting the imbalance. As reported in the FAIR newsletter *Extra!*:

> Many PBS stations air three weekly programs hosted by editors of the rightwing *National Review* magazine: *Firing Line, The McLaughlin Group* and *One On One*. Protestors asked for a weekly show hosted by a partisan journalist of the left. The business agenda is featured on regular PBS programs such as Louis Rukeyser's *Wall Street Week, Adam Smith's Money World* and the *Nightly Business Report*. Public broadcasting protestors are seeking at least one weekly program addressing the public interest agenda—consumer, labor, ecology, peace, civil rights. (November–December 1988, p. 2)

In the same issue of *Extra!*, Pat Aufderheide argues that although 45 percent of the households who view PBS are white- or blue-collar workers, labor and public interest voices are not represented. She attributes this phenomenon to PBS's three "money masters": "the government, individual donors, and corporate and foundation donors" (ibid., 12). Aufderheide notes some of the PBS series and programs that business has funded and indicates that labor has far fewer resources to devote to media production. Federal government defunding of independent film and video production also contributes to the paucity of critical voices on the public broadcast system.

During the Reagan years, whenever a documentary or program appeared on PBS that the Right claimed had a liberal or left-wing "bias," a right-wing group was allowed to offer a rebuttal—often at the public's expense. As liberals and radicals were allowed no such rebuttals, public broadcasting is currently serving to bolster conservative ideological hegemony. For example, the right-wing was allowed to produce (again, at the public's expense) "rebuttals" to the PBS series on Vietnam and to a documentary on Nicaragua, but I know of no progressive rebuttal to the right-wing documentary on the Miskito Indians in Nicaragua produced by a group affiliated with the ultrarightist Reverend Moon, nor to any other PBS program.

Although PBS offers some programming that is vastly superior to commercial network programming, much of it is elitist and dull, and local PBS programming tends to be second rate and mediocre. Furthermore, an inordinate amount of programming is imported from Britain rather than produced in the United States. Thus PBS programming tends to be aimed at an upscale "cultural" audience rather than being produced for the whole public. This was especially true during the Reagan administration, which defunded programming made by progressives, women, people of color, Native Americans, and other minority cultures (Aufderheide 1983, 1988).

There is not much of a tradition of investigative reporting in public broadcasting. Some excellent documentaries have been produced, such as Bill Moyers' 1988 program on the Iran/Contra scandal and his 1989 series on the politics of the image, as well as a superb "Frontline" documentary on the botched execution of the Grenada invasion, but these are exceptions. The nightly PBS newscasts are also generally lacking in investigative reporting, and the official spokespersons are usually moderate representatives of opposing positions. "The MacNeil/Lehrer News Hour" is funded by AT&T, one of many major corporations that finance PBS's information and entertainment programs. For example, in the late 1980s a series on space was sponsored by an aircraft manufacturer, and a series devoted to drinking in France was sponsored by an exporter of French wines.

Such underwriting amounts, in effect, to self-serving promotion, and the sponsor-funding information at the beginning of some PBS shows is becoming ever longer and more pictorial. In general, such corporate underwriting usually precludes the development of series or programs that critically present or confront corporations. For example, Du Pont provides 75 percent of the funding for the popular series "Newton's Apple." It also produces many carcinogenic chemicals and is a major corporate polluter. It manufactures 25 percent of the world's ozone-eating chlorofluorocarbons, thus putting obvious pressure to exert caution on those producing a show about, say, "the greenhouse effect" (*In These Times*, March 15, 1989, p. 4). By providing "major funding," Du Pont is thus subtly able to encourage programming that is favorable to its interests and to ensure that producers won't bite the hand that feeds it.

The paucity of public investment in U.S. public television compared to that of other countries is another national scandal (comparable to the pitifully low investment made in public health). The United States spends less public money per person on television than almost any country in the so-called developed world and accordingly has one of the weakest systems of public broadcasting. In 1983, for instance, Japan spent $10.09 per person on public television, whereas the United States spent only $3.02 (*TV Guide*, May 17, 1986, p. 3). Aufderheide claims that by 1988 the United States was spending "around 77 cents per capita on public broadcasting; in Japan it's $14; in Canada (for national services alone), $23.60; and in Britain, $24.52" (1988, 12). Furthermore, of the $173 million which the Corporation for Public Broadcasting received in 1985, only $29 million went directly into programming; the rest generated a large and self-serving bureaucracy. Indeed, the average PBS station spends only 3 to 6 percent of its budget buying programs from PBS's Station Program Cooperative.

This is a national disgrace that an enlightened public should struggle to improve. Indeed, increased investment in public television is necessary if the citizenry is to be informed, actively interested in politics, and able to participate in democratic discussion and decisionmaking. Public television should, on principle, be defended against commercial broadcasting, and there should be political agitation for the level of public television found in West Germany, Britain, France, Italy, and most European countries. But improvement of the system of public broadcasting requires major reforms.

Robert Cirino proposes a distinction between a "paternalistic, elite model of management operation" and a democratic, "spectrum-sharing model" of public broadcasting (1987, 568ff.). In the paternalist model, such as one finds in the United States, England, and Japan, elite boards determine the structure and content of public broadcasting and are often influenced by the dominant political forces of the day. By contrast, the Netherlands uses a spectrum-sharing model, wherein each group that is able to gain a certain number of members is allowed a proportionate access to the public broadcasting system, whose board of governors has been chosen from a diverse range of political and social groups. Cirino advocates such a democratic spectrum-sharing model for the United States and proposes that four public broadcasting systems be funded to supplement the current system—namely, socialist, liberal, conservative, and libertarian networks. Each could be allowed a certain amount of free time on the public broadcasting system. In this way, different political groups could be given access to public broadcasting time to present their views; time could also be reserved for cultural programming and other general-interest programs that could be produced by politically and culturally diverse groups.

Such a system would make available to the public a diversity of political opinion that could help revitalize public debate and provide a more informed citizenry. It would also help foster a more pluralist cultural system. But if such a revitalized system is to be viable, an alternative mode of financing needs to be devised that would ensure that the system was free from direct governmental pressure and control. As Garnham argues: "It is the quantity of the funding and the nature of the financing source that is the most fundamental determining constraint on a broadcasting structure" (1978, 53). The attacks on PBS during the Nixon and Reagan administrations made it clear that long-term funding is needed and that a system of public broadcasting must be established that is free from political pressures and influence. A public broadcasting system could not serve a watchdog function or engage in serious investigative reporting if it is dependent for funds on those it is supposed to monitor (i.e., business and government, the two most powerful sectors of a capitalist democracy, which currently fund and implicitly control the broadcast media, both private and public).

Also necessary is a new structure for the public broadcasting system that would make it less subject to political manipulation, more diverse, and more responsive.[9] A genuinely independent system of public broadcasting would require something like a ten-year funding program and establishment of a corporation for public broadcasting similar to the Dutch and West German systems, which include representatives from all major political parties, labor and business, public interest groups, women, and people of color. Appointments to the board should be made by a bipartisan panel independent of government and should strive to achieve ideological balance and overall diversity. Members of the board could be appointed for initial two-year terms and, if they successfully fulfill their mandates, could be reappointed for five-year terms, perhaps with a twelve-year limit.

Financing for revitalized public broadcasting could be obtained through a variety of measures. In the late 1970s, as part of an effort to reform the broadcasting system, Congressman Lionel Van Deerlin (D-Calif.) proposed that public broadcasting be financed by a yearly license fee paid by each user of the broadcast spectrum. Van Deerlin's reforms were never realized (Reel 1979, 180ff.), but other serious proposals have been advanced. For instance, Senator Ernest Hollings (D-S.C.) proposed taxing the sales of television stations, cable systems, and networks to fund public broadcasting. Hollings' proposal reached the final stages of congressional action in 1987, but "at the last moment, the proposal to levy such a tax was deleted from the bill. . . . [Hollings] acknowledged that the media owners are more powerful than Congress: 'We had unanimity,' he said, 'but the broadcasters

are way more powerful' " (Schiller 1989, 109–110). The "spectrum use fee,"
whereby broadcasters would pay a tax for use of the spectrum, could also
help. Another proposal would be to tax television advertising and use the
proceeds to finance the public access system. A Benton Foundation publication has proposed a taxpayer check-off system, whereby taxpayers
contribute a dollar a year with a check off on their tax returns (Shooshan
and Arnheim 1989). Or the United States, like England, could place a
small tax on the sale of radios, television sets, video recorders, and other
electronic equipment to fund public broadcasting—although this system is
more regressive than the above proposals. The best proposal, however, is
to fund programming by taxing advertising and, perhaps, to supplement
this money with a tax on the sale of television stations and other TV
properties (as Hollings has suggested). There is also merit in the spectrum
use fee and taxpayer check-off revenue. At any rate, it is a scandal that
more resources are not being devoted to public television in the United
States, and that Congress and corporations (with their own axes to grind)
are the current sources of financing.

In considering development of a new public broadcasting system, one
should not forget the importance of revitalizing public radio as well as
television. Britain has several public radio stations and recognizes the
continued importance of radio in the broadcasting mix. In the United
States, too, radio continues to be of importance and influence, even though
it is currently controlled by often crass commercial influences and is
predominantly used as an advertising medium with popular music as the
bait. This need not be so, however. National Public Radio in the United
States provides some excellent alternative programming. Localism in public
radio also seems to be far superior to local initiatives in public television,
given that many local National Public Radio stations are producing worth-
while programming. Such programming should be encouraged, and more
federal interest and support should be directed to the system of public
radio.

Guaranteed funding and a public broadcasting corporation independent
from governmental influence would free the system of public radio and
television from the influence of corporate sponsors and make possible the
creation of a genuinely democratic system of public broadcasting. It is
important to recognize that a predominantly commercial system (as in the
United States) and a state-controlled system (as in the Soviet Union) are
not the only alternatives. Other possibilities for financing and organizing
public broadcasting are available, and a system of broadcasting free from
domination by business and government (both of which currently dominate
public broadcasting in the United States) is indeed possible. And yet a
revitalized public broadcasting system would be only one component in a

new democratic broadcasting system complemented by other alternative broadcasting services.

5.3 Public Access Television

Public access television is one of the few real forms of alternative television, and it provides the best prospect for using the broadcast media to serve the interests of popular democracy. As Frantz Fanon put it, "A community will evolve only when a people control their own communications." Indeed, the rapid expansion of public access television in recent years has created new opportunities for progressives to counter the conservative programming that dominates mainstream television. Innovative access programming is now being cablecast regularly in New York, Los Angeles, Boston, Chicago, Atlanta, Madison, Austin, and hundreds of other towns or regions throughout the country. In this section, I shall discuss public access television in the context of the new possibilities for democratic intervention in broadcast media, and provide examples of alternative programming based on a media project with which I am involved in Austin, Texas.[10]

When cable television was widely introduced in the early 1970s, the FCC mandated that "beginning in 1972, new cable systems [and, after 1977, all cable systems] in the 100 largest television markets be required to provide channels for government, for educational purposes, and most importantly, for public access." This mandate suggested that cable systems should make three public access channels available for state and local government, education, and community use. The term *public access* was construed to mean that the cable company should make equipment and air time available so that literally anybody could make noncommercial use of the access channel to say or do anything he or she wished, on a first-come, first-serve basis, subject only to obscenity and libel laws. Local organizations were set up to manage the access system; and, in some cases, the cable company itself managed the access center, providing the equipment and personnel to make access programming.

In the beginning, few if any cable systems made as many as three channels available. Some systems began offering one or two in the 1970s. For the most part, the availability of access channels depends on the political clout of local governments and of committed, often unpaid, local groups to convince the cable companies (almost all of which are privately owned) to make access channels available. In Austin, Texas, for example, a small group of video activists formed Austin Community Television in 1973 and began cablecasting with their own equipment through the cable system that year. Eventually, they received foundation and CETA government grants to support their activities, buy equipment, and pay regular employees salaries. A new cable contract signed in the early 1980s required that the cable company pay $500,000 a year for access. After a difficult political struggle (which will be described later in the chapter), the access system was able to get at least $300,000 to $400,000 a year to support Austin Community Television activities.

In 1979, however, a Supreme Court decision struck down the 1972 FCC ruling on the grounds that the agency didn't have the authority to mandate access—an authority that supposedly belongs to the U.S. Congress (see *FCC v. Midwest Video Cor.* 440 U.S. 689, discussed in Koenig 1979). Nonetheless, cable was expanding so rapidly and becoming such a high-growth, competitive industry that city governments considering cable systems were besieged by companies making lucrative offers of 20 to 80 channel cable systems. In such an atmosphere, city governments were able to negotiate access channels and financial support for a public access system. Consequently, public access grew significantly during the 1980s, and more than 1,000 access centers now cablecast regular programming.

Where there are operative public access systems, individuals have a promising, though not sufficiently explored, opportunity to produce and cablecast their own television programs. Shown in Austin, for example, are weekly antinuclear programs, black and chicano series, gay programs, countercultural and anarchist programs, an atheist program, feminist programs, labor programs, and a weekly progressive news magazine, "Alternative Views," which produced more than 400 hour-long programs between 1978 and 1990 on a wide variety of topics, thus providing a conduit for perspectives ("alternative views") usually excluded from the broadcasting spectrum.

"Alternative Views"

Our show originated in 1978 and immediately started producing a weekly program by using video equipment and tapes at the University of Texas as well as the broadcast and editing facilities of Austin Community Television. In fact, a group does not require technical experience or even financial resources to begin producing access programming, especially when there is an access system in place that will provide equipment, technical personnel, and video tapes. A few systems charge a fee for the use of facilities or air time; but owing to competitive bidding between cable systems for the most lucrative franchises, many cable systems offer free use of equipment, personnel, and air time; occasionally they even provide free videotapes. Many public access systems also offer training programs on how to use the media, directed to groups or individuals who want to make their own programs from original conception through final editing. As equipment costs have rapidly declined, it is even possible for some groups to purchase their own video equipment. (See below for more details on how to organize public access production.)

From the beginning, those of us involved in "Alternative Views" were convinced that our programs would prove of interest to the community; indeed, we gained a large and loyal audience.[11] On our first program in October 1978, our guest was an Iranian student who discussed opposition to the shah and the possibility of his overthrow; we also featured a detailed discussion of how the Sandinista movement was struggling to overthrow Somoza—weeks before the national broadcast media discovered these movements. We then offered two programs on nuclear energy and energy alternatives, featuring, among other guests, Austinite Ray Reece (1980), whose book later became a definitive text on corporate control and suppression of solar energy. On early shows we broadcast in-depth interviews with former Senator Ralph Yarborough, a Texas progressive responsible for such legislation as the National Defense Education Act. (In the process, we learned that he had never before been interviewed for television.) We also aired an interview with former CIA official John Stockwell, who described how he had been recruited into the CIA at the University of Texas. Stockwell (1978) discussed not only the CIA's activities but also his own experiences in Africa, Vietnam, and then Angola, which led him to quit the CIA and write a book (*In Search of Enemies*) that exposed the Angola operation he had been in charge of. He then detailed a long history of CIA abuses and provided arguments as to why he thought the CIA should be shut down and a new intelligence service developed.

Other interviews included discussions with American Atheist founder Madalyn Murray O'Hair, who expounded her views on religion and told of how she had successfully brought lawsuits to eliminate prayer from schools, thus preserving the constitutional separation between church and state; with Jim Hightower, who discussed agribusiness and oil corporations; with Benjamin Spock, who discussed the evolution of his theory of child-rearing, his political radicalization, and his adventures in the 1960s as an antiwar activist; with Stokeley Carmichael (now Kwame Ture), who discussed his 1960s militancy and theories of black power, his experiences in Africa, and his perspectives on world revolution; and with Nobel Prize winner George Wald, former Attorney General Ramsey Clark, antinuclear activist Helen Caldicott, and many other well-known intellectuals, activists, and social critics.

As our connections grew, we began receiving documentaries from various filmmakers and devised a documentary and talk show format. We also presented a regular news section that utilized material from mostly non-mainstream news sources. These stories, largely ignored by the establishment media, provided interpretations of events different from those in the mainstream. We received very positive responses to our show and began regularly taping interviews with people who visited Austin as well as with local activists involved in various struggles. We began varying our format using documentary films, slide shows, raw video footage, and other material to enhance the visual aspect of our program. In addition, one of our members, Frank Morrow, became skilled at editing and developed some impressive montages of documentary and interview material to illustrate the topics being discussed.

Once the project got under way, we had little difficulty finding topics, people, or resources. We discovered that almost everyone we wished to interview was happy to appear on our program, and, after we began gaining recognition, local groups and individuals called us regularly to provide topics, speakers, films, and other video material. We encouraged some local groups to make their own weekly shows, and a variety of peace, countercultural, gay, anti-nuke, chicano, anti-klan, women's, and other groups have done so. Indeed, we have continued to serve as an umbrella organization for more than 100 local groups that have used their speakers and film or video materials to produce programs.

Aside from hour-long interviews with the nationally known individuals already mentioned, various feminists, gays, union activists, and representatives of local progressive groups have appeared as guests on our show. We have also carried through in-depth interviews with officials from the Soviet Union and Nicaragua, Allende's former government in Chile, members of the democratic front in El Salvador, and participants in other Third World revolutionary movements. And in addition to the documentaries and films provided by various filmmakers and groups, we ourselves have made video documentaries on a variety of topics. We have also received raw video footage of the bombing of Lebanon and the aftermath of the massacres at Sabra and Shatilla, of the assassinations of five communist labor organizers by the Ku Klux Klan in Greensboro, North Carolina, of daily life in the liberated zones of El Salvador, and of counterrevolutionary activity in Nicaragua.

Most of this material would not have been shown on network television; at the least, it would have been severely cut and censored. Hence it is probably true that the best existing possibility for producing alternative television is through public access/cable television. Obviously, progressive groups who want to carry out access projects must make a sustained commitment to media politics and explore local possibilities for intervention.

Public Access Television: Challenges and Problems

When progressive public access television became widespread and popular in Austin, it was subjected to political counterattacks. The establishment daily newspaper, the *Austin American-Statesman*, published frequent denunciations of public access television, claiming that it was controlled by the "lunatic" fringe of "socialists, atheists, and radicals" and that it was not representative of the community as a whole (an interesting claim given that many conservative church groups, business groups, and political groups also make use of access). The "poor technical quality" of public access television was attacked along with the "irresponsibility" of many of the programs (in fact, technical quality has been steadily improving). In 1983 these criticisms were repeated in editorials and in articles on Austin Community Television (ACTV) in the more liberal monthly magazines, *Texas Monthly* and *Third Coast*. Representatives of these publications wanted to get part of the access pie and thus attacked the group currently in control—as did some members of the local public broadcasting system.

Eventually, the criticisms became threatening. Austin Community Television was applying for a five-year renewal of its contract as access manager, but certain interests in the community were attempting to replace it with another access manager and system controlled by city government and local media interests. After an intense political struggle, the city cable commission and the city council approved the renewal of the ACTV access management. For the time being, the community remains in control of the access system, which is open to anyone who wants to use it, either on a regular or an occasional basis.

Other U.S. cities have not been so fortunate.[12] Some cable companies have either taken over the access center or leased access channels for commercial purposes. Some city governments have also taken over access centers and have been known to shut them down, lease them commercially, or use them exclusively for government purposes. Many access centers are severely underfunded, and some major cities (e.g., San Francisco) have only one access channel. Some access centers, such as the one in Houston, charge fees for use of equipment and airtime. And since there is no cable law that mandates access, some centers will be threatened with shutdown when current franchise contracts expire.

Furthermore, many cable companies have never provided access channels, whereas others rigidly control the access channels and would probably not permit a program like "Alternative Views" to be cablecast. But many cities *do* have relatively open access channels. Where possible, progressives should start using this vehicle of political communication with an eye toward developing a national public access network in which tapes can be exchanged and circulated. Steps in this direction have been discussed in various groups, including our own, which has now developed a national access network. In the spring of 1984 we began distributing "Alternative Views" program tapes to access centers in Dallas and San Antonio, and in the fall of 1984 we added Fayetteville, Atlanta, Minneapolis, Pittsburgh, and Urbana to our evolving network. After that, we made contact with access systems and groups in New York, Boston, Portland, San Diego, Marin County, Fairfax and Arlington counties in Virginia, Cincinnati, San Francisco, Columbus,

Chicago, New Haven, Durham, and many other cities. This project involves contacting local groups or members of an access center who are interested in sponsoring our program on a regular weekly basis, and duplicating and sending packages of five tapes to the access systems in these cities. Administration of this project has required the heroic labor of Frank Morrow, who has managed to provide tapes to as many as fifty different access centers and to keep track of which programs have been distributed to the various centers (i.e., to avoid duplication and to provide variety).

At the Union for Democratic Communications conference in Washington in October 1984, several access groups explored the possibility of leasing weekly satellite time so that progressive access programming could be beamed all over the country. This would mean that the millions of people who own home satellite receivers could watch progressive public access programming. Preliminary inquires suggest that the cost of renting satellite time for access programming is not prohibitive; indeed, a grant of $100,000 to $150,000 a year might yet make it possible for additional millions of people all over the country to receive progressive television in their homes.

During 1985–1986, Paper Tiger Television, a New York–based access project founded by DeeDee Halleck, received grants that made possible a ten-week satellite access project. "Deep Dish TV," as it was called, broadcast via satellite ten programs (on such topics as militarism, agriculture, racism, Central America, and children's TV) to access systems and private dishes across the country. It is hoped that this effort will eventually lead to a Left-leaning satellite channel that can compete with the multitude of religious, business, and other satellite outlets that tend to present the ideologies and agendas of the Right. Access centers must be convinced to carry progressive access programs, as Paper Tiger has done. Indeed, it claims that more than 300 systems carry its Deep Dish TV series. During a second season, Deep Dish TV produced a new series of programs on selected topics; as of 1990, a third season is being planned.

In the next section, we shall examine some of the ways in which individuals might make use of public access television in situations where cable television already exists. After that, we shall consider proposals for a progressive satellite television system.

How to Produce Local Access Programming

Individuals and groups wishing to produce progressive television programming must first explore the availability of an access channel and approach the people in charge of it. They should make clear what type of programming they want to produce, and inquiries should be made concerning what equipment, training, and tapes are available from the access center. Next, a group must decide if it wishes to produce only occasional programs or to develop a regular weekly, biweekly, or monthly series. "Alternative Views" started out by producing weekly one-hour programs and then developed its programming organization, philosophy, and projects as it went on. In some cases, however, more fully developed projects should be outlined before one begins.

In many respects, it is preferable to undertake a weekly program, played at the same day and time every week, in order to build up an audience. A talk show format is, of course, the easiest to adopt, even though more imaginative uses of video might be developed as experience and expertise expand. Paper Tiger Television in New York, for example, combines critiques of various types of corporate media by media critics with imaginative sets, visuals, editing, and so on. A labor-oriented program in Pittsburgh, "The Mill Hunk News," combines news reports of labor issues with documentary interviews and uses music videos as well as other creative visuals.

An alternative television project can also draw on the many progressive films and videos already produced. Many groups are happy to provide copies of their films and video cassettes for broadcast on public access. If the films and duplicating equipment are available, this, too, is a good way to begin. Then, as the project progresses, the group may want to begin developing its own documentaries and perhaps mix documentary, film, and discussion formats by editing in titles, slides, and other images in order to make use of the video format.

Once the project gets under way, the group should consider incorporating as a nonprofit corporation and applying for tax-exempt status from the IRS. Doing so will help in fund-raising activities because the donations then become tax-deductible; tax-exempt status also makes possible the purchase of nonprofit bulk-mailing permits, which can be useful for fund raising and communicating with the audience by mail. An access project can be funded through regular benefits, solicitation of contributions, and various local and national foundation grants. A few access systems actually pay for programming, but they are unfortunately exceptions. Indeed, the development of progressive access systems will eventually involve struggling for funding from the cable systems and the city government. In this way, members of access groups could be paid for their activity and would have a budget to purchase cassettes of films and video programming from independent producers. Both public access television and independent film and video could thus be established on a financially secure foundation.

Of course, public access television is not a substitute for political organization and struggle; rather, it is a vehicle through which participants and local political groups can provide information about their activities and involve people in their efforts. Almost every one of the 100 or so groups that have appeared on "Alternative Views" have reported that they received many phone calls and letters indicating interest in their groups and that appearing on public access television was a useful organizing and recruiting tool. Public access videotapes can also be made available to high schools, university campuses, churches, and other local groups. Our tapes on Central America, for instance, have been frequently shown in churches and elsewhere for educational and organizing purposes. Thus public access programming is a useful tool for political education; indeed, it goes beyond regular broadcasting by reaching into community politics and organizing.

Public access television is still in a relatively early stage of development in the United States, and it is just beginning in Europe; but it contains the promise of providing a different type of alternative television. Despite obstacles to its use, public access provides one opening in the commercial and state broadcasting systems that is at least potentially receptive to progressive intervention. It is self-defeating to dismiss the broadcast media as tools of manipulation and to think that the print media are the only tools of communication and political education open to progressives. Surveys have shown that people take more seriously individuals and groups that appear on TV; thus the use of television could help progressive movements and struggles gain legitimacy and force in the shifting and contradictory field of U.S. politics. After all, the Right has been making effective use of new technologies and media of communication, and progressives can no longer afford to remain aloof. As to the question of whether viewers would actually watch alternative television, surveys indicate that interesting public access programs gather a respectable percentage of the audience, often getting more viewers than PBS programs (see the sources in note 11). By 1990, *Alternative Views*, for instance, had gained a national audience, and we received stacks of letters and many phone calls everyday. Viewers seem to be ready for more socially critical, controversial, and investigative television, thus it is probable that a public interest network would have a large and devoted following.

The possible breakup of conservative hegemony in the 1990s confronts progressives with both new challenges and new dangers. But if the Left is to produce a genuine alternative to the Right, progressives must increase their mass base and circulate their struggles to more segments of the population. After all, most people get their news and information from television, and the broadcast media arguably play a decisive role in defining political realities, shaping public opinion, and determining what is to be taken seriously. If progressives want to play a role in U.S. political life, they must come to terms with the realities of electronic communication and develop strategies to make use of new technologies and possibilities for intervention.

There is the risk, of course, that the time and energy spent in other projects may be lost in occasionally frustrating media politics. But this risk must be taken if progressives want to intervene more effectively in the changing technological and political environment of the future. To ensure that we get the full free flow of information that an informed democratic citizenry requires to participate intelligently in the political process, I believe we need an expanded system of public access television that could be funded from revenues received from cable systems (as is currently the case in Austin, Texas, and elsewhere in the country). Yet, the new satellite television technology also holds the potential for a greatly expanded democratic communication system.

5.4 Satellite Television and Some Utopian Proposals

All too briefly, cable and satellite television offered possibilities for a significantly improved broadcasting system. What I call the "golden age of cable and satellite television" in the early 1980s went far beyond the "golden age of television" in the 1950s in terms of diversity of innovative programming. Whereas 1950s television broadcast, at best, a few quality live dramas and anthology drama series, 1980s television aired a wide range of new programming services. For instance, in 1980, the Cable News Network (CNN) began a 24-hour-a-day news service that was joined shortly thereafter by CNN2, which provided a 30-minute news service. Viewers could therefore receive news reports at any time of the day or night. In addition, the CNN channel frequently broadcast live congressional hearings, news conferences, and other events. These news services were supplemented in the 1980s with C-SPAN, which provided live broadcasts of congressional sessions, videotapes of significant conferences or lectures, political discussion and call-in shows, and other political television; this service was supplemented in 1987 by a second C-SPAN channel that broadcast live Senate proceedings.

In 1982 CBS Cable offered an exciting experimental cultural channel for cable television systems. It produced innovative television that included the best European movies, documentaries, provocative talk shows, and intelligent artistic productions. At the same time, The Entertainment Network cablecast quality television from England, and Tele-France presented several hours a day of the best in French film, television, and culture on the SPN network. The Arts Network also broadcast quality cultural programming, and many movie services (HBO, Cinemax, Showtime, etc.) featured contemporary and classical films, uncut and without advertising. The Black Entertainment Network and two national Spanish-language networks were implemented, and channels for the hearing-impaired, children, and businesspeople began operation. For rock music enthusiasts, MTV was available; sports fans could turn to all-sports channels; news enthusiasts could watch around-the-clock news channels; and religious buffs could ingest all the old-time religion and right-wing politics that they desired.

These services were generally supported by revenues accrued from advertising and the expansion of cable television, which had a boom period in the early 1980s. Unfortunately, CBS Cable, after losing $35 million in its first year, shut down operations in 1983, as did the Tele-France service; meanwhile, the Arts and Entertainment channels merged into one service that is still operative. The cable channels that survived, having received adequate advertising and cable industry support, were the more commercial networks such as USA, which showed network reruns and programming similar to those of commercial broadcasting. Specialty networks such as MTV, ESPN, and CNN, as well as channels funded by corporations such as the Disney Channel and the Playboy Channel, also survived. Obviously, the commercial system could not support quality cultural services or a different kind of television programming, such as was found all too briefly on CBS Cable. Thus, the promise of quality and alternative television on cable soon receded as cable became increasingly commercial and more and more like network television.

In the mid-1980s another new technology promised the ultimate in television variety and diversity: satellite television. Indeed, the home satellite industry began booming, and by 1986 more than 1.5 million Americans owned satellite dishes and were able to receive at least 100 channels on 16 or so active satellites. Moreover, new channels appeared almost every month. Movie-lovers could choose from hundreds of movies, sports fans could see almost every major sporting event, religious junkies could get their fix of evangelical religion, and news buffs could see unedited live reports broadcast from satellites to the networks—and could then determine which stories got on the evening news and in what form. Those with diverse tastes could find a variety of programming previously unimaginable. Superstations in New York, Chicago, Atlanta, New Jersey, Dallas, and San Diego provided viewers programming and news from these areas, and satellites offered programming from Mexico and Canada. In addition, one could view live news feeds, hear off-color jokes during the commercial breaks in some live network programs, and pick up satellite conferences ranging from corporate meetings attended by Coca-Cola bosses trying to deal with the disaster of the unpopular "new Coke" to gatherings of scientists concerned with the dangers of nuclear war. The Global Village seemed to have arrived.

But on January 15, 1986 (a day of infamy for the U.S. broadcasting system), HBO-Cinemax began full-time "scrambling" of its satellites signals, which the owners of home satellite dishes had previously been receiving free of cost. By the end of 1986 several other movie services and cable channels had followed suit, and as of 1990 almost every single cable network has scrambled its service. To be sure, one can buy an expensive decoder and pay for monthly satellite services, which tend to cost somewhat more than cable prices; but this television alternative is prohibitively expensive for most families. Consequently, the satellite industry has significantly slowed down after a period of rapid expansion. Once again, the imperatives of corporate profit and control of the communications system have limited the democratizing potential of a new communications technology that has been absorbed into the old system.

Just as there were earlier attempts to suppress FM radio, UHF television, and cable and pay TV in favor of maintaining the status quo in the broadcasting industry, business and government have worked together to halt the growth of the satellite industry, which threatened the interests of the major broadcasting powers and the cable industry. The FCC permitted scrambling and Congress failed to take any positive action to limit it. Although there were persistent allegations of scandal, concerning pressure from cable owners that forced satellite channels to scramble their programs, these allegations were never investigated. In short, Congress never really examined whether scrambling was in the public interest—but this was a typical abrogation of congressional responsibility during the Reagan/Bush years.

Toward a System of Democratic Cable/Satellite Television

Yet satellite television remains the technological foundation for a national system of alternative television—for a democratic, innovative, and diverse television system. A combination of cable and satellite technologies would make possible the creation of a truly excellent system of communications. But it would also require an immediate halt to satellite scrambling and allow a free flow of information and entertainment to satellite dishes. Although the U.S. government has consistently followed a communications policy in the field of international communications based on a "free flow of information" policy, it has not allowed a free flow to its own citizens. The scrambling situation has progressed to the point that even most PBS channels, the American Arms Forces Services television, and some CBS transponders have scrambled. Once again, then, commercial interests have ridden roughshod over the public interest, and the FCC and Congress have either sanctioned the process or allowed the most powerful corporate interests to control the communications spectrum.

But reversal of this process so as to permit an unscrambled satellite system would make possible a truly diverse system of broadcasting. Here is my proposal: In an age of cable and satellite television, with more than 60 percent of the nation wired for cable and more than 2.5 million homes with satellite dishes, why not make a satellite channel available to various groups who want to broadcast their political views and information? A public interest satellite channel could be provided to representative groups free of charge so that Democrats, Republicans, workers, blacks, hispanics, women, gays, socialists, anarchists, and any number of other groups could present their political views and programs every day. Time could be allotted according to the number of members in each group applying for access. This national political channel could then be picked up by every cable system in the country, and people could be assured of getting real debate over issues of public concern.

To be effective, such a channel would have to be legislated as a required channel for cable systems, to guarantee its maximum distribution. This requirement would be easy to implement and relatively inexpensive to maintain, as every cable company in the country has satellite reception dishes and most have dishes that can be used free of charge by the various groups of the public interest satellite channel. Eventually, the channel could be expanded to make possible a genuine public interest system of democratic communications. The government could dedicate an entire satellite to public broadcasting and make available the twenty-four transponders currently on each satellite to the various groups that would constitute the public broadcasting system. In this case, of course, individuals would have to own home satellite dishes; but the cost of such dishes would inevitably fall. Such a revitalized and democratized public broadcasting system could greatly expand the current spectrum of ideas and information, and allow open discussion of issues of interest and importance.

Some claim that an increased diversity of media voices will produce a "tower of Babel" that would fragment and polarize the country and undercut efforts at establishing public dialogue and articulation of common interests (Barber 1982). These consequences are possible, but at present and for the foreseeable future the major commercial networks dominate the broadcast spectrum and, as Barber states (1982, 22), create a bland, massified, ideological, and stereotypical discourse. So far, the "unity" and "consensus" brought about by broadcasting have come at the expense of radical and alternative voices and visions. Moreover, the current limitation of the opinion spectrum and the tightened corporate control over news and information have made it necessary to increase the range of voices and opinions if democracy is going to survive. Thus, I think that the risks must be taken and that diversification is less dangerous than total corporate hegemony.[13]

These, in summary, are the steps needed to transform and democratize our broadcast system: (1) Expand and democratize the current public broadcasting system; (2) expand and strengthen the public access system; (3) use cable and satellite television to produce new public broadcasting channels open to groups currently excluded from national communication; and (4) develop an entire satellite and cable system of broadcasting that would allow a significant range of alternative voices and political opinions to be broadcast. Steps 1 and 2 could be undertaken immediately, and steps 3 and 4 are both technologically and financially feasible. Yet development of such an alternative democratic communications system would require educating the public and government about the real possibilities for democratic communication inherent in cable and satellite television.

Toward Democratic Communication and Information

If we do not radically transform our media system, matters will only get worse. The rule by media managers and political handlers will continue, and democracy in the United States will be further imperiled. In the words of Max Weber: "The question is: how are freedom and democracy in the long run possible at all under the domination of highly developed capitalism? Freedom and democracy are only possible where the resolute will of a nation not to allow itself to be ruled like sheep is permanently alive. We are 'individualists' and partisans of 'democratic' institutions 'against the stream' of material constellations" (Weber, cited in Gerth and Mills 1975, 71).

It is a historical irony that the 1980s marked the defeat of democracy by capitalism in the United States and the triumph of democracy over state communism in the Soviet bloc countries. At present, the "free" television media in the United States are probably no more adversarial and no less propagandistic than *Pravda* or the television stations in the Eastern European countries. Hence the very future of democracy is at stake—and development of a democratic communications system is necessary if democracy is to be revitalized. If radical transformation of the system of communications and broadcasting is not undertaken, segments of the society will be condemned to perpetual information poverty; they will lack access to communications and social power. Indeed, the empowerment of individuals to participate in a democratic society must be an important part of a democratic communications system.

Other possibilities for expanding a system of democratic communications can be found in new computer and information technologies. The future may bring a merger of entertainment and information centers whereby all print media information becomes accessible by computer and all visual media entertainment and information resources become available for home computer/entertainment-center access. But the threat, and likelihood, is that this information and entertainment material will be thoroughly commodified, available only to those who can afford to pay. Progressive and investigative media face another threat, however, from data bases—exclusion. Many national data bases do not include Left periodicals such as *In These Times*, *The Guardian*, *Zeta Magazine*, or other publications that are significantly outside the mainstream. It is therefore important that a progressive politics of information struggle to get alternative media sources listed in the major data bases or to develop alternative data bases. Otherwise, once again, progressive voices will be excluded from the information systems of the future. Accordingly, public alternatives to these private/corporate information and entertainment systems of the future must be devised.

Given the growing importance of computers and information in the new technocapitalist society, new information networks and systems are essential ingredients of a progressive communication system. The computerization of the United States is well under way, and new information networks and computer communication systems are emerging. To avoid corporate and government monopolization and control of information, new public information networks and centers will have to provide access to the information needed to intelligently participate in a democratic society. Computers, like broadcasting, can be used either for or against democracy.

Indeed, computers are a potentially democratic technology. While broadcast communication is unidirectional, computer communication is potentially bi- or even omnidirectional. Individuals can use computers to do word-processing that communicates with other individuals; or they can communicate directly via modems, which use the telephone to link individuals with each other. Modems in turn can tap into community bulletin boards or computer conference programs, which make possible a new type of public communication. Progressives should intervene in these information modes as well as in broadcasting. For instance, many computer bulletin boards have a political debate program whereby individuals can type in their opinions and other individuals can read them and respond. This constitutes a new form of public dialogue and interaction.

Individuals can also use their computers to tap into information systems. (In a democratic communication system individuals need free access to all sources of information.) Vast amounts of information are computerized already, but much of it is commodified and accessible only to those who can purchase it. Thus every community needs a Community Information Center that would subscribe to numerous information services and make them available to the public free of charge or at minimal expense. Such an establishment could also provide free computer training classes (so that all individuals could attain the requisite computer skills and literacy for the new information age) and a community bulletin board and information system (so that individuals with home modem devices could tap into the new information systems and receive needed information free of charge). It might even offer the services of information ombudspeople who could help individuals discover appropriate information sources and access the information sought. Such centers already exist in Oakland (the pioneering Community Memory Center) and New York, but they should be developed in every city of the country.

National information networks could also be established via modems so that individuals and groups could communicate with others via national bulletin boards and information systems. Many cities now offer a diversity of computer bulletin boards, and many national groups and services (such as Peace-Net) are setting up international information-distribution systems (see Downing in Downing et al. 1990). Such systems should be expanded, democratized, and open to all.

In addition, democratic data bases and information services should make available all existing information sources, regardless of politics or viewpoint. Many data bases and information services omit leftist, radical, and other alternative information sources from their listings, thus in effect shutting out radical alternatives (much as the broadcasting networks exclude dissident voices from broadcast communication). Leftist groups and alternative publications should struggle to make sure that their information sources and services are listed in data-base bibliographies and source material.

The information and communications revolutions pose both threats and promises to American democracy. Thus far in its history, capitalism has been the major threat to democracy (Wolfe 1977; Cohen and Rogers 1983; Bowles and Gintis 1986), and some of the major struggles of the last decades have been waged over property rights versus democratic rights, over the rights of capital versus the rights of the people. This contradiction is at the center of our communications system as well, and capitalism has thus far prevailed over democracy—to an alarming degree in the 1980s. It follows that the United States has really never had a democratic system of mass communications, by the people, for the people, and of the people. Instead, television and other mainstream media have been used by the capitalist class to maintain their hegemony.

As noted, however, new communications technologies and their use by public interest and citizens groups can help produce an alternative democratic communications system. Individuals and groups are already using new technologies such as computers, desk-top publishing, video, and cable television to promote democratic communication.

Moreover, as video cameras and recorders are increasingly light, inexpensive, and accessible to a wide range of individuals, it has become possible for individuals and groups to inexpensively make their own documentaries and to show to other individuals their own and other political tapes. Political videos, duplicated and circulated to interested individuals and groups, have been an effective mode of opposition to the mainstream media in Chile, the Eastern European countries, and other places where there is tight state or corporate control of the media. In these ways, individuals can use video to produce a new type of political communication, outside of the distribution circuits controlled by broadcast corporations or the state.

Every progressive public interest group and political movement wishing to produce social change should thus devise a media politics to get its message to the public, ranging from PR material and press conferences to production and distribution of its own print and broadcast material. As I have argued, public access television is an excellent arena for political intervention, and progressive groups should use computer technologies and information services to advance their goals and agendas, as did the Right during the late 1970s and 1980s.

In addition, progressive groups should make media politics part of their political agenda, organizing against the broadcast networks when they distort or omit messages concerning issues central to these groups. There should be more monitoring of the mainstream media and more development of alternative media during an era in which politics will be fought out in the new broadcast public sphere. In a media age political struggles are mediated through the media, and those who are not players in this realm are likely to be excluded from the major issues and struggles of the future.

The future of democracy thus depends upon the use of new technologies to promote democracy and to counter capitalist control of the state and broadcast media. Ultimately, then the struggle for a democratic communications system is a struggle for democratic society. The technologies are there, but imagination, will, and struggle will be needed to realize the democratic potential that still exists in a system organized for the hegemony of capital in an era of conservative political rule. Yet liberation from the yoke of capital remains possible. It is also possible to imagine how a truly democratic society could be organized. Such a vision may be utopian, but, as Bertolt Brecht (1967) remarked, "[i]f you think that this is utopian then I would ask you to reflect upon why you think this is utopian."

Notes

1. On the GE/NBC defense and nuclear energy connections, see INFACT 1988; on Tisch's "passionately pro-Israel" stance, see Boyer (1988); and on McWethy as Defense Department apologist, see the discussion in section 4.3.

2. Adequate analysis of the failure of deregulation would involve scrutiny of the S&L and banking crises, deterioration of the airlines industry, and commercialization of broadcasting. The S&L crisis was described on "The MacNeil/Lehrer News Hour" of December 12, 1989, as the greatest economic crisis in the United States since the stock market crash of 1929 and the ensuing Depression. Network coverage of the S&L crisis in 1990 has so far merely targeted individuals charged with wrongdoing, rather than exploring how government policy encouraged the criminal activity; there have also been no investigations of the Bush "bailout" program and why individual taxpayers should pay for the gambling debts of the wheelers and dealers of the Reagan era. On the other hand, the S&L crisis is so

massive and its potential effects are so destructive that scapegoating and reassuring may not be possible if the crisis produces protracted economic hardships.

3. I have adapted the Oz parable from a talk given by Patrick Esmonde-White (1989) at the Union for Democratic Communications Conference in New York in October 1989; he also sent me an unpublished paper, "Beyond Representation: American Democracy in the 1990s," which I have drawn upon in this chapter. On the effects of Reagan's first term on redistribution of wealth and power in the United States, see Ferguson and Rogers, who write: "The combination of social-spending cuts, other budget initiatives, and the massively regressive tax bill produced a huge upward distribution of American income. Over the 1983–85 period the policies reduced the incomes of households making less than $20,000 a year by $20 billion, while increasing the incomes of households making more than $80,000 by $35 billion. For those at the very bottom of the income pyramid, making under $10,000 per year, the policies produced an average loss of $1,100 over 1983–85. For those at the top, making more than $200,000 a year, the average gain was $60,000. By the end of Reagan's first term, U.S. income distribution was more unequal than at any time since 1947, the year the Census Bureau first began collecting data on the subject" (1986, 130). For a summary analysis of how the Reagan years strengthened the position of the corporate class, see Ducat (1988, 10ff).

4. A vast literature exists on the new social movements and struggles for democratization that are currently under way in the United States and the other Western capitalist democracies. See, for example, Boyte (1981), Barber (1984, 264–265), and Boggs (1986).

5. On teledemocracy, see Wolff (1970), Barber (1984), and Atherton (1987). Atherton discusses both the current debates being waged over television democracy and a series of teledemocracy projects already undertaken.

6. An equal and perhaps greater amount of money is squandered on packaging, promotions, and other marketing ploys. For a sketch of a critical theory of advertising that documents the enormous expenditures on advertising and suggests remedies to this shameful situation, see Harms and Kellner (1991).

7. Most current leftist anthologies and texts that delineate programs for radical societal transformation usually exclude discussions of alternative politics of information and communication. Likewise, most leftist critics of television refrain from proposing significant alternatives to the system of commercial broadcasting. Now is the time, I would argue, to begin developing a new democratic communications philosophy and proposals for the democratization of communication and information. See the sources in Note 10 below.

8. For studies of PBS, see Barnouw (1975, 1978). Brown's (1971) discussion of PBS's beginnings is excellent, as are his proposals for a revitalized public broadcasting system. For other proposals for alternative funding of a public broadcasting system, see Geller (1989).

9. For critiques of the structure of the Corporation for Public Broadcasting and the need for reconstruction of the entire system, see Network Project (1971) and Shooshan and Arnheim (1989).

10. For an earlier discussion of the need for a radical media politics and for intervention in the broadcast media, see Kellner (1979, 1981), Downing (1984), and

Mattelart and Siegelaub (1979, 1983). The latter collections contain a vast amount of material on leftist media politics and projects, but they provide no interventionist consideration of the potential progressive uses of public access television. (A forthcoming third volume will contain studies addressing this issue.) On the early history of access in the United States, see Shapiro (1976). On the history of alternative media, see Armstrong (1981). On attempts by the broadcast industries and government to suppress access, and on liberal proposals for a more democratic communications system, see Johnson (1970). A directory of access systems put out by the National Federation of Local Cable Programmers, *The Video Register 1988–9*, claims that there are more than 1,000 access facilities operative in the United States at present. Some of these systems, however, are limited to a channel that presents teletypes of time, weather, and announcements of local activities. Thus, it is quite difficult to ascertain how many full-blown access centers are operatives; it is clear, however, that the number is growing.

11. A survey by the ELRA Group of East Lansing, Michigan, indicates that access is rated the fifth most popular category of television programming (ahead of sports, women's and children's programs, religious programs, etc.); and that 63 percent of those surveyed had an interest in access programming. Local surveys in Austin have confirmed that access programs have a potentially large audience. Two surveys, one undertaken by the cable company and another commissioned by it, indicated that between 20,000 and 30,000 Austin viewers watch "Alternative Views" each week, and that public access programming in general receives about 4.7 percent of the audience; another recent cable company survey indicated that the viewership of access was on a par with that of the local PBS station. National surveys of viewer preferences for cable programs also indicate that public access is a high priority for many viewers. Thus there is definitely a receptive and growing audience for public access television, and the possibility of making alternative television programs by progressives should be a much higher priority for radical media politics.

12. It is difficult to get up-to-date information on the state of local access projects. Journals such as *Access, The Independent, Alternative Media,* and *Community Television Review* and newsletters such as those published by The National Federation of Local Cable Programmers and other local access groups have some material, but an overview is hard to obtain. Material on ten access projects in the mid-1970s is surveyed in Anderson (1975), who also offers suggestions on how to develop grass-roots video projects. Material on early access projects can be found in various issues of *Radical Software* (1970–1975), in Shamberg (1971), and in Frederiksen (1972); a good review and critique of these projects is found in Jacobson (1974). Suggestions on how to set up an access system and provide quality community programming are found in Price and Wicklein (1972). For information on setting up a community media center, see Zelmer (1979). The National Federation of Local Cable programmers also provides guides concerning how to produce access television.

13. Barber (1984) is a progressive who advocates "strong democracy"; but, as Karp (1982) points out, many of the critics who are worried about the effects of fragmentation and diversification in the new broadcasting systems are precisely those conservatives who see these developments as a threat to their current hegemony. Thus I would champion increased diversification and access as possible ways to strengthen—indeed, preserve—democracy in the United States.

Appendixes

The only thing necessary for the triumph of evil is for good men to do nothing.
—Edmund Burke

Without publicity on the entire governmental process, no good is permanent; under the auspices of publicity, no evil can continue. Publicity, therefore, is the best means of securing public confidence.
—Jeremy Bentham

We are a democracy, and there is only one way to get a democracy on its feet in the matter of the individual, its social, its municipal, its national conduct, and that is by keeping the public informed of what is going on. There is not a crime, there is not a dodge, there is not a trick, there is not a swindle, there is not a vice which does not live by secrecy. Get these things out in the open, describe them, ridicule them in the press, and sooner or later public opinion will sweep them away.
—Joseph Pulitzer

The obscure we see eventually. The completely apparent takes a little longer.
—Edward R. Murrow

In the appendixes, I shall document a wide variety of stories concerning scandals of the Reagan/Bush years that were published in the investigative press and underdeveloped, or ignored, by the mainstream media. The point of this exercise is to demonstrate the limits of the mainstream media and the ways in which they maintained a conservative hegemony in the 1980s by omitting, or downplaying, stories that could have ended the reign of the Right in the United States. By "mainstream media" I am referring to the television networks, to *Time* and *Newsweek*, and to major national newspapers such as the *New York Times* and the *Washington Post*. The "investigative press" includes *The Nation, The Progressive, The Guardian, In These Times, The Village Voice, Rolling Stone, Mother Jones, The Los Angeles Weekly, The Utne Reader, Zeta Magazine,* and other journals and newspapers that practice investigative and socially critical journalism.

The large number of important stories published in the 1980s by the investigative press and ignored by mainstream media leads me to conclude that we have two media systems in the United States: the mainstream, capitalist media, which tend to be working with—and indeed are a part of—the existing power structure, in contrast to the investigative media, which maintain the honorable tradition of a free and independent press. Mainstream media are primarily commercial media, focused on profit and the "bottom line," as well as on legitimating the existing society. During the 1980s they dutifully served the powers that be by cutting back on critical, investigative reporting that might have "disturbed" their customers. The investigative press, by contrast, at its best follows the ethic of critical journalism and is committed to seeking out the truth no matter where it may lead and no matter how disturbing. Accordingly, there are now two publics in the United States: one that gains its information from the mainstream media and is thus information poor, in contrast to a public that is relatively well informed, depending on its access to alternative media.

In addition to the crisis of democracy in the United States, then, there is a crisis of journalism and investigative reporting. Part of the reason is financial. Investigative reporting is expensive, and in a climate of cost cutting and "bottom-line" profits, there is a tendency to streamline news production and to eliminate more costly investigative reporting. But a shift in news values and focus, especially in network television, has also occurred. As I have reported, not only were news personnel severely cut back during the 1980s, but there was a greater emphasis on light news and more entertaining stories, as the line between news and entertainment blurred. Finally, the conservative political climate of the 1980s, in conjunction with the "bottom-line" mentality, meant that mainstream news operations— especially television—did not want to offend and lose its audiences with critical reporting.

Conversations with members of both the mainstream and the investigative media suggest that many individuals working in mainstream journalism do not read the alternative press, or are afraid to draw on such stories in their conservative working environments. In an overview of the media coverage of the Iran/Contra affair, Scott Armstrong argues that the lesson of the lapses in press coverage can be attributed in part to press failure to read and follow up on some of the most important revelations published and broadcast in the mainstream media but ignored by the media establishment (1990, 29 and 34–35). Armstrong points out that despite the introduction of computer data bases such as Nexis and Dialogue, there was little cumulative reporting and failure to put the pieces together. In preparing these appendixes, by contrast, I have searched the relevant data bases accessible to me for all references to the major scandals of the Reagan/ Bush eras; all leads were pursued, and I have attempted to present the most compelling evidence in the following pages. Yet many alternative media sources are not included in the most widely used computer data bases, thus effectively shutting out some sources from the "official" information pool; consequently, conscientious researchers must also search through alternative media sources for crucial information often ignored in the mainstream.

Consequently, a combination of ignorance, servility, and cowardice explains why the mainstream media have failed to fully develop, or even investigate, some of the most explosive political stories of the epoch. To dramatize the differences between "official" and "alternative" versions of political reality during the 1980s, I shall present some of the major stories neglected by television and the mainstream media. My conclusion is that during the 1980s the mainstream media systematically sacrificed their journalistic integrity and became lapdogs of conservative hegemony—that is, ideological tools of the corporate power elite. The historical legacy of independent, critical journalism thus fell to the investigative press, to the so-called alternative media. Since only a relatively small number of people read the alternative media, many people today are ignorant of some of the major events of the 1980s, which have been ignored, or downplayed, by mainstream media. This is a national tragedy that threatens the very future of democracy in the United States. I would hope that journalists, writers, and citizens read the alternative press and look into the sources I have listed at the end of the Appendixes, upon which I have drawn in the following discussions. I have also drawn on work connected with "Alternative Views" (see section 5.3) and on interviews and conversations undertaken in the course of producing that TV series.

I should also point out that since the 1960s, when I began systematically reading the progressive and investigative press, these alternative media have had an excellent "track record," providing otherwise neglected information about the Kennedy assassinations, Vietnam, the Nixon administration, the arms race, the dangers of nuclear weapons and nuclear energy, racism and sexism, environmental pollution, the CIA and U.S. foreign policy, and the Reagan administration. Stories first published in investigative media were repeatedly confirmed and taken up in scholarly articles and books, and sometimes (in watered-down form) in the mainstream media itself. In other words, the stories related below appeared in publications that, in the past, provided accurate information well before it filtered into critical and respectable historical and academic texts. The magnitude of the scandals that I shall now discuss suggests that television and the mainstream media have been seriously negligent in supplying the information that a free society needs to make intelligent and informed political decisions and judgments. This situation, I believe, constitutes a crisis of journalism and democracy in the United States that can be overcome only with the assertion of more vigorous investigative reporting and the courageous search for the truth, no matter where it might lead.

Appendix A: The "October Surprise"

The "October Surprise" is perhaps the most explosive scandal of the Reagan years and the one that has been most studiously avoided by television and the mainstream media.[1] Investigative reporters who have researched the story claim that the Reagan election team in 1980 cut a deal with the Iranian ayatollahs to continue holding the Americans hostage in Tehran until after the 1980 election. The Reagan team was deeply concerned that if the hostages were released before the election, Carter would benefit from the patriotism and positive feelings that a hostage release might produce and would therefore win the election. Accordingly, the Reagan team bargained for the hostages to be held in Iran until Reagan's inauguration, and in return the Reagan team agreed to supply spare parts and weapons systems. At the time, the Iranians were fighting a deadly war with Iraq and were deprived of U.S. spare parts and replacements for their weapons systems because of an arms embargo in response to the hostage taking.

In retrospect, the "October Surprise" episode suggests that secret U.S. weapons and hostage dealings with Iran under the Reagan administration began before Reagan even took office, well before the Iran/Contra scandal of the mid-1980s. The story first broke in *The Miami Herald* in a story by the excellent reporter Alfonso Chardy published on April 12, 1987. His story opens:

"A month before Ronald Reagan trounced Jimmy Carter in the 1980 presidential election, two high-ranking Reagan campaign aides conferred secretly with a man who said he represented the Iranian government and offered to release to Reagan the 52 American hostages held in Tehran."

"The two aides, Richard Allen and Laurence Silberman, said Robert McFarlane, then a Senate aide and Reagan supporter, arranged and attended the meeting at a Washington hotel. Allen and Silberman, then top foreign policy advisers to Reagan, said the objective of the offer from the purported Iranian envoy was to ensure Carter's defeat" (Chardy 1987a, 1).

Both Allen and Silberman admitted attending the meeting, though both claimed that they rejected the Iranian offer. Chardy then notes that one-time Iranian president, Abolhassan Bani-Sadr, "said he learned after the hostage release that two of the Ayatollah Ruhollah Khomeini's closest advisers had been involved in negotiations with the Reagan camp. The negotiations were to delay release of the hostages until after Reagan became president, he said in a series of telephone interviews from exile in France. . . . In addition, Bani-Sadr said that several months after the hostages were freed he received a military report saying that after taking office, the Reagan administration had given assurances to Tehran that Iran would receive U.S. military equipment." (ibid.)

Later articles fleshed out in more detail why the Reagan team and Iranians might make such a deal, including articles published in *The Nation* and *In These Times* in June 1987. The latter report began by noting that, "[i]n October 1980, nothing worried the Reagan campaign so much as the possibility that the 52 hostages held by Iran might come home. The Reagan camp feared that the public perception of President Carter's weakness would evaporate if he could win the captives' release before the election— what Reagan staffers called an 'October Surprise' " (Honegger and Naureckas 1987, 12).

One of the authors, Barbara Honegger, had been a researcher at the Reagan campaign headquarters and later took a job with the administration. She reported that in the campaign's closing weeks, the mood of anxiety turned to elation with the report that "Dick cut a deal." The authors point out that " 'Dick' was Richard Allen, Reagan's chief foreign policy adviser. And the 'deal,' research by *In These Times* suggests, was an agreement that Reagan would guarantee post-election arms shipments to Iran in exchange for delaying the hostages' release until after the November 4 election" (Honegger and Naureckas 1987, 12).

Much of the ITT story was based on the 2,413-page Albosta Report (1984), which documented congressional investigations into allegations that members of the Reagan election campaign stole the Carter debate book in 1980. Documentation in the report makes it clear that the Reagan campaign team was obsessed with fears of an "October Surprise" hostage release, and that the Reagan team had William Casey, George Bush, and others monitoring intelligence operations, U.S. aircraft and ship movements, and other signs that a hostage release might be in the works. Although this congressional report is highly critical of the Reagan team's efforts in the 1980 election, there was little media discussion of the report and little further public or mainstream investigations of the events in question.

As noted in the *In These Times* article, the Albosta Report documents that the Reagan election team had about 120 agents who had penetrated the Carter administration, including many in high places in the CIA, Pentagon, and Defense Department who were actively working for Reagan's election, sabotaging Carter's efforts to release the hostages, and informing the Reagan team of all these efforts. The report thus documents the establishment of an "October Surprise" team consisting of top officials in the Reagan election campaign who held meetings with Iranian officials in which the holding of hostages until after the election was allegedly discussed. The *In These Times* story reports that an agreement was indeed reached with the Iranians and that Israeli weapons shipments to Iran began in 1981, soon after Reagan took office. In fact, the hostages were released precisely at the minute that Reagan was inaugurated, and a later report indicated that a former Savak officer working for the Iranian government was given orders not to let the plane full of the released hostages leave Tehran until Reagan's inauguration (*In These Times*, July 20–August 2, 1988, p. 5).

Christopher Hitchens reported in *The Nation* on June 20, 1987, that a plane "loaded with weapons in transit from Israel to Iran" crashed in Turkey on July 19, 1981. It was loaded with U.S. weapons and spare parts that, in retrospect, could have been sent to Iran as part of the payoff for the Iranians holding the hostages until after the election (p. 842). In several follow-up articles over the next two years, Hitchens provided summaries of new information on the case and continued to press for further investigations (see *The Nation* July 4/11, 1987; August 1/8, 1987; October 24, 1987; November 21, 1987; September 19, 1988; and October 31, 1988).

Chardy published two more articles in the *Miami Herald* that added some details to his original account. In an article published at the beginning of Oliver North's Iran/Contra hearings testimony, Chardy alleged that the secret government within the Reagan administration "traces its roots to the last weeks of Reagan's 1980 campaign" (1987b, 14A). Chardy linked the secret government to the October Surprise team organized by William Casey, Reagan's campaign manager and later CIA chief, and to the theft of Carter's debate book. In an August 9, 1987, report, syndicated by the Knight-Ridder News Service, Chardy reported on another interview with Bani-Sadr who said, "that 'as a deal was about to be made with the Carter administration' over the hostages in October 1980, 'suddenly the negotiations stopped. I now believe this happened because of secret contacts between President Reagan and Khomeini representatives" (in *Austin-American Statesman*, August 9, 1987, p. 8).

In other interviews, Bani-Sadr claims that he was trying to negotiate a deal himself for the hostages' release with the Carter administration, and that his efforts were undercut by Rafsanjani, Beheshti, and others in their circle who eventually forced him to give up power and flee the country. Flora Lewis published an op-ed piece in the *New York Times* on August 3, also based on an interview with Bani-Sadr, who told her that Iran was desperate in 1980 to restore relations with the United States in order to buy spare parts for its weapons system. Shortly thereafter, in an August 6 speech to the Senate, Democratic Majority Leader Robert Byrd referred to Lewis's column and stated: "This opens up disturbing questions about the longevity of this ill-conceived arms-for-hostages strategy. It needs further investigation." Representative John Conyers (D-Mich.), who chairs the subcommittee on criminal justice, considered an inquiry into the matter and appointed a Rutgers professor, Frank Askin, to investigate the case.

Nothing substantial emerged from these efforts, however (*In These Times*, July 20–August 2, 1988, p. 4).

Some newspapers and several weekly papers, magazines, and journals ran the "October Surprise" story, but it was never taken up by the mainstream media or the Democrats either in the aftermath of the Iran-Contra hearings or during the 1988 campaign. Both the Tower Commission Report and the Iran/Contra hearings limited themselves to investigations of the 1985–1986 period and did not delve into either earlier relations with Iran or the origins of the Contra war. The "October Surprise" story was thus ignored despite the fact that former president Jimmy Carter told reporters:

> We have had reports since late summer 1980 about Reagan campaign officials dealing with Iranians concerning delayed release of the American hostages. I chose to ignore the reports. Later, as you know, former Iranian President Bani-Sadr has given several interviews stating that such an agreement was made involving Bud McFarlane, George Bush and perhaps Bill Casey. By this time, the elections were over and the results could not be changed. I have never tried to obtain any evidence about these allegations but have trusted that investigations and historical records would someday let the truth be known. (Hoffman and Silvers 1988, 74)

Carter reiterated this position on Larry King's CNN talk show on June 15, during the Democratic party convention, and in a July 8 interview with Sondra Gair on Chicago's National Public Radio. When asked by King if he would speak out on the issue, Carter replied that he'd be willing to if Mike Dukakis asked him, but the Democrats chose to remain silent—and so did the mainstream media.

In September 1988, two months before the election, a popularized version of the story was published in *Playboy* (October 1988, pp. 73–74, 150–155). The article, by Abbie Hoffman and Jonathan Silvers, is framed by an epigraph by Edward R. Murrow: "The obscure we see eventually. The completely apparent takes a little longer." The authors open with a letter from Jimmy Carter (cited above) indicating that he had heard stories of negotiations to prevent a hostage release that might help his election chances. The article then documents the impressive array of intelligence operatives who formed the Reagan team's "October Surprise" group. This group had infiltrated the Carter government and had fed highly classified information, especially information concerning the fate of the hostages, to the Reagan team:

> By the fall of 1980, the Carter White House was riddled with moles, spies and informers. But preoccupied by the continuing crises and the campaign,

the President's advisors remained ignorant of the dirty tricks being played
by the Reagan-Bush team. "We were aware that we had made enemies," says
Jody Powell, "but we didn't think they were inside, chipping away at our
foundation." Given the sensitivity of the stolen documents and the impunity
with which the moles acted, the President's defenses, like those at the embassy
in Tehran, were pitifully inadequate. (Hoffman and Silvers 1988, 151)

The article then documents the contacts between the Iranians and the
Reagan team, and Bani-Sadr's claims that the deal was initially cut in
Washington and finalized in the Hotel Raphael in Paris in October 1980.
Bani-Sadr claimed that Rafsanjani (now president of Iran), Beheshti (head
of the radical Hezbollah group), and several arms merchants including
Hashemi, Ghorbanifar, and Hakim (all of whom turned up in later Iranian
arms sales) represented the Khomeini government, whereas the U.S. del-
egation included none other than Reagan's vice-presidential candidate, former
head of the CIA, George Bush. Subsequent reports claim that William
Casey (later head of the CIA), Donald Gregg (who worked with Bush at
the CIA and later became a top assistant in his White House office), and
Robert McFarlane were also present (see Appendix C.3). The article concludes
with a discussion of the Israeli connection and situates the story as the
beginning of illegal arms deals with Iran that continued throughout the
Iran/Contra affair.

Although the media lavished attention on the *Playboy* story published
in the previous year that exposed TV-evangelist Jim Bakker's sexual escapade
with Jessica Hahn and his alleged homosexual encounters, the Hoffman/
Silvers story was completely ignored by the mainstream media. Reporters
for *In These Times* called major news agencies to see if they were familiar
with the story and, if so, whether they planned to investigate it; although
some had heard of it, no one seemed interested in pursuing it (September
7–13, 1988, pp. 4–5). Meanwhile, both *In These Times* and *The Nation*
published a series of further developments in the story. It was in its October
12–18 issue that *In These Times* published its most comprehensive and
explosive version of the story. "Deal of the Decade," by Joel Bleifuss, is
prefaced by a summary of the already-published reports concerning the
scandal. The article focuses on the Paris meeting in which the deal was
allegedly finalized on October 19 and 20, 1980. Bleifuss's chief new source
is Richard Brenneke, an international arms dealer with CIA connections,
who claims that he was present at the meeting to discuss the technical
details of the payment and delivery of the weapons that would be exchanged
for hostages, who would be held until after the election and then released
on the day of Reagan's inauguration. Brenneke claims that Casey and Gregg
were also present.

Soon after, the pilot who had flown Casey to Paris, Heinrich Rupp,
claimed that he also saw Bush at the Paris airport at that time. U.S. and

French intelligence sources claimed that they, too, had information that Bush was present in Paris to finalize the deal (*In These Times*, November 2, 1988, p. 4; December 7, 1988, pp. 4–5). In his book *All Fall Down*, Gary Sick, Carter's National Security Council expert on Iran, affirmed that on October 22, 1980 (two days after the alleged Paris meetings), Iran changed its negotiating position with the Carter officials, demanding that its assets be unfrozen, whereas previously they had demanded weapons and spare parts in exchange for the release of the hostages. Furthermore, the Carter team soon found that their negotiations had unraveled completely, despite the expansion of Iran's war with Iraq. (Iran seemed to desperately require replenished weapons supplies.)

Television ignored the story completely—except for Larry King's interview with Carter, which raised the story via a caller. On October 9, 1988, the *Washington Post* published an op-ed piece on the story by *London Sunday Times* correspondent Mark Hosenball, who concluded that evidence for the deal was "too shaky to be taken seriously." Yet Hosenball accepted at face value McFarlane's version of the initial meeting, failing to point out that McFarlane had admitted to perjuring himself at congressional hearings. Several newspapers, however, did investigate the charges in some detail, including the *Boston Globe*, *Los Angeles Times*, *Portland Oregonian*, *Oakland Tribune*, and the *Rocky Mountain News*.

One article was distributed nationally by the *Los Angeles Times Service*. Written by Doyle McManus (co-author of *Landslide* [1988], one of the most exhaustive accounts of the second Reagan administration), the article contains a detailed analysis of the story. The article opens with an account of the alleged Reagan/Khomeini deal, points to some "serious problems" with the charges, and then delineates "a set of intriguing circumstances" that suggest the need for further investigation (*Austin American-Statesman*, October 30, 1998, p. A8). And yet the mainstream media have thus far refused to look into the allegations of what might be one of the major political scandals of the century. A group of thirteen of the original American hostages chose to take the story seriously, however, and attempted to bring legal action against those responsible for delaying their release (*In These Times*, November 2–8, 1988, p. 4). But television—which broadcasts hour after hour of silly fluff and carefully selected "news" stories—isn't interested. The fate of democracy in the United States seems of little importance to capital's private ministry of information.

Appendix B: The Iran/Contra Scandal

By reflecting on which stories and reports did or did not appear during the period of the Iran/Contra affair, we can determine how the mainstream media contain and cover up explosive stories (see section 4.1). In general, the media (sometimes cautiously) air stories that severely compromise U.S.

policy or personnel. Then, they either focus attention on individuals who are scapegoated and forced out of public office or they obscure the full extent of the scandal. Although many of the stories discussed below were mentioned or cited in mainstream media (so that the media could later claim they had indeed "covered them"), they were never fully researched, developed, or debated. Only when the details of a complex story such as Iran/Contra have been frequently repeated, explained, and contextualized do they reach the threshold of public understanding. Although the alternative press fully explored some of the most explosive aspects of Iran/Contra, they were ignored, barely mentioned, or glossed over by the establishment media.[2]

The Senate Iran/Contra hearings were even more timid in their pursuit of the story than the mainstream media, failing (unlike the Watergate hearings) to uncover many dramatic new revelations while actively participating in the cover-up. The hearings did elevate Fawn Hall and Oliver North to national celebrity status, but they did not unearth much in the way of new information or new interpretations of the events. If anything, they provided conservatives with a last-ditch attempt to make appeals for more Contra aid and, momentarily at least, resurrected what was believed to be a lost ultraright cause that had failed to gain popular support. Thus, with respect to the following stories, one must turn to investigative journals to get information neglected by the mainstream media.

The Contra Drug Operations

In 1985 two Associated Press (AP) reporters, Brian Barger and Robert Parry, diligently researched allegations that Contras were involved in big drug operations, selling cocaine, marijuana, and other drugs to finance their war against the Sandinista government in Nicaragua (see the discussion in Cockburn 1988). With the exception of Barger and Parry's AP wire service reports on the Contra drug connections, there were few discussions of the scandal (despite persistent rumors) in 1985 and 1986. The major newspapers and weekly news magazines neglected the story, as did the television networks. In the November 24, 1986, New Republic, Parry and Barger published a detailed account of the illegal Contra supply operations run by North and his associates. They noted that there were wide-spread reports of drug trafficking, which financed the Contra arms operations (1986, 25–27). An issue of In These Times (December 2, 1986) carried an even more detailed account of the drug operation in which illegal arms shipments to the Contras were supplemented and in part financed. According to this account, arms were sent to the Contras at U.S.-controlled bases in Costa Rica, Honduras, and El Salvador, thus providing a "safe" sanctuary for the illegal arms deliveries previously banned by Congress in the Boland Amendment. The Contra supply operation planes then picked up drugs that had been delivered to these sites from Colombia and returned to bases in the United States, including military bases and airports at which officials had been instructed not to interfere with the Contra supply network. In this way, the Contras were reportedly able to bring large amounts of drugs into the country, thus financing their military operations and no doubt enriching some of the participants.

The Contra drugs story continued to be almost completely ignored by the mainstream media. It was also neglected in the Iran/Contra hearings, with a couple of brief exceptions. To its credit, CBS's news magazine "West 57th Street" ran three well-documented segments on the Contra drug operation on March 31, 1987, April 6, 1987, and July 11, 1987, but the story was still not picked up by the mainstream media. In the first installment of the CBS show, thirty-six sources confirmed the story, and three additional on-camera sources claimed that they had flown planes in the arms/drug operation and could verify that the planes that had dropped illegal weapons to the Contras and returned to the United States were filled with illegal drugs.

The second "West 57th Street" installment ran interviews with a man, currently in prison, who laundered the money for the Contras and provided information on a dummy corporation that helped run the operation. It also interviewed Senator John Kerry of Massachusetts, who has been investigating the scandal, and a public defense attorney who claimed that the federal government had blocked investigation of certain drug operations, that had allegedly involved people in the Contra arms operation. Finally, the show interviewed individuals involved in the operation itself who confirmed that the Contra supply network was involved in drug running.

Another excellent report by Bill Moyers (November 4, 1987) on the PBS program, "Constitution in Crisis," used Senator Kerry and others as sources for the story and put the Iran/Contra scandal in the context of previous CIA covert operations, such as the overthrow of democratically elected governments in Iran (1953) and Guatemala (1954). Going against conventional wisdom, Moyers and those interviewed presented these "successful" CIA operations as a long-term debacle for U.S. interests and the well-being of the citizens of these countries. In this way, the Moyers documentary argued against covert operations and the institution of a National Security State. Yet no other mainstream media picked up this line of inquiry and never really investigated the Contra drug operation—an operation whose full extent, and connection to George Bush and the Reagan administration, will be the focus of Appendix C.3.

The Christic Institute Lawsuit and Investigation

The mainstream media also ignored the allegations of the Christic Institute, which were well publicized in the alternative media and by its own members and supporters. The Christic Institute, a public interest law firm based in Washington, D.C., began publicizing claims in 1986 that a team of individuals inside and outside the government had been engaging in illegal drug sales, political assassinations, and covert (often illegal) support of right-wing causes for several decades. The Institute initiated its suit on behalf of investigative reporters Tony Avigon and Martha Honey. Avigon had been injured at a bombing in La Penca, Nicaragua, in May 1984, where Contra leader Eden Pastora was holding a press conference to announce his separation from the other Contra forces and to denounce their connection to the CIA and to terrorist activities. The bombing had obviously been an attempt to assassinate Pastora, and a carefully orchestrated propaganda ploy was concocted to make it appear that the Sandinista Nicaraguan government was behind the assassination, in order to turn public opinion against the Sandinistas and perhaps even to help legitimize an invasion of Nicaragua.

On June 1, 1984, "ABC World News Tonight" had run a lengthy report by John McWethy, its Pentagon correspondent, claiming that a Basque "terrorist" group and the Nicaraguan Sandinistas were behind the bombing. (The same story had been broadcast the previous night, though not as aggressively, on PBS's "MacNeil/Lehrer News Hour.") It has since been revealed that this story was a disinformation plant, concocted by the Reagan administration, that ABC and PBS wittingly or unwittingly went along with (Carlisle 1988). The Christic Institute, by contrast, alleged that the bomb had been planted by a well-known international terrorist, who was identified as present at the press conference. It claimed that the terrorist was connected with Oliver North's aide, Robert Owens, and with John Hull, whose ranch in Costa Rica had been used in a Contra arms/drug-running operation. It also claimed that Hull had supplied the terrorist with materials for the bomb.[3]

The Christic Institute further claimed that some of the main players in the Iran/Contra affair—including Richard Secord, Felix Rodriguez, and Ted Clines—had been involved in such past operations as the Bay of Pigs, CIA plans to assassinate Fidel Castro, illegal drug operations and political assassinations in Vietnam, illegal arms shipments to Iran and other areas of the Mideast in the 1970s, and numerous other shadowy operations. According to the Christic Institute, the same "secret team" was involved in the arms shipments to Iran, the illegal arms shipments to the Contras, and the return drug operation.

Little of this story surfaced in the mainstream media. Although the Christic Institute "secret team" hypothesis glossed over the conflicts between members of this group and made it appear that only a few renegade individuals, rather than the National Security State apparatus and its policies, were responsible for the worst crimes of U.S. foreign policy over the last several decades, there were enough well-substantiated allegations in its indictment to merit investigation by the mainstream media and discussion of the issues.[4] Although Representative Jack Brooks (D-Tex.) attempted to bring up these charges in the Iran/Contra hearings, the story was never really aired and discussed by mainstream print and broadcast media.

FEMA

During the Iran/Contra hearings, Alfonso Chardy published an article in the *Miami Herald* (July 5, 1987) claiming that Oliver North was involved in drawing up a Federal Emergency Management Administration plan (FEMA), which, in effect, would suspend civil liberties in the case of a "national emergency." This plan would suspend the Constitution and impose martial law in response to certain "contingencies" such as mass opposition to a U.S. military operation abroad. In other words, it stipulated that if the United States were engaged in an unpopular foreign intervention (such as an invasion of Nicaragua), civil liberties could be suspended and opponents of U.S. policy could be arrested and put in concentration camps. The locations of these camps were stipulated, and plans were implemented to suspend civilian government and to replace timid politicians with tough military personnel. In this way, the Reagan administration could attempt to cut off an antiwar movement such as the one that created strong opposition to the Vietnam war in the 1960s.

Once again, Representative Jack Brooks brought up the FEMA issue with North during the Iran/Contra hearings. But the "liberal" Senator Daniel Innoye (D-Hawaii) cut him off, saying that this was a topic for "executive session," not for the press and public. The scene provided a dramatic highlight of Barbara Trent's documentary "Cover-Up," on the extent of the Iran/Contra scandal and the complicity of Congress and the media in the cover-up. This spectacle dramatically illustrates how even the Democrats were concerned about covering up the worst excesses of the Reagan years. Consequently, we still don't know the extent of the Reagan/North FEMA program or whether, as some claim, Reagan implemented some of the plans in a secret Executive Order.

Limits to Congressional Investigations

Investigative reporter Seymour Hersh (1990) published a study detailing the limits to congressional investigations during the Iran/Contra hearings, through analysis of certain stories and issues omitted from the hearings. As Hersh notes, the congressional committees protected Reagan insasmuch as they had decided from the beginning not to seek evidence that would lead to impeachment hearings. Hersh's investigations reveal, for instance, that one of Oliver North's associates, James Radzimski, saw two memoes that listed the details of the illegal diversion of funds from the Iran arms sales to the Contras that were directed to President Reagan. Radzimski was scheduled to testify after North, but North's popularity reportedly led the Iran/Contra committee to cancel his presentation.

Hersh also notes that the White House had a computer back-up system that would have allowed retrieval of all documents pertaining to the case (such as the ones that Radzimski claims to have seen). But the White House refused, on "national security" grounds, either to put this retrieval system into operation or to provide the committees with its documents. Meanwhile, discussion of the computer system led to the revelation that Reagan regularly taped his phone calls with foreign leaders, but this material, too, was not demanded by the "investigating" committees.

Hersh also revealed that the committee had learned of a second illegal diversion of funds from the Iranian arms sales "to Israel, via a Swiss bank account, for covert operations in the Middle East—for which there was no legal authority. After initiating investigations of these operations, the committees chose not to discuss them in public or to consider any of the constitutional questions they raised in public hearings" (Hersh 1990, 47). Hersh's investigations further reveal that the committees did not want to risk disruption of relations with Israel, nor did they wish to pursue investigations of the various Israeli operations for the United States in places like the Middle East or Central America.

Thus, the Iran/Contra hearings were clearly part of a government cover-up of scandalous wrong-doings. In fact, both the Tower Commission and the Iran/Contra hearings failed to investigate allegations that U.S. arms deals with Iran began shortly after Ronald Reagan was elected president, and that these deals were the pay-off for an arrangement whereby the Iranians would hold the American hostages in Iran until the 1980 election—thus ensuring the defeat of Jimmy Carter, who was desperately trying to cut a deal to release them (see Appendix A). The neglect of these and many other scandals of the Reagan years points up the limits of the mainstream press, outside of which the timid establishment media fear to tread. Armstrong (1990) argues that although the media uncovered some of the pieces of the Iran/Contra puzzle from 1981 to 1986 and did some good investigative reporting from November 1986 to March 1987, they failed to properly develop the story in the Iran/Contra hearings and let the story drop in the 1988 election. In addition, Armstrong claims that the mainstream media failed to adequately cover and interpret the later North and Poindexter trials and have thus never really presented the full ramifications of the Iran/Contra scandals to the public. In particular, the media role in the Iran/Contra affair reveals a systematic co-optation of Congress, the media, the courts, and segments of the intelligentsia, who either participated in the Great Cover-up of the 1980s or failed to disclose and attack what future historians will probably interpret as some of the most explosive scandals in U.S. history. Failure of the mainstream media to investigate these stories during the 1988 election helped ensure the election of George Bush to the presidency.

Appendix C:
The Big Cover-Up: Bush and the 1988 Election

A wide range of stories were not reported during the 1988 election campaign, or were broadcast briefly and then dropped, that could have greatly damaged Bush's bid for the presidency. They include stories concerning Bush and the CIA; Bush and an illegal arms supply operation to the Contras that was also connected with Noriega, the Colombia drug cartel, and the shipping of illegal drugs to the United States; Bush and the "October Surprise" deal with the Iranians; and Bush's role in the Iran/Contra scandal. These stories were fully investigated in the alternative press but generally ignored in the mainstream press. If they has been fully reported in the mainstream media during the 1988 election, George Bush might currently be facing a day in court and even imprisonment rather than the prestige of the White House. Their omission requires reflection on the impact of corporate control of the media and the current crisis of democracy and journalism in the United States.

Appendix C.1: Bush and the CIA

During the 1988 presidential campaign, allegations surfaced that Bush had worked for the CIA as early as 1963. In an article in *The Nation* (July 16/23, 1988, p. 37ff.), Joseph McBride reported the discovery of a memorandum from J. Edgar Hoover, then chief of the FBI, stating that: "Mr. George Bush of the Central Intelligence Agency" had been briefed by the Bureau on November 23, 1963, about the reaction of anti-Castro Cuban exiles in Miami to the assassination of President John F. Kennedy. "A source with close connections to the intelligence community" told McBride "that Bush started working for the agency in 1960 or 1961, using his oil business as a cover for clandestine activities" (ibid.). Bush denied that he had worked for the agency during this period, and the CIA claimed that it had another George Bush working for them at the time and that the memo must have referred to him. The mainstream press briefly mentioned both the memo and the CIA explanation, and dropped the story. McBride, however, tracked down the other George Bush (to whom the memo had referred, according to the CIA) in MacLean, Virginia. He stated that he had indeed worked for the CIA, but insisted to McBride that the memo must have referred to "the other George Bush," for he was "just a lowly researcher and analyst," and had never received interagency briefings or memos from J. Edgar Hoover himself (*The Nation*, August 13/20, 1988, p. 117).[5]

Although the mainstream media aired the original story and the CIA retraction, they never did a follow-up, nor did they pursue the "other George Bush" who had denied the CIA version. The mainstream media also never aired allegations to the effect that, during Bush's directorship of the CIA in 1976, the CIA was involved in such activities as a coverup of the assassinations of Orlando Letelier (a leading exile figure in Chilean politics) and Ronni Mofitt (a colleague from the Institute for Policy Studies) who were car-bombed in Washington, D.C., on September 21, 1976. A later Justice Department investigation revealed that the victims had been assassinated by agents of the Chilean secret police working with Cuban-Americans. Many individuals who researched the affair claimed that Bush had participated in a cover-up of the crime, and, on several occasions, had diverted investigations away from the role of Chilean agents and Cuban-American terrorists (Armstrong and Nason 1988, 47; Levin 1988, 15).

In the conclusion to their *Mother Jones* story on Bush and the CIA, Scott Armstrong and Jeff Nason contended that Bush

> was successful in stalling, if not in actually preventing, the prosecutions of those associated with the CIA's role in Chile, the Wilson affair [i.e., former CIA agent Edwin Wilson, charged with illegal arms sales and other crimes, was eventually jailed for selling arms illegally to Libya], and the assassination of Orlando Letelier. Eventually, these cases would be acted upon more vigorously by Jimmy Carter's director of central intelligence, Stansfield Turner. When Turner began his own internal investigations of the incidents, however, he would find Bush's closest aides to be among those most resistant to his efforts. (1988, 47)

Earlier, as head of the Republican National Committee during the Watergate scandal, Bush had specialized in covering up the political misdeeds and crimes of the Nixon administration; thus his work in covering up past and current CIA scandals fits into the pattern of willing participation in cover-ups of government wrong-doing that has marked his career. As Armstrong and Nason argue, "while director of the Central Intelligence Agency, Bush played the role of a cheerleader and a front man—willfully ignorant of unpleasant news. He ignored repeated signals that rogue, 'off-the-books' operations by former agents were out of control, leading to Agency acquiescence in illegal activities" (ibid.).

Indeed, the mainstream press—and the Democrats—failed to raise the obvious question concerning the implications of having an ex-CIA director as president of the United States. Might not a major player in the CIA be vulnerable to potential blackmail by individuals who had been involved in illegal operations that the CIA had sanctioned? Might not an ex-CIA chief overly rely on CIA sources and covert operations, to the extent that the CIA would have an undue influence on foreign and domestic policy? To my knowledge, the only attempt to raise these sorts of questions within the mainstream media was Tom Wicker's *New York Times* op-ed piece of April 29, 1988, in which he asked: "Do the American people really want to elect a former director of the C.I.A. as their President?" Wicker then continued: "That's hardly been discussed so far; but it seems obvious that a C.I.A. chief might well be privy to the kind of 'black' secrets that could later make him—as a public figure—subject to blackmail. Given the agency's worldwide reputation for covert intervention and political meddling, moreover, one of the former directors in the White House certainly would be the object of suspicion and mistrust in numerous parts of the globe. And well he might be."

Wicker's fears are well-founded, as the following examination of one of the most important stories neglected by the mainstream media should make clear.

Appendix C.2: Bush, Noriega, and Black Eagle

The mainstream press downplayed allegations to the effect that, when Bush was CIA director, he first became involved with Manuel Noriega and later used him as an "asset" during the Reagan administration—even though there was copious evidence that Noriega had been involved in serious drug dealing. In addition, no sustained investigations during the 1988 campaign were made into earlier allegations that an illegal Contra arms ring (also involved in drug dealing) was run out of Bush's office, and that Bush's Noriega connection was intimately bound up with the illegal Contra arms/ drug ring.

Allegations that Bush's office was running the illegal Contra supply network first surfaced in October 1986, when Eugene Hasenfus was captured by the Sandinistas after his plane (which was attempting to deliver weapons and supplies to the Contras) was shot down over Nicaragua.[6] Hasenfus told the Nicaraguans that his resupply operation was run by the CIA and supervised by "Max Gomez" and "Ramon Medina." On October 11, 1986, Doyle McManus published an article in the *Los Angeles Times* that appeared in the *Washington Post* with the headline: "Bush is Linked to Head of Contra Aid Network." The article discussed the "Max Gomez"/Bush connection and indicated that "Gomez" was indeed the head of a Contra supply network and that he had told associates that he reported directly to Bush and had met twice with the vice-president. ("Max Gomez" is the pseudonym of Felix Rodriguez, an anti-Castro Cuban who had been involved in covert actions against Castro and allegedly helped track and murder Che Guevara.) Bush's office admitted that the vice-president had met with "Gomez" but insisted that the two had not discussed the Contra supply network.

Gomez/Rodriguez was linked in the article with Donald Gregg, a former CIA official then serving as Bush's national security adviser. Gregg had recommended Gomez to the El Salvador military, which allowed him to run the Contra supply network from a base in Illopango, El Salvador. Stories published in the *Washington Post* over the next two weeks (October 12, 13, 24, and 26) contained more material on Gomez/Rodriguez's background, his close Vietnam ties with Gregg, and his frequent communications with Bush's office. The emergence of the Iran/Contra scandal during this period greatly overshadowed the connection between Gregg, Bush, and the illegal Contra supply operation, although CBS reported the links in two December newscasts.

In addition, there was little serious investigation during the Iran/Contra scandal into allegations that the Contras were involved in running drugs to help support their activities, with the exception of a three-part series on the CBS news magazine "West 57th Street" (see Appendix B and Cockburn 1988). The other mainstream media, however, generally ignored the story during 1987 (the year of the Iran/Contra cover-up by the mainstream media [see section 4.1]); and, to my knowledge, the only attempt that year to systematically document Bush's involvement in the Contra supply network was Allain Nairn's (1987) article in *The Progressive*, which provided detailed information on the Gregg/Rodriguez connection and on the logistics of the illegal Contra arms/drugs operation.

During 1988, however, when Bush was actively running for president and was quickly becoming the Republican front-runner, the question of his connection with the Iran/Contra scandal began to be discussed once more in the mainstream and investigative media. On January 7, 1988, the *Washington Post* detailed Bush's involvement in the Iran/Contra affair, and his involvement was also scrutinized in *The Nation* and by Judy Woodruff in a "MacNeil/Lehrer News Hour" segment (see the account in Armstrong 1990, 31). Later in the month Bush engaged in a widely viewed shouting match with Dan Rather on CBS that was instigated by Rather's questions concerning Bush's involvement in Iran/Contra. Bush testily refused to discuss the matter. On February 8, 1988, *Newsweek* published an article entitled "What Did Bush Know? Questions about Iran/Contra Haunt the Candidate." The article documents Bush's probable connection with both scandals, notes Bush's denials, and then asks interview questions concerning his knowledge of the scandals and his relationships with Gregg, Oliver North, and others. Shortly thereafter, *The Progressive* published another article by Allain Nairn, "George Bush's Secret War" (March 1988, pp. 22–

25), based in part on an interview with arms dealer Richard Brenneke, who claimed that he was a member of the illegal Contra supply network. Brenneke describes how he flew arms to the Contras and had detailed discussions over the operations with Donald Gregg, who appeared to be running the supply network out of Bush's office.

During April and May 1988 the mainstream media broadcast several reports that might well have ended Bush's candidacy had they been pursued. On ABC's "World News Tonight" report of April 7, 1988, Richard Threlkeld broke an explosive story linking the illegal arms/drug network to the Reagan administration. Threlkeld's report began:

> For three years . . . from 1983 to 1986 . . . the Contras fought the Marxist government of Nicaragua with weapons . . . made in the Communist bloc . . . bought by Israeli agents with American financial support . . . and delivered by a U.S.-Israeli airlift which wound up . . . incredibly enough . . . delivering illegal drugs to the United States. That's the astonishing story told to ABC News by American, . . . Israeli and Panamanian sources . . . some of whom insist on remaining anonymous . . . including this American . . . we'll call Harry . . . who helped purchase the arms and deliver them.

The report went on to document how the illegal arms were financed by covert-operation funds and delivered to the Contras. It also claimed that the supply network involved "a makeshift air cargo network experienced in running illegal drugs. . . . After dropping off their weapons . . . the planes and contract pilots of this makeshift Israeli-American airlift went back to business as usual . . . smuggling illegal Colombian cocaine across the U.S. border."

As on-camera sources, the Threlkeld report used the arms merchant "Harry" (later revealed to be Richard Brenneke) and a former associate of Noriega, José Blandon, who had testified to Congress in detail about Noriega's drug operation, which he claimed was connected with U.S./Contra supply operations. The report raised some questions concerning the implications of these reports and closed by stating that "a Senate Subcommittee will be meeting next week to demand some answers." The story immediately disappeared from the mainstream media and was ignored until an April 25 *New Yorker* "Talk of the Town" column cited the failure of mainstream media to investigate the story as an example of the flaccid state of investigative journalism. Although the *New Yorker* commended ABC for running the story, it criticized the network for omitting to mention that Felix Rodriguez, who was in charge of a Contra supply network in Central America and had been named in the story, was a close friend of Donald Gregg, Bush's national security adviser and a former deputy to Bush when he was chief of the CIA.

In mid-May a flurry of reports surfaced, linking the Reagan administration and Bush's office to this arms/drugs network. In a UPI report of May 15, 1988, Brian Barger claimed: "White House officials brokered weapons sales to the Nicaraguan Contras from an arms dealership tied to drug trafficking, according to government documents, U.S. officials, and arms brokers involved in supplying weapons to the rebels." The UPI report linked the network to Oliver North's office and to Donald Gregg, thus implicating high officials in the Reagan administration. On the next day, the story broke in many newspapers and was taken up by both CBS and ABC News. Both reports linked the operation to Bush. Dan Rather opened his CBS story by saying: "There are additional reports now that a top aide to vice president George Bush had ties to a secret operation that was deeply involved in international gun-running and drugs. The aid is a man with long ties to the CIA whose name has come up many times before in cases of guns and drugs. As he has before, Bush today tried to shrug off the reports as 'old news.' " The reporter, Eric Engberg, detailed the allegations and then cut to Bush's denial:

> *Vice President Bush:* "This is old news—it's not even news . . . and you just get bombarded by these si— insinuations and tired stories. . . . I—and it's just pure unadulterated—and I gotta watch my language."
>
> *Engberg:* "Gregg, Bush's aide, maintains he does not know Brenneke and has never spoken to him. He says he played no role in the supply operation, even though Gregg was a close associate of Felix Rodriguez, the ex-CIA man who helped set it up; but, as other evidence accumulates bit by bit, new questions are raised about Bush's and Gregg's links to North's secret operations. Item: in early 1985 (January 28, 1985), a few days after a Rodriguez-Bush meeting in Washington, a top CIA official apparently called North to talk about Rodriguez's ties to the Vice President. Item: an entry in North's diaries mentions a September 1985 meeting with Gregg to discuss 'logistics' and 'maintenance' at the air base where Rodriguez and the Contra network were headquartered. Then days later (September 20, 1985), North flashed the go-ahead to Rodriguez to begin setting up the secret Contra aid flights. Gregg has testified he was not at that September meeting, despite North's written record. Gregg maintains a full year went by before he was to learn of Rodriguez's secret work for the Contras; and even then, Gregg says, he did not tell the Vice President."

ABC broadcast an equally detailed report that day, and in a May 17 story it linked the illegal arms/drugs network to the U.S. government, Noriega, and the Contras while highlighting Donald Gregg's role. Newspapers all over the country also picked up the story. At the same time, stories began to circulate concerning Bush's relations with Noriega (dating back to the time when he was head of the CIA) and Noriega's connection with drug-dealing.[7] The *Christian Science Monitor* (May 19, 1988) connected the Noriega and Contra/drugs stories, asking: "•Were members of Bush's staff aware of a Contra arms supply operation in Honduras from 1984 to 1986, and the fact that it was financed in part with drug money? •Was Bush aware that the Panamanian strong man, Gen. Manuel Antonio Noriega, was involved in the drug trade at the same time that he was receiving aid from the U.S.?" (pp. 1, 32). The article then summarized the stories that had circulated concerning the Bush/Noriega connection and the Contra drug/arms ring and its possible connection with Bush's office.

In the same vein, *Newsweek* (May 23, 1988) published a potentially damaging story linking Bush to the arms/drug operation of Gregg, Rodriguez, and Noriega. The story concluded by noting that former Noriega aide "[José] Blandon has testified to [Massachusetts Senator John] Kerry's committee that Noriega boasted to him that he knew things that 'could affect the elections of the United States,' and Noriega's former sidekick, Col. Roberto Diaz Herrera, put that more bluntly to *Newsweek*: Noriega told him, he said, that 'I have Bush by the balls.' In the vocabulary of the spook shop he once headed, Bush still has deniability on the Contra connection. Whether it is plausible is another matter—one that will surely come up in the fall campaign" (ibid., p. 23).

The Bush/Contras/drugs connection was also discussed in a PBS documentary directed by Andrew and Leslie Cockburn. Ms. Cockburn had earlier helped produce CBS's "West 57th Street" reports on the illegal Contra arms/drug ring, and her 1988 book *Out of Control* remains the classic account of the arms/drug-ring operations. During the documentary's interview, Ramon Milian-Rodriguez, currently in federal prison on drug charges, detailed how the drug/arms operation worked and how he had personally laundered the money and had given the Contras a cut. He explained that he had been approached by Felix Rodriguez and was asked to work with the operation. The interview continued as follows:

> *Question:* Who was Felix Rodriguez working for, or with, when he approached you?
> *Milian-Rodriguez:* Well, the only government mention he made was Vice President Bush.
> *Question:* And what was his relationship with Bush as you understood it?
> *Milian-Rodriguez:* He was reporting directly to Bush. I was led to believe he was reporting regularly to the Vice President. . . . The request for the contribution [i.e., for drug dollars from the drug cartel to the Contras] made a lot more sense because Felix was reporting to George Bush. If Felix had come to me and said I'm reporting to anyone else, let's say, you know, Oliver North, I might have been more skeptical. I didn't know who Oliver North was, I didn't know his background. But you know, if you have a . . . let's

say we'll call him an ex-CIA operative, even though it's not true you know, he's a current operative. . . .

Question: Who is?

Milian-Rodriguez: Felix . . . Yeah, there's nothing ex about him. But if you have a CIA, what you consider to be a CIA man coming to you saying "I want to fight this war, we're out of funds, can you help us out. I'm reporting directly to Bush on it," I mean it's very believable. . . . Here you have a CIA guy reporting to his old boss.

The only other television exploration of the Contra arms/drugs ring and its connection with the Bush office was an interview on May 26, 1988, with arms dealer Richard Brenneke on CNN's "Larry King Live" show. The interview once again detailed Brenneke's involvement with the arms/ drug operation. For the next several weeks, the story circulated in newspapers and other periodicals; but the television networks backed off from the story and never pursued it again—one of the great scandals in the history of American mainstream journalism. As I shall argue in the next section, the mainstream media and the Democratic party during the 1988 election backed away from stories that had already broken during the early days of the Iran/Contra affair and had surfaced again during April and May 1988. Subsequently, the mainstream media "teflonized" Bush, and only the investigative media pursued the Bush scandals further—often with startling revelations, which were nevertheless ignored by the mainstream media.

Throughout the summer of 1988, the investigative press continued to pursue the Bush scandals. A story by Jim Naureckas and Richard Ryan in *In These Times* (June 8, 1988) alleged that Bush's office had worked with Israel's Mossad, Colombian cocaine dealers, Panama's Noriega, and an Iranian diplomat to illegally arm the Contras. The source was Richard Brenneke, who said that he had not only delivered illegal arms to the Contras but had also flown drugs on a return flight to Amarillo, Texas. Brenneke claimed that Gregg was the Washington contact for the arms network and that Gregg had discussed purchase and delivery plans with him in detail. Brenneke also claimed that he had warned Gregg about the Contra supply network drug connections and that Gregg had replied: "You do what you were assigned to do. Don't question the decision of your betters" (p. 7).

The investigative press also uncovered evidence concerning Bush's earlier involvement with the CIA (see Appendix C.1), more information on Bush's connections with Noriega and the Contra supply ring, a report on Bush's extra-marital affairs ("The Mistress Question"), and allegations concerning Bush's involvement in the "October Surprise" (see Appendix A) during the summer and fall of 1988.[8]

One of the more detailed stories appeared in *Rolling Stone.* In "The Dirty Secrets of George Bush," by Howard Kohn and Vicki Monks (1988), the authors claim that an illegal Contra supply operation had been set up in 1982 by CIA Director William Casey and was run from George Bush's office by Donald Gregg. These events occurred at least two years before the infamous North/Secord "Enterprise," whose activities were documented in the Iran/Contra hearings; sources included key operatives in the network, military and intelligence sources, and foreign government sources. As Kohn and Monks (1988) put it:

> After meetings with Casey in the summer of 1982, Bush agreed to use the vice-president's office as a cover for Black Eagle, according to a retired army covert operative assigned to Black Eagle. Gregg, a veteran CIA official, was assigned to work out of Bush's office as the Washington liaision to Black Eagle operatives in Central America, coordinating financial and operational details. Gregg made regular status reports on Black Eagle to Bush, who relayed them to Casey. "Bush and Gregg were the asbestos wall," says the career military man, who used the code Lew Archer. "You had to burn through them to get to Casey." (ibid., p. 42)

During 1982–1983, the Israelis played a key operational role in supplying illegal weapons to the Contras, but a bizarre error led to Noriega's increased involvement (ibid., pp. 47ff.). The Israelis had been sending weapons to a warehouse in San Antonio, from which they were sent on to the Contras, but by mistake some crates were stamped with the label "CIA WAREHOUSE." The weapons then came to the attention of U.S. customs officials, and the supply route was discovered and exposed. The central transfer point was shifted to El Salvador and Panama. Already working for Noriega was a former Mossad agent, Michael Harari, who was assigned to the Black Eagle operation. Noriega allowed Contras to train in Panama and permitted Black Eagle supply planes to land in his country on the condition that they be available for his drug smuggling ring. According to Kohn and Monks:

> Soon after Noriega was brought into the Black Eagle operation, he began to commandeer Black Eagle planes and pilots for drug-running flights to the southern United States, according to Lew Archer, who'd been assigned to keep the Panamanian strong man under surveillance. Instead of immediately demanding that the drug trafficking cease, says Blandon [a former Noriega associate who emigrated to the United States and testified to Congress concerning Noriega's drug running], U.S. policy makers struck a devil's bargain with Noriega. Under terms of the deal, one percent of the gross income generated by the drug flights was set aside to buy additional weapons for the *contras*. This eventually amounted to several million dollars. (ibid., p. 48)

During this period, José Blandon claims, Noriega amassed a great deal of blackmail material on those involved in the Black Eagle and other operations, compiling a large dossier on the role of Bush and his staff in the operations. Sources interviewed said that both Bush and his assistant Gregg were fully aware of the drug involvement in the arms network, and that the Contra arms network was the topic of a famous conversation between Bush and Noriega in their meeting in 1983. Eventually, the Israelis pulled out of the operation. The United States then distanced itself from Noriega, setting up its own supply operation run by North and Richard Secord, who surfaced as the major players in the Iran/Contra hearings.

The *Rolling Stone* story of November 3, 1988, contained the most detailed account thus far of Felix Rodriguez (who directed the arms/drugs operation in El Salvador) and his relationship with Donald Gregg, whose involvement dated back to their service together in Vietnam. The article provided a detailed history of the operation and the involvement of Gregg and Bush. The Kohn/Monks article, in turn, provides the first detailed account of the involvement of Panama's General Noriega in the operation, the connection with the Colombia drug cartel, and eventual feuds between North and Rodriguez that allegedly required Bush's mediation (ibid., pp. 48ff.). The article raises interesting questions pertaining to the incredible risks Bush took during the Panama invasion, and raises the specter that a deal might be cut between Bush and Noriega in light of the potentially explosive revelations that could emerge from a Noriega trial.

Despite these serious allegations, the mainstream press ignored the story completely, just as they had ignored the "October Surprise" story. To this day, few people are familiar with the terms *Black Eagle* and *October Surprise;* nor are many people aware of the compelling claims that illegal Contra operations were run out of George Bush's office. The mainstream media— and the U.S. government—have scapegoated John Poindexter and Oliver North for operations that were run by Bush and William Casey and possibly had the sanction of Ronald Reagan.[9] It is quite possible, therefore, that a systematic cover-up has been carried out by Congress, the media, and the judiciary system to gloss over the involvement of Reagan, Bush, and other high officials in some of the greatest political scandals in U.S. history.

Appendix C.3:
George Bush: Son of Teflon

During the Reagan years the media coined the term *teflon president,* meaning a president from whom the most damning allegations would wash off and disappear without harming his presidency. I am suggesting here that the mainstream media also "teflonized" Bush, by refusing to investigate some of the serious scandals in which he was involved. As noted, although some reports emerged in October 1986 and April and May 1988 in the mainstream media concerning Bush's connections with the illegal Contra supply operation and the Panamanian dictator Manuel Noriega, the mainstream media failed to fully investigate these reports and completely ignored the "October Surprise" and Black Eagle stories.

During the 1988 campaign, in fact, the mainstream media failed to investigate Bush's background, particularly his years in the CIA and his involvement in the Iran/Contra affair. The investigative press released allegations of Bush's involvement in serious scandals, but these allegations were not explored on network television or in the mainstream press despite (or because of) the fact that George Bush was running for president—presumably an office that a democratic society would want filled by someone of high moral character, free of the taint of scandal.

For instance, the mainstream media failed to explore allegations, raised repeatedly by the investigative press, that Bush was a major player in the Iranian arms-for-hostages deal. Bush has repeatedly claimed that "it is simply false" that the Reagan administration was bartering weapons for the release of U.S. hostages held by Iranian-influenced groups in the Middle East. Bush has also repeatedly denied active participation in the Iranian arms initiatives, claiming that, until he was briefed by Senator David Durenberger of the Senate Intelligence Committee in December 1986 (following the revelation of the arms sales to the Iranians and after diversion of the profits to the Contras had been made public), he had not known most of the details concerning the arms deal with Iran. In his autobiography Bush wrote: "What Dave had to say left me with the feeling that I'd been deliberately excluded from key meetings involving details of the Iran operation." To the contrary, in *Los Angeles Weekly* (October 14–20, 1988, p. 24) Frank Snepp and Jonathan King claim that Bush was at the center of the key meetings from the beginning and, in opposition to Secretary of State George Shultz and Secretary of Defense Caspar Weinberger, repeatedly supported the initiative. "Sen. Edward Kennedy has asked, 'Where was George?' If the focus is the U.S. arms sales to Iran, the answer has to be: he was there—at almost every crucial stopping point on the road to the decision. Given that, the more important question is: what was George doing?" (ibid.).

Peter Dale Scott, co-author of *The Iran-Contra Connection* (Marshall et al. 1987), suggests that Vice-President Bush not only supported Reagan's secret arm shipments to the Iranians but may very well have promoted the entire Iran initiative, taken part in key negotiations, and assigned Oliver North the powers necessary to carry it out. Scott (1988) argues that Bush's primary concern in early 1986 was to stabilize falling crude oil prices by promoting a common price policy between the United States and the oil producers of the Gulf, especially Iran and Saudi Arabia. This required relations with Iran. The price of better Iranian relations, Scott contends, was provision of weapons to Iran to help it carry out its war with Iraq. "Manipulating the price of oil upward, in fact, reflected the concerns of Bush, a former Texas oilman with close ties to the oil industry, more than those of Ronald Reagan, a free market advocate" (ibid., p. 87).

Scott traces Bush's involvement back to the meeting on January 17, 1986, of the president's national security advisers at which President Reagan signed the controversial finding authorizing the arms sale. This meeting was attended by Bush and three other known supporters of the arms sale initiative: Chief of Staff Donald Regan, National Security Director John Poindexter, and Poindexter's deputy.

Scott then points out that, three months later, Oliver North and Robert McFarlane traveled to Iran to negotiate the deal, while Shultz and Weinberger were allegedly kept in the dark about the whole affair. Not only did Bush know about this deal, but he was also at the meeting that planned the operation and, according to Scott, had helped schedule the trip. Moreover, it is well documented that Bush took a trip to Saudi Arabia, where he successfully lobbied the Saudi leadership to help stabilize oil prices that had fallen to less than $10 a barrel. He succeeded with the Saudis, who in turn scheduled a meeting with the Iranian oil minister in the fall of 1986. The two countries agreed to follow the U.S. line to push OPEC to raise oil prices to $18 a barrel.

Investigations by the alternative media thus reveal that George Bush was involved in a series of scandals that raise serious questions concerning not only his fitness to govern but also the issue of whether the mainstream media are guilty of seriously undermining democracy in the United States. A comparison of reports on Bush in the investigative media with reports in the mainstream media discloses the limits of establishment media and the extent to which they have actively served to develop conservative hegemony in the 1980s. The fact that these stories involving Bush were never fully aired in the mainstream media (despite their documentation in the investigative press) raises serious questions concerning the effects of ownership of the media by giant capitalist conglomerates.

As noted, during the 1980s all three major television networks merged with other communications conglomerates and giant transnationals such as General Electric. Indeed, GE/NBC did the least amount of reporting on the stories cited in the Appendixes and generally presented Reagan and Bush in the most favorable light. NBC's documentary (with Tom Brokaw) on Reagan during the last week of his term as president was embarrassingly adulatory and failed to deal with the many scandals of the Reagan years. The networks' failure to provide any critical investigations of Reagan and Bush makes clear the consequences of having major corporations own and control network television.

Indeed, the major broadcast corporations now possess some of the most potent tools in history to mold U.S. society and culture in their interests. During the 1980s major corporations took over a vast array of culture industries, and the mergers during this period gave immense power to the largest media conglomerates (Schiller 1989). All industry publications indicate that even more concentration of media power is likely in the future. The information and entertainment industries are central forces in the emerging technocapitalist order, and corporate control of these forces provides their owners with fantastic and unparalleled powers of social control.

The story of the 1980s is thus increased corporate control over the state, the media, and other aspects of U.S. society. A small number of corporations now control information, entertainment, and our political culture and can determine which ideologies, political parties, and candidates prevail. It thus appears that network television and the other mainstream media are increasingly becoming the corporate voices of those who control them, inasmuch as they present views that coincide with those of the dominant forces in corporate capitalism while eliminating more discordant and troubling views.

The take-over and control of television and the mainstream media by transnational capital thus constitute both a crisis of democracy and a crisis of journalism. If the mainstream media fail to explore the most disturbing and scandalous stories of the era and allow a man to become president who was centrally involved in some of the most disturbing scandals of the century, then the claim of the media to present independent, critical voices and to serve as a balance of power to the dominant economic and political forces is a sham. *Broadcasting* magazine, the most respected and widely read organ of the television industry, calls television the "fifth estate"—as if it were an independent, responsible journalistic force. My studies of the role of television during the 1980s suggest, on the contrary, that television and other mainstream media have become incorporated into the capitalist power structure and that they are best interpreted as capitalist media serving as major forces of conservative hegemony during the 1980s.

The tighter relations between big business and big media during an era when the media are becoming ever-more powerful forces of governance and social control are frightening in their implications. The media not only decide who will and will not become president, by selecting or avoiding what they broadcast and print, but they can also gloss over the crimes of governing elites whom they have supported—with potentially disastrous consequences for the country. In the case of George Bush, for instance, if the stories in the investigative press are true concerning his involvement in the Reagan-era scandals, then he is beholden to some of the world's most corrupt and reactionary forces, and the health of democracy in the United States is in jeopardy.

For if Bush was involved in the operations alleged in the stories in the investigative press, then the CIA, Noriega, the Contras, Israel, the Iranians, and many other forces have blackmail material on Bush, thus binding him to their demands if he fails to do their will or acts against their interests. Indeed, the day after Bush's election, at his first press conference, he pointedly referred to his continuing support of Contras and continued to support them despite efforts by the Central American governments to end the war and the regional destabilization. During the same press conference, when asked what would be different about his presidency, Bush indicated that he would call the CIA directly for daily briefings to keep on top of things. It was not by accident that he approved support of continued CIA backing for the Afghan rebels, even after the Soviets withdrew from Afghanistan. The Israelis are still able to deny the Palestinians' statehood, and if it is true that the Iranians have blackmail material on Bush, he will not be able to make demands or take action that might lead forces in Iran to reveal the facts concerning Bush's involvement in the "October Surprise" and Iran/Contra scandal.

The United States is a captive nation.

Appendix D: The Crisis of Democracy

In a sense, the Trilateral Commission managed to put through its agenda (see the Preface). Jimmy Carter, a member of the commission, was elected president in 1976, and his cabinent consisted largely of commission members (Sklar 1980). George Bush, also a member of the commission, was chosen as Reagan's vice-president in 1980 and was elected in 1988. During this period, the media went from playing what many considered to be an "adversary" role to being faithful supporters of the status quo that rigorously advanced conservative interests. Meanwhile, as I have argued throughout this book, democracy in the United States has been seriously imperiled.

George Bush is the perfect representative of Trilateral neoconservativism. Unlike Reagan, who was far to the Right and had to be disciplined during Iran/Contra, Bush is a centrist by inclination—albeit one drawn to covert action and to an ultra-imperialist foreign policy, as demonstrated by the Panama invasion and his sending troops to Saudi Arabia after the Iraqi invasion of Kuwait. Indeed, it is shocking that the "center" and the "Hard Right" are increasingly occupying the same ground in U.S. politics. Bush is also the first full-fledged member of the establishment ruling class to assume the presidency since Roosevelt. Thus far he has followed Reagan's deregulatory policy and has faithfully advanced the interests of corporate capital, while continuing to practice an interventionist covert foreign policy and to strengthen the National Security State.

The television networks, meanwhile, are seeking a tremendous bonzana denied them by Reagan. GE/NBC, in particular, has aggressively sought a rescindment of the laws that prohibit networks from producing, owning, and syndicating television entertainment (*Forbes*, April 17, 1989, p. 127). Currently, Hollywood production studios produce television series that are sold to the networks; the mega-profits that accrue from syndication thus go to the production companies. The networks want a big slice of this pie. Because of Reagan's close ties to the Hollywood production community, he did not allow the networks to enter the privileged domain of his Hollywood friends. Deregulator Mark Fowler, the head of Reagan's FCC, went to Reagan to rescind the ownership/syndication rule but was sharply rebuffed (Brown 1984, 38ff.).

The networks hope that the Bush administration will cancel the rules and let them enter into entertainment production and syndication. Indeed, it has been predicted that global information and entertainment will be big profit centers for the next decade, and the communications giants who control television want to get into the game. Eventually, television may well become global as national television networks lose their hegemony, cross-national television production increases, and the proliferation of channels continues and increases. This may, however, lead to control of entertainment and information throughout the world by a handful of corporations who would enjoy unparalleled cultural power. One can thus expect continued communications mergers, a growing involvement on the part of the network behemoths in the entertainment and information industries, and little criticism of George Bush if his administration fulfills their dreams of expanded empire.

One can also expect little coverage of the network conglomerates' own corporate crimes and failings. In November 1989 reporter Peter Karl of an NBC affiliate in Chicago reported that "General Electric engineers discovered they had a big problem—one out of [every] three bolts from one of their major suppliers was bad." These bolts held together the GE-manufactured engine components used in Stealth bombers, nuclear power plants, and civilian aircraft. According to the report, GE had been buying the bolts from the supplier for eight years without any certification that the bolts were adequate. The report also indicated that the National Transportation Safety Board had listed seventy-five airline accidents over the last four years as having involved deficient bolts from this supplier, including the GE engine that failed over the Iowa cornfield in July 1989. Furthermore, the Nuclear Regulatory Commission reported that defective bolts had been used in half of the nuclear power plants in the United States. (See the report on this story by Joel Bleifuss in *In These Times*, December 13, 1989, pp. 4–5.)

According to Bleifuss, after the show was aired in Chicago, it was picked up on NBC's "Today" show, in an edited version with all references to GE deleted! Tom Shales of the *Washington Post* reported that Karl and others in Chicago were furious over the editing. Although NBC News Vice-President Tom Ross denied that the network had edited the show on orders from GE, he admitted that he had informed GE that the segment would run on "Today." As GE is a major defense contractor and a major producer of nuclear weapons and energy, and as it is heavily involved in Star Wars defense projects, NBC is unlikely to cover these issues in a critical and socially responsible fashion.

To demonstrate their allegiance to the new administration, GE/NBC broadcast a publicity puff-piece on Bush "A Day in the Life of the White House"—an attempt to humanize Bush also undertaken by ABC. During the Panama invasion the following exchange took place on NBC on December 20, 1989:

Question: "Do we bring him [i.e., Noriega] here and put him on trial . . . or do we just neutralize him in some way?"—John Chancellor.

Answer: "I think you bring him here and you make it a showcase trial in the war on drugs and justice prevails"—Tom Brokaw.

Upon hearing that "only" nine U.S. soldiers were reported dead in the initial official body count, John Chancellor approvingly commented: "We lose numbers like that in large training exercizes" (these quotes are found in *Extra*, January/February 1990, p. 6). When Salvadorean ex-President Jose Napoleon Duarte died of cancer, Tom Brokaw eulogized that the top ally in the region of the Reagan/Bush administrations "fought for democracy in his own country. . . . He promised to end the long civil war, stop the right-wing death squads and replace the military dictatorship with true democracy. . . . To the Reagan administration he was a champion of democracy . . . Duarte will be remembered for his attempt to bring democracy to his country." Brokaw fails to mention that more than 20,000 civilians were killed by government forces while Duarte was a member of the ruling junta and that thousands more were killed when he was president by the army and death squads (ibid., p. 13). With media support like this, a government hardly need hire press secretaries or public relations specialists.

Indeed, coverage of the Iraqi invasion of Kuwait and Bush's immediate dispatch of troops to Saudi Arabia made it appear natural that only a military response to the Iraqi invasion was viable and tended to support Bush's military policy, making it appear that war in the Middle East was inevitable. During the first two weeks of the crisis, the only voices opposing the U.S. intervention were Middle East politicians and intellectuals, often interviewed live when the networks sent their correspondents to the region to get "on the scene" reports. By Sunday, August 19, 1990, on the morning talk shows, some critical questions were being raised by the network correspondents to administration officials, mostly citing establishment reservations to Bush's rash reaction. Cokie Roberts of ABC, for instance, raised Jeane Kirkpatrick's concern on the "David Brinkley Show" that the U.S. military response was far in excess of U.S. interests in the region, and Pierre Salinger, on the same show, raised Henry Kissinger's concern that the U.S. might get bogged down in a hopeless military occupation in the Middle East that could be a catastrophe. (Salinger failed to note, however, that Kissinger was recommending instead a quick "surgical strike" at Iraq and the total elimination of Hussein.)

In the August 27, 1990, Newsweek, Zbigniew Brzezinski states that: "My greatest fear about the ongoing crisis is that it could get out of hand. The way it has been played in the media, and even by some officials, will create a mass hysteria" (p. 32). When the polity has to depend on hardline conservatives like Kirkpatrick and Brzezinski to counter media war hysteria, the country—indeed the world—is in serious trouble. Yet GE, one of the world's largest defense contractors, should be proud of the way that its network, and its two competitors, have been promoting military intervention and the need for a strong military. Dwight Eisenhower warned about the military-industrial complex taking over the polity, and we now see that they own at least one television network. Meanwhile, as I send this book to press in August 1990, the world moves closer to war, and the TV networks are promoting military solutions to complex economic and political problems. The world is now a significantly more dangerous place to live, and the television networks are part of the problem.

The television networks are thus the tools of corporate interests and only an informed and organized public will be able to reform the communications systems and save democracy in the United States. If corporate hegemony over television continues unabated, the crisis of democracy will intensify. Corporate control of the media in the United States is approaching the degree of state control in the communist world. Militant struggle against that oppressive system brought dramatic changes to the communist countries in the late 1980s. It is to be hoped that struggles for *glasnost, perestroika,* and democratization will also occur in the capitalist world in the 1990s. Otherwise, our democracy will be lost, and a long reign of total capitalist hegemony will be the fate of the United States as it enters the next century.

Notes

1. Curiously, *Penthouse* magazine published an article on "The October Surprise" by Carl Carlson in their November 1984 issue that documented the infiltration of the Carter White House by the Reagan team during the 1980 election. Although the article hints of sabotage of the hostage negotiations between the Carter administration and the Iranians, the story did not document the details of the deal

that later allegedly took place. Honegger (1989) published a book on *The October Surprise* that has thus far been neglected by the mainstream media. Hoffman and Silvers (1988) contains the most complete journalistic account.

2. On the Iran/Contra affair and the aspects of it ignored by the mainstream media, see Cockburn (1988), Chomsky (1988), and Marshall, Scott, and Hunter (1988).

3. The chief sources on the Contra arms/drugs networks are Cockburn (1988), publications by the Christic Institute, periodicals such as *In These Times* and *The Nation*, broadcasts on CBS News's "West 57th Street," and PBS documentaries produced by Moyers and the Cockburns. Also worth examining is the series of articles in the *San Francisco Examiner* on March 16, 1986, p. A1; March 18, 1986; June 23, 1986, p. A1; and June 24, 1986. In addition, see the *San Francisco Chronicle*, July 16, 1987, p. 9. In the spring of 1990 the Costa Rican government sought indictments against Oliver North, John Hull, and others in the illegal arms/drugs network for drug smuggling, political assassination, and other crimes; see Bernstein and King (1990).

4. The Christic Institute's claims were generally ignored by the mainstream media and were skeptically, and even critically, received by the alternative press—in part because of the flamboyant personality of its representative Daniel Sheehan, and in part because of its misstatements and lack of documentation of certain claims. Resentment was also expressed over the amount of money raised by the institute.

5. Emile de Antonio speculates that Bush might be a deep-cover CIA operative who joined the intelligence force as early as the 1950s. Bush's father Prescott had connections with the intelligence service, was involved in the secret investment bank of Harrington and Brown, and, like his son, was a member of the secret Skull and Bones society at Yale. George Bush was established in business in Texas during the 1950s by his father's friend Neil Mallon, who also had intelligence connections and was a member of Skull and Bones. Bush's Zapata oil company was active in the Caribbean, where there was much CIA interest and activity, and the memo from J. Edgar Hoover to CIA member George Bush turned up in a Freedom of Information Act file. (See the interview with de Antonio for "Alternative Views," October 1989.)

6. For a full account of the Hasenfus connection, see Cockburn (1988).

7. Rumors concerning Noriega's ties to the CIA and his drug-running, political-assassination, and other criminal activities began appearing in the mainstream media in mid-1986. An article by Seymour Hersh published in the *New York Times* (June 12, 1986, pp. 1, 6) claimed that Noriega was involved in drugs, illegal arms sales, illicit money laundering, and political assassination of his opponents; Hersh details charges that Noriega had long-time intelligence connections with the CIA and claims that he was also involved with Cuban intelligence, playing both sides of the fence. A *Washington Post* story (June 10, 1987) alleged that Noriega had been involved in political assassinations, including the killing of General Torrijos, the previous president of Panama, as well as drug running and other crimes. The story relied on the testimony of an official who had worked with Noriega, Colonel Diaz Herrara, who was at one time second in command to Noriega. Diaz claimed that Noriega

" 'was directly involved' in the July 31, 1981, death of Torrijos, a popular nationalist, in a crash of a private plane in the jungle. Diaz charged that Noriega arranged for a small bomb to be planted on the plane and that he 'sent a message' to Vice President Bush about Torrijos' death." As CIA critic John Stockwell noted in an interview (January 1990, Austin, Texas), Max Hugel, director in charge of covert operations of the CIA at the time, was soon dismissed because of charges concerning CIA assassinations of political leaders. If Noriega was indeed involved with the CIA, was the CIA involved in this assassination? And what was Noriega's "message" to his old CIA boss George Bush? What *is* the extent of the Bush/Noriega relationship? Many articles have appeared concerning Bush's connections with Noriega, but no book or definitive study has thus far systematically investigated either those connections or Noriega's drug running and connections with the Reagan administration.

8. The *Los Angeles Weekly* published a series of critical articles about Bush in its October 14–20 issue. Among them were stories by Jay Levin ("The Covert George Bush"); by Frank Snepp and Jonathan King ("The Iran Connection" and "The Vice President and the Contras"); and by Richard Ryan ("The Mistress Question"). The *New Republic* published a rather critical article concerning Bush's involvement in the Reagan-era scandals entitled "Incurious George" (October 17, 1988, p. 7) and, as noted, *Playboy* published the "October Surprise" story, *Mother Jones* published a systematic account of Bush's tenure as CIA director, the *Rolling Stone* published the Black Eagle story, and other stories in the investigative press elaborated on these and other scandals involving Bush. But to no avail. The curious reader who has not yet become familiar with these stories is directed to the references listed below.

9. The first major histories of the Reagan era, though sharply critical of Reagan, have failed to investigate Bush's complicity in the scandals of the administration. See the whitewash of Bush in Mayer and McManus (1988) and in Schieffer and Gates (1989). Likewise, Donald Regan's (1988) book contains nothing but positive references to Bush and fails to implicate him in any of the major scandals of the Reagan administration.

References

Armstrong, Scott (1990) "Iran/Contra: Was the Press Any Match for All the President's Men?" *Columbia Journalism Review* (May/June), pp. 27–35.

Armstrong, Scott, and Jeff Nason (1988) "Company Man." *Mother Jones*, (October), pp. 20–25, 42–47.

Bernstein, Dennis and Janet King (1990) "Hostile Acts." *The Progressive* (March), pp. 25–29.

Bleifuss, Joel (1989) "In Short." *In These Times* (December 13), pp. 4–5.

Brown, Les (1984) "Who's Really Running the FCC?" *Channels of Communication* (January–February), pp. 38–39.

Carlisle, Johan (1988) "Anatomy of a Disinformation Campaign." *Propaganda Review* 3, pp. 5–9.

Carlson, Carl E. (1984) "The October Surprise." *Penthouse* (November), pp. 69–70, 142, 150.

Chardy, Alfonso (1987a) "Reagan Aides Had Hostage Meeting in '80." *Miami Herald* (April 12), pp. 1A, 26A.

Chardy, Alfonso (1987) "Reagan Advisers Ran 'Secret Government.' " *Miami Herald* (July 5), pp. 1A, 14A.

Chardy, Alfonso (1987) "CIA Knew of '81 Israel-Iran Arms Deal." *Austin American-Statesman* (August 9), p. 8A.

Chomsky, Noam (1988) *The Culture of Terrorism*. Boston: South End Press.

Conason, Joe, and John Kelly (1988) "Bush and the Secret Noriega Report." *Village Voice* (October 11), pp. 31–32, 114.

Hersh, Seymour (1990) "The Iran/Contra Committees: Did They Protect Reagan?" *New York Times Magazine* (April 29), pp. 47ff.

Hitchens, Christopher (1987) "Minority Report." *The Nation* (June 20, July 4, August 1, October 24, November 21).

Hitchens, Christopher (1988) "Minority Report." *The Nation* (September 19).

Hoffman, Abbie, and Jonathan Silvers (1988) "An Election Held Hostage." *Playboy* (October), pp. 73–74, 150–155.

Honegger, Barbara (1989) *The October Surprise*. New York: Tudor Publishing Co.

Honegger, Barbara, and Jim Naureckas (1987) "Did Reagan Steal the 1980 Election?" *In These Times* (June 24), pp. 12–13.

Kohn, Howard, and Vicki Monks (1988) "The Dirty Secrets of George Bush." *Rolling Stone* (November 3), pp. 42–50, 120.

Judis, John (1988) "Bush's Teflon on Anti-Semitic Links." *In These Times* (September 28–October 4), pp. 6–7.

Levin, Jay (1988) "The Covert George Bush," *Los Angeles Weekly* (October 14/20), pp. 14–15, 40.

McManus, Doyle (1986) "Bush Is Linked to Contra Aid Network." *Washington Post* (October 11), pp. 1, A20.

McBride, Joseph (1988a) " 'George Bush,' C.I.A. Operative." *The Nation* (July 16/23), pp. 37, 41–42.

———— (1988b) "Where Was George? (cont.)." *The Nation* (August 13/20), pp. 117–118.

Nairn, Allan (1987) "The Bush Connection." *The Progressive* (May), p. 1923.

———— (1988) "George Bush's Secret War." *The Progressive* (March), pp. 22–25.

Naureckas, Jim, and Richard Ryan (1988) "Bush's Network: All the Vice President's Men." *In These Times* (June 8–21), p. 7.

Parry, Robert (1988) "What Did Bush Know?" *Newsweek* (February 8), pp. 24–25.

Parry, Robert, and Brian Barger (1986) "Reagan's Shadow CIA." *New Republic* (November 24), pp. 23–27.

Parry, Robert, with Rod Norland (1988) "Guns for Drugs?" *Newsweek* (May 23), pp. 22–23.

Ryan, Richard (1988) "The Mistress Question." *Los Angeles Weekly* (October 14/20), pp. 21, 39–40.

Scott, Peter Dale (1988) "Bush Had Oil Policy Interest in Promoting Iran Arms Deals." *Pacific News Service* (December 21, 1987), summarized in *Utne Reader* (September–October), pp. 87–88.

Sick, Gary (1985) *All Fall Down*. New York: Random House.

Snepp, Frank, and Jonathan King (1988a) "The Vice President and the Contras." *Los Angeles Weekly* (October 14/20), pp. 16–18, 26–38.

Snepp, Frank, and Jonathan King (1988b) "The Iran Connection." *Los Angeles Weekly* (October 14/20), pp. 24, 43–44.

Bibliography

Adorno, T. W. (1957) "Television and the Patterns of Mass Culture." In Rosenberg and White 1957.

Altheide, David L. (1976) *Creating Reality*. Beverly Hills and London: Sage.

Althusser, Louis (1971) *Lenin and Philosophy*. New York: Monthly Review Press.

Anderson, Chuck (1975) *Video Power*. New York: Praeger.

Anderson, Kent (1978) *Television Fraud*. Westport, Conn.: Greenwood Press.

Ang, Ien (1990) "The Nature of the Audience." In Downing et al., 1990, pp. 155–165.

Archer, Gleason (1938) *History of Radio to 1926*. New York: American Historical Society; reprinted by Arno Press, 1971.

———. (1939) *Big Business and Radio*. New York: American Historical Society; reprinted by Arno Press, 1971.

Arlen, Michael J. (1969) *Living Room War*. New York: Viking.

Armstrong, David (1981) *A Trumpet to Arms: Alternative Media in America*. Boston: Houghton Mifflin; reprinted by South End Press, 1981.

Aronowitz, Stanley (1972) *False Promises*. New York: McGraw-Hill.

Atherton, F. Christopher (1987) *Teledemocracy*. Beverly Hills: Sage.

Aufderheide, Pat (1983) "Public Television's Prime-Time Politics." *American Film* (April), pp. 53–57, 62.

———. (1988) "What Makes Public TV Public?" *The Progressive* (January), pp. 35–38.

———. (1989) "Re-regulating Sleazy Kid Stuff." *In These Times* (August 2), p. 28.

Baehr, Helen, and Gillian Dyer (1987) *Boxed In: Women and Television*. London: Pandora.

Bagdikian, Ben (1987) *The Media Monopoly*, 2nd ed. Boston: Beacon Press.

———. (1989) "The Lords of the Global Village." *The Nation*, June 12, 1989, pp. 805–820.

Baran, Paul and Paul Sweezy (1966) *Monopoly Capital*. New York: Monthly Review Press.

Barber, Benjamin (1982) "The Second American Revolution." *Channels of Communication* (February–March), pp. 21–25, 62.

———. (1984) *Strong Democracy*. Berkeley: University of California Press.

Barnet, Richard J., and Ronald E. Müller (1974) *Global Reach*. New York: Simon and Schuster.

Barnouw, Erik (1966) *A Tower in Babel*. New York. Oxford University Press.

———. (1968) *The Golden Web*. New York: Oxford University Press.

————. (1970) The Image Empire. New York: Oxford University Press.

————. (1975) Tube of Plenty. New York: Oxford University Press.

————. (1978) The Sponsor. New York: Oxford University Press.

Barron, Jerome (1973) Freedom of the Press for Whom? Bloomington: University of Indiana Press.

Baudrillard, Jean (1978) For a Critique of the Political Economy of the Sign. St Louis: Telos Press.

————. (1983a) Simulations. New York: Semiotext(e).

————. (1983b) In the Shadows of the Silent Majority. New York: Semiotext(e).

Beard, Charles (1965; orig. 1913) An Economic Interpretation of the Constitution of the United States. New York: The Free Press.

Bedell, Sally (1981) Up the Tube. New York: Viking Press.

Bell, Daniel (1973) The Coming of Post-Industrial Society. New York: Basic Books.

————. (1976) The Cultural Contradictions of Capitalism. New York: Basic Books.

Benjamin, Walter (1969) Illuminations. New York: Schocken.

Berger, Peter, and Thomas Luckmann (1972). The Social Construction of Reality. Garden City, N.Y.: Doubleday Anchor Books.

Berkman, Dave (1988) "A Lesson from the History of Broadcasting." Monthly Review (February), pp. 34–41.

Best, Steven, and Douglas Kellner (1987) "(Re)Watching Television: Notes Toward a Political Criticism." Diacritics (Summer), pp. 97–113.

————. (1990) Postmodern Theory. London: Macmillan.

Black, Norman (1984) "The Deregulation Revolution." Channels of Communication (September–October), pp. 52–56.

Boddy, William (1987) "Operation Frontal Lobes Versus the Living Room Toy: The Battle Over Programme Control in Early Television." Media, Culture and Society, Vol. 9, pp. 347–368.

Bogart, Leo (1956) The Age of Television. New York: Ungar.

Boggs, Carl (1984) The Two Revolutions. Boston: South End Press.

————. (1986) Social Movements and Political Power. Philadelphia: Temple University Press.

Boorstin, Daniel (1962) The Image. New York: Harper and Row.

Boot, William (1989) "Campaign '88: TV Overdoes on the Inside Dope." Columbia Journalism Review (January–February), pp. 23–29.

Bower, Robert T. (1985) The Changing Television Audience in America. New York: Columbia University Press.

Bowles, Samuel, and Herbert Gintis (1986) Democracy and Capitalism. New York: Basic Books.

Boyer, Peter J. (1988) Who Killed CBS? New York: Random House.

Boyte, Harry (1981) The Backyard Revolution: Understanding the New Citizen Movement. Philadelphia: Temple University Press.

Braestrup, Peter (1977) Big Story: How the American Press and Television Reported and Interpreted the Crisis of Tet 1968 in Vietnam and Washington. Boulder, Colo.: Westview Press.

Brantlinger, Patrick (1983) Bread and Circuses. Ithaca: Cornell University Press.

Brecht, Bertolt (1967) "Der Rundfunk als Kommunikationspparat." In *Gesammelte Werke*, Vol. 18. Frankfurt: Suhrkamp.

Broadcasting/Cable Yearbook (1989). New York: Broadcasting.

Bronner, Stephen Eric, and Douglas Kellner (1989) *Politics and Society: A Critical Theory Reader*. New York. Routledge.

Brown, Les (1971) *Television: The Business Behind the Box*. New York: Harcourt Brace Jovanovich.

———. (1981) "Fear of Fowler." *Channels of Communication* (December–January), pp. 21–22.

———. (1982) "The FCC Proudly Presents the Vast Wasteland." *Channels of Communication* (March–April), pp. 27–28.

———. (1984) "Who's Really Running the FCC?" *Channels of Communication* (January–February), pp. 24–25.

Buckley, William (1951) *God and Man at Yale*. Chicago: University of Chicago Press.

Bunce, Richard (1977) *Television in the Corporate Interest*. New York: Praeger.

Carey, James (1988) *Media, Myths, and Narratives*. Beverly Hills: Sage.

Carnegie Commission on Educational Television (1967) *Public Television: A Program for Action*. New York: Harper and Row.

Cater, Douglass (1959) *The Fourth Branch of Government*. Boston: Houghton Mifflin.

Charney, Mitchell (1948) *News by Radio*. New York: Macmillan.

Chomsky, Noam (1989) *Necessary Illusions*. Boston: South End Press.

Cirino, Robert (1971) *Don't Blame the People*. New York: Random House.

———. (1974) *Power to Persuade*. New York: Bantam.

———. (1977) *We're Being More Than Entertained*. Honolulu, Hawaii: Lighthouse Press.

———. (1987) "An Alternative American Communications System." *College English*, Vol. 38, no. 8 (reprinted in Lazere, 1987).

Cohen, Jeff (1989) "The Centrist Ideology of the News Media." *Extra* (October–November), pp. 12–14.

Cohen, Joshua, and Joel Rogers (1983). *On Democracy*. London and Baltimore: Penguin Books.

Cole, Barry, and Mal Oettinger (1978). *Reluctant Regulators*. Reading, Mass.: Addison Wesley.

Cockburn, Leslie (1987) *Out of Control*. New York: Atlantic Monthly Press.

Compaine, Benjamin M., ed. (1979) *Who Owns the Media?* New York: Harmony Books.

Comstock, George (1980) *Television in America*. Beverly Hills and London: Sage.

Comstock, George, et al., eds. (1972) *Television and Social Behavior*. Rockville Md.: National Institute of Mental Health.

Cowan, Geoffrey (1978) *See No Evil*. New York: Simon and Schuster.

Crawford, Alan (1980) *Thunder on the Right*. New York: Pantheon.

Crozier, Michel, Samuel Huntington, and Joji Watanuki (1975) *The Crisis of Democracy*. New York: NYU Press.

Czitrom, Daniel (1982). *Media and the American Mind*. Chapel Hill: University of North Carolina Press.

Danziger, Kurt (1971) *Socialization*. Baltimore and Middlesex: Penguin.

Deaver, Michael (1987) *Behind the Scenes*. New York: Morrow.

Debord, Guy (1975) *The Society of the Spectacle*. Detroit: Black and Red.

Donahue, Jim (1989) "Shortchanging the Viewer." Washington, D.C.: Essential Information, pp. 1–29.

Douglas, Susan (1987) *Inventing American Broadcasting: 1899–1922*. Baltimore: Johns Hopkins University Press.

Dowie, Mark (1985) "How ABC Spikes the News." *Mother Jones* (November–December), pp. 33–39, 53.

Downing, John (1984) *Radical Media*. Boston: South End Press.

———. (1990) "Alternative Media and the Boston Tea Party." In Downing et al., 1990, pp. 180–191.

Downing, John, Ali Mohammadi, and Annabelle Sreberny-Mohammadi (1990) *Questioning the Media. A Critical Introduction*. Newbury Park, CA: Sage Publications.

Drier, Peter (1987) "The Corporate Complaint Against the Media." In Donald Lazere, ed., *American Media and Mass Culture*. Berkeley: University of California Press.

Ducat, Stephen (1988) *Taken In: American Gullibility and the Reagan Mythos*. Tacoma, Wash.: Life Sciences Press.

Edwards, Mickie (1986) "FCC Changes Cut Public's Access to News." *Miami News* (September 2), p. 15A.

Esmonde-White, Patrick (1989) "Beyond Representation: American Democracy in the 1990s." Unpublished paper presented at Union for Democratic Communications, New York.

Efron, Edith (1972) *The News Twisters*. New York: Manor Books.

Ellison, Harlan (1975) *The Glass Teat*. New York: Pyramid Books.

ELRA Group of East Lansing, Michigan (1982). Survey discussed in *CableVision*, April 26.

Emery, Edwin (1972) *The Press and America*. Englewood Cliffs, N.J.: Prentice-Hall.

Emery, Michael C., and Ted Curtis Smythe (1972) *Readings in Mass Communication*. Dubuque, Iowa: Wm. C. Brown Company.

Engelhardt, Tom (1987) "Children's Television." In Gitlin 1987.

Enzensberger, Hans Magnus (1974) *The Consciousness Industry*. New York: Seabury.

———. (1977) "Television and the Politics of Liberation." In Douglas Davis, ed. *The New Television: A Public-Private Art*. Cambridge, Mass.: MIT Press.

Epstein, Edward (1973) *News from Nowhere*. New York: Random House.

Ewen, Stuart (1976) *Captains of Consciousness*. New York: McGraw-Hill.

FAIR (1989). *Exposé of* Nightline. New York.

Faulk, John Henry (1964) *Fear on Trial*. New York: Simon and Schuster.

Ferguson, Thomas, and Joel Rogers (1986) *Right Turn*. New York: Hill and Wang.

Feshbach, Seymour, and Robert D. Singer (1971) *Television and Aggression*. San Francisco: Jossey-Bass Inc.

Fly, James, and Clifton Durr et al. (1959) *Broadcasting and Government Regulation in a Free Society*. Santa Barbara, Calif.: Center for the Study of Democratic Institutions.

Forester, John (1985) *Critical Theory and Public Life*. Cambridge: MIT Press.

Foucault, Michel (1977) *Discipline and Punish.* New York: Pantheon.

Fox, Frank (1975) *Madison Avenue Goes to War.* Provo, Utah: Brigham Young University Press.

Frederiksen, H. Allan (1972) *Community Access Video.* Menlo Park, N.J: Nowells Publications.

Friendly, Fred (1967) *Due to Circumstances Beyond Our Control.* New York: Random House.

——— . (1977) *The Good Guys, the Bad Guys, and the First Amendment.* New York: Vintage.

Gans, Herbert (1974) *Popular Culture and High Culture.* New York: Basic Books.

——— . (1979) *Deciding What's News.* New York: Random House.

Garnham, Nicholas (1978) *Structures of Television.* London: British Film Institute.

Geller, Henry (1989) *Financing Public Television.* Washington, D.C.: The Benton Foundation.

Gerbner, George (1977) "Television: The New State Religion." *et cetera* (June), pp. 3–13.

Gerbner, George, and Larry Gross (1976) "Living with Television: The Violence Profile." *Journal of Communications* (Spring), pp. 173–199.

Gerbner, George, Larry Gross, Michael Morgan, and Nancy Signorielli (1982) "Charting the Mainstream: Television's Contributions to Political Orientations." *Journal of Communication,* Vol. 32, No. 2; reprinted in Lazere 1987, pp. 441–464.

Gerth, H. H., and C. Wright Mills (1946) *From Max Weber.* New York: Oxford University Press.

Gibson, William (1987) *The Perfect War: Technowar in Vietnam.* New York: Random House.

——— . (1980) "Network News. Elements of a Theory." *Social Text,* Vol. 3, pp. 88–113.

——— (n.d.) "World War II: The Beginnings of the Permanent Mobilization of American Society." Unpublished manuscript.

Gilbert, Dennis (1988) *Compendium of Public Opinion.* New York: Facts on File.

Ginsberg, Benjamin (1986) *The Captive Public.* New York: Basic Books.

Gitlin, Todd (1972) "Sixteen Notes on Television and the Movement." In George White and Charles Newman, eds., *Literature and Revolution.* New York: Holt, Rinehart and Winston.

——— . (1978) "Media Sociology: The Dominant Paradigm." *Theory and Society,* Vol. 6, pp. 205–253.

——— . (1980) *The Whole World's Watching.* Berkeley: University of California Press.

——— . (1983) *Inside Prime Time.* New York: Pantheon.

——— , ed. (1987) *Watching Television.* New York: Pantheon.

Goldman, Robert, and Satya Rajagopal (1990) *Mapping Hegemony.* Norwood, N.J.: Ablex Publishing Company.

Goldsen, Rose (1978) *The Show and Tell Machine.* New York: Delta.

Gomery, Douglas (1989) "The Reagan Record." *Screen* (Winter–Spring), pp. 92–99.

Gouldner, Alvin (1976) *The Dialectic of Ideology and Technology.* New York: Seabury.

Gramsci, Antonio (1971) *Prison Notebooks*. New York: International Publishers.

Habermas, Jurgen (1975) *Legitimation Crisis*. Boston: Beacon Press.

———. (1989; orig. 1962) *The Structural Transformation of the Public Sphere*. Cambridge: MIT Press.

Halberstam, David (1979) *The Powers That Be*. New York: Knopf.

Hall, Stuart, et al. (1980) *Culture, Media, and Language*. London: Hutchinson.

Hallin, Daniel (1985) "The American News Media: A Critical Theory Perspective." In Forester 1985.

———. (1986) *The "Uncensored War."* New York: Oxford University Press.

———. (1987) "We Keep You on Top of the World." In Gitlin 1987.

Harms, John, and Douglas Kellner (1990) "Toward a Critical Theory of Advertising." *Critical Perspectives in Social Theory* (in press).

Hay, James (1989) "Rereading Early Television Advertising." *Journal of Film and Video*, Vol. 41, No. 1 (Spring), pp. 1–17.

Head, Sidney (1976) *Broadcasting in America*. Boston: Houghton Mifflin.

Herman, Edward (1981) *Corporate Control, Corporate Power*. Cambridge: Cambridge University Press.

Herman, Edward, and Noam Chomsky (1988) *Manufacturing Consent*. New York: Pantheon.

Herschensohn, Bruce (1976) *The Gods of Antenna*. New Rochelle, N.Y.: Arlington House.

Hertsgaard, Mark (1988) *On Bended Knee*. New York: Farrar, Straus, and Giroux.

Hill, George H. (1985) *Blacks on Television*. Metuchen, N.Y.: Scarecrow Press.

Hirsch, Paul, and Horace Newcomb (1987) "Television as a Cultural Forum." In Horace Newcomb, ed., *Television: The Critical View*. New York: Oxford University Press.

Hocking, William Ernest (1947) *Freedom of the Press*. Chicago: University of Chicago Press.

Hodgson, Godfrey (1976) *America in Our Time*. New York: Random House.

Hofstadter, Richard (1955) *The Age of Reform*. New York: Random House.

Horkheimer, Max, and Theodor Adorno (1972; orig. 1947) *Dialectic of Enlightenment*. New York: Seabury.

Horowitz, Robert (1989) *The Irony of Regulatory Reform*. New York: Oxford University Press.

Hulteng, John L., and Roy Paul Nelson (1983) *The Fourth Estate*. New York: Harper and Row.

Huntington, Samuel (1975) "The Democratic Distemper." In Michel Crozier et al., eds., *The Crisis of Democracy*. New York: NYU Press.

Infact (1988) *Infact Brings GE to Light*. Boston: Infact.

Iyengar, Shanto, and Donald Kinder (1987) *News That Matters*. Chicago: University of Chicago Press.

Jacobson, Bob (1974) "Video at the Crossroads." *Jump Cut* 1 (May–June).

Jay, Martin (1973) *The Dialectical Imagination*. Boston: Little, Brown and Company

Jewett, Robert, and John Lawrence (1988) *The American Monomyth*, 2nd ed. Lanham, Md.: University Press of America.

Johnson, Nicholas (1970) *How to Talk Back to Your Television Set.* Boston: Little, Brown and Company.

Kahn, Frank, ed. (1978) *Documents of American Broadcasting.* Engelwood Cliffs, N.J.: Prentice-Hall.

Karp, Walter (1983) "The Lie of TV's Political Power." *Channels* (May–June), pp. 37–40.

――――. (1989) "Who Decides What Is News? (Hint: It's not Journalists)." *Utne Reader* (November–December), pp. 60–68.

Katz, Elihu, and Lazarsfeld, Paul (1955) *Personal Influence.* New York: Free Press.

Kellner, Douglas (1978) "Ideology, Marxism, and Advanced Capitalism." *Socialist Review,* Vol. 42, pp. 37–65.

――――. (1979) "TV, Ideology, and Emancipatory Popular Culture." *Socialist Review,* Vol. 45, pp. 13–53.

――――. (1980a) "Television Research and the Fair Use of Media Images." In Lawrence and Timberg 1980; 1989, pp. 146–164.

――――. (1980b) "Television Images, Codes, and Messages." *Television,* Vol. 7, No. 4, pp. 2–19.

――――. (1981) "Network Television and American Capitalism." *Theory and Society,* Vol. 10, No. 1, pp. 31–62.

――――. (1982) "Television Myth and Ritual." *Praxis,* Vol. 6, pp. 133–155.

――――. (1987) "Baudrillard, Semiurgy, and Death." *Theory, Culture, and Society,* Vol. 4, pp. 125–146.

――――. (1989a) *Critical Theory, Marxism, and Modernity.* London and Baltimore: Polity Press and Johns Hopkins University Press.

――――. (1989b). *Jean Baudrillard: From Marxism to Post-Modernism and Beyond.* London and Baltimore: Polity Press and Johns Hopkins University Press.

――――. (1990) "Postmodernism and Identity." In Jonathan Friedman and Scott Lash, eds., *Modernity and Identity.* London: Basil Blackwell.

Kellner, Douglas, and Michael Ryan (1988) *Camera Politica: The Politics and Ideology of Contemporary Hollywood Film.* Bloomington: Indiana University Press.

Kendrick, Alexander (1969) *Prime Time: The Life of Edward R. Murrow.* New York: Avon.

King, Elliot, and Michael Schudson (1987) "The Myth of the Great Communicator." *Columbia Journalism Review* (November–December), pp. 37–39.

Klein, Paul (1972) "Entertainment." Discussion in The Network Project: "Feedback 5." *Performance,* No. 3 (July–August), p. 43.

Koenig, Josh (1979) "Court Strikes Down FCC Access Rules." *Community Television Review* (Spring) pp. 4–5.

Laclau, Ernesto, and Chantel Mouffe (1983) *Hegemony and Socialist Strategy.* London: Verso.

Lang, Kurt, and Gladys Lang (1968) *Television and Politics.* Chicago: Quadrangle Books.

――――. (1983). *The Battle for Public Opinion.* New York: Columbia University Press.

Lash, Scott, and John Urry (1987) *The End of Organized Capitalism.* Cambridge: Polity Press.

Lashner, Marilyn A. (1984) *The Chilling Effect in TV News*. New York: Praeger.

Lawrence, John, and Bernard Timberg (1989) *Fair Use and Free Inquiry*. Norwood, N.J.: Ablex.

Lazere, Donald, ed. (1987) *American Media and Mass Culture*. Berkeley: University of California Press.

Lee, Martin A., and Norman Solomon (1990) *Unreliable Sources*. New York: Lyle Stuart.

Lefever, Ernest W. (1974) *TV and National Defense*. Boston, Va.: Institute for American Strategy.

Lichter, S. Robert, Stanley Rothman, and Linda S. Lichter (1986). *The Media Elite*. Bethesda, Md.: Adler and Adler.

Lowi, Theodore J. (1979) *The End of Liberalism*. New York: Norton.

Luke, Timothy (1989) *Screens of Power*. Champaign, Ill.: University of Illinois Press.

Luke, Timothy, and Stephen White (1985) "Critical Theory, the Informational Revolution, and an Ecological Path to Modernity." In Forester 1985, pp. 22–56.

MacDonald, J. Fred (1979) *Don't Touch That Dial! Radio Programming in American Life, 1920–1960*. Chicago: Nelson-Hall.

_____. (1983) *Blacks and White TV: Afro-Americans in Television since 1948*. Chicago: Nelson-Hall.

_____. (1985) *Television and the Red Menace: The Video Road to Vietnam*. New York: Praeger.

_____. (1990) *One Nation Under Television*. New York: Pantheon Books.

Mandel, Ernest (1975) *Late Capitalism*. London: Verso.

Mander, Jerry (1978) *Four Arguments for the Elimination of Television*. New York: William Morrow.

Marc, David (1984) *Demographic Vistas*. Philadelphia: University of Pennsylvania Press.

Marcuse, Herbert (1964) *One-Dimensional Man*. Boston: Beacon Press.

Marshall, Jonathan, Peter Dale Scott, and Jane Hunter (1987). *The Iran Contra Connection*. Boston: South End Press.

Marx, Karl, and Friedrich Engels (1978) *The Marx-Engels Reader*. New York: Norton.

Mattelart, Armand (1983) *Transnationals and the Third World*. South Hadley, Mass.: Bergin.

Mattelart, Armand, and Seth Siegelaub, eds. (1979) *Communication and Class Struggle*. Vol. 1.: *Capitalism, Imperialism*. Paris: International General.

_____. (1983) *Communication and Class Struggle*. Vol. 2: *Liberation, Socialism*. Paris: International General.

Mayer, Jane, and Doyle McManus (1988) *Landslide*. Boston: Houghton Mifflin.

Mayer, Martin (1972) *About Television*. New York: Harper and Row.

McGinniss, Joe (1969 and 1988) *The Selling of the President*. New York: Simon and Schuster; Baltimore: Penguin.

McLuhan, Marshall (1964) *Understanding Media*. New York: McGraw-Hill.

Meyrowitz, Joshua (1985) *No Sense of Place*. New York: Oxford University Press.

Miege, Bernard (1989) *The Capitalization of Cultural Production*. Paris and New York: International General.

Mills, C. Wright (1959) *Power, Politics and People*. New York: Oxford University Press.

Minow, Newton (1964) *Equal Time*. New York: Atheneum.

Minow, Newton, John B. Martin, and Lee M. Mitchell (1973) *Presidential Television*. New York: Basic Books.

Modlesky, Tania (1982) *Loving with a Vengeance*. New York: Metheun.

Montgomery, Kathryn C. (1989) *Target: Prime Time*. New York: Oxford University Press.

Morrow, Frank (1985) "The U.S. Power Structure and the Mass Media." Ph.D. dissertation, University of Texas.

Mosco, Vincent (1979) *Broadcasting in the United States*. Norwood, N.J.: Ablex.

Mosco, Vincent, and Janet Wasko (1990) *Democratic Communications in the Information Age*. Toronto: Garamond Press.

Moynihan, Daniel (1973) *Coping: On the Practice of Government*. New York: Vintage.

Mueller, Claus (1973) *The Politics of Communication*. New York: Oxford University Press.

National News Council (1975) *In the Public Interest*. New York: National News Council.

Network Project (1971) *The Fourth Network*. New York: The Network Project.

———. (1973a) *Directory of the Networks*. Notebook Number Two.

———. (1973b) *Control of Information*. Notebook Number Three.

———. (1974) *Government Television*. Notebook Number Nine.

Newcomb, Horace, ed. (1987) *Television: The Critical View*. New York: Oxford University Press.

Nimmo, Dan, and James E. Combs (1983) *Mediated Political Realities*. New York: Longman.

O'Connor, James (1973) *The Fiscal Crisis of the State*. New York: Saint Martin.

Parenti, Michael (1986) *Inventing Reality*. New York: Saint Martin.

Parry, Robert, and Peter Kornbluh (1988) "Iran-Contra's Untold Story." *Foreign Policy* (Fall), pp. 3–30.

Pells, Richard (1973) *Radical Visions and American Dreams*. New York: Harper and Row.

Peterson, Theodore (1956) "The Social Responsibility Theory." In Fred S. Siebert et al., eds., *Four Theories of the Press*. Urbana: University of Illinois Press.

Phillips, Kevin (1975) *Mediacracy*. New York: Doubleday.

Postman, Neil (1985) *Amusing Ourselves to Death*. New York: Viking.

Powledge, Fred (1971) *The Engineering of Restraint*. Washington, D.C.: Public Affairs Press.

Price, Monroe, and John Wicklein (1972) *Cable Television: A Guide for Citizen Action*. Philadelphia: Pilgrim Press.

Raboy, Marc, and Peter Bruck, eds. (1989) *Communication For and Against Democracy*. Montreal and New York: Black Rose Books.

Radical Software (1970–1975).

Rapping, Elayne (1987) *The Looking Glass World of Nonfiction TV*. Boston: South End Press.

Read, William H. (1976) *America's Mass Media Merchants*. Baltimore: The Johns Hopkins University Press.

Reel, A. Frank (1979) *The Networks: How They Stole the Show*. New York: Scribner's.

Regan, Donald T. (1988) *For the Record*. New York: Harcourt, Brace, Jovanovich.

Report of the International Commission for the Study of Communication Problems (1980) *Many Voices, One World*. Paris: UNESCO.

Robinson, Michael (1975) "American Political Legitimacy in an Era of Electronic Journalism: Reflections on the Evening News." In Richard Adler, ed., *Television as a Social Force*. New York: Praeger.

Robinson, Michael, and Maura E. Clancey (1985) "Network News, 15 Years After Agnew." *Channels* (January–February), pp. 34–39.

Rogin, Michael (1987) *Ronald Reagan, the Movie*. Berkeley: University of California Press.

Roper, Burns (1981) *Evolving Public Attitudes Toward Television and Other Mass Media 1959–1980*. New York: Television Information Office.

Rorty, James (1934) *Our Master's Voice: Advertising*. New York: John Day.

Rosenberg, Bernard, and David White (1957) *Mass Culture*. Glencoe, Ill.: Free Press.

Rowan, Ford (1984) *Broadcast Fairness*. New York: Longman.

Rusher, William A. (1988) *The Coming Battle for the Media*. New York: William Morrow and Company.

Saldich, Anne Rawley (1979) *Electronic Democracy*. New York: Praeger.

Schieffer, Bob, and Gary Paul Gates (1989) *The Acting President*. New York: Dutton.

Schiller, Daniel (1981) *Objectivity and News*. Philadelphia: University of Pennsylvania Press.

Schiller, Herbert (1969) "The Mass Media and the Public Interest." In *Television Today*. Washington, D.C.: Institute for Policy Studies.

––––––– . (1971) *Mass Communications and American Empire*. Boston: Beacon Press.

––––––– . (1973) *The Mind Managers*. Boston: Beacon Press.

––––––– . (1976) *Communications and Cultural Domination*. White Plains, N.Y.: M.C. Sharpe.

––––––– . (1989) *Culture, Inc.* New York: Oxford University Press.

Schorr, Daniel (1977) *Clearing the Air*. Boston: Houghton Mifflin.

Schulte-Sasse, Jochen (1987–1988) "Electronic Media and Cultural Politics in the Reagan Era." *Cultural Critique*, Vol. 8, pp. 123–152.

Schwartz, Tony (1983) *Media: The Second God*. New York: Doubleday.

Shamberg, Michael (1971) *Guerrilla Television*. New York: Holt, Rinehart and Winston.

Shapiro, Andrew (1976) *Media Access*. Boston: Little, Brown and Company.

Shooshan, Harry M., and Louise Arnheim (1989) *Public Broadcasting*. Washington, D.C.: Benton Foundation.

Siebert, Fred. S. (1956) "The Authoritarian Theory." In Fred S. Siebert, et. al, eds., *Four Theories of the Press*. Urbana: University of Illinois Press.

Siepmann, Charles A. (1946) *Radio's Second Chance*. Boston: Little, Brown and Company.

––––––– . (1950) *Radio, Television, and Society*. New York: Oxford University Press.

Simmons, Steven J. (1978) *The Fairness Doctrine and the Media*. Berkeley: University of California Press.

Simons, Howard, and Joseph Califano (1979) *The Media and Business.* New York: Vintage.

Sklar, Holly, ed. (1980) *Trilateralism.* Boston: South End Press.

Sklar, Martin (1988) *The Corporate Reconstruction of American Capitalism, 1890–1916.* Cambridge and New York: Cambridge University Press.

Skornia, Henry (1965) *Television and Society.* New York: McGraw-Hill.

———. (1968) *Television and the News.* Palo Alto: Pacific Books.

Smythe, Dalls W. (1981) *Dependency Road: Communications, Capitalism, Consciousness and Canada.* Norwood, N.J.: Ablex.

Stein, Ben (1979) *The View from Sunset Boulevard.* New York: Basic Books.

Sterling, Christopher H., and John M. Kitross, *Stay Tuned.* Belmont, Calif.: Wadsworth Publishing Company.

Stevenson, Robert L., et al. (1973) "Untwisting the News Twisters: A Replication of Efron's Study." *Journalism Quarterly,* Vol. 50, pp. 211–219.

Stockwell, John (1978) *In Search of Enemies.* New York: Norton.

Stoler, Peter (1986) *The War Against the Press.* New York: Dodd, Mead.

Stone, David (1985) *Nixon and the Politics of Public Television.* New York: Garland Publishing Company.

Swingewood, Alan (1977) *The Myth of Mass Culture.* London: Macmillan.

Tebbel, John (1974) *The Media in America.* New York: Thomas Crowell.

Toffler, Alvin (1980) *The Third Wave.* New York: William Morrow.

Tuchman, Gaye (1974) *The TV Establishment.* Englewood Cliffs, N.J.: Prentice-Hall.

Tunstall, Jeremy (1986) *Communications Deregulation.* Oxford: Oxford University Press.

United States Commission on Civil Rights (1977) *Window Dressing on the Set: Women and Minorities in Television.* Washington, D.C.: U.S. Commission on Civil Rights.

Waldrop, Frank C., and Joseph Borkin (1938) *Television: A Struggle for Power.* New York: William Morrow.

Weber, Max (1946) *From Max Weber,* edited by Hans Gerth and C. Wright Mills. New York: Oxford University Press.

Williams, Raymond (1975) *Television: Technology and Cultural Form.* New York: Schocken.

Winston, Brian (1990) "How Are Media Born?" in Downing, et al., 1990, pp. 55–72.

Wolfe, Alan (1973) *The Seamy Side of Democracy.* New York: McKay.

———. (1977) *The Limits of Legitimacy.* New York: Free Press.

Wolff, Robert Paul (1970) *In Defense of Anarchy.* New York: Harper and Row.

Woodward, Bob (1987) *Veil.* New York: Simon and Schuster.

Zelmer, A.C. Lynn (1979) *Community Media Handbook.* Metuchen, N.J.: Scarecrow Press.

About the Book and Author

Douglas Kellner offers a systematic, critically informed political and institutional study of television in the United States. Focusing on the relationships among television, the state, and business, he traces the history of television broadcasting, emphasizing its socioeconomic impact and its growing political power. Acknowledging that television has long served the interests of the powerful, he points out that it has dramatized conflicts within society and has on occasion led to valuable social criticism.

Kellner's examination of television in the 1980s and, in particular, its role in the 1988 presidential election yield the conclusion that in our time television has worked increasingly to further conservative hegemony. In so doing, Kellner argues, contemporary television has helped produce a crisis of democracy.

But *Television and the Crisis of Democracy* goes beyond description and diagnosis. In a discussion that is both analytical and comparative, Kellner presents alternative models to the existing structure of commercial broadcasting and shows how new technologies might be used to create a more democratic future for television—one that could enhance political knowledge and participation.

Douglas Kellner is professor of philosophy at the University of Texas, Austin. He is the author of many books and essays, including *Herbert Marcuse and the Crisis of Marxism*, *Jean Baudrillard*, and *Critical Theory, Marxism, and Modernity*.

Index